Structured
ANS COBOL

Books in the Paul Noll COBOL Series

Structured Programming for the COBOL Programmer
The Structured Programming Cookbook
Structured ANS COBOL, Part 1
Structured ANS COBOL, Part 2
Report Writer

Development Team

Director/author: Mike Murach
Advisor/author: Paul Noll
Writer/editor: Judy Taylor
Programmer: Doug Lowe
Art director/designer: Michael Rogondino
Production coordinator: Debbie Zoldoske

Structured ANS COBOL

Part 1: A Course for Novices

MIKE MURACH

PAUL NOLL

Mike Murach & Associates, Inc.

4222 West Alamos, Suite 101
Fresno, California 93711
(209) 275-3335

Thanks to International Business Machines Corporation for permission to reprint the following materials: figures 1-1, 1-3, 1-18, 3-29, 5-19, 6-2, 6-4, 6-5, 6-7, and 6-11.

Acknowledgment

The following information is reprinted from *COBOL Edition 1965*, published by the Conference on Data Systems Languages (CODASYL) and printed by the U.S. Government Printing Office:

Any organization interested in reproducing the COBOL report and specifications in whole or in part, using ideas taken from this report as the basis for an instruction manual or for any other purpose, is free to do so. However, all such organizations are requested to reproduce this section as part of the introduction to the document. Those using a short passage, as in a book review, are requested to mention "COBOL" in acknowledgment of the source, but need not quote this entire section.

COBOL is an industry language and is not the property of any company or group of companies, or of any organization or group of organizations.

No warranty, expressed or implied, is made by any contributor or by the COBOL Committee as to the accuracy and functioning of the programming system and language. Moreover, no responsibility is assumed by any contributor, or by the committee, in connection therewith.

Procedures have been established for the maintenance of COBOL. Inquiries concerning the procedures for proposing changes should be directed to the Executive Committee of the Conference on Data Systems Languages.

The authors and copyright holders of the copyrighted materials used herein

FLOW-MATIC (Trademark of Sperry Rand Corporation), Programming for the Univac (R) I and II, Data Automation Systems copyrighted 1958, 1959, by Sperry Rand Corporation; IBM Commercial Translator Form No. F28-8013, copyrighted 1959 by IBM; FACT, DSI 27A5260-2760, copyrighted 1960 by Minneapolis-Honeywell

have specifically authorized the use of this material in whole or in part, in the COBOL specifications. Such authorization extends to the reproduction and use of COBOL specifications in programming manuals of similar publications.

Contents

Preface

COBOL is the most widely used programming language for business applications. This language is available on nearly all medium- and large-sized computer systems, and each year it becomes available on more small systems. At present, there are well over 100,000 COBOL programmers working in industry. And each year thousands of new COBOL programmers are trained.

With all this COBOL activity, there are dozens of books and courses available for COBOL training. Nevertheless, COBOL training is a continual problem in industry because training requirements for the COBOL programmer are continually changing. As a result, training materials that were acceptable three years ago are no longer acceptable. And few training managers would say that they are satisfied with their COBOL training programs. To better understand the training problem (and the need for this book), let me briefly describe the changing nature of the COBOL environment.

The development of COBOL

COBOL, which stands for *COmmon Business Oriented Language*, is one of the oldest programming languages, first introduced in 1959. By the mid-sixties, COBOL had established itself as the most widely used language for business applications. Before 1968, however, there was no standard COBOL language. Although all versions of COBOL were based on the same set of language specifications, there were major COBOL differences as you moved from one type of computer to another.

Then, in 1968, the American National Standards Institute (ANSI) approved a standard COBOL language. Theoretically, this meant that one standard language could be used on all types of computer systems. In practice, however, the standards didn't put an end to COBOL variations because the standards didn't provide for all of the capabilities that computer users wanted. As a result, each manufacturer added *extensions* to the language that provided the additional capabilities. Furthermore, the 1968 standards allowed these extensions. As long as the rest of the language conformed to the standards, a manufacturer could refer to his version of COBOL as

1

standard no matter how many extensions were added. Needless to say, the end result was that the 1968 COBOL standards did *not* lead to widespread standardization of the COBOL language.

In 1974, the American National Standards Institute released a new set of COBOL standards. These standards deleted some of the 1968 standards, modified others, and, most important, added most of the capabilities that computer users had wanted in the 1968 standards. COBOL that is based on the new standards is usually referred to as ANS 74 COBOL, while ANS 68 COBOL refers to COBOL that is based on the old standards. In contrast to ANS 68 COBOL, ANS 74 COBOL for one computer system is usually very similar to that for another computer system. In the best cases, you can convert an ANS 74 COBOL program from one system to another by making only minor changes to the program. On the other hand, extensions to the standards are still allowed. So in the worst cases, extensive changes must be made to an ANS 74 COBOL program to convert it from one system to another.

Because it takes time to develop new compilers, a few years usually pass between the time a new set of standards is released and the time compilers that conform to those standards are available. For instance, IBM didn't release a 1974 ANS compiler for its most popular computer, the System/370, until 1977. And at this writing IBM still hasn't announced an ANS 74 COBOL compiler for its Disk Operating System, which is widely used on small System/360s and System/370s.

After a new COBOL compiler becomes available, it usually takes another few years before computer users convert to it. Why? Because it costs a lot of money to make the conversion. Programmers have to be taught how to use the new language. And eventually all programs written in the earlier version of the language have to be converted to the new language so they will compile correctly when they are modified to meet changing business conditions. In general, then, computer users delay the conversion to the new standards until the new compiler gives them some capability that they want but can't get through extensions on their current compiler. Because IBM extensions to the 1968 standards gave the System/360 and System/370 user all of the significant capabilities provided by the 1974 standards, there is little reason for System/360-370 users to want to convert to the new ANS 74 compiler. As a result, most COBOL programs for the System/360-370 are still being written in ANS 68 COBOL. Yet already we're getting rumors about new standards, perhaps becoming official in 1984.

From an instructor's point of view, this continual change presents many problems. In general, every company that has been programming in COBOL for any length of time has many programs (hundreds and even thousands) written in 1968 COBOL. As a result, every new programmer should be familiar with this language. Until these programs are converted to ANS 74 COBOL, they must be maintained in 1968 COBOL; and all programs require periodic maintenance. On the other hand, most companies are likely to switch to ANS 74 COBOL eventually. So new programmers (and old) should become familiar with this version of COBOL. At the least, a programmer should be aware of ANS 74 COBOL so he can write programs in ANS 68 COBOL in a way that will make them easy to convert later on.

To complicate the trainer's problem, new programming techniques are having an effect on COBOL training. In particular, it has become apparent that the techniques of structured programming can have a major effect on programmer productivity. As a result, the COBOL trainer must teach more than just the COBOL language. In addition, the trainer must teach techniques for using this language that make the resulting programs easier to code, test, debug, and maintain. In general, this forces the trainer to include structured design within the COBOL course. And this by itself has destroyed the usefulness of most of the traditional training materials for COBOL instruction.

What this book does

This book is the first in a two-part series for COBOL training in industry. It is designed to teach a novice how to develop structured programs in a professional manner. In terms of COBOL, the book covers a professional subset of COBOL plus COBOL and job-control language for handling sequential files on tape or direct-access devices. As a result, a student who successfully completes this course will have the qualifications of an entry-level programmer in industry.

To handle the problem of what version of COBOL to teach, 1968 or 1974, this book teaches a subset of the two sets of standards that will run on either a 1968 or a 1974 compiler. By using this subset, you won't have to modify the programs you write in ANS 68 COBOL when your shop converts to ANS 74 COBOL. Whenever language is presented that is only available under the 1974 standards, it is clearly identified so you can avoid using it if you are using a 1968 compiler.

Because we feel that it's impossible to teach a student how to code structured programs without also teaching him how to design structured programs, this book gives extensive coverage to modern design techniques. In fact, structured design and documentation are covered in detail in chapter 3, right after you learn how to use an introductory subset of the COBOL language. Thereafter, you should be able to design and code simple programs using structured techniques. In my opinion, this material on structured design is essential to a structured COBOL course even though COBOL and design have traditionally been treated as independent courses.

Who this book is for

Since this book is designed for a complete beginner, it assumes no prior knowledge of computing or data processing. Chapter 1, then, provides the minimum hardware and software background that the beginner requires before he can start learning how to program. As a result, if a person has education or experience in the data processing field, he can probably skip much of the material in chapter 1.

Although this book deals primarily with standard COBOL, both 1968 and 1974, it is specifically designed for users of the Disk Operating System (DOS) and the full Operating System (OS) on IBM's System/360 or System/370 (or the new Series 30). For this reason, this book teaches the IBM extensions to the standards whenever they are required for effective coding on one of these systems. In general, then, you can learn DOS ANS COBOL or OS ANS COBOL using this book alone; no reference manuals should be needed.

Even though it has an IBM orientation, this book should also be useful to users of other types of systems. As I said, the emphasis in this book is on a standard COBOL subset as presented in the 1968 and 1974 ANSI standards. So with minor modifications, any program shown in this book will run on any system that has a standard COBOL compiler. However, the non-IBM user will want to supplement this book with reference materials for the system he is using.

How this book was developed

Because this book wasn't developed in the traditional way, I think you might be interested in how it was developed. To begin with, a major portion of the content in this book is taken from two earlier books: (1) *Standard COBOL*, Mike Murach, Science Research Associates, 1975, and (2) *Structured Programming for the COBOL Programmer*, Paul Noll, Mike Murach & Associates, 1977. That's why Mike Murach and Paul Noll are credited as the authors of this book.

In fact, however, Paul and I didn't do any of the writing in this book. Instead, a team of people worked on it. I was responsible for the organization of the book and the coordination of the team. Paul Noll, a software specialist and trainer from industry, was the technical advisor and technical coordinator. Judy Taylor did the rewriting and new writing that was required...a major effort. And Doug Lowe wrote all of the programs that are used in this book based on the programming standards supplied by Paul.

Because of this team approach, I think this book has some strengths that aren't found in competing products. First, because the educational approach used in this book is adapted from *Standard COBOL*, I'm confident that the book will be effective in terms of instruction. *Standard COBOL* has been used by thousands of students in more than 200 colleges and universities in the last few years. It has also been used in dozens of businesses for inhouse training; and it has been used by thousands of professionals for self-instruction. As a result, the method of instruction used in this book has been proven effective many times over.

Second, because the structured programming content is taken from Paul's book, *Structured Programming for the COBOL Programmer*, I'm confident that the techniques presented here can have a major effect on programmer productivity. Paul's structured programming book is currently in use in hundreds of businesses for inhouse training. And many companies have adopted its principles as their standard for program development. In short, though there is considerable debate about which are the best methods for implementing structured programming, you can be sure that the methods presented here are widely used.

Finally, because Paul was responsible for the technical excellence of this product, I'm confident that it is without equal in this respect. At present, Paul is responsible for the training of 150 programmers at Pacific Telephone in San Francisco; he is assistant manager of the COBOL group within GUIDE (an association of large IBM users); and in my opinion, he is one of the top COBOL experts in the country. To the benefit of this book, Paul has taken pains to see that the COBOL presented here is not only accurate, but that it also represents the practices that are currently in use in the best COBOL shops in America. As a result, if you compare the programs in this book with those taken from any competing book or course, I think you'll find a significant difference in program quality.

How to use this book if you're a student

If you are reading this book on your own (not as part of a course), you should realize that the chapters don't have to be read in sequence. Instead, they are grouped into five parts as indicated by table 1. This means that you can continue with any other part in the book after completing the first two parts. If, for example, you want to compile and test a program after you complete part 2, you can skip to either chapter 8 or 9 to learn how to use the related job-control language. Similarly, if you want to learn about the proper sequence of program development before learning about sequential file handling, you can skip to chapter 10 immediately after chapter 5.

If you would like a recommended sequence of study, I suggest the following:

Chapters 1–5	The Core Content
Chapter 8 or 9, Topics 1 and 2	DOS or OS Job-Control Language
Chapters 6–7	Sequential File Handling
Chapter 8 or 9, Topic 3	JCL for Sequential Files
Chapter 10	Structured Program Development

But don't feel that you should rigidly adhere to this sequence. Whenever a subject arouses your interest, read the appropriate material. There is no better atmosphere for learning than the one created when you study something in search of an answer.

To help you learn from this book, each topic is followed by terminology lists, behavioral objectives, problems, and solutions. The intent of the terminology lists is not that you be able to define the words, but that you feel you understand them. So after you read a topic, you can glance at the list and note any word whose meaning is unclear to you. Then, you can reread the related material.

The behavioral objectives describe the activities (behavior) that you should be able to demonstrate upon completion of a topic. The theory is that you will be a more effective learner if you know what you are expected to do. Since structured COBOL programming is concerned with problem solving, most of these objectives ask you to apply knowledge rather than just to list, describe, or explain what you've been taught.

For each objective that asks you to apply what you've learned, you will find one or more problems and their solutions. Problems are intended to get you involved based on this maxim: I hear and I forget, I see and I remember, I *do* and I understand. If there is one message that has come from research in education, it is that meaningful learning depends on what the learner does—not on what he sees, hears, or reads. At times, then, I hope the problems will help you to experience the joy of discovery and to receive the reward of deeper understanding.

Part	Chapters	Title	Prerequisite Parts
1	1	Required Background	—
2	2-5	COBOL: The Core Content	1
3	6-7	Sequential File Handling	1, 2
4	8-9	DOS and OS Job-Control Language	1, 2
5	10	Programming Techniques	1, 2

Table 1   The organization of this book

Solutions are presented right after the problems. This allows you to confirm that you are right when you are right. And it helps you learn from being wrong. By checking the solution when you finish a problem, you can discover when you are wrong and correct false notions right away.

How to use this book if you're an instructor

If you're an instructor or if you're in charge of training for your company, I think you'll find that this book represents a complete first course in structured COBOL for the programming novice . . . a course that will outperform any competing course at any price. In fact, you have my word on it. If you try this book in your training program and it doesn't teach your students how to write structured COBOL programs at an entry level for industry, you can return any or all books for a complete refund no matter how long you've had them.

From a practical point of view, then, you only need to do two things to make effective use of this book. First, since the book doesn't have to be read in sequence (see table 1), you must plan the sequence that is best for your course. Second, assuming you will want to measure the success of the course, you will have to develop a method for testing students upon completion of the course.

If you are training students for a non-IBM system, you will want to supply reference materials for the system your students will be using. Similarly, if you are training students for a DOS or OS system, you will probably want to provide the COBOL reference manual and programmer's guide for the compiler your students will be using. Except when debugging, however, your students should have little need for these manuals. So you can probably get by with one set of manuals for each group of students, rather than one set

Title	Order Number
Reference manuals:	
DOS Full ANS COBOL	GC28-6394
OS Full ANS COBOL	GC28-6396
VS COBOL for OS/VS	GC26-3857
Programmer's guides:	
DOS Version 3 COBOL Programmer's Guide	SC28-6441
DOS/VS COBOL Programmer's Guide	SC28-6478
OS Version 3 COBOL Programmer's Guide	SC28-6437
OS Version 4 COBOL Programmer's Guide	SC28-6456
OS/VS COBOL Programmer's Guide	SC28-6483

Table 2   COBOL manuals for the DOS and OS compilers

for each student. For your convenience, the order numbers for the current COBOL manuals for DOS and OS compilers are given in table 2.

Related products

As I mentioned earlier, this book is part 1 of a two-part series for COBOL training. The second book, *Structured ANS COBOL, Part 2,* is designed to train an entry-level COBOL programmer to use advanced COBOL features. This course covers table handling, subprograms, the COPY library, character manipulation, the debugging verbs, sort, ISAM files, and the related DOS and OS JCL. Since many practicing programmers are unable to use some of these COBOL capabilities, this course may be of value to them as well as to entry-level programmers.

One of the major training problems today is to train the experienced COBOL programmer to use the improved productivity techniques that are related to structured programming. For this purpose, Paul Noll developed the book called *Structured Programming for the COBOL Programmer.* This book first tries to motivate the reader to want to master the new techniques. Then it presents a practical method for designing, documenting, coding, and testing structured programs in COBOL. It also covers related techniques like structured walkthroughs and chief-programmer teams. Because this book presents material on design and documentation that isn't covered in part 1 or part 2 of *Structured ANS COBOL,* this book is valuable for programmer trainees as well as for experienced programmers.

After a new programmer is trained in COBOL or an experienced programmer is trained in structured programming, he all too often fails to use much of what he's been taught. For this reason, we developed *The Structured Programming Cookbook*. This book has two purposes. First, it presents standards and guidelines for program development in a structured COBOL shop. This part of the Cookbook functions as an instant standards manual, and many companies have adopted these standards with little or no modification. Second, the Cookbook presents complete program solutions for four problems that are taken from the four major classes of business problems: (1) input editing, (2) report extraction, (3) sequential file updating, and (4) random file updating. These solutions include structure chart, module documentation, and complete COBOL coding. By using these solutions as guides for new program development, a programmer doesn't have to start each program from scratch. For instance, when Paul Noll develops a master-file update program, he finds that he can use the structure chart, some module documentation, and even some of the COBOL code from the model update program in the Cookbook. In this way, the Cookbook can have a major effect on the productivity of a typical COBOL programmer.

To order any of these books, you can write, call, or use the order form near the back of this book. If you don't find them to be worth many times more than your purchase price, you can return them at any time for a full refund.

Conclusion

In this book, we have tried to do something that I don't think has been done effectively before. That is, we have tried to integrate the teaching of structured design with the teaching of COBOL. Although Paul has used this approach with programmer trainees in his shop for several years now, I think this is the first book that uses this approach. If this approach is successful, it means that a programmer trainee can begin writing professionally structured programs right from the start.

As always, we welcome your comments, criticisms, suggestions, or questions. If you have any, feel free to use the postage-paid comment form near the end of this book. With the help of your comments, I hope we can improve not only this product, but also future products.

Mike Murach, Publisher
Fresno, California
May, 1978

PART ONE

Required Background

Before you can start learning about COBOL, you need to understand some basic concepts. As a result, this part presents the
minimum background you'll need before you can learn how to program in COBOL. If you have already written programs in another
language or if you have had a course in computing or data processing, you probably are familiar with most of the material in this part.
If so, you can use this material as a review.

1

Preliminary Concepts and Terminology

Before you can learn to write COBOL programs, you must be familiar with a certain amount of background information. This chapter, which consists of four topics, is designed to provide that background. Topic 1 introduces the System/360-370 computer system; topic 2 explains the coding used in punched cards and describes the operation of a keypunch; topic 3 describes the sequence of steps a programmer performs when writing a structured COBOL program; and topic 4 introduces you to the major functions of an operating system.

If you are already familiar with these subjects through a previous course or job experience, you probably won't need to study this chapter. To help you determine whether or not to skip a topic, review the terminology lists, the behavioral objectives, and the problems at the end of each topic.

TOPIC 1 Introduction to the System/360-370

To begin with, a *computer* is a machine that accepts input data, processes it, and gives output data. For example, a computer can read sales data from punched cards, process this data, and provide output in the form of a printed sales report. A computer can also accept

13

many other forms of input, such as magnetic tapes or checks recorded in magnetic ink, and give many other forms of output, such as data on magnetic disks or displays on television-like devices. Because a computer's processing depends on the sequence of instructions (the *program*) that it is given prior to doing a job, it can process data in an almost endless variety of ways.

In general, a computer, also known as a *computer system*, consists of one or more input devices, one or more output devices, and a *central processing unit (CPU)*. A small system consists of a CPU and only a few *input/output (I/O) devices*, while a large system consists of a CPU and dozens of I/O devices. Theoretically, at least, the components of a computer system are chosen to fill the needs of the user: the system should be large enough to do all the jobs required by the user but not so large that processing capacity goes to waste.

The System/360 and the System/370

The IBM System/360 has been the most widely used computer system in history. Because its CPUs are available in many different sizes and can be combined with many different I/O devices, the System/360 can be used in relatively small businesses as well as in the largest businesses in the world. For example, the user of a small computer might have a System/360 Model 22, while the user of a large computer might have a 360 Model 195. Between the Model 22 and the Model 195 are Models 25, 30, 40, 50, and so forth.

The IBM System/370 is the successor to the 360. Because it makes use of more recent technological developments, the cost of computer processing can be lower with the 370 than with the 360. Like the 360, the System/370 is available in many model sizes—the Model 115, the 125, the 135, and so forth—and can be combined with many different I/O devices

Because the 370 was designed to be compatible with the 360, they are conceptually the same from a programmer's point of view, even though electronic components or other equipment elements may differ. In fact, programs written for the System/360 will run on a 370 without any changes as long as the same I/O devices are used. This makes it easy for a computer user to switch from a 360 to a 370.

On the other hand, the System/370 has some capabilities that go beyond those of the 360. If these capabilities are used, a 370 program will not run on a System/360. As a result, this book carefully notes any instances when the variations between the System/360 and the System/370 might cause programming or operational variations.

A small System/370

Figure 1-1 illustrates a typical, small-sized System/370, Model 135. It consists of a CPU, a card reader and card punch in the same physical unit (called a *reader/punch*), a printer, four tape drives, a disk unit consisting of five disk drives, and a console typewriter. The model numbers for the I/O devices are shown near the units so you can become familiar with these numbers. In this case, the components are a Model 135 CPU, a 2540 reader/punch, a 1403 printer, four 3400 tape drives, a 2314 disk unit, and a 3215 console typewriter.

The 2540 *card reader* has one input hopper and can stack cards in any of three output stackers. As the cards are read, one at a time, they pass from the input hopper to one of the stackers. The 2540 can read cards at a maximum speed of 1000 cards per minute.

The 2540 *card punch* also has one input hopper and can stack cards in any of three output stackers. Usually, blank cards are placed in the input hopper and data is punched into them during operation. In general, card punches are somewhat slower than card readers. The 2540, for example, can punch cards at a maximum speed of 300 cards per minute.

The 1403 *printer* can print at a maximum speed of 1100 lines per minute. To operate at such high speed, the 1403 prints on continuous rather than cut forms. *Continuous forms* are attached to each other in a continuous band of paper as illustrated in figure 1-2. They are fed through the printer by a mechanism that fits into the tiny holes on both sides of the forms. After the forms are printed, the sides can be removed and the forms themselves separated, usually at perforations. Because a printer can be adjusted to forms of many widths and lengths, it can be used to print very small forms such as mailing labels as well as 14-inch wide management reports.

A *tape drive* is an I/O device that can read data from or write data on a magnetic tape. The magnetic tape is a long strip of plastic tape that is wound on a reel; it is the big brother of the tape used for home tape recorders. When the reel of tape is mounted on the tape drive, data can be read from it and written on it at speeds much faster than those of card or printing operations. A 3400 tape drive, for example, typically operates at a speed of 60,000 characters of data per second, the equivalent of about 45,000 cards per minute. Tape drives and tape operations will be covered in detail in chapter 6.

The 2314 disk facility can read data from or write data on disk packs mounted on *disk drives*, or *spindles*, within the unit. The facility shown in figure 1-1 consists of five separate disk drives. The *disk packs* consist of several platters (disks), somewhat similar to

Figure 1-1   A System/370 Model 135

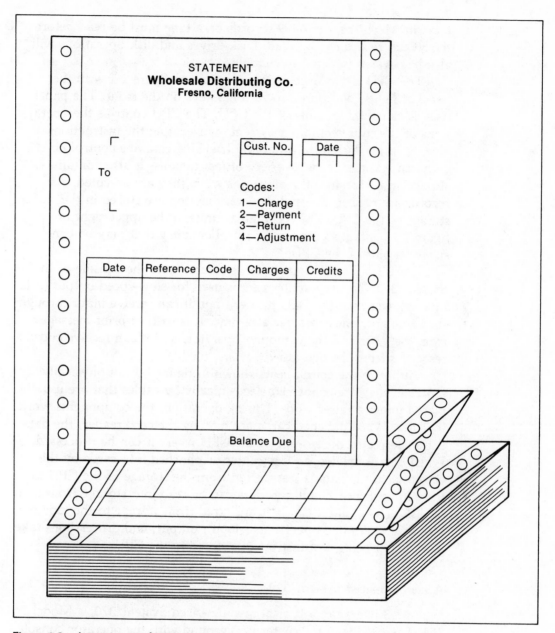

Figure 1-2 A continuous-form statement

phonograph records, that are stacked on a central spindle. The unique characteristic of the disk is that any one of the records stored on the device can be accessed without reading the other records. For example, 64,000 records might be stored on a disk pack for the 2314, yet any one of these records can be accessed and read in an average of about 88/1000 of a second. Contrast this with magnetic tape, in which the first 4999 records on a tape must be read before the 5000th record can be read. Disk drives and disk operations will also be covered in detail in chapter 6.

The CPU is the large rectangular unit in figure 1-1 with the panel of lights, dials, and operational keys on the front. The panel itself is called the *console* of the CPU. The CPU controls the operations of the entire computer system by executing the instructions given it in the form of a program. The CPU contains control circuitry so it can execute a variety of instructions. It also contains storage so it can store the programs while they are executed. As records are read from input devices, they too are stored in the storage of the CPU. The rectangular units in the upper right of figure 1-1 contain storage and control circuitry that may be considered a part of the CPU.

The 3215 *console typewriter* is located near the console of the System/370. This typewriter can be used for slow-speed output (it is much slower than the 1403 printer), and it can receive input through the keyboard, one character at a time. It is used to print messages from the system to the computer operator, and it can receive coded responses from the operator.

Although the components shown in figure 1-1 are physically separate, they are connected electronically by cables that are usually placed under a raised floor. During operation, the components work together. When punched cards are read by the card reader, the data is transferred to the storage of the CPU where it can be processed. When data is printed on the printer or punched into cards by the card punch, the data is transferred from the storage of the CPU to the output device. Similarly, data can be read into storage from tape or disk drives, and it can be transferred from storage to the tape or disk drives. And all operations—input, output, and processing—take place under control of instructions stored in the CPU.

A medium-sized System/370

Figure 1-3 illustrates a typical medium-sized System/370, a Model 158. The CPU is in the center background with the operator console at its right front corner. On this system, the operator console includes a television-like video screen on which messages to the operator are displayed. A keyboard below the screen allows the operator to enter responses or initiate messages to the system.

A 3505 card reader and 3525 card punch are located to the left of the CPU in figure 1-3. The card reader is available in 800 and 1200 card-per-minute models and the card punch in three models at 100, 200, or 300 cards per minute.

Figure 1-3   A System/370 Model 158

In the foreground are three printers. The two leftmost ones are the 1403 printers. The printer on the right is a 3211 printer, which is capable of a maximum speed of 2000 lines per minute. Frankly, not all 370 systems are large enough to require three printers. Many System/370s use a 3211 printer alone, or perhaps a 3211 plus one 1403.

The row of eight tape drives in the left background are 3420 units. At the near end of the row, you can see the tape control unit that controls the transfer of data to or from any one of the drives. The 3420 tape drive is available in several models that range from a moderate read/write speed of 120,000 characters per second to a very high speed of 1,250,000 characters per second.

The most heavily used input/output units of a System/370 are the disk drives. The system in figure 1-3 includes two types of direct-access devices, both located in the right background. The unit nearest the front of the photograph is a 2305 Fixed Head Storage Unit. It is a very high speed device used on larger systems to store programs that must be quickly and frequently retrieved from direct-access storage. The rear unit is a 3330 Direct Access Storage Facility that can mount up to eight disk packs, one on each of the eight individual drives contained within it.

The 3330 is actually a successor to the 2314 Direct Access Storage Facility that was originally developed for the System/360. The two devices are similar, but the more expensive 3330 is much faster and stores much more data. Details on both the 2314 and 3330 are presented in chapter 6.

Loading and executing a program

Before a computer can be used to process data, it must be given a detailed sequence of instructions called a program. In other words, the equipment (or *hardware*) must be combined with programs (or *software*). A separate program is required for each job that a computer does; thus, a typical computer installation has hundreds of different programs. Because of the time required to write programs, the amount of money spent for programming in a typical installation is usually far more than the amount spent for computer rental.

Before a program can be *executed* by a computer system, it must be *loaded* into the CPU. From an operator's point of view, this process is generally quite simple. On a small System/360 or 370, for example, the operator puts *job-control cards* in the card reader for each program to be executed; these cards indicate what programs are to be loaded and executed and what input or output files are required by the programs. If a program is supposed to read input cards, the input (data) cards follow the job-control cards for that program. When the operator pushes the start button on the card reader, the job-control cards are read and the computer system begins loading and executing the programs specified.

Before a computer system can execute a program, however, the files required by the program must be available to the system. If, for example, cards are to be punched by a program, the operator must put blank cards in the card punch and push the start button on that device; this means the card output file is ready for processing. Similarly, if a special form is needed, the operator changes the continuous form in the printer and pushes the printer's start button. And if tapes or disk packs are required by the program, the operator must mount the required tapes on appropriate tape drives and the required disk packs on appropriate disk drives. After they are mounted, the operator must push the start buttons on these devices. When all files are available to the system and the I/O devices are ready for operation, the computer system executes the program. If the I/O devices aren't ready when a computer system starts to execute a program, the system will print messages to the operator telling him what files must be mounted on what devices.

To illustrate these operational procedures, suppose that a small System/370 is to prepare payroll checks from two input tapes—one containing weekly payroll data and one containing year-to-date totals. To load and execute the program, the operator will put the job-control cards for this program in the card reader and push its start button. As soon as this is done, the cards will be read and the job information will be stored until the computer system is ready for the program. When it is ready, the program will be loaded into the CPU of the system. Before the program can be executed, however, the operator must prepare the I/O devices required by the program. This means mounting the required tapes on the appropriate tape drives and pushing the start buttons on these devices. It also means adjusting the continuous-form payroll checks in the printer of the system and pushing its start button. When all I/O devices are ready for operation, the computer system executes the check-writing program, thus reading the input tapes and printing the payroll checks.

Discussion

It should be clear by now that computer systems vary tremendously as to the components that make them up, their capabilities, and their price. A small system like the one in figure 1-1 will rent for around $10,000 to $25,000 per month, while a large system may cost well over $100,000 per month. Purchase prices for computer systems vary accordingly; generally, they are about forty-five times as much as the monthly rental price. The System/360 or 370 user has the option of renting or buying the system.

Although System/370s are now installed in thousands of businesses, there are still thousands of System/360 installations operating today. A typical System/360 is much like the system shown in figure 1-1. It will consist of a 2540, a 1403, several 2400 tape drives, and a 2314. The console typewriter, however, will be a 1052 on a System/360 in contrast to the 3215 of the System/370.

New models of computers are being developed, too. In 1978, IBM started delivery on three new CPUs: the 3031, 3032, and 3033. Each one is a CPU that is plug-to-plug compatible with the System/370; in other words, one CPU can be exchanged for another without changing the system's I/O devices, the operating system, or the programs that are run on the computer. The advantage of the models in this 30 series is that they produce more power at a lower cost. For example, two System/370 model 168s have a relative power factor of 1.7 at a current price of about $190,000 per month. In contrast, two 3033s offer a power factor of 4.0 at a price of $140,000 per month. Because of the increased capabilities and lower cost, many System/370 users will switch to series 30 CPUs in the years to come.

This book is designed to teach you how to write COBOL programs for the System/360, 370, or series 30. Because the System/360 and 370 are conceptually the same, they are generally spoken of as if they were the same, even though there are some technological differences. Throughout this book, then, you will find them spoken of as one system that is referred to as the System/360-370. Furthermore, all references to the System/370 will apply to the series 30 computers as well.

Terminology

computer
program
computer system
central processing unit
CPU
input/output device
I/O device
reader/punch
card reader
card punch
printer
continuous form

tape drive

disk drive

spindle

disk pack

console

console typewriter

hardware

software

executing a program

loading a program

job-control card

Objectives

1. List the components of a typical System/360-370.
2. Describe what is meant by a *continuous form*.
3. Describe typical operator's procedures for loading and executing a program on a small System/360-370.

Problems

1. Identify the computer system and I/O devices of the system for which you will be writing COBOL programs.

TOPIC 2   The Punched Card and Keypunching

At one time or another, you have probably come into contact with a standard punched card—perhaps in the form of a payroll check, a utility bill, or a student registration card. The question is: Can you decode the data that is punched in a card?

Figure 1-4 shows the basic characteristics of a standard punched card. The card has eighty vertical *columns*, numbered from left to right. A hole can be punched in twelve different positions in each card column. For the purpose of illustration, each of these punching positions is punched in column 1 of the card. From bottom to top, these punches are called the 9-punch, 8-, 7-, 6-, 5-, 4-, 3-, 2-, 1-, 0- (zero), 11-, and 12-punch. As you can see at the right edge of the card, the 0- through 9- punches are called *digit punches*; and the 12-, 11- and 0-punches are called *zone punches*. The 0-punch, therefore,

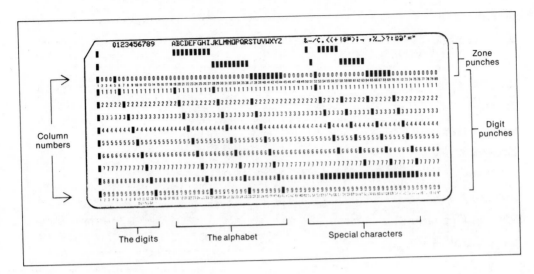

Figure 1-4 The standard punched card

can be either a zone or a digit punch: it is a digit punch when no other punch is recorded in the column, but it is a zone punch if a digit punch is recorded below it.

Each column of a punched card can contain one character of data; namely, a number (0 through 9), a letter (A through Z), or a *special character* (such as an asterisk, a dollar sign, or a decimal point). In the illustration, the numbers are punched in columns 5–14, the letters in columns 19–44, and twenty-six special characters in columns 50–75. The character punched in each column is printed at the top of the card directly over the column.

The combinations of punches used to represent characters in a punched card make up a code called *Hollerith code*, named after Herman Hollerith, inventor of the punched card. As you can see in the illustration, the numbers 0 through 9 are represented by the corresponding digit punch, and the letters by the combination of a zone and a digit punch. The special characters are represented by one, two, or three punches in a single card column. For example, a decimal point consists of a 12-, 3-, and 8-punch, while a hyphen (-) consists of an 11-punch only. You can find the punches used for any character by looking at the IBM "green card" for the System/360 (form X20-1703) or the "yellow card" for the 370 (form GX20-1850).

When a punched card is used to represent business data, groups of adjacent columns, called *fields*, are used to represent specific data items. For instance, columns 21–40 may be used for the description of a product, while columns 76–80 are used for the number of the customer who bought the product. In the card in figure 1–5, there

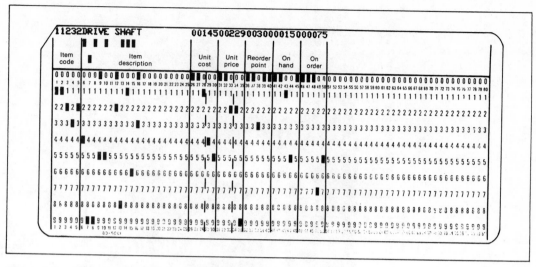

Figure 1-5   An inventory balance-forward card

are seven fields in columns 1–50. From left to right, they are the item-code field, the item-description field, the unit-cost field, the unit-price field, the reorder-point field, and so on.

If you study the fields in figure 1–5, you can see that they are punched differently, depending on whether they are numeric or *alphanumeric*. (An alphanumeric field may contain letters, numbers, or special characters.) For an alphanumeric field, the data begins in the leftmost column of the field and continues to the right. When there are no more characters to be punched, the remainder of the field is left blank. Thus, the item-description field contains DRIVE SHAFT in columns 6–16 and blanks in columns 17–25. This can be referred to as *left-justifying* the data in the field.

In contrast, numeric fields are punched to correspond with an assumed decimal point—the decimal point itself isn't punched. For example, the unit-price field in figure 1–5 assumes two decimal places, as indicated by the dotted line. Thus, the unit price of $2.29 is punched as the number 229 in columns 33–35. Since all columns of a numeric field should be punched with a digit, zeros are punched in columns 31 and 32 to fill the unit-price field. When a numeric field doesn't have a decimal point, its data is *right-justified*; again, any blank columns in the left part of the field are punched with zeros.

In some cases, a numeric field in a card may contain a negative number. This is normally indicated by an eleven-punch in the rightmost column of the field. For example, a customer may have a credit balance of $12.85 in his accounts-receivable record with a company. If the balance field is in columns 51–56, the field would

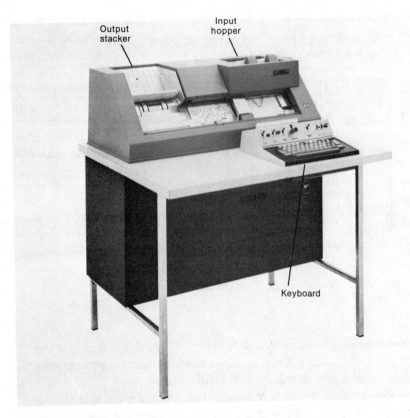

Output
stacker

Input
hopper

Keyboard

Figure 1-6   The 129 keypunch

contain 00128N. Since N is the combination of an eleven-punch and a 5-punch and two decimal places are assumed, it would indicate a negative 12.85.

A corner cut, as illustrated in figure 1-5, is used to be sure that all cards in a deck are facing the same way. For example, if a card is turned upside down in a deck with right corner cuts, that card will stick out at the right corner. The corner cut can be on either the left or the right, but all corner cuts should be on the same side for any one deck of cards.

The keypunch

The *keypunch*, shown in figure 1-6, is used to record data in punched cards. The keypunch operator places blank cards in the input hopper of the machine and sits at the typewriter-like keyboard. To the left of the operator are printed documents, called *source documents*, from which data is to be keypunched. As the operator's fingers strike the keys, the corresponding Hollerith codes are punched into the columns of the cards, one column per keystroke. At the end of the job, the newly punched cards are in the stacker on the left of the machine.

During the keypunching operation, some functions take place automatically—for example, feeding cards, skipping over fields that aren't going to be punched, and duplicating data from one card into the following card. This increases the speed at which an operator can keypunch data. Since the automatic functions can be changed quite easily at the beginning of each job, the keypunch can be used to punch cards in any format. In general, keypunches print (or *interpret*) the data being punched over the card column in which it is punched; however, some of the older keypunches do not print data on the cards at all.

The verifier

To ensure that the data punched in the cards is accurate, the keypunch operation is usually followed by a verifying operation. The *verifier* can be a separate machine that looks much like a keypunch, or it can be the same machine as the keypunch. In this second case, the machine is changed to verifying mode by the flip of a switch.

Regardless of what type of machine is used, verifying is similar to the keypunching operation. The verifier operator uses the same source documents that were used during keypunching. He or she places the keypunched cards in the input hopper of the verifier and keys data on the keyboard of the verifier exactly as if operating the keypunch. The difference is that the verifier, instead of punching, checks to see that the holes in the card correspond to the keys that the operator strikes. If all the characters of data that the operator keys for a card agree with the characters already punched in the card, a correct-card notch is cut on the right side of the card indicating that its data has been verified.

Suppose, however, that the verifier operator keys the digit 3 for column 12 of a card, but the column contains the digit 2. In this case, the keyboard locks and an error light turns on. The operator checks the source document to be sure that the digit 3 is correct, pushes a button to release the keyboard, and strikes the digit 3 again. If the character in the card and the character keyed do not agree this time, the keyboard again locks and the error light turns on. The operator then repeats the process one more time to be absolutely sure that the correct character is 3 and, if so, keys it again. If the verifier still detects an error, an error notch is cut over the card column, and the verifier moves on to the next column. Once an error card is detected, a new card is punched, either as part of the verifying operation or as a separate step later on, depending on what type of equipment is used.

Discussion

Although keypunches are used primarily to punch data into cards, they can also be used to punch programs. For instance, the programs you write for this course could be punched into cards. In addition, a keypunch could be used to punch your job-control cards. However, on your system you may be able to enter your programs directly into the computer through data-entry devices called *terminals*. If that's the case, you'll only need the keypunch for punching data cards.

Although a professional programmer should rarely have to do his own keypunching (the keypunching department does it), he or she should be able to use a keypunch when necessary. In practice, a programmer often uses a keypunch to punch a few correction cards for a COBOL source deck or to punch job-control cards. This book doesn't give specific instructions for using a keypunch since there are many different models. However, keypunching is quite easy to learn on your own.

Terminology

column

digit punch

zone punch

special character

Hollerith code

field

alphanumeric

left-justified

right-justified

keypunch

source document

interpreted card

verifier

terminal

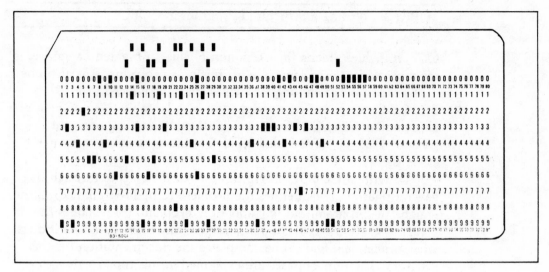

Figure 1-7   An accounts-receivable card

Objectives

1. Given an uninterpreted punched card, tell what data is punched in specified fields of the card. No special characters will be included.

2. Describe how a keypunch operator records data in punched cards.

3. Describe how a verifier operator verifies the data punched into cards.

Problems

1. (Objective 1) Refer to the punched card in figure 1-7.

    a. What data is punched in the customer-name field, columns 13–35, of the card?

    b. What data is punched in the reference-number field, columns 36–40?

    c. What value is punched in the amount field, columns 47–52 with two decimal positions?

Solutions

1. a. NATIONAL HARDWARE

    b. 49333

    c. -49.98

TOPIC 3   Writing a Structured Program in COBOL

COBOL, which stands for *CO*mmon *B*usiness *O*riented *L*anguage, is the most widely used language for business problems. It is also one of the oldest programming languages, first introduced in 1959. Because the language was designed to be adaptable to equipment of all manufacturers, COBOL is available on most computers. In general, COBOL can be used on all but the very small computer systems.

To write a COBOL program, a programmer goes through five general phases: (1) he defines the problem to be programmed; (2) he designs the program that will solve the problem; (3) he codes the program in COBOL; (4) he tests his program to be sure that it does what is intended; and (5) he completes the documentation for the program. These five phases are explained in this topic.

Problem definition

Defining the problem is simply making sure that you know what the program you are going to write is supposed to do. You must understand what the input is going to be, what the output of the program must be, and what calculations or other procedures must be followed in deriving the output from the input. Two documents that are often used for defining card input and printer output are the *record layout form* and the *print chart*.

Record layout forms have many different formats. The one you will see throughout this book is illustrated in figure 1-8. Although it can be used for any kind of record—card, tape, or disk—the example in figure 1-8 gives the format for an inventory-balance card. By studying the field-name and position entries, you can see that the item-code field is in card columns 1-5, the unit-cost field is in columns 26-30, and so on. (The characteristics and usage entries will be explained in chapter 2.)

A print chart, such as the one in figure 1-9, shows the layout of a printed report or other document. It indicates the print positions to be used for each item of data on the report and the headings to be printed. As indicated in figure 1-9, the heading INVESTMENT REPORT is to be printed in print positions 15-31, the column heading ITEM CODE is to be printed in lines 4 and 5 in print positions 7-10, and so on. Similarly, the item code for each data line (as opposed to a heading line) is to be printed in print positions 6-10 and the amount invested is to be printed in positions 41-49. At the end of the report, the total amount invested is to be printed after skipping two lines; this total is indicated by two asterisks printed in

File name ___BALCDS___   Record name ___BAL-FWD-CARD___   Date ___April 3, 1978___
Application ___Inventory Control___   Designer ___DAL___
Comments _____

Field Name	Item Code	Item Description	Unit Cost	Unit Price	Reorder Point	On Hand	On Order	Unused
Characteristics	X(5)	X(20)	999V99	999V99	9(5)	9(5)	9(5)	X(30)
Usage								
Position	1-5	6-25	26-30	31-35	36-40	41-45	46-50	51-80

Figure 1-8 A record layout form

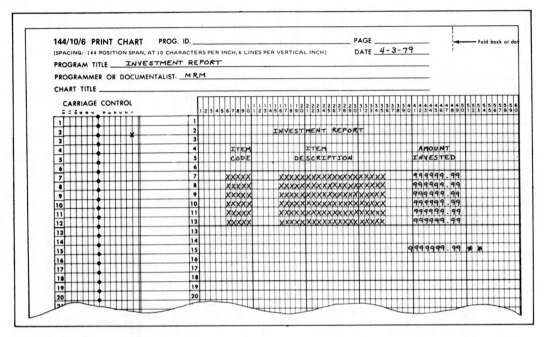

Figure 1-9   A print chart

positions 51 and 53. Although figure 1-9 indicates only 60 print positions from left to right, a complete print chart usually has 132 or more—at least as many as are available on the printer being used.

A print chart may also have an area that can be used to show what punches should be made in the *carriage-control tape* for the job. A carriage-control tape is a paper tape that is placed in the carriage-control mechanism in the printer. This tape, which can be punched in twelve different positions, moves in conjunction with the continuous form that is being printed, so the tape can control the skipping of the form. In an invoicing job, for example, a 1-punch may correspond to the first address line of the invoice, a 2-punch to the first line in the body of the form, and a 3-punch to the total line of the form. Then, if the printer is instructed to skip to a 1-punch, the continuous form is skipped to the first address line of the invoice. If it is instructed to skip to a 2-punch, the continuous form skips to the first body line of the invoice. And so on.

In general, you will only use punches 2 through 12 when printing special forms like invoices or payroll checks. When printing standard forms, you can always assume that a carriage-control tape is present in the printer with a 1-punch to represent the first printing line on the form. This is standard operating procedure. Since the programs in this book do not require the use of special forms, the print charts used from now on will not have a carriage-control area.

In addition to the record-layout form and print chart, a programmer may be given other written program specifications before writing a program. For example, he may be given formulas to be used for calculating output results or a narrative summary of the processing to take place.

To further define the problem, a programmer usually questions the person who assigns the program to him, since certain aspects of the problem are likely to be indefinite. For instance, suppose you are asked to write a program that prepares a report like the one in figure 1-9 from a deck of input cards with the format shown in figure 1-8. What additional information would you need from the person who assigned the problem to you? Here are some ideas:

1. How is the amount invested calculated? Is it the on-hand balance multiplied by unit cost, or is it on-hand balance multiplied by unit price?

2. Should the input records be sorted to be sure they're in numerical sequence by item number? (Since input decks are usually considered to be out of sequence, this is a common programming practice.)

3. Is one line supposed to be printed for each card in the input deck or would it be better to print a line for only certain items—say those items with an inventory investment over $10,000?

The point is that you must know exactly what the program is supposed to do before you can write it. Often, an error in testing a program stems from not completely understanding what the program is supposed to do.

Program design

Design is a critical stage in the process of program development because it affects the stages that follow. With good design, a program can be coded and tested with maximum efficiency. With poor design, coding is likely to be inefficient and testing is often a nightmare.

In recent years, programming has moved toward a new method of program design called *structured design*. The idea here is to solve a problem by first breaking it down into its functional parts, or *modules*. The program can then be thought of as a series of small, manageable problems rather than as one large, complicated problem.

As the programmer divides a structured program into its functional modules, he creates some sort of *structure chart*, or *structure diagram*. The purpose of this chart is to show the program modules and their relationships to each other.

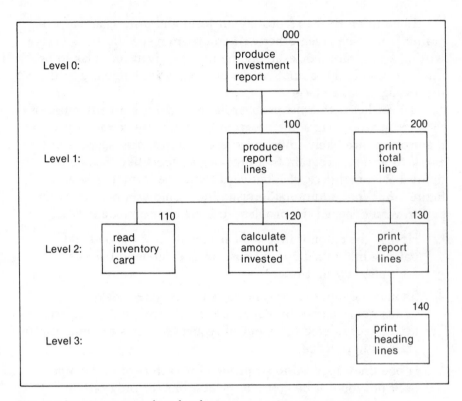

Figure 1-10   A structure chart for the investment-report program

To illustrate, suppose a program is to be written that prepares an investment report like the one charted in figure 1-9 from a deck of cards with the format given in figure 1-8. The structure chart in figure 1-10 divides this program into seven modules at four levels. At the top level, level 0, there is one module that represents the entire program. At level 1, the top-level module is divided into two modules, one to produce the report lines and one to print the total line after all the report lines have been printed. Level 2 breaks the produce-report-lines module, module 100, into three more modules: module 110 reads the input cards, module 120 does the necessary calculations for figuring the investment amount, and module 130 prints the lines on the output report. Finally, level 3 consists of a module that will print heading lines on each page of the report.

If a program is large, the programmer further subdivides it into as many levels as are necessary. When the structure chart is complete, each of the modules should be small enough that it can be easily coded and tested. The large, complex program thus becomes a collection of small, manageable modules. And both coding and testing are simplified.

Once the structure chart is created, it is the overall guide to program development. However, each of the modules must be documented before coding. Module documentation will be explained in detail in chapter 3.

Coding

Coding a program in COBOL involves writing the code that eventually is translated into a machine-language program—that is, a program that can be run by the computer. The major purpose of this book, of course, is to teach you how to code in COBOL.

When coding in COBOL, special coding sheets are used. Then, if the program is to be keypunched when it is finished, one card is punched for each coding line. The resulting deck of cards is called the *source deck*.

Before the source deck is punched, however, the programmer should *desk check* his coding sheets to catch and correct any programming or clerical errors he might have made. Then, once the deck has been punched, it should be key verified as described in topic 2. When the programmer is sure that the source deck is as accurate as possible, he is ready to have it *compiled*.

Compiling a COBOL source deck means converting the source code of the source deck into an *object program*. The object program may be punched into cards, called an *object deck*, but it is usually stored on magnetic disk. In any case, the object program contains machine-language instructions that can be executed by the computer system itself.

The translation of source code into object code is called a *compilation* and is done by the computer under control of a translator program called a *compiler*. A typical compilation is illustrated in figure 1-11. This compilation takes place in two steps:

1. The COBOL compiler, which is stored on magnetic disk, is loaded into the computer.

2. The computer executes the COBOL compiler, thus processing the source deck and creating the object program, which is written on a disk ready to be loaded and executed. During the compilation, *compiler output* is printed by the computer.

The compiler output includes a *source listing* (a listing of the source deck) as well as various reference tables to which you will be introduced in chapters 4, 8, and 9. If any errors are detected by the compiler during the compilation (as is usually the case), one or more *diagnostic messages* (or just *diagnostics*) are printed on a *diagnostic listing* as part of the compiler output, and the object program is not created. Each diagnostic on the diagnostic listing calls attention to a possible source-deck error.

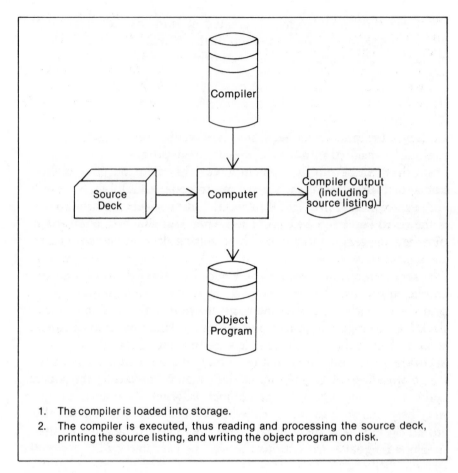

Figure 1-11   Compilation

If there are diagnostics, the programmer makes the necessary corrections to the source deck and the deck is recompiled. This process is repeated until there are no more diagnostics or until the only remaining diagnostics are those that do not indicate true source-deck errors. This last compilation then is referred to as a *clean compilation*. At this stage, the object program is ready to be tested.

Testing

To test a program, the programmer tries his object program on some *test data*. This test data is intended to simulate all of the conditions that may occur when the program is actually used. For card-to-printer programs, the test data is punched into cards; but for more complex programs, the test data may include card decks, tapes, disks, and any other form of input used. When the program is executed, the programmer compares the actual output with the output that he expected to get. If they agree, he can assume that the program does what it is intended to do.

More likely, however, the actual output and the intended output will not agree. The programmer must then *debug* the program. He must find the errors (bugs), make the necessary corrections to the source deck, recompile the source program, and make another *test run*. This process is continued until the program executes as intended.

In actual practice, a series of test runs is made using different sets of test data. The test data for the first test run is usually low in volume—perhaps a dozen input records or less—and should be designed to test only the main processing functions of the program. After the program is debugged using this data, it should be tested using data that tries all conditions that may possibly occur during the execution of the program. This set of test data is usually much greater in volume than the first one. After the program executes correctly with this data, a test run may be made using actual, or "live," test data. Then, an entire group of programs may be tested together to be sure that the output from one program is valid input to the next. Only after a program has proved itself under conditions that are as close to real as possible is the program considered ready for use.

Documentation

In data-processing terminology, *documentation* refers to the collection of records that specifies what is being done and what is going to be done within a data-processing system. For each program in an installation, there is a collection of records referred to as *program documentation*. One of the jobs of a programmer is to provide this documentation.

Why is programming documentation necessary? Data-processing requirements change. For example, tax laws change: the percent used to calculate social security tax has increased periodically over the last several years as has the maximum amount of social security tax that must be paid in any one year. Company policies also change: discounts may vary from year to year, production departments may switch to new forecasting techniques, and accounting practices may change. For each change, all affected programs must be modified.

Change is so common, in fact, that large companies have special maintenance programmers whose entire job is to modify existing programs. This frees other programmers to work on new programs without interruption. Without adequate documentation, however, maintenance programmers could not make changes within a reasonable period of time. Even when a programmer modifies his own programs, documentation is valuable. Three months after writing a program, you may barely remember it.

Some of the more important documents likely to be required by a company's documentation standards are the following:

1. Specifications that give the detailed requirements of the program

2. Layouts of all input and output records on special layout forms

3. A structure chart

4. Specifications for the processing to be done by each of the modules in the structure chart

5. The source listing created during the last compilation

6. Listings of the input data used for testing and listings of the output results of the test runs

Most of these documents, of course, are prepared and used as the program is developed. Nevertheless, a programmer normally spends some time refining and finishing documentation when he completes a program.

Discussion

Traditionally, the major emphasis of a programming course has been on the coding phase of program development. In other words, the typical programming course dealt primarily with the programming language to be taught. In recent years, however, it has become clear that design has more effect on programmer productivity than any other phase of program development. As a result, this course emphasizes design as well as coding. And it gives heavy emphasis to testing and debugging, another critical stage in the process of program development.

Although you have been introduced to structured design in this topic, it is only one of several techniques that are associated with *structured programming*. These techniques involve design, documentation, coding, and testing. Since this book teaches structured programming as well as COBOL, most of these techniques are explained in this book. For instance, chapter 3 presents detailed techniques for structured design and documentation. Chapters 4 and 10 present structured techniques for testing. And the techniques for structured coding are presented throughout this book. As a result, though you may have only a hazy notion of what structured programming is all about right now, you will be able to design, document, code, and test structured COBOL programs by the time you finish this book.

Terminology

COBOL

record layout form

print chart

carriage-control tape

structured design

module

structure chart

structure diagram

source deck

desk checking

compile

object program

object deck

compilation

compiler

compiler output

source listing

diagnostic message

diagnostic

diagnostic listing

clean compilation

test data

debug

test run

documentation

program documentation

structured programming

Objectives

1. Given the record layout form and the print chart for a programming problem with card input, identify the card columns or print positions of any input or output data item.

2. Explain the purpose of a channel-1 punch in a carriage-control tape.

3. In general terms, describe how a COBOL source deck is compiled into an object program.

4. List the five phases a programmer goes through when writing a COBOL program.

Problems

Note: If you have not previously been introduced to record layout forms or print charts, you should do the problems that follow. Otherwise, you will probably want to skip them since they are quite elementary. As you work your way through this book, you will be presented with progressively more complex examples and problems involving the analysis of layout forms and print charts.

1. (Objective 1)

   a. In the card layout shown below, which columns contain the hourly-rate field?

Field Name	Employee Number	Employee Name	Hourly Rate	Hours Worked	Unused
Characteristics	X(5)	X(20)	99V99	99V9	X(48)
Usage					
Position	1-5	6-25	26-29	30-32	33-80

   b. What data is punched in columns 6-25?

2. (Objective 1)

   a. Based on the print chart in figure 1-12, in what print positions should the first heading line, OVERTIME REPORT, be printed?

   b. In what print positions is the final total of overtime hours supposed to be printed?

   c. In what print positions is the message, END OF JOB, supposed to be printed?

   d. What character is supposed to print in print position 40 of each detail line?

   e. Should the headings be printed on all pages or only on the first page of the report?

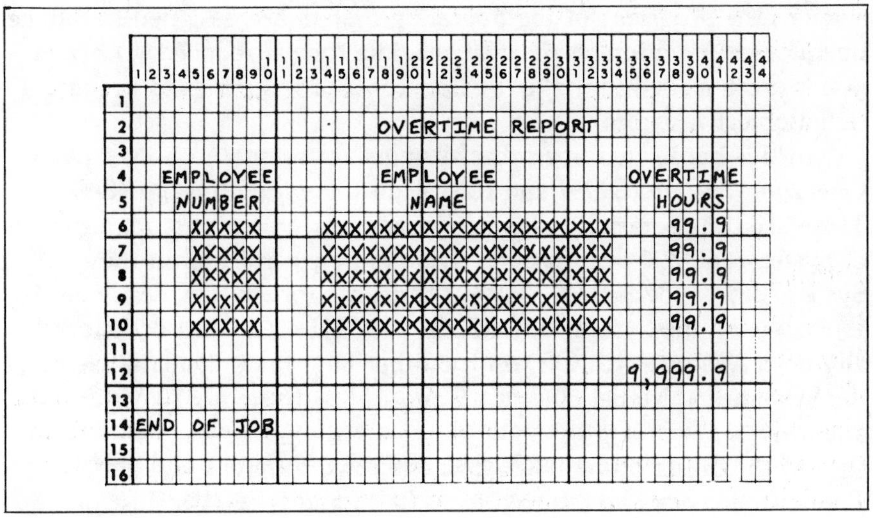

Figure 1-12   Print chart for overtime report

Solutions

1. a.   Columns 26-29

    b.   Employee name

2. a.   Positions 18-32

    b.   Positions 35-41

    c.   Positions 1-10

    d.   A decimal point

    e.   You can't tell from a print chart, but it is common to print the headings on all pages of a report.

TOPIC 4   Introduction to the DOS and OS Operating Systems

At one time, computer manufacturers first designed a computer and then decided what programming support, such as COBOL or FOR-TRAN compilers, should be supplied with it. About the mid-1960s, however, most manufacturers realized that the programming support, or software, was almost as important as the equipment, or hardware. One result was the development of operating systems, which are supplied along with all major computer systems.

An *operating system* is a collection of programs designed to improve the efficiency of a computer installation. These programs affect both operating and programming efficiency. For instance, some of the programs of the operating system are designed to reduce operator intervention so the system's idle time is reduced. Other programs are designed to make it easier for a programmer to prepare a tested object program.

In this book, two operating systems are presented: IBM's *Disk Operating System (DOS)* and IBM's full *Operating System (OS)*. These are the operating systems that are used in the vast majority of System/360-370 installations. DOS is in general use on the System/360 Model 22, 25, 30, 40, and occasionally on the Model 50, as well as on the System/370 Model 115, 125, 135, and occasionally on the Model 145. OS, on the other hand, is in general use on the System/360 Model 50 and up and on the System/370 Model 145 and up.

At the present time, DOS comes in two different versions. These versions can be referred to as DOS and DOS/VS. Just plain DOS is the version used on all System/360s, while DOS/VS is the version used on all System/370s. The primary difference between these two versions is that DOS/VS offers a capability called *virtual storage* (thus, the VS), while DOS doesn't. (If you're not familiar with virtual storage, you'll find a description of it later on in this topic.) From an operational point of view, both versions are alike, the only difference being the advanced capabilities of DOS/VS. As a result, you can interpret any reference to DOS in this book as a reference to either DOS or DOS/VS unless specific differences are noted.

OS also comes in several versions. Two are designed for the System/360 and two are for the System/370. The two versions for the System/360 are referred to as OS/MFT (Multiprogramming a Fixed number of Tasks) and OS/MVT (Multiprogramming a Variable number of Tasks). (If you're not familiar with multiprogramming, you'll find a description of it later on in this topic.) The two versions for the System/370 are called OS/VS1 and OS/VS2 where VS stands for Virtual Storage. All four of these versions are much alike from an operational point of view, with the primary differences being the advanced functions offered by each. As far as this book is concerned, then, everything that refers to OS can be interpreted as referring to any of these four versions of OS unless specific differences are noted. (Incidentally, you'll often hear the OS dropped when a programmer talks about one of these operating systems; that is, they're referred to as MFT, MVT, VS1, and VS2.)

Before you start the next chapter, you should be familiar with five capabilities of an operating system that are in common use on both DOS and OS systems. These include stacked-job processing, multiprogramming, link editing, spooling, and virtual storage. As a result, they are presented now. If you are already familiar with these functions, you can check the objectives at the end of this topic to see whether you need to study this material any further.

Stacked-job processing

Before *stacked-job processing* was developed, a computer system stopped when it finished executing a program. The operator removed the program output, such as card decks or magnetic tapes, and made ready the I/O units for the next program. He or she then loaded the program—usually in the form of an object deck—and placed any cards to be processed in the card reader. The program was then ready to be executed.

The trouble with this intervention by the operator between programs is that it wastes computer time. If a company runs 120 programs a day and the operator takes thirty seconds to set up each program, one hour of computer time is lost. With computer time on a medium-sized system costing $100 or more per hour, that lost time can be very costly.

When stacked-job processing is used, the computer rather than the computer operator loads programs. To make this possible, all of a company's programs are stored in *libraries* on a *system-residence device,* which is usually a disk device. As a result, programs can be directly accessed from the system-residence device and loaded into storage at a high rate of speed.

At the start of a day's computer operations, then, a *supervisor program* (or just *supervisor*) is loaded into the storage of the CPU, and control of the computer is transferred to this program. The supervisor program, which is one of the programs of the operating system, is responsible for loading all of the other programs to be executed from the system-residence device. The supervisor program, which may require 20,000 storage positions or more, remains in storage during the execution of all other programs.

Before I go on, I want to define a couple of terms relating to computer storage. On the System/360-370, each storage position in the CPU is referred to as one *byte.* And on all systems, one *K* refers to approximately one thousand storage positions. To be precise, one K is 1,024 bytes, so 16K is 16,384 bytes of storage. But in normal conversation, the excess storage positions are dropped. This is common terminology, and I'll be using it whenever appropriate from now on.

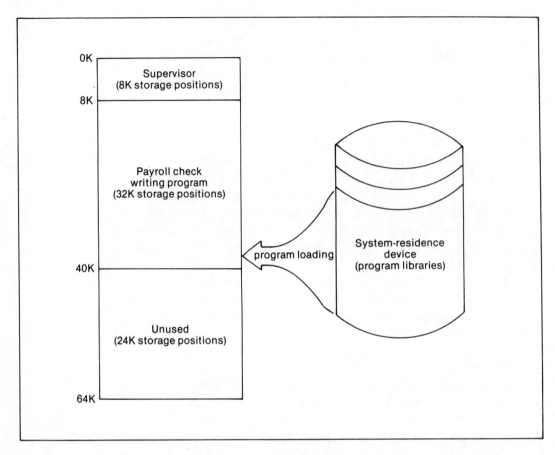

Figure 1-13   Internal storage during execution of an application program on a small
DOS system

Figure 1-13 illustrates the storage of a small computer while a
payroll program is being executed. In this case, total storage consists
of 64K with the supervisor occupying 8K positions and the payroll
program occupying 32K positions; 24K isn't used while this program
is being executed. When the payroll program finishes its execution, it
passes control to the supervisor program so the next program can
be loaded.

To tell the supervisor which programs are supposed to be executed, the operator places a stack of job-control cards, such as the
stack in figure 1-14, in the card reader. These cards give the names
of the programs to be executed, along with information such as
which tape should be mounted on which tape drive. There are usually several job-control cards for each program to be executed, and,

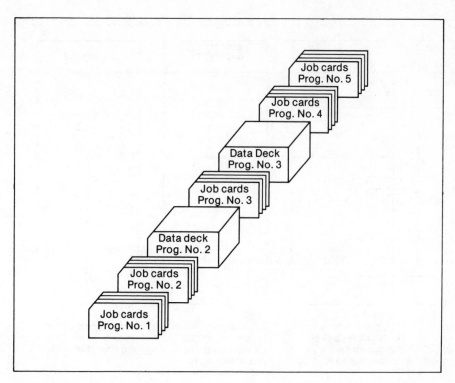

Figure 1-14   A job deck

if a program requires card input, the data deck follows the job-control cards. In the illustration, programs 2 and 3 require card input, while programs 1, 4, and 5 do not. The stack of job-control cards is commonly referred to as a *job deck*.

When the computer finishes executing one program, loading and executing the next one typically takes place in four steps as illustrated in figure 1-15. First, control of the computer passes from the completed program to the supervisor program. Second, the supervisor loads a program called the *job-control program* from the system-residence device and passes control to it. This job-control program is one of the programs of the operating system. Third, the job-control program reads and processes the job-control cards for the next program. If there are any errors in the job-control cards or if any necessary information is omitted, the job-control program prints or displays a message so the problem can be corrected. When all job cards for the next program are processed, control passes back to the supervisor. Finally, the supervisor loads the next program from the system-residence device and passes control to its first instruction.

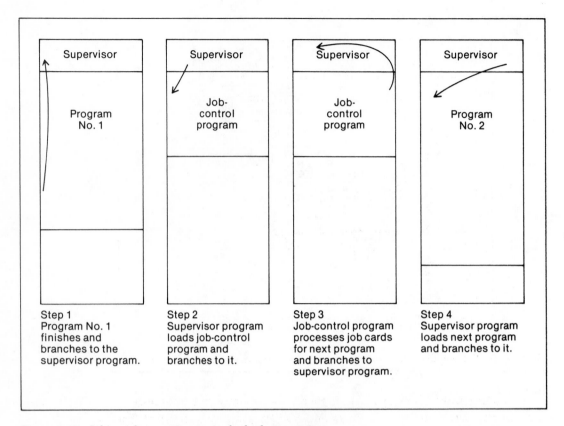

Figure 1-15   Job-to-job transition in stacked-job processing

Multiprogramming

Multiprogramming means the simultaneous execution of more than one program. Actually, this is misleading, because what really happens is that, simultaneously, multiple programs are present in separate parts of storage, but only one program executes at any given time. The others wait for input or output operations to be completed, or simply wait to be given control by the supervisor.

Multiprogramming can increase the overall productivity of a computer system, because CPU operations such as arithmetic operations can be executed thousands of times faster than input or output operations. Since it is the nature of business programs to have little internal processing between I/O operations, the CPU is normally idle a great percentage of the time with the program waiting for an I/O operation to be completed. In an effort to make use of this idle time, multiprogramming systems allow additional programs to be in storage so their instructions can be executed while the first program waits for its I/O operations to be completed.

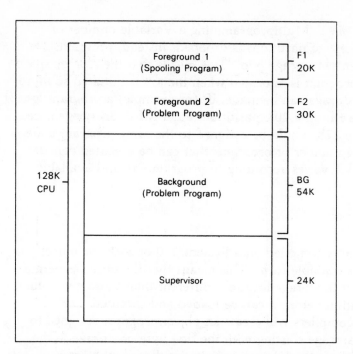

Figure 1-16   Storage allocation in a multiprogramming DOS system

In a standard DOS system, for instance, up to three programs may be multiprogrammed at one time. Under supervisor control, the storage area above the supervisor is divided into three *partitions* called *background* (BG), *foreground 1* (F1), and *foreground 2* (F2). Although they can be altered by special operator commands, the sizes of these partitions are assigned standard values at the time the system is generated. Figure 1-16 shows the storage allocations for the three partitions in a typical multiprogramming system. The supervisor then has the added responsibility of deciding which partition will begin processing after the supervisor has started an I/O operation. To solve this problem, a priority system is used, with the supervisor always giving control to the F1 program first. If the F1 program is waiting for an I/O operation to finish, the supervisor then gives control to the F2 program. If F2 is also waiting, control is given to the BG program.

Like DOS, OS/MFT (Multiprogramming a Fixed number of Tasks) uses partitions for multiprogramming. Both the number and size of these partitions are set when the system is generated, but they can be altered by the operator for any special processing requirements. Under MFT, up to 15 different programs can be executed concurrently. However, practical considerations such as CPU storage and I/O devices usually limit this to from two to seven programs executing concurrently.

Under OS/MVT (Multiprogramming a Variable number of Tasks), the concept of partitions is dropped. Instead, programs are executed in a general storage pool. This means that the storage space required for a program is allocated when the job is initiated so more efficient use of storage can be made. If, for example, a program requiring 12K is run in a 20K paritition under MFT, 8K goes unused. In contrast, only 12K would be assigned to the same program under MVT. Thus, the number of programs that can be executed concurrently under MVT varies according to program size and available storage space.

Link editing

When a program is compiled on a System/360 or 370, the object program is in relocatable form. This means that the object program must be assigned to storage locations different than those given during the compilation before it can be loaded and executed. For instance, most compilers will create an object program designed to be loaded into storage starting with the first byte of storage in the computer. However, the supervisor occupies these first storage bytes. As a result, the object program must be reassigned to the partition or area of the storage pool in which it will actually be loaded and executed.

Under DOS and DOS/VS, this is done by the *linkage-editor program* (or just *linkage editor*). The input to this program is the object program; the output is a module called a *load module* that can be loaded and executed. To compile and test a COBOL program, then, takes three steps. First, the source code is compiled into an object program. Second, the object program is link edited into a load module. Third, the load module is loaded and executed, thus testing the COBOL program.

Under OS, programs are loaded by the *loader program*. This program can load either object modules or load modules. Before it can load an object module, however, it must reassign the object program to the storage locations in which it will be loaded. Here again, three separate steps are required to compile and test a COBOL program. First, compilation; second, relocation and loading by the loader program; and third, execution of the load module resulting from the original COBOL program.

All OS systems also provide a linkage editor. When it is used to convert an object program into a load module, compiling and testing a COBOL program takes the same three steps as under DOS. First, compilation; second, link editing into a load module; and third, loading and execution of the load module.

Besides converting a single object program into a load module, a linkage editor can combine two or more segments of an object program (called *object modules*) into a single load module. For instance, a programmer who is writing an inventory program may want to make use of an available object module that calculates square roots; otherwise, he would have to write this routine himself. In this case, the inventory program is the main program and the square-root module is a *subprogram*. Before testing the inventory program, then, the linkage editor would be used to combine the main program and subprogram into a single load module. Since the use of subprograms isn't covered in this book, the linkage function of the linkage editor program will not be mentioned again. As a result, you need only be familiar with the relocation function of the linkage editor.

Spooling

Even with multiprogramming, there is still usually more CPU time available than can be used because of the difference between internal processing speed and the speed of the I/O units. In a further effort to make better use of the available CPU time, *spooling programs* serve as an interface between the very slow I/O devices—the card readers, punches, and printers—and the processing programs. When the processing program attempts to print a line on the printer, for example, a spooling program causes the line to be written as a record on a tape or disk file instead. Since these devices are much faster than the printer, they allow the problem program to resume processing much sooner. Later, when little is being done by the computer, the spooling program prints out the lines that were temporarily stored on tape or disk.

The same spooling procedure is used in reverse for card input files. The spooling program first places the data in the cards on tape or disk. Then, when the processing program tries to read a card from the card reader, it is actually read from the tape or disk, and the program thus waits a much shorter time for I/O completion. A spooling program is usually run in the F1, or top priority, partition, so the I/O operations will keep running regardless of the other demands on CPU time.

Figure 1-17 is a schematic illustration of the concept of *spooling*. Quite simply, the job deck, which consists of job-control statements plus data decks, is read by the spooling program and converted to a number of disk files. The disk files of job-control statements can then be processed by the job-control program and the data files on disk can be processed by the processing programs. When an application program is executed, it processes the appropriate disk file for the original card deck just as though it was the card deck itself. For

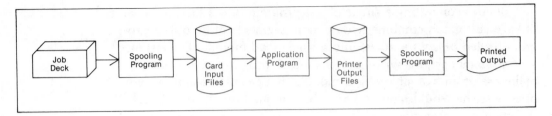

Figure 1-17   Spooling

output, the lines intended for the printer are written in a disk file area reserved for printer output. Later, when the spooling program processes the output disk file for this application program, the disk file is converted to printed output.

Incidentally, spooling takes place even though the programmer may be completely unaware of it. In fact, the processing programs are written as though they were using card input and printer output, even though they are actually using disk input and output. The operating system itself makes the necessary adjustments so that spooling takes place automatically.

Virtual storage

Virtual storage (VS) is another capability of advanced operating systems that you should know about. It allows simulation of a very large CPU on a much smaller one by using disk storage as an extension of internal storage. In a typical virtual storage system, for example, a computer with 256K bytes of *real storage* might appear to the user to have 512K bytes; it is thus said to consist of 512K bytes of virtual storage.

During processing, only small portions of the programs being executed are present in real storage. The parts of the program that aren't currently being used are stored on disk. As additional portions of programs are required, parts that are no longer needed are written out on the disk and the new ones replace them in real storage.

Virtual storage is accomplished in different ways on different computer systems. Figure 1-18 illustrates the relationships and terms used for DOS/VS and OS/VS1. Here, real storage consists of a supervisor area plus a *page pool*. The page pool area consists of portions of programs currently being multiprogrammed. These portions are fixed-size blocks, 2K bytes long, called *pages*, and the 2K blocks of real storage they occupy are called *page frames*. As a program is executed, the required pages are brought into real storage from disk after the pages that are no longer needed are written back on the disk. This shuttling of pages back and forth from CPU storage to

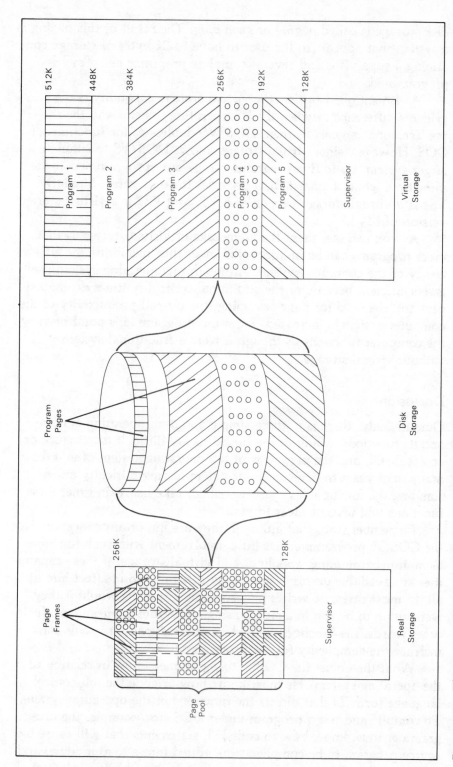

Figure 1-18   The concept of virtual storage on the IBM System/360-370

disk storage is called *paging* or *swapping*. The result of this paging is a system that appears to the user to have 512K bytes of storage containing a supervisor and several complete programs being multiprogrammed.

As I mentioned earlier, the virtual storage capability is the primary difference between the VS operating systems and their predecessors. In general, then, DOS/VS duplicates the functions of DOS. However, since virtual storage allows DOS/VS to simulate a larger system, up to five programs can be multiprogrammed at the same time while standard DOS provides for only three. Similarly, VS1 is a virtual storage version of MFT, and VS2 is a virtual storage version of MVT.

As you can see, then, the advantage of virtual storage is that more programs can be multiprogrammed, thus increasing the efficiency of the computer system. Although the operating system itself is less efficient because of the additional control routines demanded of it and the need for page swapping, the overall productivity of the computer system is increased. From the programmer's point of view, the computer functions as though it were a traditional system without virtual storage.

Discussion

Quite frankly, there is nothing simple about an operating system and its functions. Many of the functions are difficult to visualize or comprehend; and the programs of the operating system often take many man-years to develop. So if you're having difficulty understanding the functions I've just described, take heart. In time, these functions will become clear to you.

Remember, too, that although they are important conceptually, the COBOL programmer has little involvement with such functions as multiprogramming, spooling, and virtual storage. If these capabilities are available on his system, they generally don't affect him at all. In most cases, he writes his programs just as he would if they were going to be run in a simple, single-program environment. In other words, the functions take place automatically, so they don't increase the complexity for the programmer.

What then must the COBOL programmer know in relation to the operating system? He must know how to code the job-control language (or *JCL*) that directs the functions of the operating system. To compile and test a program under DOS, for example, the programmer must know how to code JCL statements that will cause his source program to be compiled, link edited into a load module, and then loaded and executed. In terms of difficulty, this is a relatively manageable task.

Rather than get into job-control language now, however, all of the JCL that you will require for this course is explained in chapter 8 for DOS users and chapter 9 for OS users. So when you're ready to compile your first COBOL program, you will go to topic 1 of these chapters for the required JCL. Then, at various times as you progress through the course, you will refer to other topics in these JCL chapters. Sooner or later, though, you will want to read the entire JCL chapter for your system, since everything it covers will be of use to you in your job as a COBOL programmer.

Terminology

operating system

Disk Operating System

DOS

Operating System

OS

stacked-job processing

library

system-residence device

supervisor program

supervisor

byte

K

job deck

job-control program

multiprogramming

partition

background

foreground 1

foreground 2

link editing

linkage-editor program

linkage editor

load module

loader program

object module

subprogram

spooling program

spooling

virtual storage

VS

real storage

page pool

page

page frame

paging

swapping

JCL

Objectives

1. Describe the purpose of each of the following programs:

    supervisor

    job-control program

    linkage editor

    loader program

2. Explain how stacked-job processing, multiprogramming, spooling, and virtual storage help to increase the productivity of a computer system.

Problems

1. Find out what operating system or systems you will be writing COBOL programs for. Also, find out whether multiprogramming, spooling, and virtual storage are used on your system.

PART TWO

COBOL: The Core Content

This part presents the critical material of your COBOL training. If you master it, you will be able to design and code complete COBOL programs in a professional style. Furthermore, it will be relatively easy for you to add to this *core content* by learning how to use other COBOL facilities. As a result, you should be prepared to put far more effort into the mastery of the material in this part than you will put into subsequent parts of your COBOL training.

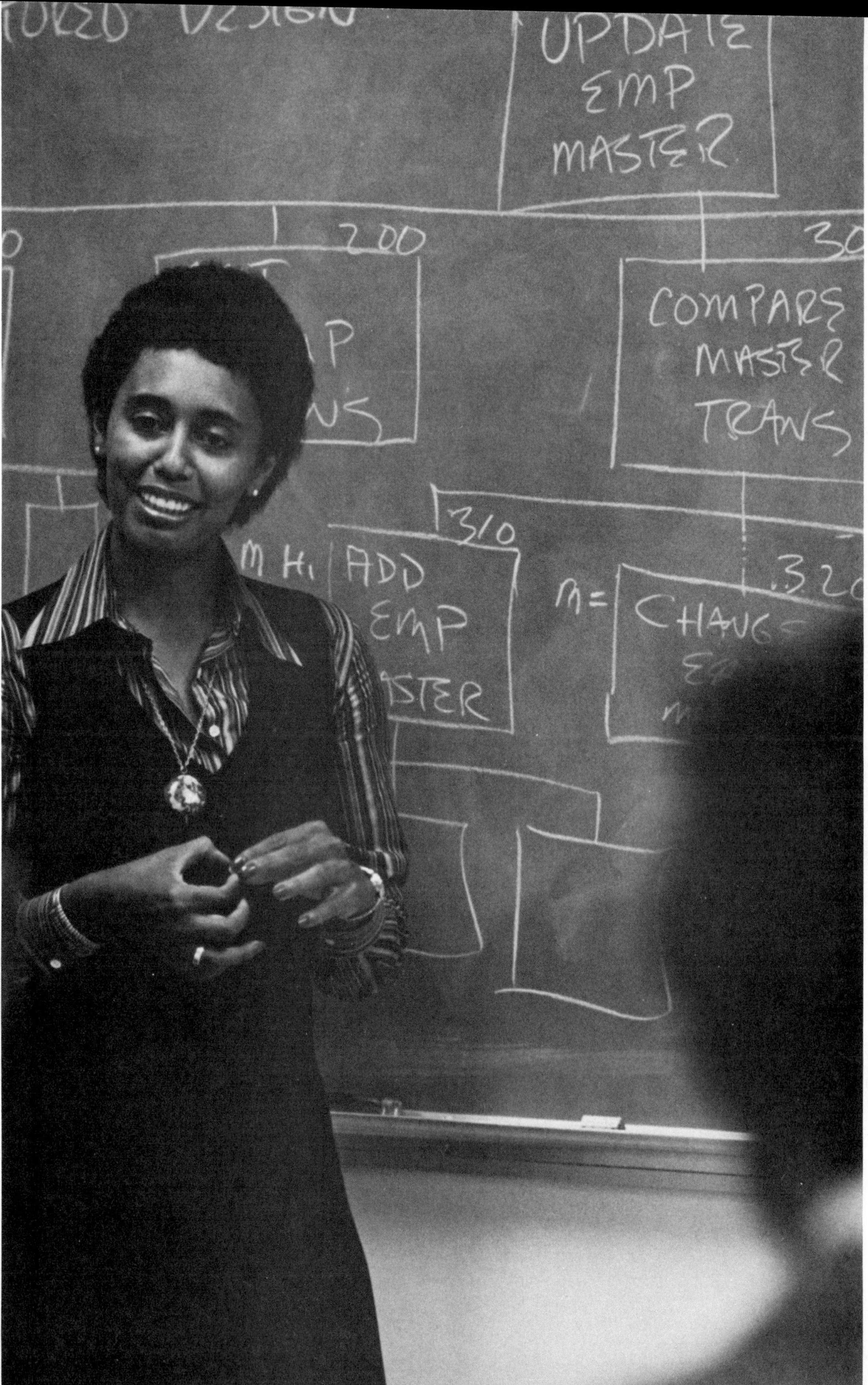
UPDATE EMP MASTER
200
COMPARE MASTER TRANS
310
ADD EMP

2

A Basic Subset of ANS COBOL

This chapter introduces you to American National Standard (ANS) COBOL. It does so by presenting programming problems and the COBOL solutions for these problems. Since the solutions use COBOL code that represents the basic capabilities of the language, the code presented can be called a *subset* of the complete ANS COBOL language.

Because effective COBOL programming requires some knowledge of how a computer executes a stored program, topic 1 presents the concept of the stored program and its relationship to the COBOL program. If you are already familiar with the System/360-370 instructions and their execution, you can probably skip this topic. Then topic 2 introduces the first subset of the COBOL language. Finally, topic 3 presents elements that complete the basic COBOL subset.

The purpose of this chapter is to get you to see the complete picture right away—that is, how the elements of COBOL work together in a complete program. When you have completed this chapter, you should be able to write complete COBOL programs of considerable complexity. The remaining chapters will then build on this base of knowledge.

TOPIC 1   COBOL and the Stored Program

When a program is loaded into a computer, it is placed in the storage of the CPU. That's why a computer program is often referred to as a stored program. Small computers may have only a limited amount of storage—say 8000 *storage positions*—while some of the largest computers have several million storage positions.

Associated with each of the storage positions of a computer is a number that identifies it, called the *address* of the storage position. A 16K computer, for instance, has addresses ranging from 0000 to 16,383. You can therefore talk about the contents of the storage position with address 180 or the contents of storage position 14,482.

In the System/360-370, each storage position is commonly referred to as a *byte* of storage. Within these storage bytes, data can be stored in four different forms. To keep this explanation simple, however, let's consider only the form in which one character is stored in each storage byte. To illustrate this form, suppose the following boxes represent the 20 bytes from 480 to 499:

Contents: | G | E | O | R | G | E | 3 | 4 | 3 | 9 | 9 | 8 | 2 | | * | 1 | 1 | 2 | 1 | 4 |

Addresses: 48_0 48_5 49_0 49_5

You can then say that byte 480 contains the letter G, byte 487 contains the number 4, byte 494 contains an asterisk, and byte 493 contains a blank. Or you can say that there is a 2 at address 497 and the number 343 is stored in bytes 486 through 488. This is simply the way data-processing people talk about storage and its contents.

Several bytes in a row that contain one item of data such as an item number or unit price are commonly referred to as a *field*. For instance, in the above example, bytes 486–490 (which is read as 486 through 490) might represent a balance-on-hand field, while bytes 495–499 represent an item-number field. To address a field, a System/360-370 instruction specifies the address of the leftmost byte as well as the number of bytes in the field. Thus, address 486 with a length of 5 would address the field in bytes 486–490, while address 1024 with a length of 20 would address the field in bytes 1024–1043.

Of course, a storage positon, or byte, isn't really a small box with a character of data in it. Instead, each byte consists of a number of electronic components called *binary components* because they can be switched to either of two conditions, commonly referred to as "on" and "off".

On the System/360, the binary component used is the *magnetic core*. This tiny, doughnut-shaped component can be magnetized in either of two directions: clockwise or counterclockwise. When magnetized in one direction, a core is said to be *on*; when magnetized in the other direction, a core is said to be *off*. A string of cores makes up one byte of storage in a computer, and thousands of cores in planes make up a computer's storage. Because most storage on older systems consists of magnetic cores, you will often hear storage referred to as *core storage*.

In order to represent data, the cores at a storage byte are turned on or off in selected combinations by wires that run through the center of the cores. Each combination of on and off cores represents a digit or digits, a letter, or a special character. Figure 2-1, for example, might represent three storage positions. By decoding the combinations of on and off cores at each storage position, it can be determined that the characters B, 2, and 9 are stored. (The shaded cores are on; the white cores are off.)

On some models of the System/370, magnetic cores are *not* used for storage. Instead, transistor-like solid materials are used as the binary components. Regardless of this variation, however, the principles are the same: a fixed number of binary components makes up one storage byte and one or more bytes represent a field in storage.

Instructions

While a program is being executed, both the instructions of the program and the data being processed are contained in storage. The instructions, in coded form, indicate the operations that are to be performed and give the addresses of the storage bytes that hold the data to be operated upon. The number of storage bytes required to store an instruction varies from computer to computer and from instruction to instruction. In the System/360-370, instructions are two, four, or six storage positions in length, depending on the function of the instruction.

Although a program may consist of thousands of instructions, there are basically only four types that a computer can execute, plus some miscellaneous ones. As a result, a program with 6000 instructions consists of the same types of instructions being executed over and over again. These basic types are (1) input and output (I/O), (2) data-movement, (3) arithmetic, and (4) logical (or program-control) instructions.

I/O instructions

An I/O instruction specifies the type of input or output operation to be performed and the storage bytes to be used in performing the

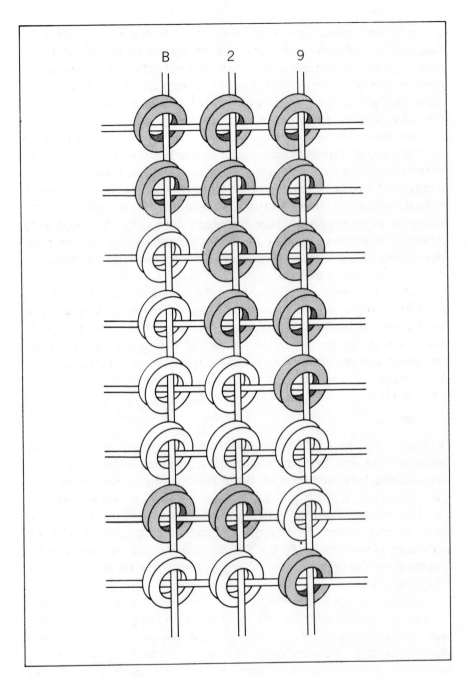

Figure 2-1   Core storage

operation. For example, an input instruction such as a card reading
instruction might specify that a card is to be read and its data is to
be stored in the 80 storage bytes beginning with address 5501. In this
case, storage bytes 5501–5580 are called the *card input area*, or just

the *input area*, of storage. When the read instruction is executed, the data that is read from a card replaces the data that the card input area originally contained. The data from card column 1 is stored in storage byte 5501, the data from card column 2 is stored in byte 5502, and so on, until the data from card column 80 is stored in byte 5580.

Similarly, an output instruction such as a write instruction for a printer specifies the storage bytes from which the output line is to be printed (called the *printer output area*, or just *output area*, of storage). If a write instruction specifies that a line should be printed from locations 5601 through 5700, the content of storage byte 5601 is printed in print position 1 on the printer, the content of byte 5602 is printed in print position 2, and so on. Since a typical printer may have up to 132 print positions between the left and right margins, the printer output area may require up to 132 storage positions.

Other I/O instructions enable a computer to make use of the other I/O capabilities of the system. For example, a write instruction for a card punch will cause a card to be punched from an output area. Similarly, instructions for tape units will cause tape records to be read into input areas or to be written from output areas, and instructions for disk devices will cause disk records to be read into input areas or to be written from output areas.

Data-movement instructions

Data-movement instructions allow a computer to move data from one field in storage to another. The basic data-movement instruction, commonly called the move instruction, causes the data from one field to be moved unchanged to another field. If, for example, a move instruction specifies that the contents of storage bytes 541–545 should be moved to bytes 701–705, the execution of the instruction can be shown as follows:

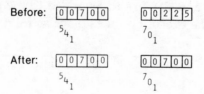

The effect is that the data in the first field is duplicated in the second field.

Another basic data-movement instruction is the edit instruction. The main purpose of this instruction is to move data into a printer output area in a form that will be easier to read when printed. For instance, $3.25 is more understandable than 00325.

In its simplest form, the edit instruction may operate like a move instruction except the insignificant zeros (zeros to the left of a number such as the italicized zeros in *00*140) are suppressed (changed to blanks). If, for example, the contents of bytes 536–540 are moved with zero suppression to bytes 671–675, the execution takes place as follows:

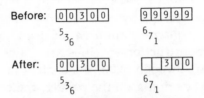

Depending on the codes stored in the receiving field, the edit instruction may also cause decimal points and commas to be inserted into a field, dollar and credit signs to be placed before and after the number, etc.

Other System/360-370 data-movement instructions are used to convert data from one form to another. Since three or more forms of data are likely to be used when your COBOL programs are compiled, a significant portion of a System/360-370 program may be made up of data-conversion instructions.

Arithmetic instructions

In general, there are two different ways in which arithmetic instructions operate in the System/360-370. In the format discussed here, the instruction specifies the arithmetic operation (addition, subtraction, multiplication, or division) and the two fields to be operated upon. The result of the arithmetic operation replaces one of the fields specified, while the other field remains unchanged.

For example, to illustrate the add instruction, suppose that the contents of bytes 546–550 are to be added to the contents of bytes 701–705. Then, the execution takes place as follows:

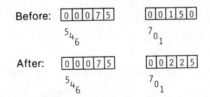

Actually, another form of data storage is used for data involved in arithmetic operations, but conceptually this is what happens. When the subtract, multiply, or divide instructions are executed in this two-field form, the operation takes place in basically the same way.

Because the result of a multiplication or addition may be larger than either field operated upon (for instance, 555 plus 500 equals 1055), one of the fields is usually moved to a larger field before the calculation takes place. Similarly, because the result of a division has a remainder, the number that is divided must be placed in a larger field, part of which becomes the quotient and part of which becomes the remainder.

Logical instructions

The basic logical instruction and the basis of logic in the computer is the branch instruction. When a program is initially loaded into storage, the load module specifies in which storage bytes the instructions are to be stored and at which storage byte the computer is to begin executing the program. When the computer finishes executing one instruction, it continues with the next instruction in storage. After executing the instruction in bytes 1000–1005, for example, the computer executes the instruction starting with address 1006. The only exception to this sequence results from use of the branch instruction. When the branch instruction is executed, it can cause the computer to break the sequence and jump to the instruction beginning at the address specified in the branch instruction.

For instance, one type of branch instruction tells the computer to branch whenever it is executed. This is called an *unconditional branch*. Suppose then that an unconditional branch instruction, which is stored in bytes 4032–4035, specifies a branch to address 801. When the branch instruction is executed, the computer will continue with the instruction starting at address 801.

Conditional branch instructions cause branching only when specified conditions are met. For example, one type of conditional branch instruction specifies a branch if the result of an arithmetic instruction is negative. Suppose this instruction occupies storage positions 2044–2047 and specifies that the computer should branch to address 1000 if the result of the preceding arithmetic instruction is negative. If the result is zero or positive, the computer continues with the instruction starting at address 2048, the next instruction in storage. If the result is negative, however, the computer continues by executing the instruction starting at address 1000.

Other branch instructions specify that a branch should take place when the result of an arithmetic calculation is zero, when the result of an arithmetic calculation is larger than the result field, or when an I/O device isn't working. Perhaps the most used branch instruction, however, specifies a branch based on the results of a comparison between two fields in storage. This branch instruction is used in conjunction with the second type of logical instruction, the compare instruction.

The compare instruction specifies that two fields are to be compared. When it is executed, the computer determines the relationship between the two fields: Are they equal? Is the first field greater in value than the second? Is the first field less than the second? The branch instruction then specifies a branch based on any of these three conditions. If, for example, the compare instruction compares two fields representing ages, the branch instruction can specify that a branch should take place if the first age is less than the second.

A compare instruction can operate on alphanumeric as well as numeric fields. For example, if two fields containing alphabetic names are compared, the branch instruction can specify that a branch take place when the second name is higher in alphabetic sequence than the first name. Or, if a one-position alphanumeric character is compared with a storage position containing the character M, the branch instruction can specify that a branch take place when the characters are equal.

Discussion

Understanding the nature of the stored program is important because a COBOL program is related to its object program. For instance, the COBOL READ and WRITE statements are compiled into input and output instructions. When executed, the instructions resulting from a READ statement cause data to be read from an input device into an input area in storage; the instructions resulting from a WRITE statement cause data to be written on an output device from an output area in storage.

Similarly, a COBOL arithmetic statement such as

```
ADD TR-ON-HAND TO TR-ON-ORDER
```

will cause one or more arithmetic instructions to be compiled into the object program. A COBOL MOVE statement such as

```
MOVE TR-ITEM-NUMBER TO PR-ITEM-NUMBER
```

will cause one or more data-movement instructions to be compiled. And a COBOL IF statement such as

```
IF AVAILABLE IS LESS THAN BF-REORDER-POINT
      PERFORM PROCEDURE-1
ELSE
      PERFORM PROCEDURE-2
```

will cause a compare instruction and two or more branch instructions to be compiled. By understanding the general nature of the System/360-370's instructions, you will be better able to understand what happens when COBOL statements are compiled and executed.

Terminology

subset

storage position

address

byte

field

binary component

magnetic core

core storage

card input area

input area

printer output area

output area

unconditional branch

conditional branch

Objectives

1. Identify these terms: *storage position, storage address, byte*.

2. Describe one way in which a field in storage can be identified
    by a System/360-370 instruction.

3. List the four basic types of instructions that can be executed by
    a typical computer system, and describe the execution of typical
    instructions within each group. For instance, describe the execu-
    tion of the move instruction within the data-movement group of
    instructions.

4. Explain what an input or output area in storage is.

TOPIC 2   Introduction to Structured COBOL

COBOL is by far the most widely used programming language for
business applications. The language has been popular since the mid-
1960s, and tens of thousands of programmers have been trained in
it. COBOL is now available on nearly all medium- and large-sized
business computers, and it is available on many small-sized computers as well.

Although all COBOL compilers are based on a single set of
language specifications, each computer manufacturer's version of
COBOL has its own peculiarities. As a result, you cannot take a
COBOL program for one system—say an IBM System/370—and
compile it on another system—say a Univac 1100. Instead, a series
of changes first has to be made to the source program.

In an attempt to standardize COBOL, the American National
Standards Institute approved a standard COBOL language in 1968.
These standards were designed so a standard COBOL compiler could
be implemented for computers of varying sizes. This could be done
by implementing only a portion (a subset) of the complete language.
Thus, subset compilers have been developed for small computer
systems, while full standard compilers have been developed for large
systems. As you might guess, a subset of standard COBOL can be
compiled on a full compiler, but full COBOL cannot be compiled on
a subset compiler.

Because of the criticism of the 1968 standards and changing
requirements in the computer industry, the 1968 standards were
revised in 1974. These new standards deleted some of the capabilities
of the old standards, modified others, and added a number of
capabilities. The new specifications can be referred to as ANS
COBOL 1974 in contrast to ANS COBOL 1968. COBOL is continually being reviewed by user committees, and we can expect a
revised set of the current COBOL standards in the 1980s.

In spite of the attempts at standardization, however, ANS
COBOL variations still exist from one manufacturer to another. In
general, these variations are caused by *extensions* to the standard
specifications. These extensions are designed to provide some
capability that isn't provided for by the ANS specifications. The
1968 and 1974 standards, in fact, allow such extensions. No matter
how many extensions a manufacturer incorporates into his compiler,
he can still refer to it as "standard" as long as the rest of the
language conforms to the standards.

Because it takes time and money to develop new compilers,
computer manufacturers do *not* release new compilers as soon as
new standards are released. For example, IBM didn't release an ANS
74 compiler for the System/360-370 until 1977. Furthermore, because
it takes a computer user time and money to convert his existing programs from one compiler to another and to retrain his programmers,
new compilers are *not* readily accepted when they are released.
That's why it will be several more years before the 1974 standards
are widely used on the System/360-370.

At present, seven different IBM ANS COBOL compilers are
available with the System/360-370, and this book is designed to
teach you to create structured COBOL programs using any of these

compilers. For the most part, the ANS COBOL language is the same for all of them, so you should have no problems. When variations do exist from one compiler to another, the differences will be carefully explained.

The seven ANS compilers currently in use on the System/360-370 are as follows:

X 1.   DOS Subset COBOL (1968)
  2.   DOS COBOL, Version 3 (1968)
  3.   DOS/VS COBOL (1968)
X 4.   OS COBOL, Version 2 (1968)
  5.   OS COBOL, Version 3 (1968)
  6.   OS COBOL, Version 4 (1968)
  7.   OS/VS COBOL (1968 or 1974)

The first six compilers are based on the 1968 standards. The seventh compiler offers both 1968 and 1974 ANS COBOL, but only one at a time; a compiler option allows you to change from one set of standards to the other. Be sure to find out which compiler you will be using so you can take note of any specific references to it. The heading at the top of the first page of any COBOL source listing will tell you what compiler produced the listing. (Incidentally, IBM no longer supports DOS Subset COBOL or Version 2 OS COBOL, so their users should eventually upgrade to the next COBOL compiler.)

Because you are almost certain to encounter changes in your COBOL compiler in the years ahead, we have made every effort to present a subset of the COBOL language that will be in use ten or more years from now. As a result, all of the language presented in this book is within both the 1968 and 1974 standards. So if you are using a 1968 ANS compiler, you will have no problem upgrading to a 1974 ANS compiler. In the same way, we have tried to present elements of the COBOL language that are almost certain to be included in future revisions of the ANS COBOL standards.

A Sample ANS COBOL Program

Figure 2-2 gives the characteristics of a reorder-listing program that is to be written in COBOL. The input consists of a deck of balance-forward cards, one card per inventory item. The output of the program is a listing of those items in inventory that need to be reordered. The illustration indicates the card columns and characteristics of each input field and the print positions for each item to be printed on the output listing. As you can see from the processing specifications, a line is printed whenever an item's available stock

Input record layout:

Field Name	Item No.	Item Description	Unit Cost	Unit Price	Reorder Point	On Hand	On Order	Unused
Characteristics / Usage	9(5)	X(20)	999V99	999V99	9(5)	9(5)	9(5)	X(30)
Position	1-5	6-25	26-30	31-35	36-40	41-45	46-50	51-80

Print chart:

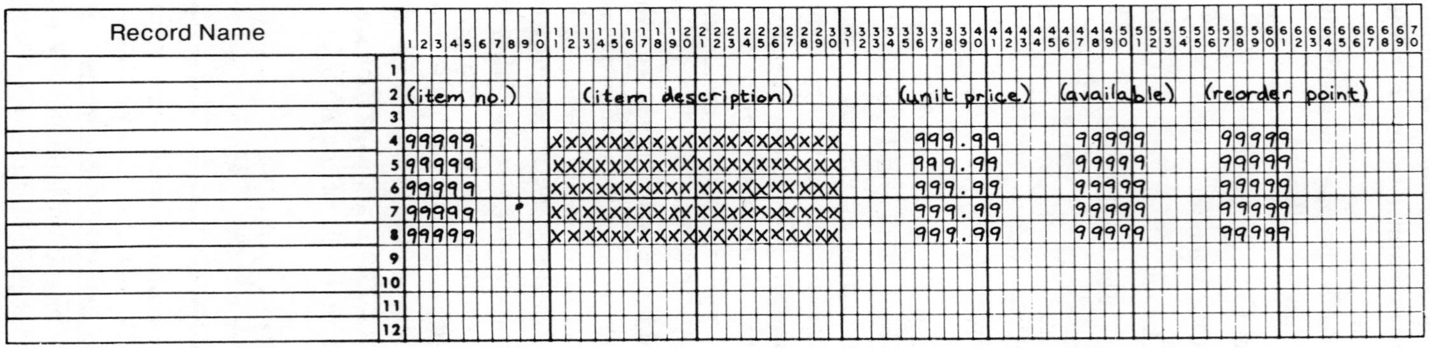

Narrative:
1. Add on-hand to on-order to derive available.
2. Print a line on the reorder listing only when available is less than the reorder point.

Figure 2-2 The reorder-listing problem

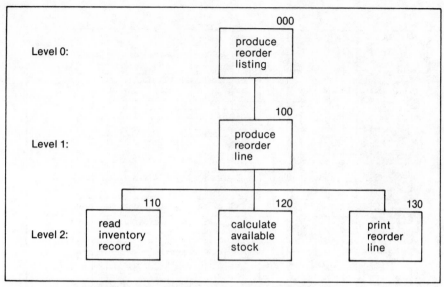

Figure 2-3   A structure chart for the reorder-listing problem

(on-hand plus on-order) is less than its reorder point. To simplify your introduction to COBOL, no headings or totals are to be printed on this report.

The structure chart   Figure 2-3 gives a structure chart for this program. The top-level module represents the entire program, so its functional description is "produce reorder listing." It has only one module beneath it, a module that will produce one line of the reorder listing. This module in turn is broken down into three modules: one that reads input cards, one that calculates the available stock for an inventory item, and one that prints the reorder lines when the available stock is less than the reorder point. You will soon see how the COBOL program relates to this structure chart. Then, in chapter 3, you will learn how to create structure charts of your own.

The COBOL coding form   When a COBOL programmer codes this program, he uses a coding form like the one in figure 2-4. The form in the illustration, in fact, is the first page of the reorder-listing program. If you study the form, you will see that 80 columns are indicated from left to right. When the program is complete, one source-deck card is keypunched for each coding line.

The first three columns are used for the page number of the coding form; the next three columns are used for the line number of the coding line. Thus, 001020 in the first six columns of a source card represents the line numbered 020 on page 001, and 005010

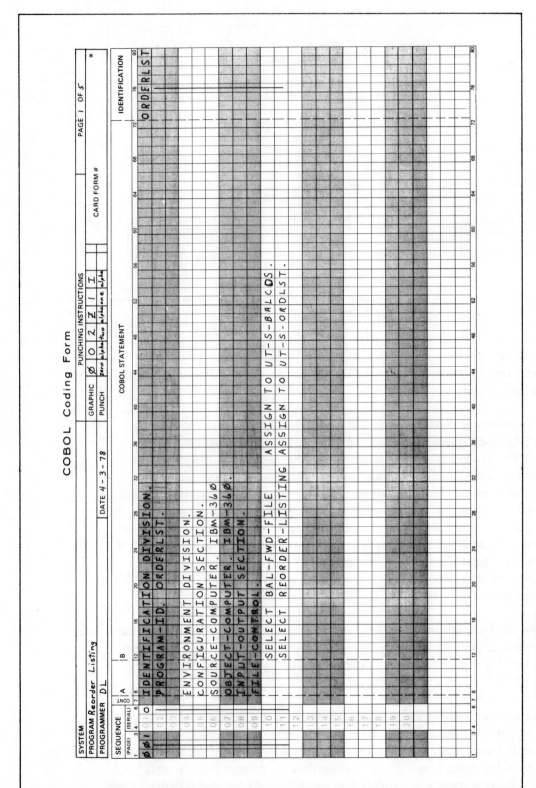

Figure 2-4 The COBOL coding form

represents the line numbered 010 on page 005. Although lines can be numbered consecutively (001, 002, 003), it is more common to number by tens (010, 020, 030). Then, if a line of coding has to be added to a program, it can be done by using a number of appropriate numerical value. For example, line number 165 would fall between 160 and 170.

The last eight columns of the source-deck cards are used to identify the cards. For example, in this program ORDERLST would be punched in columns 73–80 of each card in the source deck. Although the identification columns should contain the program name, the punches in these columns do not affect compilation or the resulting object program in any way.

Column 7 of the coding form is used to indicate that certain types of coding lines are to be ignored by the compiler. This will be explained in topic 3 of this chapter, so forget this column for now.

The actual program is coded in columns 8–72. Within these columns, only column 8, called the *A margin*, and column 12, called the *B margin*, require special mention. In general, each line of COBOL coding starts in one of these two margins, depending on the function of the coding. In figure 2-4, the first eight lines of the coding start in the A margin, and the coding on lines 100 and 110 begins at the B margin. Although all the System/360-370 compilers give the leeway of starting A-margin coding lines anywhere between column 8 and column 11, you should always start them in column 8. Likewise, you should start all B-margin sentences in column 12, though the compilers allow them to begin anywhere between column 12 and column 72.

The heading of the COBOL coding form gives information such as program name, date, and programmer. In addition, it gives punching instructions that show the keypunch operator which symbols are likely to be confusing and tell what they represent. In figure 2-4, for example, the programmer is telling the keypunch operator that a Ø represents the number zero while O represents the letter O. Similarly, a Z is written with a bar through it (Ƶ) to distinguish it from a 2, and the number one is written as a vertical line to distinguish it from the letter I, which is written with top and bottom cross members.

The COBOL program listing   Since columns 1–6 and columns 73–80 of a source deck can be disregarded without affecting the program, a COBOL program can be illustrated as in figure 2-5. The far left margin of the listing is therefore the A margin, and the B margin starts four spaces to its right. In the remainder of this book, this is how most programs will be illustrated.

Take a minute to look at the program in figure 2-5. It is the

```
        IDENTIFICATION DIVISION.
        PROGRAM-ID. ORDERLST.
        ENVIRONMENT DIVISION.
        CONFIGURATION SECTION.
        SOURCE-COMPUTER. IBM-360.
        OBJECT-COMPUTER. IBM-360.
        INPUT-OUTPUT SECTION.
        FILE-CONTROL.
            SELECT BAL-FWD-FILE     ASSIGN TO UT-S-BALCDS.
            SELECT REORDER-LISTING ASSIGN TO UT-S-ORDLST.
        DATA DIVISION.
        FILE SECTION.
        FD  BAL-FWD-FILE
            LABEL RECORDS ARE STANDARD
            RECORDING MODE IS F
            RECORD CONTAINS 80 CHARACTERS.
        01  BAL-FWD-CARD.
            02  BF-ITEM-NO          PICTURE IS 9(5).
            02  BF-ITEM-DESC        PICTURE IS X(20).
            02  FILLER              PICTURE IS X(5).
            02  BF-UNIT-PRICE       PICTURE IS 999V99.
            02  BF-REORDER-POINT    PICTURE IS 9(5).
            02  BF-ON-HAND          PICTURE IS 9(5).
            02  BF-ON-ORDER         PICTURE IS 9(5).
            02  FILLER              PICTURE IS X(30).
        FD  REORDER-LISTING
            LABEL RECORDS ARE STANDARD
            RECORDING MODE IS F
            RECORD CONTAINS 132 CHARACTERS.
        01  REORDER-LINE.
            02  RL-ITEM-NO          PICTURE IS Z(5).
            02  FILLER              PICTURE IS X(5).
            02  RL-ITEM-DESC        PICTURE IS X(20).
            02  FILLER              PICTURE IS X(5).
            02  RL-UNIT-PRICE       PICTURE IS ZZZ.99.
            02  FILLER              PICTURE IS X(5).
            02  RL-AVAILABLE-STOCK  PICTURE IS Z(5).
            02  FILLER              PICTURE IS X(5).
            02  RL-REORDER-POINT    PICTURE IS Z(5).
            02  FILLER              PICTURE IS X(71).
        WORKING-STORAGE SECTION.
        01  SWITCHES.
            02  CARD-EOF-SWITCH     PICTURE IS X.
        01  WORK-FIELDS.
            02  AVAILABLE-STOCK     PICTURE IS 9(5).
```

Figure 2-5 The reorder-listing program in COBOL (part 1 of 2)

```
PROCEDURE DIVISION.
000-PRODUCE-REORDER-LISTING.
    OPEN INPUT  BAL-FWD-FILE.
    OPEN OUTPUT REORDER-LISTING.
    MOVE 'N' TO CARD-EOF-SWITCH.
    PERFORM 100-PRODUCE-REORDER-LINE
        UNTIL CARD-EOF-SWITCH IS EQUAL TO 'Y'.
    CLOSE BAL-FWD-FILE.
    CLOSE REORDER-LISTING.
    STOP RUN.
100-PRODUCE-REORDER-LINE.
    PERFORM 110-READ-INVENTORY-RECORD.
    IF CARD-EOF-SWITCH IS NOT EQUAL TO 'Y'
        PERFORM 120-CALCULATE-AVAILABLE-STOCK
        IF AVAILABLE-STOCK IS LESS THAN BF-REORDER-POINT
            PERFORM 130-PRINT-REORDER-LINE.
110-READ-INVENTORY-RECORD.
    READ BAL-FWD-FILE RECORD
        AT END
            MOVE 'Y' TO CARD-EOF-SWITCH.
120-CALCULATE-AVAILABLE-STOCK.
    ADD BF-ON-HAND BF-ON-ORDER
        GIVING AVAILABLE-STOCK.
130-PRINT-REORDER-LINE.
    MOVE SPACE              TO REORDER-LINE.
    MOVE BF-ITEM-NO         TO RL-ITEM-NO.
    MOVE BF-ITEM-DESC       TO RL-ITEM-DESC.
    MOVE BF-UNIT-PRICE      TO RL-UNIT-PRICE.
    MOVE AVAILABLE-STOCK    TO RL-AVAILABLE-STOCK.
    MOVE BF-REORDER-POINT   TO RL-REORDER-POINT.
    WRITE REORDER-LINE.
```

Figure 2-5   The reorder-listing program in COBOL (part 2 of 2)

complete program for printing the reorder listing from the balance-forward cards. It is written for a System/360 computer operating under OS, but as you will see, only two lines of coding would have to be changed in order to compile the program on the System/360-370 operating under DOS.

If you scan the program, you can see that it is made up of four divisions: the Identification, Environment, Data, and Procedure Divisions. Although the Identification and Environment Divisions are first, the Data and Procedure Divisions are the essence of the program.

The Identification Division

The Identification Division is used to identify the program. It does not cause any object code to be compiled and requires only two coding lines. In figure 2-5, the programmer has written

```
IDENTIFICATION DIVISION.
PROGRAM-ID.   ORDERLST.
```

Except for ORDERLST, which is the *program name* made up by the programmer, these two coding lines will be the same for all COBOL programs.

For the System/360-370 operating under DOS or OS, program names should be made up of eight or fewer letters or numbers and must start with a letter. Thus, ORDERLST, INV0147A, and AR3 are valid program names, but 73AR and INV# are not. Although a program name of up to thirty letters, numbers, and dashes is valid in terms of COBOL, the operating system will ignore all but the first eight characters, it will convert a lead digit to a letter, and it will convert the dashes to zeros. So always limit your program names to eight letters and numbers, and start your names with a letter. This also makes it possible to code the name in columns 73–80 of the source deck so the deck will be easy to identify.

The Environment Division

The Environment Division of a COBOL program specifies the hardware components that are to be used for the compilation and for the execution of the object program. As a result, this division shows the greatest variance from one computer manufacturer to another. When converting from DOS to OS or vice versa, this division must always be changed.

The Environment Division for the reorder-listing program in figure 2-5 is as follows:

```
ENVIRONMENT DIVISION.
CONFIGURATION SECTION.
SOURCE-COMPUTER.   IBM-360.
OBJECT-COMPUTER.   IBM-360.
INPUT-OUTPUT SECTION.
FILE-CONTROL.
    SELECT BAL-FWD-FILE    ASSIGN TO UT-S-BALCDS.
    SELECT REORDER-LISTING ASSIGN TO UT-S-ORDLST.
```

This format will be the same for all programs that use card input and printer output. As a result, though it may look confusing, this division is quite routine.

The Configuration Section

In the Configuration Section, SOURCE-COMPUTER specifies the computer that will be used for the compilation. In most cases, this will be the same as the computer used for executing the object program, known as the OBJECT-COMPUTER. In the example, the computer used is the System/360, always indicated as IBM-360.

If you are writing a program for the System/370, you can code the source and object computers as IBM-370. When this is done for the object computer on some IBM compilers, System/370 instructions are compiled into the object program. Then, the object program cannot be run on a System/360. In contrast, an object program compiled when IBM-360 is specified can be executed on either the System/360 or the System/370.

When you use the VS compilers, you will automatically get System/370 instructions in your object code. On other compilers, you will only get System/370 instructions if you specify IBM-370 for the object computer. If your installation has both 360s and 370s, I recommend specifying IBM-360 for the object computer so you won't have conversion problems as you move from one machine to the other. This increased flexibility offsets a rather trivial loss in object program efficiency.

On all IBM compilers, you can omit the SOURCE-COMPUTER and OBJECT-COMPUTER coding lines altogether. This means you can omit the Configuration Section entirely, unless your program requires a SPECIAL-NAMES paragraph as shown in topic 3. Remember, however, that on non-VS compilers you must include this section and specify IBM-370 for the object computer if you specifically want System/370 instructions in your object program.

The Input-Output Section

In the Input-Output Section, the programmer codes SELECT statements that give symbolic *file names* to the I/O devices that will be used by the program. The format for the SELECT statement is as follows:

```
SELECT file-name ASSIGN TO system-name
```

Here, the capitalized words are always the same (they are part of the COBOL language), while the lowercase words represent names that are assigned by the programmer.

When a programmer makes up a file name, it must conform to these rules:

1. It must be thirty characters or less and consist entirely of letters, numbers, and hyphens.

2. It must not end or begin with a hyphen and cannot contain blanks.

3. It must contain at least one letter.

In figure 2-5, then, BAL-FWD-FILE is the file name for the deck of input cards, and REORDER-LISTING is the file name for the output report. (Although you might not commonly think of a printed listing as a file, it is considered one in COBOL, and each line on the listing is treated as a record in the file.)

The *system name* given in the SELECT statement pertains to the I/O device that is going to be used for a file. Since this name must meet the specifications of the computer manufacturer, system names must be changed as you move from one type of computer to another. Before writing a COBOL program, then, you have to find out the system names for the I/O devices that your program will use.

In this book, some of the program examples used are for DOS systems, some for OS systems. In general, the only code that would have to be changed to get a DOS program to compile on an OS system or vice versa is to change the system names in the SELECT statements. For instance, if you wanted to run the program in figure 2-5 on a DOS system, only the system names would have to be changed.

DOS system names   For the Disk Operating System, the system name has this format when using card or printer devices:

```
SYSnnn-UR-device-S
```

(Here again, the capital letters are always the same; the small letters are replaced by specifications supplied by the programmer.) For device, the programmer inserts the number of the I/O device that is to be used—such as 2540R for the IBM 2540 Card Reader, 2540P for the IBM 2540 Card Punch, 1403 for the IBM 1403 Printer, or 2501 for the IBM 2501 Card Reader. For card and printer system names, UR refers to Unit Record and S to Sequential organization.

The SYS number is simply a number between SYS000 and SYS221—a number used by the Disk Operating System. As you will see in chapter 8, each of these numbers can be used to represent a different I/O device. In fact, each DOS system has standard assignments in which specific devices are represented by specific SYS numbers. From a practical point of view, you should find out what these standard assignments are so you can use them when you create your DOS system names in your SELECT statements.

In any event, this book assumes standard assignments in which SYS005 is assigned to a card reader, SYS006 is assigned to a printer, and SYS007 is assigned to a card punch. Under DOS, then, the SELECT statements for running the reorder-listing program might be as follows:

```
SELECT BAL-FWD-FILE     ASSIGN TO SYS005-UR-2540R-S.
SELECT REORDER-LISTING ASSIGN TO SYS006-UR-1403-S.
```

The SYS and device numbers show that the BAL-FWD-FILE would be assigned to the 2540 card reader and the REORDER-LISTING to the 1403 printer. If different models of these I/O devices were to be used, the device numbers in the system names would be changed accordingly.

OS system names   For IBM's full Operating System, the system name can have one of two different formats when using card or printer devices. One of these formats is somewhat similar to the format for DOS:

```
UR-device-S-ddname
```

Here, device is the I/O device itself, as it is under DOS, while *ddname* refers to the *external name* by which the file is known to the OS operating system. The ddname must consist of eight or fewer letters or numbers and must start with a letter. As you will see in chapter 9, the ddname is used in the job-control language needed for program execution. Using this format, then, the SELECT statements for the reorder-listing program might be as follows:

```
SELECT BAL-FWD-FILE     ASSIGN TO UR-2540R-S-BALCDS.
SELECT REORDER-LISTING ASSIGN TO UR-1403-S-ORDLST.
```

The second format for an OS system name is this:

```
UT-S-ddname
```

This format, which can be used for tape and disk files as well as for card and printer files, substitutes UT (UTility) for UR. When using UT, the device does *not* have to be specified in the system name. Instead, the device can be given in the job-control language for running the program. This means that at execution time, the operator can specify an alternate device if the intended device isn't available. Since this format gives the operator greater flexibility, you should use it in all of your OS programs. You can see it used in both SELECT statements in figure 2-5.

Incidentally, it is acceptable under OS to use the same name for the file name and the ddname. Thus, the SELECT statements for the reorder-listing program could be written like this:

```
SELECT BALCDS ASSIGN TO UT-S-BALCDS.
SELECT ORDLST ASSIGN TO UT-S-ORDLST.
```

In fact, some programming managers require that these names be the same since this reduces the chance for confusion. In this book, all OS examples from this point on will use file names that match the ddnames.

The Data Division

The Data Division can consist of two sections. The first section, called the File Section, gives the characteristics of the input and output files and records. The Working-Storage Section describes the other fields of storage required by the program.

The File Section

The card file   The file and record descriptions for the balance-forward cards are as follows:

```
FD   BAL-FWD-FILE
     LABEL RECORDS ARE STANDARD
     RECORDING MODE IS F
     RECORD CONTAINS 80 CHARACTERS.
01   BAL-FWD-CARD.
     02  BF-ITEM-NO              PICTURE IS 9(5).
     02  BF-ITEM-DESC            PICTURE IS X(20).
     02  FILLER                  PICTURE IS X(5).
     02  BF-UNIT-PRICE           PICTURE IS 999V99.
     02  BF-REORDER-POINT        PICTURE IS 9(5).
     02  BF-ON-HAND              PICTURE IS 9(5).
     02  BF-ON-ORDER             PICTURE IS 9(5).
     02  FILLER                  PICTURE IS X(30).
```

FD stands for file description and is followed by the file name that was originally created in the SELECT statement of the Environment Division. The next three lines give information about the file.

The LABEL RECORDS clause is required in every FD statement. For most files, the label records are either STANDARD or OMITTED—that is, either the file has beginning and ending labels in a standard format or it doesn't have beginning and ending labels at all. Since card and printer files don't have labels, it may seem logical to code LABEL RECORDS ARE OMITTED. In fact, some compilers—like the DOS compiler—require this.

Many compilers, however, are like the OS compiler—they allow you to code STANDARD labels for card and printer files. Then, if a card device or printer isn't available when the program is run, the file can be directed to a tape or direct-access device. STANDARD labels will be specified for all files in the OS programs in this book.

RECORDING MODE IS F means that the records in the file are of constant (F for Fixed) length. Card files are always F mode. In contrast, tape and direct-access files may have other recording modes, such as V for Variable. Although the RECORDING MODE clause is not a part of the ANS COBOL standards (it is an IBM extension), it is recommended for DOS and OS COBOL because it provides a check on the actual recording mode of the file. If there's a discrepancy, a diagnostic message will print, allowing you to correct the error before you test the program.

RECORD CONTAINS 80 CHARACTERS means just what it says. This is obvious here since all card records are 80 characters long. For tape and direct-access files, however, you will have to adjust this coding to the actual lengths of the records used. Again, as you will see in a moment, this clause provides a check on the actual length of the record.

The line starting with 01 begins the description of the card record. The 01 level number indicates that the name following is the name for an entire record. In other words, BAL-FWD-CARD is the *record name*. The rules for forming a record name are the same as those for forming a file name—up to thirty letters, numbers, or hyphens and containing at least one letter.

The 02 level numbers indicate that the lines describe fields within the 01 record. Following the 02 numbers are *data names*, which are made up using the rules for file or record names, or the word FILLER, which is used for those fields or card columns that are not used by the program. For example, the first two 02 lines give the data names BF-ITEM-NO and BF-ITEM-DESC to the item-number and item-description fields of the input cards. The third 02 line, which is FILLER, indicates that the third field in the input card will not be used by the program. If you refer to figure 2-2, you can see that the third field is the unit-cost field, which is not required on the output record.

Although the programmer could have used names like S241 and B11 for item number and item description, he made up names that reflect their use. In this program, BF in a name refers to the input file—Balance Forward—and the remainder of the name refers to the field. Thus, BF-ITEM-DESC indicates the item-description field in the balance-forward file. This is a common naming technique.

One point to remember when creating names such as file names, record names, or data names is that you must avoid duplicating COBOL *reserved words*. For example, the words SELECT, LABEL, RECORDS, ARE, and STANDARD are reserved words—words that are a part of the COBOL language. As a result, you cannot use any of these words for a name that you make up. If LABEL is used as a file name, for instance, the COBOL compiler will diagnose an error. Since you will use a prefix like BF for most of the names you create (as in BF-ITEM-NO), you normally have little chance of duplicating

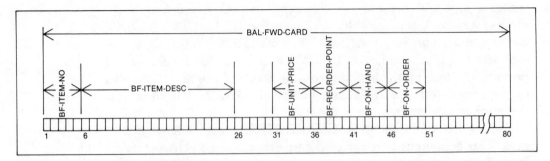

Figure 2-6   The card input area

a reserved word. You can find a complete list of the reserved words for your compiler in the compiler's reference manual.

The PICTURE IS clauses that follow the data names give the characteristics of the fields and correspond to the characteristics entries in the record-layout form. The number or letter outside the parentheses tells what kind of data the field contains; the number inside parentheses tells how long the field is. For example, 9(5) means the field is numeric and consists of five columns. And X(20) means that the field is alphanumeric and consists of twenty columns. (An alphanumeric field can contain letters, numbers, or special characters.)

Do you understand so far? The data names give each of the fields in the card a symbolic name that can be used later in the Procedure Division. The PICTURE IS clauses, which may start one or more spaces after the data names, indicate the nature of the data and the size of the field.

Now, look a little further. The PICTURE for the field named BF-UNIT-PRICE is 999V99. This means that the field is five columns long (there are five 9s) and contains numeric data with a decimal point two places from the right. In other words, a 9 indicates one numeric column and the V indicates the position of the assumed decimal point. (Remember that the decimal point usually isn't punched in an input card.)

When the source program is compiled, the computer adds up the number of columns indicated in the PICTURE clauses for a record and compares the sum to the character count in the RECORD CONTAINS clause. If they don't match, a diagnostic message is printed. For the BAL-FWD-CARD, the sum of the PICTUREs is 80. Since this is the count in the RECORD CONTAINS clause, no error is indicated. Figure 2-6 illustrates the names assigned to the card input area and the fields within it.

The printer file   The next file description is for the report that is to be printed on the printer. Its coding lines are as follows:

```
FD  REORDER-LISTING
    LABEL RECORDS ARE STANDARD
    RECORDING MODE IS F
    RECORD CONTAINS 132 CHARACTERS.
```

Except for the file name, REORDER-LISTING, the four lines of coding are like those for the card input file. They say that the file either has standard labels or none at all and that the file contains fixed-length records that are 132 characters long. Most printers have a print line that is 132 characters long, but you may have to adjust the RECORD CONTAINS clause for the printer you will be using.

The record description that follows the FD statement is this:

```
01  REORDER-LINE.
    02 RL-ITEM-NO              PICTURE IS Z(5).
    02 FILLER                  PICTURE IS X(5).
    02 RL-ITEM-DESC            PICTURE IS X(20).
    02 FILLER                  PICTURE IS X(5).
    02 RL-UNIT-PRICE           PICTURE IS ZZZ.99.
    02 FILLER                  PICTURE IS X(5).
    02 RL-AVAILABLE-STOCK      PICTURE IS Z(5).
    02 FILLER                  PICTURE IS X(5).
    02 RL-REORDER-POINT        PICTURE IS Z(5).
    02 FILLER                  PICTURE IS X(71).
```

Here, the 01 line assigns the name REORDER-LINE to the output record. Thus, REORDER-LINE is the record name.

As you can see, the 02 levels and the PICTURE clauses define the fields of the printed line just as they did the fields of the input cards. The only new symbols used are the Z as in Z(5) and the decimal point as in ZZZ.99. Z(5) means that a five-digit numeric field is to be printed and the high-order zeros should be zero-suppressed. ZZZ.99 means that a five-digit numeric field is to be printed with two decimal places and a decimal point. The high-order zeros to the left of the decimal point are to be zero-suppressed. Thus, the number 00718 will print as 7.18; the number 00003 will print as .03. The data names in these descriptions begin with RL, which refers to the record name, REORDER-LINE.

The total number of characters in the PICTURE clauses for the printer area equals 132, which is the number of print positions on the printer. It is also the count given in the RECORD CONTAINS clause. As a result, no error is indicated. Figure 2-7 illustrates the names assigned to the output area and the fields within it. Notice that the FILLER lines in the printer description determine the spacing of the output report.

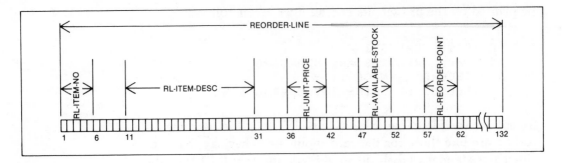

Figure 2-7   The printer output area

The Working-Storage Section

The Working-Storage Section of the Data Division defines all other data fields that are to be used by the program. For this program, the Working-Storage Section is as follows:

```
WORKING-STORAGE SECTION.
01   SWITCHES.
     02   CARD-EOF-SWITCH      PICTURE IS X.
01   WORK-FIELDS.
     02   AVAILABLE-STOCK      PICTURE IS 9(5).
```

Here, the 01 levels, SWITCHES and WORK-FIELDS, aren't record names for input or output areas. Instead, they are used to logically group the fields the program will need during the processing of the balance-forward cards.

We define a *switch* as a field that can have one of two possible values; these values indicate the switch is either "off" or "on." In this book, a value of N is used to mean "off;" a value of Y is used to mean "on." Whenever you move one of these values to a switch field, you are "setting the switch."

The one switch in this program, CARD-EOF-SWITCH, indicates when all the cards in the input file have been read. (Since EOF is a commonly used abbreviation for end-of-file, you are likely to see it often.) Like all switches, CARD-EOF-SWITCH is described as a one-position alphanumeric field. It will have a value of either Y or N moved to it during the course of this program, depending on whether any input cards remain to be read. Switches are quite common in structured programs, so you will learn more about how and when to use them as you go through this book.

WORK-FIELDS hold the results of calculations that must be made to produce the output data from the input data. In this program, AVAILABLE-STOCK, a five-position numeric field, will hold the result when the available stock for each balance-forward card is calculated. This result will then be used to decide whether a line should be printed on the reorder listing.

Incidentally, when coding a PICTURE clause, 9(5) and 99999 are equivalent. Similarly, 9(3)V9(2) and 999V99 are equivalent as are Z(3).9(2) and ZZZ.99. In general, the programmer chooses the form that is easier for him to code or to understand. As a rule of thumb, use parentheses when four or more characters in a row are required.

The Procedure Division

As you will see in chapter 3, a programmer begins to document the modules of a program after he has designed its structure chart. At that time, he creates many of the file, record, and data names he will use to code the Environment and Data Divisions. In addition, he creates names for the groups of instructions that make up the Procedure Division. These names are called *procedure,* or *paragraph, names.* Since they always start at the A margin, they are easy to identify. In figure 2-5, for example, 000-PRODUCE-REORDER-LISTING, 100-PRODUCE-REORDER-LINE, 110-READ-INVENTORY-RECORD, and so forth are the procedure names used. These names are formed using the same rules as for file names with one exception: they need not contain any letters.

In general, there should be one paragraph name for each module in the structure chart for a program. As a result, there are five paragraph names in the Procedure Division of figure 2-5, one for each of the five module blocks in figure 2-3. As you can see, a paragraph name is created by taking the block number and the module description from the structure chart and separating the number and words by hyphens. The paragraphs are in sequence by module number, so it is easy to locate a paragraph in a large program when you know its paragraph name.

The lines of coding that start in the B margin of the Procedure Division are COBOL statements that specify operations that are to take place on the fields, records, and files previously defined. These symbolic statements follow consistent formats, some of which are given in figure 2-8. To use any of these statements, the programmer substitutes the names of the files, records, or fields that are to be operated upon for the lowercase words in the statement formats. The capitalized words in each statement are written just as they appear in the statement format. To execute a procedure named 110-READ-INVENTORY-RECORD, for example, the programmer codes

```
PERFORM 110-READ-INVENTORY-RECORD.
```

```
                    PROCEDURE DIVISION FORMATS

        I/O Statements:
                OPEN INPUT file-name.

                OPEN OUTPUT file-name.

                READ file-name RECORD
                    AT END
                        imperative-statement.

                WRITE record-name.

                CLOSE file-name.

        Data-Movement Statements:
                MOVE SPACE TO data-name.

                MOVE literal TO data-name.

                MOVE data-name-1 TO data-name-2.

        Arithmetic Statements:
                ADD data-name-1 TO data-name-2.

                ADD data-name-1 data-name-2
                    GIVING data-name-3.

                SUBTRACT data-name-1 FROM data-name-2.

                SUBTRACT data-name-1 FROM data-name-2
                    GIVING data-name-3.

                MULTIPLY data-name-1 BY data-name-2.

                MULTIPLY data-name-1 BY data-name-2
                    GIVING data-name-3.

                DIVIDE data-name-1 INTO data-name-2.

                DIVIDE data-name-1 INTO data-name-2
                    GIVING data-name-3.

        Sequence-Control Statements:
                IF condition
                    statement-1
                [ELSE
                    statement-2].

                PERFORM procedure-name.

                PERFORM procedure-name
                    UNTIL condition.

        Miscellaneous Statements:
                STOP RUN.
```

Figure 2-8   Simplified statement formats showing recommended indentation

```
000-PRODUCE-REORDER-LISTING.
    OPEN INPUT  BAL-FWD-FILE.
    OPEN OUTPUT REORDER-LISTING.
    MOVE 'N' TO CARD-EOF-SWITCH.
    PERFORM 100-PRODUCE-REORDER-LINE
        UNTIL CARD-EOF-SWITCH IS EQUAL TO 'Y'.
    CLOSE BAL-FWD-FILE.
    CLOSE REORDER-LISTING.
    STOP RUN.
```

Figure 2-9   Module 000: Produce Reorder Listing

The problem for the beginning programmer, then, is to learn the format and function of each of the available COBOL statements.

In the remainder of this topic, I will explain the operation of each of the paragraphs in the reorder-listing program. Although this may be somewhat confusing at first, you should understand the operation of this program by the time you complete this topic.

Module 000: Produce Reorder Listing

The top-level module in the structure chart in figure 2-3 represents the entire program. Its primary function is to determine which of the level-1 modules should be executed and how many times these modules should be executed. Since there is only one level-1 module for this program, module 000 determines how many times module 100 should be executed. In addition, it gets the input and output files ready for processing at the start of the program, and it deactivates the files at the end of the program. The COBOL code for this module is duplicated in figure 2-9.

The OPEN statement   An OPEN statement is required for each file that is to be read or written by a program. Therefore, the OPEN statements usually are found in the top-level module. If you look at the formats for the OPEN statement in figure 2-8, you can see how the OPEN statements in figure 2-9 relate to the formats. The programmer simply substitutes into the OPEN statements the file names defined in the Environment Division. The word INPUT is used for an input file, the word OUTPUT for an output file.

Although the OPEN statements are required, they don't actually cause any processing to be done for card or printer files. You can think of the OPEN statement as checking to be sure a device is ready to operate. For tape and disk files, however, the OPEN statement does considerably more.

The MOVE statement   The MOVE statement that follows the OPEN statements is this:

```
MOVE 'N' TO CARD-EOF-SWITCH.
```

It sets the field named CARD-EOF-SWITCH to a value of N, for "no," meaning that the end of the card file has *not* been reached. As you will see later, this switch is set to a value of Y, for "yes," when all of the input cards have been read. In this program, then, when CARD-EOF-SWITCH is equal to N it means there are still some more cards to be processed. When it is equal to Y, it means there are no more cards to be processed.

The PERFORM UNTIL statement   The PERFORM UNTIL statement in module 000 is this:

```
PERFORM 100-PRODUCE-REORDER-LINE
     UNTIL CARD-EOF-SWITCH IS EQUAL TO 'Y'.
```

It will cause the paragraph named 100-PRODUCE-REORDER-LINE to be executed until CARD-EOF-SWITCH has a value of Y. In other words, module 100 will be executed until there are no more input cards to be processed. The program will then continue with the next statements in sequence, the CLOSE statements.

If you compare this PERFORM UNTIL statement with the format in figure 2-8, you'll see that the *condition* in the statement is this:

```
CARD-EOF-SWITCH IS EQUAL TO 'Y'
```

Each time the statement is executed, the program tests the value of CARD-EOF-SWITCH to see whether the condition has been met *before* performing 100-PRODUCE-REORDER-LINE. Thus, module 100 will not be performed the first time CARD-EOF-SWITCH is found to be equal to Y.

Conditions are formed by using the general format shown in figure 2-10. In other words, two values can be compared to see whether value-A is greater than value-B, value-A is equal to value-B, or value-A is less than value-B. The values can be values stored in fields or values specified in the statement itself (*literals*). In the condition in figure 2-9, the first value is the value stored in the field named CARD-EOF-SWITCH; the second value is the literal value Y.

Topic 3 of this chapter will explain in detail how to create literals. For now, accept the fact that a non-numeric literal is expressed by enclosing the literal value in single quotation marks. Thus, the literal in the condition is 'Y'; the literal value is Y.

Condition format:

$$\begin{Bmatrix} \text{literal-1} \\ \text{data-name-1} \end{Bmatrix} \quad \begin{Bmatrix} \text{IS [NOT] GREATER THAN} \\ \text{IS [NOT] EQUAL TO} \\ \text{IS [NOT] LESS THAN} \end{Bmatrix} \quad \begin{Bmatrix} \text{literal-2} \\ \text{data-name-2} \end{Bmatrix}$$

Examples:

```
CARD-EOF-SWITCH IS NOT EQUAL TO 'Y'
ITEM-CODE-1 IS GREATER THAN ITEM-CODE-2
TR-CODE IS LESS THAN 5
'N' IS NOT GREATER THAN EMP-NAME
```

Figure 2-10   Basic condition tests

NOT is an optional word in a condition. It is used to state the negative of a condition. Thus, the PERFORM UNTIL statement could be written like this with the same results:

```
PERFORM 100-PRODUCE-REORDER-LINE
    UNTIL CARD-EOF-SWITCH IS NOT EQUAL TO 'N'.
```

Module 100 would still be executed until CARD-EOF-SWITCH is equal to Y.

The CLOSE statement   Just as files must be opened at the start of a program, they must be closed at the end. As a result, module 000 uses these CLOSE statements:

```
CLOSE BAL-FWD-FILE.
CLOSE REORDER-LISTING.
```

After CLOSE statements are executed, the files are no longer available for processing. You should realize, however, that the real significance of the CLOSE statement, like the OPEN, pertains to tape and direct-access files.

The STOP statement   STOP RUN means that the program has finished and the computer system should go on to the next program. It causes a branch to the supervisor so the next program can be loaded into storage and executed.

```
100-PRODUCE-REORDER-LINE.
    PERFORM 110-READ-INVENTORY-RECORD.
    IF CARD-EOF-SWITCH IS NOT EQUAL TO 'Y'
        PERFORM 120-CALCULATE-AVAILABLE-STOCK
        IF AVAILABLE-STOCK IS LESS THAN BF-REORDER-POINT
            PERFORM 130-PRINT-REORDER-LINE.
```

Figure 2-11   Module 100: Produce Reorder Line

Module 100: Produce Reorder Line

Module 100 is the level-1 module in figure 2-3. Its coding is shown
in figure 2-11. Its primary function is to see that all the level-2
modules that it controls are executed in the proper sequence. Each
time module 100 is given control by module 000, it is executed one
time; then control passes back to the PERFORM UNTIL statement in
module 000. Remember that the PERFORM UNTIL statement will
cause module 100 to be executed again and again until CARD-EOF-
SWITCH is equal to Y. Thus, it will be executed once for each
balance-forward card.

The PERFORM statement   The PERFORM statement causes one
paragraph to be executed. The program then continues with the first
statement following the PERFORM statement. As a result, the first
statement in module 100 causes the paragraph named 110-READ-
INVENTORY-RECORD to be executed. After this, the IF statement
that follows the PERFORM statement is executed.

The IF statement   The IF statement is the logical statement of the
COBOL program. It usually compares two values and continues
based on the results of the comparison. Some examples follow:

```
1.   IF VALID-TRAN-SWITCH IS EQUAL TO 'Y'
            PERFORM 240-PRINT-SALES-LINE
        ELSE
            PERFORM 250-PRINT-ERROR-MESSAGE.

2.   IF SR-SALES-QUOTA IS GREATER THAN TOTAL-SALES
            MOVE 'C' TO COMMISSION-CODE
            PERFORM 320-CALCULATE-COMMISSION-1
        ELSE
            MOVE 'A' TO COMMISSION-CODE
            PERFORM 320-CALCULATE-COMMISSION-1
            PERFORM 330-CALCULATE-COMMISSION-2.
```

In these examples, the programmer has used indentation to show that the IF-ELSE structure provides for two conditions—true and false. If the condition in the IF statement is true, all statements before the ELSE are executed; if the condition is false, all the statements after the ELSE are executed. Notice that only one period is used in the IF-ELSE structure, after the last statement of the ELSE clause. The condition formats you can use are summarized in figure 2-10.

If you look at the IF-statement format in figure 2-8, you'll see that the ELSE clause is enclosed in brackets. This means that the clause is optional. As a result, IF statements like these can be coded:

```
1.    IF ER-HOURS-WORKED IS GREATER THAN 40
            PERFORM 320-CALCULATE-OVERTIME-PAY.

2.    IF TRAN-EOF-SWITCH IS NOT EQUAL TO 'Y'
            PERFORM 120-ACCUMULATE-CUST-TOTAL.
```

Here, if the condition is true, the statements following the condition are executed. If the condition is false, processing continues with the statement following the IF statement.

Nested IF statements   When an IF statement contains one or more other IF statements, they are referred to as *nested IF statements*. In figure 2-11, nested IF statements are used in module 100 as follows:

```
IF CARD-EOF-SWITCH IS NOT EQUAL TO 'Y'
    PERFORM 120-CALCULATE-AVAILABLE-STOCK
    IF AVAILABLE-STOCK IS LESS THAN BF-REORDER-POINT
        PERFORM 130-PRINT-REORDER-LINE.
```

Once again, indentation is used to show the relationships between the parts of the IF statements.

Figure 2-12 shows how these nested IF statements operate when executed. In brief, if CARD-EOF-SWITCH isn't equal to Y (meaning there are still cards to be processed), the available stock is calculated. Then, if the available stock is less than the reorder point, a reorder line is printed. If, however, the condition in either IF statement is *not* true, processing should continue with the next statement after the IF. As a result, ELSE clauses aren't required.

Because COBOL allows many levels of nesting, nesting can become very confusing if it isn't handled correctly. To better understand it, look at figure 2-13. It shows the logic of IF statements nested within both the IF and ELSE portions of a primary IF statement.

One key point to remember when nesting is that the compiler will pair each ELSE with the first IF that precedes it that doesn't already have an ELSE, regardless of how you have paired IFs and

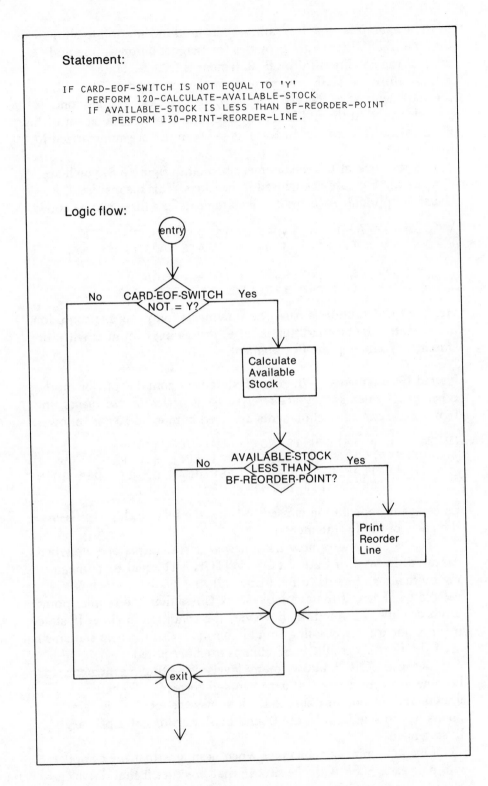

Figure 2-12   Operation of the nested IF statements in module 100

Coding:

```
IF condition-1
    IF condition-2
        statement-group-A
    ELSE
        statement-group-B
ELSE
    IF condition-3
        statement-group-C
    ELSE
        statement-group-D
```

Logic flow:

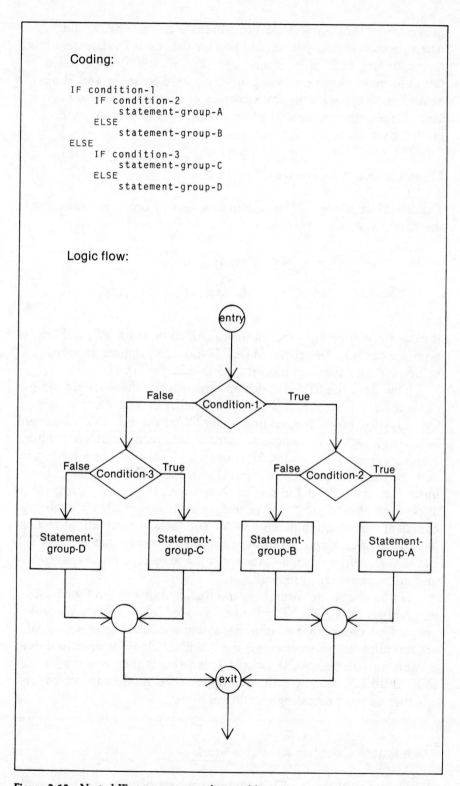

Figure 2-13   Nested IF statements—coding and logic

ELSEs through indentation. So to eliminate errors when coding nested IF statements, you should be sure that each IF statement has a corresponding ELSE if it requires one. You should also use indentation to make sure you have properly paired your IFs and ELSEs, as well as to show the logical structure of the nesting. If you do both of these things, several levels of nesting can be used with limited confusion.

Module 110: Read Inventory Record

The READ statement   This module consists of only one statement, the READ statement:

```
READ BAL-FWD-FILE RECORD
    AT END
        MOVE 'Y' TO CARD-EOF-SWITCH.
```

It causes one inventory record (one card) to be read. When there are no more cards to be processed (AT END), the program moves a value of Y into the field named CARD-EOF-SWITCH.

How does the READ statement know when there are no more cards to be processed? This varies somewhat by operating system. On a System/360-370 operating under DOS, the AT END clause will be executed when the computer reads a card with a slash in column 1 and an asterisk in column 2. Thus, the /* card (slash-asterisk card) must be the last card in any input deck. Under OS, the end of the input may be indicated in one of three ways: (1) by a /* card; (2) by a job-control card (any card beginning with //); or (3) by a job comment card (beginning with //*). You'll learn more about coding JCL in chapters 8 and 9. For now, simply be aware that the AT END clause is executed when an attempt is made to read another record and no more records are available.

If you check the format for the READ statement in figure 2-8, you will see that AT END must be followed by an *imperative statement*. That means that conditional statements like the IF statement are not allowed. In most cases, the AT END clause is used to move a value into an end-of-file switch. This value is then tested by a PERFORM UNTIL statement in a higher-level module to determine whether or not processing should continue.

Module 120: Calculate Available Stock

Arithmetic statements   This module consists of only one statement, an ADD statement:

```
ADD BF-ON-HAND BF-ON-ORDER
    GIVING AVAILABLE-STOCK.
```

It adds the contents of BF-ON-HAND to the contents of BF-ON-ORDER and stores the result in AVAILABLE-STOCK.

In general, there are two formats for each type of arithmetic statement (see figure 2-8). In the first format, the result of the arithmetic operation replaces the contents of the second field named (data-name-2), while the contents of the first field named are unchanged. For instance,

```
ADD BF-ON-HAND TO BF-ON-ORDER
```

would execute this way:

Field name:	BF-ON-HAND	BF-ON-ORDER
Contents before:	00050	00070
Contents after:	00050	00120

The second format, which uses GIVING and a third data name, is the one used in module 120. By using GIVING, the statement has the effect of a move and an add instruction, so neither data-name-1 nor data-name-2 is changed. For example, the ADD statement in module 120 would execute this way:

Field name:	BF-ON-HAND	BF-ON-ORDER	AVAILABLE-STOCK
Before:	00070	00050	?
After:	00070	00050	00120

Although all four arithmetic statements have the same basic formats, it should be noted that the remainder in a DIVIDE statement is lost when the statement is executed. Thus,

```
DIVIDE TR-MONTHS INTO TOTAL
```

executes in this way:

Field name:	TR-MONTHS	TOTAL
Before:	10	23
After:	10	02

and

```
DIVIDE TR-MONTHS INTO TOTAL GIVING AVERAGE
```

executes in this way:

Field name:	TR-MONTHS	TOTAL	AVERAGE
Before:	10	23	?
After:	10	23	02

When using arithmetic statements, you should make sure that all result fields are large enough to store the results. Also, all fields except the GIVING field in the second format must be numeric. For now, that means that they must have PICTUREs that consist of 9s and Vs only, while a GIVING field may consist of either Zs, 9s, and a decimal point or of 9s and Vs.

Module 130: Print Reorder Line

Module 130 is the last paragraph in the program in figure 2-5. It consists of these statements:

```
MOVE SPACE             TO REORDER-LINE.
MOVE BF-ITEM-NO        TO RL-ITEM-NO.
MOVE BF-ITEM-DESC      TO RL-ITEM-DESC.
MOVE BF-UNIT-PRICE     TO RL-UNIT-PRICE.
MOVE AVAILABLE-STOCK   TO RL-AVAILABLE-STOCK.
MOVE BF-REORDER-POINT  TO RL-REORDER-POINT.
WRITE REORDER-LINE.
```

It moves the required data to the printer output area and prints one reorder line. Remember that this module is only executed when the available stock is less than the reorder point.

The MOVE statements   The first statement

```
MOVE SPACE TO REORDER-LINE
```

simply does what it says: it puts spaces, or blanks, in all 132 positions of the printer output area. (SPACE is a COBOL reserved word that represents one or more spaces.) As a result, it clears the area of any data remaining from a previous program or from a previous line of printing. A statement such as this is often used prior to statements that move data to an output area.

After the output record is cleared (set to spaces), a series of MOVE statements moves the data to the output record. These statements indicate the power of the MOVE statement in COBOL. If zero suppression or the insertion of a decimal point is necessary when a field is moved, the MOVE statement does it. For example, when BF-ITEM-NO is moved to RL-ITEM-NO, leading zeros are suppressed as follows:

Field:	BF-ITEM-NO	RL-ITEM-NO
PICTURE:	9(5)	Z(5)
Before:	00103	?????
After:	00103	103

When BF-UNIT-PRICE is moved to RL-UNIT-PRICE, a decimal point is inserted and the leading zeros before the decimal point are suppressed, as in this example:

Field:	BF-UNIT-PRICE	RL-UNIT-PRICE
PICTURE:	999V99	ZZZ.99
Before:	00449	?????
After:	00449	4.49

If 00005 were moved instead of 00449, RL-UNIT-PRICE would print as .05. As you can see, the result of a COBOL MOVE depends on the PICTUREs given for each of the fields involved in the statement.

To classify data items, most reference manuals use the terminology in figure 2-14. Alphabetic items, which have not yet been mentioned, have PICTUREs that consist of As. Since they contain letters and spaces only, they have limited use and *alphanumeric items* will always work just as well. As a result, alphabetic items aren't used in this book.

Numeric items consist primarily of 9s, but they may also have one V (decimal point) and one S (a sign as explained in the next topic). *Numeric edited items* can consist of 9s, Zs, decimal points, and any of several other editing characters that will also be covered in the next topic.

The bottom table in figure 2-14 uses this terminology to indicate which types of moves are legal, which are illegal, and which, though legal, should never be done. As you can see, it is always an error to move an alphabetic field to a numeric or numeric edited field. In contrast, it is always OK to move a numeric field to a numeric edited field. In this type of move, the number of digits (9s) in the sending field should be the same as the number of digits (9s or Zs) in the receiving field.

The moves marked "Questionable" in the chart are allowed by the compiler; however, in almost all cases they should be avoided. For example, if an alphanumeric field were moved to a numeric field, it would be treated as though it contained an integer, which might not be the case at all. As a result, the value in the receiving field would be unpredictable. In general, then, treat the

Data item table:

Item name	PICTURE contains	PICTURE examples
Alphabetic	As	A(20) AA
Alphanumeric	Xs	X(20) XXX
Numeric	S, V, and 9s	9(5) S999V99
Numeric edited	Decimal point, Zs, 9s, and other editing characters	Z(5) ZZZ.99

MOVE table:

Sending Item	Receiving Item			
	Alphabetic	Alphanumeric	Numeric	Numeric edited
Alphabetic	OK	OK	Illegal	Illegal
Alphanumeric	OK	OK	Questionable	Questionable
Numeric	Illegal	Whole numbers OK; others questionable	OK	OK
Numeric edited	Illegal	OK	Illegal	Illegal

Figure 2-14   Data items and the MOVE statement

moves marked "Questionable" as though they were illegal, and avoid them entirely.

The WRITE statement   The WRITE statement causes one line to be printed and the form to be moved up one line. In other words, after all the fields are moved to the printer output area, the WRITE statement prints the output line. Note that the format for the WRITE statement (see figure 2-8) requires the record name. In contrast, the format for the READ statement requires the file name.

Discussion

I think the key to understanding the reorder-listing program just described is in following the flow of control from one module to another. So let me recap. First, the top module (module 000) is executed only once. However, control passes from module 000's PERFORM UNTIL statement to module 100 once for each card in the input deck until at last there are no more records in the input file and Y is moved to CARD-EOF-SWITCH. Then, the program moves from the PERFORM UNTIL statement to the CLOSE statements that follow it.

Each time module 100 is executed, it causes module 110 to be executed. And as long as module 110 reads another data record, module 100 also causes module 120 to be executed. Finally, for each data card, if the available stock is less than the reorder point, module 100 causes module 130 to be executed and a reorder line is printed.

As you can see from this program, coding the Identification, Environment, and Data Divisions is a rather trivial job. The difficulties are encountered in the Procedure Division. If you don't yet understand how the reorder-listing program works, I think you will after you do the problems for this topic. Then, topic 3 will present some additional COBOL elements so you will know everything you need to write programs of considerable complexity.

Terminology

extension

A margin

B margin

program name

file name

system name

ddname

external name

record name

data name

reserved word

switch

procedure name

paragraph name

condition

literal

nested IF statements

imperative statement

alphanumeric item

numeric item

numeric edited item

Objectives

1. Identify the compiler that you will be writing programs for during this course.

2. Given the program listing in figure 2-5 and sample input data, answer questions about the execution of the object program.

3. Given the description of an input or output file, code acceptable SELECT statements (Environment Division) and data descriptions (Data Division) for it using system names that are compatible with your system.

Problems

1. (Objective 1) Find out what compiler you will be using in this course. If necessary, refer to the heading on the first page of any source listing prepared by your compiler.

2. (Objective 2) The data in the table in figure 2-15 represents six input cards for the reorder-listing program shown in figure 2-5. Assuming that columns 51–80 of all the input cards are blank, answer the following questions:

    a. Give the verbs for the first four statements that will be executed by this program.

    b. Other than module 000, list in sequence the modules that will be executed for card 1.

    c. What does the field named CARD-EOF-SWITCH contain after the first input card has been processed? What does AVAILABLE-STOCK contain?

Field name:	Item no.	Item description	Unit cost	Unit price	Reorder point	On hand	On order
Card columns:	1-5	6-25	26-30	31-35	36-40	41-45	46-50
Card 1:	00101	GENERATOR	04000	04900	00100	00070	00050
	00103	HEATER SOLENOID	00330	00440	00050	00034	00000
	03244	GEAR HOUSING	06500	07900	00010	00012	00000
	03981	PLUMB LINE	00210	00240	00015	00035	00000
	04638	STARTER SWITCH	00900	00980	00030	00016	00000
Card 6:	/*						

Figure 2-15   Input data for the reorder-listing program

d. What is the next statement to be executed after the ADD statement for card 1?

e. Other than module 000, list in sequence the modules that will be executed for card 2.

f. After module 110 has been executed for card 2, what do BF-UNIT-PRICE, BF-ON-ORDER, and AVAILABLE-STOCK contain?

g. After module 120 has been executed for card 2, what does AVAILABLE-STOCK contain?

h. After module 130 is executed for card 2, what do RL-ITEM-NO, RL-ITEM-DESC, RL-UNIT-PRICE, and RL-AVAILABLE-STOCK contain?

i. When the WRITE statement is executed for card 2, what is printed in the first 51 print positions of the printer?

j. What is the next statement to be executed after the WRITE statement for card 2?

k. Assume that the program is back at the PERFORM UNTIL statement prior to processing card 3. List in sequence the modules that will be executed up to the time that the program ends. Do not include module 000.

l. What will be printed in the first 51 print positions for card 3?

m. What will be printed in the first 51 print positions for card 4?

n. What will be printed in the first 51 print positions for card 5?

o. What happens when the READ statement is executed for card 6? What are the next two statements to be executed after this?

p. What happens when the PERFORM UNTIL statement is executed after card 6 has been processed?

q. What happens when the STOP RUN statement is executed?

3. (Objective 3) Write a SELECT statement and file, record, and field descriptions for an input card file consisting of invoice cards in this format:

Card columns	Field	Form
1	Card code	Alphanumeric
2–4	Salesman number	Numeric
5–9	Customer number	Numeric
15–19	Invoice number	Numeric
20–25	Invoice date	Numeric
26–47	Customer name	Alphanumeric
48–54	Invoice amount	Numeric (two decimal places)

4. (Objective 3) Write a SELECT statement and file, record, and field descriptions for a printer file that prints an invoice register with this line format:

Print positions	Field	Form
1–5	Invoice number	Numeric
10–14	Customer number	Numeric
19–40	Customer name	Alphanumeric
45–51	Invoice amount	Numeric (decimal point must print)

Suppress the lead zeros in all numeric fields and coordinate your descriptions with the input data descriptions of problem 2.

Solutions

1. Write the name of the compiler you will be using right here:

2. a. OPEN, OPEN, MOVE, PERFORM UNTIL

    b. 100, 110, 120

    c. N, 00120

    d. The second IF statement in module 100 (part of the nested IFs)

    e. 100, 110, 120, 130

f.   00440, 00000, and 00120

g.   00034

h.   bb103, HEATERbSOLENOIDbbbbb, bb4.40, and bbb34
(where b equals one blank)

i.   bb103bbbbbHEATERbSOLENOIDbbbbbbbbbbbbb4.40b-
bbbbbbb34 (where b equals one blank)

j.   PERFORM UNTIL

k.   100, 110, 120, 100, 110, 120, 100, 110, 120, 130, 100, 110

l.   Nothing

m.   Nothing

n.   b4638bbbbbSTARTERbSWITCHbbbbbbbbbbbbb9.80b-
bbbbbbb16 (where b equals one blank)

o.   The /* card is read and the AT END clause is executed. As
a result, Y is moved into CARD-EOF-SWITCH. Then, the
IF statement in module 100 is executed followed by the
PERFORM UNTIL statement in module 000.

p.   Control falls through to the first statement following the
PERFORM UNTIL statement.

q.   The program ends and a branch to the supervisor
takes place.

3.   This is an acceptable SELECT statement for the System/360-370
DOS compilers:

```
SELECT INVCDS ASSIGN TO SYS005-UR-2540R-S.
```

This is acceptable for the OS compilers:

```
SELECT INVCDS ASSIGN TO UT-S-INVCDS.
```

These are acceptable file and data descriptions:

```
FD  INVCDS
    LABEL RECORDS ARE STANDARD
    RECORDING MODE IS F
    RECORD CONTAINS 80 CHARACTERS.
01  INVOICE-CARD.
    02  IC-CODE          PICTURE IS X.
    02  IC-SLSMN-NO      PICTURE IS 9(3).
    02  IC-CUST-NO       PICTURE IS 9(5).
    02  FILLER           PICTURE IS X(5).
    02  IC-INV-NO        PICTURE IS 9(5).
    02  IC-INV-DATE      PICTURE IS 9(6).
    02  IC-CUST-NAME     PICTURE IS X(22).
    02  IC-INV-AMOUNT    PICTURE IS 9(5)V99.
    02  FILLER           PICTURE IS X(26).
```

4. This is an acceptable SELECT statement for the System/360-370 DOS compilers:

```
SELECT INVREG ASSIGN TO SYS006-UR-1403-S.
```

This is acceptable for the OS compilers:

```
SELECT INVREG ASSIGN TO UT-S-INVREG.
```

These are acceptable file and data descriptions:

```
FD  INVREG
    LABEL RECORDS ARE STANDARD
    RECORDING MODE IS F
    RECORD CONTAINS 132 CHARACTERS.
01  INV-REG-LINE.
    02  IR-INV-NO        PICTURE IS Z(5).
    02  FILLER           PICTURE IS X(4).
    02  IR-CUST-NO       PICTURE IS Z(5).
    02  FILLER           PICTURE IS X(4).
    02  IR-CUST-NAME     PICTURE IS X(22).
    02  FILLER           PICTURE IS X(4).
    02  IR-INV-AMOUNT    PICTURE IS Z(5).99.
    02  FILLER           PICTURE IS X(80).
```

TOPIC 3   Completing the Basic Subset

In topic 2, you were introduced to the basic structure of the COBOL program. In this topic, you will build on that base with some additional COBOL elements. This topic describes how COBOL is used for punching card output, for varying the spacing on a printed form, and so on.

Comment Cards

Occasionally, a programmer uses *comment cards*, or *comments*, in a program to explain or give extra information about a certain segment of code. A comment card has an asterisk in column 7 and a comment or note written by the programmer in the remaining columns of the card. During compilation, the contents of comment cards are printed, but otherwise the cards are ignored. Thus, they can be placed in a program without affecting the resulting object code.

Because a structured program is relatively easy to follow by virtue of its structure alone, it rarely requires any comments at all. In general, then, you should only use comments when they actually contribute to the clarity of the program. Don't use them to document or restate something that is made clear by the code itself.

```
          IDENTIFICATION DIVISION.
     *
               .
               .
     *
          ENVIRONMENT DIVISION.
     *
               .
               .
     *
          DATA DIVISION.
     *
          FILE SECTION.
     *
          FD  .
               .
               .
     *
          01  .
     *
               .
               .
     *
          PROCEDURE DIVISION.
     *
          000-PRODUCE-REORDER-LISTING.
     *
               .
               .
```

Figure 2-16   Using blank comment cards to space the source listing

Blank comment cards   In contrast to comment cards with notes
punched in them, blank comment cards should be used regularly
to help make your program listings easier to follow. A blank comment card also has an asterisk in column 7, but nothing is punched
in the rest of the card. Using blank comment cards before and after
the logical breaks in your programs will space your program listings
and make them more readable. In general, you should use blank
comment cards before and after division names, section names,
paragraph names, FD items, and 01-level items, as shown in figure
2-16. As you go through this book, you will see many examples
showing the use of blank comment cards.

     (You can also use completely blank cards, with nothing punched
in them, to space your output listing. However, the COBOL compiler has to search a blank card column-by-column to make sure

that it doesn't contain any source code. In contrast, once the compiler encounters an asterisk in column 7, it knows it can ignore the rest of the card. So for efficiency's sake, always use blank comment cards, not blank cards.)

Card Output

In COBOL, the READ and WRITE statements are used for most input and output operations. The READ is used for an input operation; the WRITE for an output operation. The only way you can tell which I/O device is actually being used is by referring to the corresponding SELECT statement in the Environment Division or, under OS, to the job-control cards for the program. For example,

```
WRITE PAYROLL-RECORD
```

could refer to a printed line, a punched card, a record on magnetic tape, or a record on magnetic disk. However, the DOS SELECT statement and file description in figure 2-17 would indicate that it is a card-punching operation using the IBM 2540 Card Punch. On the System/360-370, 2540P refers to the 2540 card punch.

To code punched-card output, then, you write the statements just as you would if coding for printer output. The differences are (1) the device number used in the DOS SELECT statement or in the job setup on an OS system and (2) the number of positions allocated to the output record (80 characters for a punched card instead of 132 for the 1403 printer).

Spacing the Printed Output Form

In many applications, the vertical spacing of a printed form must be varied. For example, when printing an invoice, the customer name and address is printed, several lines are skipped to the body of the form where one or more body lines are printed, several more lines are skipped and the total line is printed, and then the form is skipped to the heading of the next invoice. In COBOL, this skipping is generally done by using the following formats of the WRITE statement:

1.   WRITE record-name AFTER ADVANCING integer LINES.

2.   WRITE record-name AFTER ADVANCING data-name LINES.

3.   WRITE record-name AFTER ADVANCING mnemonic-name.

When the first format is used on the System/360-370, the integer must be a positive number less than 100. (An integer is simply a whole number.) When the statement is executed, the form in the

```
      ENVIRONMENT DIVISION.
          .
          .
          SELECT PAYROLL-FILE ASSIGN TO SYS007-UR-2540P-S.
          .
          .
      DATA DIVISION.
  *
      FILE SECTION.
          .
          .
      FD  PAYROLL-FILE
          LABEL RECORDS ARE OMITTED
          RECORDING MODE IS F
          RECORD CONTAINS 80 CHARACTERS.
  *
      01  PAYROLL-RECORD.
  *
          02  PR-CODE            PICTURE IS X.
          02  PR-EMP-NO          PICTURE IS 9(4).
          02  PR-EMP-NAME        PICTURE IS X(22).
          02  PR-JOB-CLASS       PICTURE IS 99.
          02  PR-HRS-WORKED      PICTURE IS 99V9.
          02  FILLER             PICTURE IS X(48).
          .
          .
          .
      PROCEDURE DIVISION.
          .
          .
          .
          WRITE PAYROLL-RECORD.
          .
          .
          .
```

Figure 2-17 Punching output cards on a DOS system

printer moves up as many lines as indicated before the output record
is printed.

In the second format, the WRITE statement uses a data name
described in the Working-Storage Section of the Data Division.
Spacing of the form depends on the value of the field at the time
that the WRITE statement is executed. For example,

```
WRITE PAYROLL-RECORD
    AFTER ADVANCING SPACE-CONTROL LINES
```

causes triple spacing if SPACE-CONTROL contains a 3 at the time of execution. The field must always contain a positive integer that is less than 100.

The third format of the AFTER ADVANCING clause provides for skipping to various punches in the carriage-control tape of the printer. When it is used, *mnemonic names* are assigned to specific carriage-control punches in the Configuration Section of the Environment Division. The rules for forming mnemonic names are the same as those for data names. As we said in chapter 1, a 1-punch is used to skip to the top of the next page when standard forms are used. So, to allow for skipping to the next page, a 1-punch can be given the mnemonic name of PAGE-TOP like this:

```
ENVIRONMENT DIVISION.
CONFIGURATION SECTION.
SPECIAL-NAMES.
    C01 IS PAGE-TOP.
```

As you can see, a paragraph named SPECIAL-NAMES is required. The COBOL reserved word C01 is needed to indicate a 1-punch (C01 stands for channel 01) in the carriage-control tape.

C01, C02, C03, and so on, up to C12 are special COBOL words created by IBM to correspond to the twelve punching positions in a carriage-control tape. Such words are referred to in COBOL literature as *implementor names* because they are created by the implementor of the compiler being used. Usually, the implementor is the computer manufacturer, so these names vary depending on the computer manufacturer.

When the third format of the WRITE statement is executed, the printer skips to the portion of the printed page that is represented by the mnemonic name. Thus,

```
WRITE PAYROLL-RECORD
    AFTER ADVANCING PAGE-TOP
```

will cause the form to be skipped to the top of the next page before printing if PAGE-TOP is assigned to a channel-1 punch in the SPECIAL-NAMES paragraph.

If you're using an ANS 74 compiler, you can skip to the top of a page without using a mnemonic name assigned in the SPECIAL-NAMES paragraph. In place of the mnemonic name, you use the reserved word PAGE. Thus,

```
WRITE PAYROLL-RECORD
    AFTER ADVANCING PAGE
```

will cause a skip to the top of the next page on a 1974 compiler. Note, however, that a 1974 compiler will also accept the use of the mnemonic name so this presents no problem when converting a 1968 program to 1974 standards.

When using the ADVANCING option of the WRITE statement, the programmer must remember two other requirements. First, if AFTER ADVANCING appears in one WRITE statement for a file, it must be used in all of the WRITE statements for the file. Second, on the System/360-370, one extra position must be described in the record description for the printed line. That extra storage position must be the first position of the record description and must not be used by the program, since it is used for controlling the spacing of the form. When the line is printed, the contents of this storage position will not be printed. For example, a record for the 1403 printer must be 133 positions long instead of 132. The first position should have a PICTURE of X and a suitable name—for example, ER-CC could be the name of the carriage-control field in an employee record.

In general, you will use only formats 2 and 3 of the WRITE AFTER statement to control spacing. Furthermore, you will use format 3 primarily for skipping to the top of a new page. On those few occasions when you work with special forms, you will assign carriage-control punches to specific lines of the form, you will give mnemonic names to these punches in the SPECIAL-NAMES paragraph of the Configuration Section, and you will use format 3 to skip to the various punches in the control tape. Because none of the programs in this book require special forms, you will only see C01 used in this book and it will always represent the top of a page.

Incidentally, the word BEFORE can be used in place of the word AFTER in any of the three formats just described. Then, the printing of the line takes place before the indicated spacing or skipping. In general, however, only one of the words should be used in any one program since mixing them can easily lead to programming errors in which one line is printed over a previously printed line. As a result, I recommend that you use the AFTER forms in all the programs you write.

Field Description in the Data Division

In topic 2 you were introduced to some basic ways of describing fields in the Data Division of the program. As you will see, however, there are a number of other clauses that can further define data fields. These include the VALUE, USAGE, and SYNCHRONIZED clauses. First, though, you'll learn how additional level numbers can be used to define fields within fields.

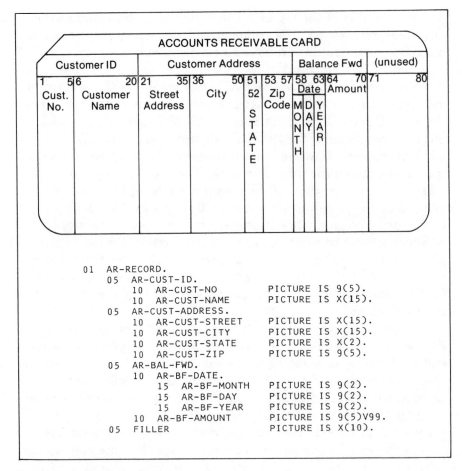

Figure 2-18   Level numbers

Level numbers

In topic 2, 01 and 02 level numbers were used in the Data Division to describe the fields within a record. Additional level numbers are used to describe fields within fields—such as month, day, and year fields within the larger date field. To illustrate, consider the accounts receivable card and its associated data descriptions in figure 2-18. Here, AR-CUST-ID refers to the first 20 card columns while AR-CUST-NO refers to columns 1-5. Similarly, AR-BAL-FWD refers to columns 58-70, AR-BF-DATE to columns 58-63, and AR-BF-YEAR to columns 62 and 63.

Notice that PICTUREs are used only for *elementary items*—data fields that are not broken down any further. *Group items*—fields that have fields within them—cannot have PICTURE clauses.

Note also that the level numbers used are 01, 05, 10, and 15, not 01, 02, 03, and 04. Although 01, 02, 03, and 04 could be used, leaving a gap between the level numbers makes it easier to further divide a record later. Thus, leaving gaps is a common programming practice.

On the System/360-370, you can use level numbers from 01 to 49 to describe items. As long as one level number is greater than a preceding level number, it is considered to be part of the larger field. By using a group item such as AR-CUST-ADDRESS as well as elementary items such as AR-CUST-STREET and AR-CUST-ZIP, you can operate on the entire field or any of its parts when writing statements in the Procedure Division.

Signed numbers

In some applications, input data may be either positive or negative. A card input field is considered negative, for instance, when the rightmost column of the field contains an 11-punch in addition to a digit punch. If an amount field in columns 41–45 of a card contains the digits 12366 along with an 11-punch in column 45, the data is read into storage as −12366. In many programs, it is also possible that the result of a calculation will be negative. For example, if 5 is subtracted from 4, the answer is −1.

In COBOL, an S should be used in the PICTURE of any input or working storage field that may be either positive or negative. The following are examples:

```
05   SALES-AMOUNT      PICTURE IS S9(4)V99.

05   NET-PAY           PICTURE IS S999V99.
```

The S doesn't require an extra card column in an input field, and it does not require an extra storage position.

If S is not specified for a field and the field becomes negative as the result of a calculation, the minus sign will be removed. Thus, −200 would be converted to an unsigned 200, which is treated as +200. If removing the sign isn't the intention of the programmer, errors are sure to occur.

In general, then, you should use an S on all numeric fields in working storage unless you deliberately intend to remove plus or minus signs that may occur during the execution of the program. This will lead to more efficient object code. As for numeric input fields, you should only use S for fields that may carry a sign.

Value clauses

Many programs require fields that have a certain starting or constant value. In COBOL, these initial values are given in the Data

Division by using VALUE clauses. For example, the following description in the Working-Storage Section of a program gives the field named INTEREST-RATE a value of .005:

```
05   INTEREST-RATE    PICTURE IS V999 VALUE IS .005
```

On the System/360-370, any numeric value up to eighteen digits long may be used in the VALUE clause as long as it doesn't exceed the PICTURE size for a field. A value can have a leading plus or minus sign as in +.005 or -32, and it can have a decimal point.

In the example above, .005 is called a *numeric literal*. In general, the numeric literal used in the VALUE clause should be consistent with the PICTURE for the field. That is, it should have the same number of decimal positions and digits; and if the field is signed, the literal should have a sign too. If the VALUE and the PICTURE for the field aren't consistent, diagnostics will occur.

A VALUE clause can also be used to give a non-numeric value to a field in storage. In this case, a *non-numeric literal* is used as in the following:

```
05   IR-TITLE    PICTURE IS X(16)
                 VALUE IS 'INVENTORY REPORT'.
```

The non-numeric literal is 'INVENTORY REPORT' and all characters between the quotation marks (') are stored in the field named IR-TITLE. In other words, IR-TITLE is given an initial value of INVENTORY REPORT.

Because the quotation mark is used to mark the beginning and end of a non-numeric literal, it cannot be used within the literal itself. As you will see in chapter 5, however, the word QUOTE can be used in those rare instances when a quotation-mark literal value is needed. With the exception of the quotation mark, all other characters can be used in the normal way within a non-numeric literal.

On the System/360-370, either the double (") or single (') quotation mark can be used to enclose a non-numeric literal, but only one or the other. This is an option of the compilers. Since the single mark is more common, it is used throughout this book.

A VALUE clause can also contain the COBOL words SPACE or ZERO. Thus,

```
05   AMOUNT    PICTURE IS 9(4)  VALUE IS ZERO.
05   BLANKS    PICTURE IS X(10) VALUE IS SPACE.
```

gives a starting value of zero to AMOUNT and a value of spaces to BLANKS.

VALUE clauses are often used for fields whose values might have to be changed from time to time. For example, in a report-printing program, you usually have to determine when you've come to the end of one page of printed output and need to skip to the top of the next page (this is called *forms overflow*). To do this, you can create a working-storage field with an appropriate name—like LINES-ON-PAGE—and assign it a value equal to the maximum number of lines per page. You can then use an IF statement to compare LINES-ON-PAGE with a field that counts the lines as they are printed, as in this example:

```
IF LINE-COUNT IS GREATER THAN LINES-ON-PAGE
```

If the condition is true, your program can skip to a new page. If the number of lines per page ever needs to be adjusted, you can quickly and easily change the value of LINES-ON-PAGE without having to recode any Procedure Division statements.

Another common use of VALUE clauses is to store data that is to be printed as the heading of a report. For example, the COBOL code in the Working-Storage Section of figure 2-19 would print this heading before processing data:

```
                    INVESTMENT  REPORT

ITEM NUMBER          ITEM NAME              INVESTMENT
```

Notice that 133 positions are allotted for the record named INVENTORY-LINE because the ADVANCING option of the WRITE statement is used.

USAGE clauses

USAGE clauses are not absolutely necessary in a COBOL program. However, they can significantly affect the efficiency of the object program that is compiled. The USAGE clause allows the programmer to specify the form in which a field of data should be stored.

On the System/360-370, the COBOL programmer normally uses three different forms of data representation. These forms are referred to as DISPLAY, COMPUTATIONAL-3, and COMPUTATIONAL. In addition, System/360-370 COBOL provides for three other data forms: COMPUTATIONAL-1, COMPUTATIONAL-2, and COMPUTATIONAL-4. These forms, however, are rarely used by the COBOL programmer and are not covered in this book.

```
     ENVIRONMENT DIVISION.
  :
     CONFIGURATION SECTION.
  :
     SPECIAL-NAMES.
         C01 IS PAGE-TOP.
             .
             .
     DATA DIVISION.
  :
     FILE SECTION.
             .
             .
     FD  INVENTORY-LISTING
         LABEL RECORDS ARE STANDARD
         RECORDING MODE IS F
         RECORD CONTAINS 133 CHARACTERS.
  :
     01  INVENTORY-LINE.
  :
         05   IL-CC          PICTURE IS X.
         05   FILLER         PICTURE IS X(3).
         05   IL-ITEM-NUMBER PICTURE IS Z(5).
         05   FILLER         PICTURE IS X(6).
         05   IL-ITEM-NAME   PICTURE IS X(20).
         05   FILLER         PICTURE IS X(6).
         05   IL-INVESTMENT  PICTURE IS Z(6).99.
         05   FILLER         PICTURE IS X(83).
  :
     WORKING-STORAGE SECTION.
  :
     01  HEADING-LINE-1.
  :
         05   HDG1-CC        PICTURE IS X.
         05   FILLER         PICTURE IS X(15)    VALUE IS SPACE.
         05   FILLER         PICTURE IS X(17)
                             VALUE IS 'INVESTMENT REPORT'.
         05   FILLER         PICTURE IS X(100)  VALUE IS SPACE.
  :
     01  HEADING-LINE-2.
  :
         05   HDG2-CC        PICTURE IS X.
         05   FILLER         PICTURE IS X(11)    VALUE IS 'ITEM NUMBER'.
         05   FILLER         PICTURE IS X(8)     VALUE IS SPACE.
         05   FILLER         PICTURE IS X(9)     VALUE IS 'ITEM NAME'.
         05   FILLER         PICTURE IS X(11)    VALUE IS SPACE.
         05   FILLER         PICTURE IS X(10)    VALUE IS 'INVESTMENT'.
         05   FILLER         PICTURE IS X(83)    VALUE IS SPACE.
             .
             .
     PROCEDURE DIVISION.
             .
             .
     270-PRINT-REPORT-HEADINGS.
  :
         MOVE HEADING-LINE-1 TO INVENTORY-LINE.
         WRITE INVENTORY-LINE
             AFTER ADVANCING PAGE-TOP.
         MOVE HEADING-LINE-2 TO INVENTORY-LINE.
         MOVE 2 TO SPACE-CONTROL.
         WRITE INVENTORY-LINE
             AFTER ADVANCING SPACE-CONTROL LINES.
             .
             .
```

Figure 2-19   Printing report headings

The USAGE clauses for the common forms of data representation are written this way:

```
USAGE IS DISPLAY

USAGE IS COMPUTATIONAL-3

USAGE IS COMPUTATIONAL
```

The USAGE clause is one of the clauses that can come after a data name, as in these examples:

```
05   FIELD-A   USAGE IS COMPUTATIONAL-3   PICTURE IS S9(3)V99.

05   FIELD-B   PICTURE IS S9(4)           VALUE IS +1244
               USAGE IS COMPUTATIONAL.

05   FIELD-C   PICTURE IS 9(5)            USAGE IS DISPLAY.
```

Notice that the sequence of PICTURE, VALUE, and USAGE clauses is not significant. However, to keep your programs clear and readable, you should align similar clauses whenever possible.

When the data from a field of one USAGE is moved to a field of another USAGE, it is converted to the form of the receiving field. As a result, the data in a field can be converted from one form to another by using the MOVE statement. However, other statements can lead to data conversion, too, and this is what can result in an inefficient object program. For example, all arithmetic takes place in one of the computational forms of storage, whether it is specified in a USAGE clause or not. So when arithmetic operations are performed on DISPLAY fields, the data in the fields must be converted to a computational form before the arithmetic can take place. Then, after the fields have been operated upon, they must be converted back to their original usage (DISPLAY) before the program can continue. Assigning the fields the proper usage (in this case, a computational one) in the Data Division would save all this data conversion and lead to a more efficient object program.

When, then, should you use each of the USAGE forms? And how does one form of storage differ from another? To answer these questions, a brief explanation of the three common forms of data representation follows along with recommendations on when to use each form.

DISPLAY   The DISPLAY form of storage (also referred to as *external decimal*) means that there is one character of data in each byte of storage. This is the form of storage that was described in topic 1 of this chapter. All card and printer fields must have DISPLAY usage.

USAGE IS DISPLAY is assumed by the compiler when the USAGE clause is omitted, so most programmers don't bother to code USAGE clauses for DISPLAY fields. As a result, USAGE IS DISPLAY is never used in the programs illustrated in this book. Since there are no USAGE clauses in the program in figure 2-5, all of the fields have DISPLAY usage.

COMPUTATIONAL-3   The COMPUTATIONAL-3 form (abbreviated COMP-3) on the System/360-370 is a compressed form of storage for numeric fields. It is usually referred to as *packed decimal,* or *internal decimal.* With the exception of the rightmost storage position, two digits are stored in each byte of a COMP-3 field. The rightmost byte stores only one digit plus the sign of the field. Thus, a one-digit field requires one byte of storage, a three-digit field requires two bytes, a five-digit field requires three bytes, and so on. For example, look at the following:

```
05   FLD-1   PICTURE IS S9        USAGE IS COMP-3.

05   FLD-2   PICTURE IS S9(3)     USAGE IS COMP-3    VALUE IS -500.

05   FLD-3   PICTURE IS S9(9)     USAGE IS COMP-3.
```

Here, FLD-1 will require one storage byte, FLD-2 two bytes, and FLD-3 five bytes.

Because a packed-decimal field always contains an odd number of digits, the PICTURE for a COMP-3 field should also carry an odd number of digits. As for use, COMP-3 should generally be used in working storage for all numeric fields that are going to be involved in arithmetic operations or numeric comparisons. Both these practices can help avoid inefficiency during compilation and execution.

COMPUTATIONAL   A COMPUTATIONAL (abbreviated COMP) field on the System/360-370 occupies two, four, or eight bytes of storage depending on the number of digits in the field. If the field has from one to four digits in its PICTURE, it occupies two bytes of storage. From five to nine digits, it occupies four bytes. And from ten to eighteen digits, it occupies eight bytes.

When arithmetic operations are performed on COMP fields, the instructions are executed faster than if COMP-3 fields are used. Nevertheless, COMP-3 is the preferred data form for most of the fields in a business program. Why? Because it is more time-consuming to convert a field (for instance, a card input field) from DISPLAY to COMP and back to DISPLAY than it is to convert the field from DISPLAY to COMP-3 and back. So whatever is gained by using COMP in arithmetic operations is lost in data conversion.

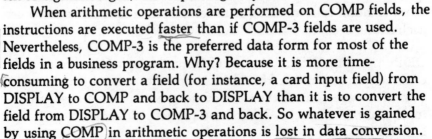

In general, then, you will use COMP sparingly in a COBOL program. However, there are a couple of cases in which you should use it. One is when you have fields that are going to be involved in a long series of arithmetic operations. Another, as you will see in chapter 5, is when you're doing repetitive processing. The one that is most important to you now, though, is when you're working on an OS system and you use a data name in the WRITE AFTER statement.

To illustrate, suppose a program contains this statement:

```
WRITE REPORT-LINE
      AFTER ADVANCING SPACE-CONTROL LINES.
```

No matter what usage is given to SPACE-CONTROL in working storage, the program has to convert the field to COMP in order to execute the WRITE statement on an OS system. So to save this conversion, a field like SPACE-CONTROL should be given COMP usage in programs that are run under OS. And any fields that are involved with SPACE-CONTROL in arithmetic operations or numeric comparisons should also have COMP usage. You will see this illustrated in an OS program at the end of the topic. Do *not*, however, use COMP for the SPACE-CONTROL field on a DOS system.

The SYNCHRONIZED clause

When COMP fields are used on the System/360, they must start at a proper *storage boundary* before they can be operated upon. Specifically, a two-byte COMP field must start at an address that is a multiple of two (such as 2, 4, 6, 8, or 10) before it can be operated upon. Similarly, a four-byte or an eight-byte COMP field must start at an address that is a multiple of four. While boundary alignment isn't required on the System/370, the COBOL compiler (which is the same for both the System/360 and the System/370) isn't aware of that. So before a COMP field is operated upon, it is moved to a proper boundary on the System/370, just as on the System/360.

In general, this type of boundary alignment isn't something that the COBOL programmer has to be concerned about. In all cases, the COBOL compiler makes sure that a COMP field is aligned properly before it is operated upon. The compiler does this by compiling extra machine-language instructions that move a COMP field to its proper boundary each time a COBOL statement refers to it. However, these extra instructions take additional time to compile and execute.

To give the COBOL programmer some control over the placement of fields within storage, COBOL provides the SYN-

CHRONIZED (abbreviated SYNC) clause that can be applied to a field in the Data Division. For instance, the following code causes the field named PRINCIPAL to be stored on a proper boundary:

```
05   PRINCIPAL   PICTURE IS S9(5)V99   USAGE IS COMP   SYNC.
```

Now PRINCIPAL will not have to be moved to a proper boundary each time it is operated upon by the object instructions. Thus, the programmer improves the operation of the object program by using this clause.

In summary, remember that if the SYNC clause is omitted entirely, the COBOL program will still compile and execute properly. However, the resulting object code will not be as efficient as it would be if the clause were used. For this reason, we recommend that SYNC be used on all fields that are defined with COMP usage. This coding will compile on all System/360-370 compilers.

The PICTURE clause and editing

When numeric data is moved to a numeric edited item, the data is normally converted to a more readable form. In group 1 of figure 2-20, for example, the numbers 12345 and 00123 are converted to 123.45 and 1.23 by using PICTURE clauses consisting of Zs, 9s, and decimal points. This conversion of a numeric item to a more readable form is often referred to as *editing*.

To further refine numeric data, editing characters such as the comma and the CR symbol are used. For example, commas are normally used when printing a field that has four or more digits to the left of the decimal point. This usage is shown in group 2 of figure 2-20. Since the numbers 001242 and 000009 do not have four or more significant digits to the left of the decimal point, the comma is suppressed along with the insignificant zeros. Otherwise, the comma prints as desired. If a field can have a value in the millions or billions, additional commas may be used; for example, ZZ,ZZZ,ZZZ,ZZZ.99.

In the examples so far, a negative field moved to a numeric edited item would be stripped of its sign and printed as if it were positive. As shown in group 3, the credit symbol (CR) is used to indicate that a field is negative. When coding, CR is placed to the right of the field that is being printed. CR is then printed to the right of the field if the number being edited is negative; if the number is positive, nothing is printed.

Group 4 illustrates the use of a fixed dollar sign. Here, one dollar sign is used as the leftmost character of an editing PICTURE. When data is moved to this numeric edited field, editing takes place

Group	Sending field		Receiving field	
	PICTURE	Data	PICTURE	Edited result
1 Basic Editing	S999V99 S999V99 S999V99	12345 00123 -00123	ZZZ.99 ZZZ.99 ZZZ.99	123.45 1.23 1.23
2 Comma Insertion	S9(4)V99 S9(4)V99 S9(4)V99	142090 001242 000009	Z,ZZZ.99 Z,ZZZ.99 Z,ZZZ.99	1,420.90 12.42 .09
3 Credit Symbol	S9(6) S9(6) S9(4)V99	001234 -001234 -001234	ZZZ,ZZZCR ZZZ,ZZZCR Z,ZZZ.99CR	1,234 1,234CR 12.34CR
4 Fixed Dollar Sign	S9(6) S9(4)V99 S9(4)V99	001234 123456 000012	$ZZZ,ZZZ $ZZZZ.99 $ZZZZ.99	$ 1,234 $1234.56 $ .12
5 Floating Dollar Sign	S9(4)V99 S9(4)V99 S9(4)V99 S99V99 S99V99	142090 001242 000009 1234 -0012	$$,$$$.99 $$,$$$.99 $$,$$$.99 $$$.99CR $$$.99CR	$1,420.90 $12.42 $.09 $12.34 $.12CR
6 Asterisk Check Protection	S9(4)V99 S9(4)V99 S9(4)V99 S9(4)V99	142090 001242 000009 123456	$*,***.99 $*,***.99 $*,***.99 **,***.99	$1,420.90 $***12.42 $*****.09 *1,234.56
7 Floating Plus Sign	S9(4)V99 S9(4)V99 S9(4)V99 S9(4)V99 S9(4)V99 S9(4)V99	142090 -142090 001242 -001242 000009 -000009	++,+++.99 ++,+++.99 ++,+++.99 ++,+++.99 ++,+++.99 ++,+++.99	+1,420.90 -1,420.90 +12.42 -12.42 +.09 -.09
8 Floating Minus Sign	S9(4)V99 S9(4)V99 S99V99 S99V99	001242 -001242 1234 -1234	--,---.99 --,---.99 ---.99 ---.99	12.42 -12.42 12.34 -12.34
9 Insertion Character 0	S9(4) S9(4) S9(4) S9(4)	1234 -1234 -0012 0012	ZZZ,Z00 ++,+++.00 ZZZ,Z00CR $$,$$$.00	123,400 -1,234.00 1,200CR $12.00
10 Insertion Character B	S9(4) S9(6) S9(6)	-1234 040339 001234	ZZZZBCR 99B99B99 ZZZB999	1234 CR 04 03 39 1 234
11 Stroke (ANS 74)	S9(6) S9(4)	040339 0775	ZZ/99/99 99/99	4/03/39 07/75

Figure 2-20 Editing numeric fields

as usual with the dollar sign remaining unchanged in the leftmost position of the field.

Group 5 represents the use of the floating dollar sign. Here, the dollar signs replace the Zs that would otherwise be used and one additional dollar sign is placed to the left of the field. Since there are four digit positions (9s) to the left of the decimal point in the first three examples, five dollar signs and one comma are used. When numeric data is moved to a field described with a floating dollar sign, the dollar sign prints just to the left of the first printed digit.

The asterisk (*), illustrated in group 6, is often used when printing checks to make sure that no one changes the amount printed. A fixed dollar sign is normally used at the far left of the field, but it may be omitted. At least one asterisk is used for each digit position to the left of the decimal point. When data with insignificant zeros is moved to a field like this, asterisks replace the zeros, and, if necessary, the commas.

A floating plus (+) or minus (−) sign may be used in place of the CR symbol to indicate whether a field is positive or negative. Groups 7 and 8 give some examples. In either case, the number of signs used in the numeric edited item is one more than the number of digit positions to the left of the decimal point in the sending item. Since there are four digit positions to the left of the decimal point in all of the examples in group 7 and in the first two examples in group 8, five plus or minus signs appear in the PICTURE for each corresponding receiving field. When the plus sign is used (group 7), it prints to the left of the result if the value is positive; a minus sign prints if the value is negative. When the minus sign is used (group 8), nothing prints if the value is positive; the minus sign prints if the value is negative.

Occasionally, a value in storage—such as 12—may represent a larger number—such as 1200 or 12,000. Then, zeros should be added to the field when it is printed. For this purpose, the insertion character 0 (zero) may be used as in group 9. When the value 1234 is moved to a field with a PICTURE of ZZZ,Z00, for example, the result is 123,400. In other words, the 0 is inserted into the result. The zero character may be used in combination with any of the other editing characters and may be placed anywhere in a field.

To insert a blank into a field, the insertion character B may be used as in group 10. Wherever the B appears in the PICTURE, a blank is inserted when the field is printed. Bs may also be used in combination with any of the other editing characters.

Group 11 illustrates the use of the *stroke* (slash) as an insertion character. This edit character is only available on the IBM ANS 74 compiler. It is used for editing date fields.

Although there are other ways in which numeric fields may be edited, those just illustrated satisfy the requirements of most business programs. When coding these PICTUREs, always try to have the same number of decimal places in the sending and the receiving fields—that is, align decimal points. Otherwise, inefficient object code is likely to result. By the same token, you should try to have as many Zs and 9s in the receiving field as there are 9s in the sending field. When using floating characters, there should be one more $, +, or − than would be used if coding Zs. Incidentally, the USAGE of the sending field doesn't affect the editing that is performed when a numeric item is moved to a numeric edited field.

When you want to edit an alphanumeric field, as opposed to a numeric field, the editing that can be done is limited. In this case, the only valid editing characters are the insertion characters: 0 (zero), B (blank), and / (stroke). Editing takes place just as in groups 9, 10, and 11 in figure 2-20; however, the picture of the sending field is described with Xs and the picture of the receiving field is described with Xs and the insertion characters as in these examples:

Sending field		Receiving field	
PICTURE	Data	PICTURE	Data
X(3)	123	XXX000	123000
X(3)	MRM	XBXBX	M R M
X(6)	123456	XX/XX/XX	12/34/56

Here again, insertion of the stroke (slash) is only available on 1974 compilers.

The BLANK WHEN ZERO clause

If a value of zero is moved to a field with this PICTURE:

        $$,$$$.99BCR

$.00 will be printed. Since this printing is usually unnecessary, the BLANK WHEN ZERO clause is often used as follows:

```
05  CR-AMOUNT-OWED    PICTURE IS $$,$$$.99BCR BLANK WHEN ZERO.
```

Here, CR-AMOUNT-OWED is converted to blanks when a value of zero is moved to it.

Procedure Division Elements

Literals in the Procedure Division

As we have seen, both numeric and non-numeric literals can be used in VALUE clauses in the Data Division. They can also be used, as shown in the reorder-listing program, in statements in the Procedure Division. The following are some examples:

```
1.  PERFORM 100-PRODUCE-REORDER-LINE
        UNTIL CARD-EOF-SWITCH IS EQUAL TO 'Y'.
```

```
2.    ADD 1.57 TO RESULT-FIELD.

3.    IF SL-ACCOUNT IS GREATER THAN 10000
          PERFORM 150-PRINT-REPORT-LINE.

4.    IF TR-TRAN-CODE IS EQUAL TO 'R'
          PERFORM 240-PROCESS-RETURN-RECORD.
```

A literal cannot, however, be used as the receiving field in an arithmetic instruction. For example,

```
ADD RESULT-FIELD TO 1.57
```

would cause a diagnostic.

Statements with items in a series

In many COBOL statements, a series of items can be coded in one statement, as in these examples:

```
1.    OPEN INPUT  BAL-FWD-FILE
          OUTPUT REORDER-LISTING.
```

(Both input and output files are opened in one statement.)

```
2.    ADD FIELD-A FIELD-B FIELD-C
          GIVING FIELD-D.
```

(Three fields are added together and the result is placed in the fourth field.)

```
3.    MOVE FIELD-1 TO FIELD-X FIELD-Y FIELD-Z.
```

(The contents of one field are moved to three fields.)

```
4.    CLOSE BAL-FWD-FILE
          REORDER-LISTING
          NEW-BAL-FILE.
```

(Three files are closed in one statement.)

By using a string of three periods, the format for a statement indicates that a series of data names can be used. For example, the expanded formats of the OPEN and CLOSE statements are

```
OPEN INPUT file-name ... OUTPUT file-name ...
CLOSE file-name ...
```

ROUNDED and ON SIZE ERROR options for arithmetic statements

For all arithmetic statements, there are two optional clauses that may be used. The first is the ROUNDED clause, which is used as follows:

```
MULTIPLY EMP-HOURS-WORKED BY EMP-HOURLY-RATE
    GIVING WS-NET-PAY ROUNDED.
```

To illustrate how this statement works, suppose EMP-HOURS-WORKED is 40.5, EMP-HOURLY-RATE is 2.25, and WS-NET-PAY is a field with two decimal places. Although the result of the multiplication is 91.125, the statement would round the result to 91.13:

	PICTURE	Value before execution	Value after execution
EMP-HOURS-WORKED	99V9	40.5	40.5
EMP-HOURLY-RATE	99V99	2.25	2.25
WS-NET-PAY	999V99	?????	91.13

Without the ROUNDED option, the third decimal place in the answer would be dropped, and 91.12 would be placed in the WS-NET-PAY field.

You should consider using the ROUNDED option whenever the result of a calculation will have more decimal places than is specified in the PICTURE of the receiving field. However, because of efficiency considerations, you should avoid using it unless you really need a rounded result.

The second arithmetic option is the ON SIZE ERROR option, which is used as follows:

```
MULTIPLY EMP-HOURS-WORKED BY EMP-HOURLY-RATE
    GIVING WS-NET-PAY
    ON SIZE ERROR
        PERFORM 330-PRINT-ERROR-MESSAGE.
```

This means that the program should perform the procedure named 330-PRINT-ERROR-MESSAGE if the result of the calculation has more digits than is specified in the PICTURE of the receiving field. For example, if WS-NET-PAY has a PICTURE of 999V99 and the result of the multiplication is 2125.90, a size error has occurred, and the program will perform the error-message procedure. Without the ON SIZE ERROR clause, the computer would continue to execute the program, but you couldn't be sure of the value in the result field; it would depend on the compiler.

In general, you should avoid using ON SIZE ERROR whenever possible. As you might guess, it affects the efficiency of the object program because a test for size overflow must be made each time a calculation is performed. As a more efficient alternative, I recommend that you check your input fields for valid values before you use them in an arithmetic statement. Then you'll know the values are small enough that size overflow won't occur.

The REMAINDER clause

All System/360-370 compilers provide for the remainder in a DIVIDE statement to be saved by using the REMAINDER clause. For instance, consider this example:

```
DIVIDE FIELD-A INTO FIELD-B
    GIVING FIELD-C
    REMAINDER FIELD-D.
```

When this statement is executed, FIELD-C will receive the quotient and FIELD-D will receive the remainder.

If the ROUNDED and ON SIZE ERROR clauses are needed, they are used as in this example:

```
DIVIDE FIELD-A INTO FIELD-B
    GIVING FIELD-C ROUNDED
    REMAINDER FIELD-D
    ON SIZE ERROR
        PERFORM 330-PRINT-ERROR-MESSAGE.
```

The rounding is done after the remainder has been stored in FIELD-D, so FIELD-D will still contain the remainder after the statement has been executed. For example, suppose FIELD-A equals 6 and FIELD-B equals 10. Then the results of the two DIVIDE statements above will differ as follows:

	FIELD-A	FIELD-B	FIELD-C	FIELD-D
Unrounded result	6	10	1	4
Rounded result	6	10	2	4

The DISPLAY statement

The DISPLAY statement can be used for infrequent printer output within a program. For example, if an END OF JOB message is to be printed at the end of a program, the DISPLAY statement, rather than the WRITE statement, can be used.

The format of the DISPLAY statement is as follows:

```
DISPLAY  {data-name}   ...
         {literal   }
```

Therefore, the following are examples of valid DISPLAY statements:

```
DISPLAY OUTPUT-DATA.

DISPLAY 'END OF JOB'.

DISPLAY 'RECORD NUMBER ' INV-ITEM-NUMBER ' IS IN ERROR.'
```

In example 1, the contents of the field named OUTPUT-DATA would be printed on the printer. In example 2, END OF JOB (a literal) would be printed. In example 3—which uses a series of a literal, a data name, and another literal—if the field named INV-ITEM-NUMBER contained 7904, this line would print:

```
RECORD NUMBER 7904 IS IN ERROR.
```

When a numeric field is displayed, it is first converted to DISPLAY usage. If the field has a sign, the rightmost digit of the number will print as a letter—the equivalent of a digit plus a zone punch in Hollerith code. In other words, the data isn't edited before being printed. Thus, +184 prints as 18D, where D is the combination of the digit 4 and the zone for the 12-punch. A −184 prints as 18M, where M is the combination of the digit 4 and the zone for an 11-punch. Of course, if Ss aren't used in the PICTUREs of the fields that are displayed, the fields will not carry signs.

Because the data printed by a DISPLAY statement is never considered to be part of a file, the printer doesn't have to be specified in a SELECT statement and an FD description isn't required. However, a DISPLAY statement is executed much more slowly than a WRITE statement. As a result, you should never use the DISPLAY statement for printing more than a few lines within a program.

In general, then, the DISPLAY statement is used for printing messages about the operation of a program during its execution. These messages should be printed on one of the printers of the system. Under DOS, the DISPLAY messages are commonly interspersed with the printer output resulting from the WRITE statement. Under OS, the messages are printed separately from the normal printer output.

In either case, it should always be easy to identify the program that issued the message, and the message should always be understandable. The message form we recommend is this:

```
program-name  {I}   message-number   message
              {A}
```

Here, the braces show that you must code either an I or an A to print as part of the message. An I means the message is only for Information, while an A is used when some outside Action is required to correct the condition causing the message. The message number refers to the numbers given in the instructions for running the program in which a complete description of the message can be found. You will see this format used in programs at the end of the topic.

Punctuation and Spacing in Your Coding

Thus far, the only punctuation mark used in the COBOL examples in this book has been the period. The System/360-370 compilers, however, allow the use of the comma and semicolon in much the same way that they would be used in English. As a result, you might see statements such as these in COBOL programs:

```
ADD FIELD-A, FIELD-B, FIELD-C, GIVING FIELD-D.

READ BALCRD RECORD; AT END MOVE 'Y' TO CARD-EOF-SWITCH.
```

When the compiler encounters a comma or semicolon, it simply ignores it.

The intent of the comma and semicolon, of course, is to improve the readability of a program. Unfortunately, they do more harm than good. In actual practice, they lead to keypunching errors and unwanted diagnostics. As a result, I recommend that the comma and semicolon be avoided, and none of the programs in this book use them.

As for spacing, the only requirement is that COBOL reserved words, names supplied by the programmer, and literals be separated by one or more spaces. As a result, statements can be written on more than one line, as they have been throughout this chapter:

```
1.    MULTIPLY EMP-HOURS BY EMP-HOURLY-RATE
          GIVING GROSS-PAY ROUNDED
          ON SIZE ERROR
              PERFORM 330-PRINT-ERROR-MESSAGE.

2.    05  INTEREST-RATE      PICTURE IS S9V99
                             VALUE IS +4.50
                             USAGE IS COMPUTATIONAL.
```

Statements can also be written one after the other as shown here:

```
290-PRINT-REPORT-HEADING.  MOVE HEADER-LINE TO
    OUTPUT-LINE.  WRITE OUTPUT-LINE AFTER ADVANCING
    PAGE-TOP.  MOVE COLUMN-HEADING TO OUTPUT-LINE.
    WRITE OUTPUT-LINE AFTER ADVANCING 2 LINES.
```

Coding in this way makes it more difficult to change the source deck, however, and thus is not a recommended programming practice. So never code more than one statement per line.

The real key to readability in a COBOL program is the proper use of indentation. For instance, the IF statement should be coded with indentation as in figures 2-12 and 2-13 to show the relationships between the true and false clauses. Similarly, conditional clauses like AT END and ON SIZE ERROR should be indented four spaces from the start of the statements that contain them. In chapter 5, you will be given some specific rules for the use of indentation in the Data and Procedure Divisions. In the meantime, you will use indentation to good advantage if you use the programs shown in this book as guides.

COBOL Reference Formats

So far, this book has used somewhat simplified formats when presenting a new COBOL element. Not all of the variations of a statement or clause have been given, and, as much as possible, the common technical notation has been avoided. In contrast, a COBOL technical manual normally expresses COBOL formats as shown in the samples in figure 2-21. Here, the following notation is used:

1. All words printed entirely in capital letters (such as DATA DIVISION) are COBOL reserved words.

2. Words that are printed in lowercase letters (such as file-name) represent names or words supplied by the programmer.

3. Braces ({ }) enclosing a stack of items indicate that the programmer must use one of the items. In the PICTURE clause, for example, the programmer can use either PICTURE or the shortened form, PIC.

4. Brackets ([]) are used to indicate that the enclosed item may be used or omitted, depending on the requirements of the program. For example, the ROUNDED clause in the ADD statement is optional.

5. The ellipsis (. . .) indicates that an element may appear once or any number of times in succession. Thus, a series of fields may be added together in the ADD statement.

6. Underlined reserved words are required unless the element itself is optional, but reserved words that are not underlined are optional. Thus, the LABEL RECORDS clause can be written

        LABEL RECORDS STANDARD

Since this notation is common to all COBOL manuals, it is used in the COBOL chapters that follow.

By studying the formats in figure 2-21, you can see that a large amount of coding can be eliminated by using shortened forms of words. For example, a COMP-3 field can be described as follows:

```
05  DATA-FIELD     PIC S999V99     VALUE +3.40     COMP-3.
```

It also reduces coding to eliminate all optional words. However, it is good practice to use the optional words if they add to the sense of a

```
DATA DIVISION.

FILE SECTION.
FD      file-name
        LABEL RECORDS ARE{OMITTED  }
                         {STANDARD }
        RECORDING MODE IS mode
        RECORD CONTAINS integer CHARACTERS.


01-49   {data-name}
        {FILLER   }

        {PICTURE}  IS character-string
        {PIC    }

          BLANK WHEN ZERO

WORKING-STORAGE SECTION.

01-49   {data-name}
        {FILLER   }

        {PICTURE}  IS character-string
        {PIC    }

                     {DISPLAY          }
                     {COMPUTATIONAL    }
        USAGE IS     {COMP             }
                     {COMPUTATIONAL-3  }
                     {COMP-3           }

        [{SYNCHRONIZED}].
         {SYNC        }

          VALUE IS literal

          BLANK WHEN ZERO

PROCEDURE DIVISION.
        ADD    {data-name-1}  [data-name-2] ...
               {literal-1   }  [literal-2  ]

               TO data-name-m [ROUNDED] [data-name-n [ROUNDED]] ...

               [ON SIZE ERROR imperative-statement]

        CLOSE file-name-1 [file-name-2] ...

        READ file-name RECORD AT END imperative-statement

                                              {integer LINES  }
        WRITE record-name[{BEFORE} ADVANCING {data-name LINES }]
                          {AFTER } {mnemonic-name}
```

Figure 2-21   Some sample COBOL formats

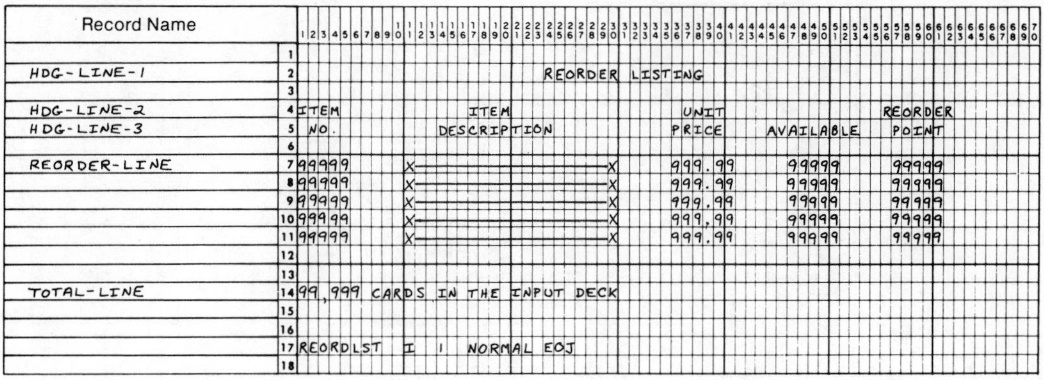

Figure 2-22 The refined reorder-listing print chart

Procedure Division statement because the program is then easier to read. As a result, a WRITE statement is usually written as

```
WRITE record-name AFTER ADVANCING SPACE-CONTROL LINES.
```

rather than

```
    WRITE record-name AFTER SPACE-CONTROL.
```

Both are acceptable COBOL, however. In the Data Division, it is common to omit all optional words in PICTURE, VALUE, and USAGE clauses and to use the shortened forms of the words PICTURE (PIC), COMPUTATIONAL (COMP), COMPUTATIONAL-3 (COMP-3), and SYNCHRONIZED (SYNC).

The Refined Reorder-Listing Program

Because it was the first program presented, the reorder-listing program in topic 2 of this chapter was much simplified. In actual practice, a program like this would print headings at the top of each page of the report and, at the end of the report, would probably print a count of the number of records processed. This count would be used to verify that all inventory records were processed—that is, no cards were missing from the input deck. These printing lines are shown on the print chart in figure 2-22. In addition, a normal end-of-job message should be displayed when the program ends. This message, too, is shown on the print chart.

Notice that I have given a record name to each type of output line on the print chart in figure 2-22. For instance, I have given the name HDG-LINE-1 to the first heading line of the report and the name REORDER-LINE to the body lines of the report. Later on, I can use these names in my HIPO diagrams and COBOL code. We

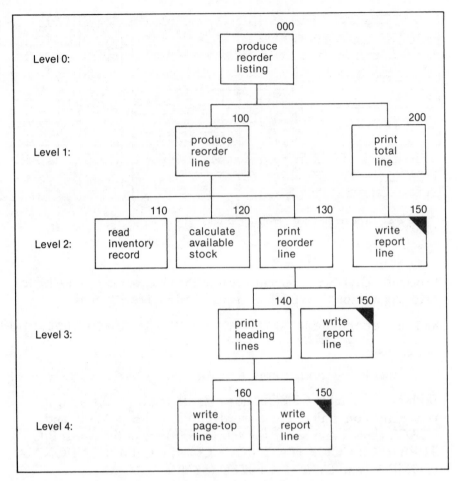

Figure 2-23 Structure chart for the refined reorder-listing program

recommend this practice because it relates one form of documentation to another. From now on, then, you will see record names given on all print charts. Incidentally, I haven't given any name to the last line on the print chart in figure 2-22, because this will be printed by a DISPLAY statement.

The structure chart

A structure chart for the refined reorder-listing program is given in figure 2-23. Here, modules 000, 100, 110, and 120 are the same as in the simplified reorder-listing program. However, since a total line is needed, module 200 is used at level 1 to print the total line after all inventory cards have been processed. Similarly, since heading lines are required on this report, module 140 has been added subordinate to module 130. It will be performed by module 130 whenever the heading lines should be printed.

Module 150 is used in three different places in the structure chart. Its function is to write a line on the report whether it be a heading, reorder, or total line. The use of this module makes it possible for only one WRITE statement to be used for writing all but the first line on each page. Since each WRITE statement generates several dozen bytes of object code, using one WRITE statement rather than several can reduce the size of the object program. In this book, a maximum of two WRITE statements will be used for each print file: one for skipping to the top of a page and printing the first heading line (module 160 in figure 2-23); and one for printing all other report lines (module 150).

To show that module 150 is used in more than one place in the program, the right corner is shaded. You will now see how this module and this structure chart are related to the COBOL coding.

The program listing

Figure 2-24 is a program listing of the refined reorder-listing program. It includes sequence codes in columns 1-6 of the source deck, and it is for an OS compiler. Because the listing illustrates many of the elements presented in this topic, let me summarize some of the main points.

1. Blank comment cards are used to vertically space the listing.

2. In the Configuration Section, both the SOURCE-COMPUTER and OBJECT-COMPUTER paragraphs are omitted, so System/360 code will be compiled. Because forms overflow is required by this program, the SPECIAL-NAMES paragraph is used to assign the mnemonic name PAGE-TOP to a channel-1 punch in the carriage-control tape. This name is used in the WRITE statement in module 160.

3. In the Input-Output Section, OS system names are used in the SELECT statements. Note that the file names are the same as the ddnames. To run this program under DOS, only the system names in the SELECT statements would have to be changed.

4. No fields are defined within the output area for the printer (PRINT-AREA). Instead, all print lines are defined in working storage. As a result, PRINT-AREA is an elementary item and it requires a PICTURE clause.

5. In the Working-Storage Section, the fields that are needed to control the processing done by the program are grouped under four different 01-levels: SWITCHES for the fields that determine the logical flow of the program; WORK-FIELDS for the fields

```
001010 IDENTIFICATION DIVISION.                              REORDLST
001020*                                                      REORDLST
001030 PROGRAM-ID. REORDLST.                                 REORDLST
001040*                                                      REORDLST
001050 ENVIRONMENT DIVISION.                                 REORDLST
001060*                                                      REORDLST
001070 CONFIGURATION SECTION.                                REORDLST
001080*                                                      REORDLST
001090 SPECIAL-NAMES.                                        REORDLST
001100      C01 IS PAGE-TOP.                                 REORDLST
001110*                                                      REORDLST
001120 INPUT-OUTPUT SECTION.                                 REORDLST
001130*                                                      REORDLST
001140 FILE-CONTROL.                                         REORDLST
001150      SELECT BFCRDS ASSIGN TO UT-S-BFCRDS.             REORDLST
001160      SELECT ORDLST ASSIGN TO UT-S-ORDLST.             REORDLST
001170*                                                      REORDLST
002010 DATA DIVISION.                                        REORDLST
002020*                                                      REORDLST
002030 FILE SECTION.                                         REORDLST
002040*                                                      REORDLST
002050 FD  BFCRDS                                            REORDLST
002060      LABEL RECORDS ARE STANDARD                       REORDLST
002070      RECORDING MODE IS F                              REORDLST
002080      RECORD CONTAINS 80 CHARACTERS.                   REORDLST
002090*                                                      REORDLST
002100 01  BAL-FWD-CARD.                                     REORDLST
002110*                                                      REORDLST
002120      05  BF-ITEM-NO          PIC 9(5).                REORDLST
002130      05  BF-ITEM-DESC        PIC X(20).               REORDLST
002140      05  FILLER              PIC X(5).                REORDLST
002150      05  BF-UNIT-PRICE       PIC 999V99.              REORDLST
002160      05  BF-REORDER-POINT    PIC 9(5).                REORDLST
002170      05  BF-ON-HAND          PIC 9(5).                REORDLST
002180      05  BF-ON-ORDER         PIC 9(5).                REORDLST
002190      05  FILLER              PIC X(30).               REORDLST
002200*                                                      REORDLST
003010 FD  ORDLST                                            REORDLST
003020      LABEL RECORDS ARE STANDARD                       REORDLST
003030      RECORDING MODE IS F                              REORDLST
003040      RECORD CONTAINS 133 CHARACTERS.                  REORDLST
003050*                                                      REORDLST
003060 01  PRINT-AREA              PIC X(133).               REORDLST
003070*                                                      REORDLST
003080 WORKING-STORAGE SECTION.                              REORDLST
003090*                                                      REORDLST
003100 01  SWITCHES.                                         REORDLST
003110*                                                      REORDLST
003120      05  CARD-EOF-SWITCH    PIC X      VALUE 'N'.     REORDLST
003130*                                                      REORDLST
003140 01  WORK-FIELDS.                                      REORDLST
003150*                                                      REORDLST
003160      05  AVAILABLE-STOCK    PIC S9(5)  COMP-3.        REORDLST
003170*                                                      REORDLST
003180 01  PRINT-FIELDS           COMP       SYNC.           REORDLST
003190*                                                      REORDLST
003200      05  LINE-COUNT         PIC S99    VALUE +99.     REORDLST
003210      05  LINES-ON-PAGE      PIC S99    VALUE +57.     REORDLST
003220      05  SPACE-CONTROL      PIC S9.                   REORDLST
004010*                                                      REORDLST
```

Figure 2-24   The refined reorder-listing program (part 1 of 4)

```
004020 01   COUNT-FIELDS.                                                 REORDLST
004030*                                                                   REORDLST
004040     05   CARD-COUNT       PIC S9(5)   COMP-3   VALUE ZERO.          REORDLST
004050*                                                                   REORDLST
004060 01   HDG-LINE-1.                                                    REORDLST
004070*                                                                   REORDLST
004080     05   HDG1-CC          PIC X.                                    REORDLST
004090     05   FILLER           PIC X(23)   VALUE SPACE.                  REORDLST
004100     05   FILLER           PIC X(15)   VALUE 'REORDER LISTING'.      REORDLST
004110     05   FILLER           PIC X(94)   VALUE SPACE.                  REORDLST
004120*                                                                   REORDLST
004130 01   HDG-LINE-2.                                                    REORDLST
004140*                                                                   REORDLST
004150     05   HDG2-CC          PIC X.                                    REORDLST
004160     05   FILLER           PIC X(4)    VALUE 'ITEM'.                 REORDLST
004170     05   FILLER           PIC X(12)   VALUE SPACE.                  REORDLST
004180     05   FILLER           PIC X(4)    VALUE 'ITEM'.                 REORDLST
004190     05   FILLER           PIC X(16)   VALUE SPACE.                  REORDLST
004200     05   FILLER           PIC X(4)    VALUE 'UNIT'.                 REORDLST
005010     05   FILLER           PIC X(15)   VALUE SPACE.                  REORDLST
005020     05   FILLER           PIC X(7)    VALUE 'REORDER'.              REORDLST
005030     05   FILLER           PIC X(70)   VALUE SPACE.                  REORDLST
005040*                                                                   REORDLST
005050 01   HDG-LINE-3.                                                    REORDLST
005060*                                                                   REORDLST
005070     05   HDG3-CC          PIC X.                                    REORDLST
005080     05   FILLER           PIC X       VALUE SPACE.                  REORDLST
005090     05   FILLER           PIC X(3)    VALUE 'NO.'.                  REORDLST
005100     05   FILLER           PIC X(9)    VALUE SPACE.                  REORDLST
005110     05   FILLER           PIC X(11)   VALUE 'DESCRIPTION'.          REORDLST
005120     05   FILLER           PIC X(11)   VALUE SPACE.                  REORDLST
005130     05   FILLER           PIC X(5)    VALUE 'PRICE'.                REORDLST
005140     05   FILLER           PIC X(4)    VALUE SPACE.                  REORDLST
005150     05   FILLER           PIC X(9)    VALUE 'AVAILABLE'.            REORDLST
005160     05   FILLER           PIC X(3)    VALUE SPACE.                  REORDLST
005170     05   FILLER           PIC X(5)    VALUE 'POINT'.                REORDLST
005180     05   FILLER           PIC X(71)   VALUE SPACE.                  REORDLST
005190*                                                                   REORDLST
006010 01   REORDER-LINE.                                                  REORDLST
006020*                                                                   REORDLST
006030     05   RL-CC            PIC X.                                    REORDLST
006040     05   RL-ITEM-NO       PIC Z(5).                                 REORDLST
006050     05   FILLER           PIC X(5)    VALUE SPACE.                  REORDLST
006060     05   RL-ITEM-DESC     PIC X(20).                                REORDLST
006070     05   FILLER           PIC X(5)    VALUE SPACE.                  REORDLST
006080     05   RL-UNIT-PRICE    PIC ZZZ.99.                              REORDLST
006090     05   FILLER           PIC X(5)    VALUE SPACE.                  REORDLST
006100     05   RL-AVAILABLE-STOCK  PIC Z(5).                             REORDLST
006110     05   FILLER           PIC X(5)    VALUE SPACE.                  REORDLST
006120     05   RL-REORDER-POINT PIC Z(5).                                 REORDLST
006130     05   FILLER           PIC X(71)   VALUE SPACE.                  REORDLST
006140*                                                                   REORDLST
006150 01   TOTAL-LINE.                                                    REORDLST
006160*                                                                   REORDLST
006170     05   TL-CC            PIC X.                                    REORDLST
006180     05   TL-CARD-COUNT    PIC ZZ,ZZZ.                               REORDLST
006190     05   FILLER           PIC X(24)                                 REORDLST
006200                           VALUE ' CARDS IN THE INPUT DECK'.         REORDLST
006210     05   FILLER           PIC X(102)  VALUE SPACE.                  REORDLST
006220*                                                                   REORDLST
```

Figure 2-24   The refined reorder-listing program (part 2 of 4)

```
007010 PROCEDURE DIVISION.                                      REORDLST
007020*                                                         REORDLST
007030 000-PRODUCE-REORDER-LISTING.                             REORDLST
007040*                                                         REORDLST
007050     OPEN INPUT  BFCRDS                                   REORDLST
007060         OUTPUT ORDLST.                                   REORDLST
007070     PERFORM 100-PRODUCE-REORDER-LINE                     REORDLST
007080         UNTIL CARD-EOF-SWITCH IS EQUAL TO 'Y'.           REORDLST
007090     PERFORM 200-PRINT-TOTAL-LINE.                        REORDLST
007100     CLOSE BFCRDS                                         REORDLST
007110         ORDLST.                                          REORDLST
007120     DISPLAY 'REORDLST  I  1  NORMAL EOJ'.                REORDLST
007130     STOP RUN.                                            REORDLST
007140*                                                         REORDLST
007150 100-PRODUCE-REORDER-LINE.                                REORDLST
007160*                                                         REORDLST
007170     PERFORM 110-READ-INVENTORY-RECORD.                   REORDLST
007180     IF CARD-EOF-SWITCH IS NOT EQUAL TO 'Y'               REORDLST
007190         PERFORM 120-CALCULATE-AVAILABLE-STOCK            REORDLST
007200         IF AVAILABLE-STOCK IS LESS THAN BF-REORDER-POINT REORDLST
007210             PERFORM 130-PRINT-REORDER-LINE.              REORDLST
008010*                                                         REORDLST
008020 110-READ-INVENTORY-RECORD.                               REORDLST
008030*                                                         REORDLST
008040     READ BFCRDS                                          REORDLST
008050         AT END                                           REORDLST
008060             MOVE 'Y' TO CARD-EOF-SWITCH.                 REORDLST
008070     IF CARD-EOF-SWITCH IS NOT EQUAL TO 'Y'               REORDLST
008080         ADD 1 TO CARD-COUNT.                             REORDLST
008090*                                                         REORDLST
008100 120-CALCULATE-AVAILABLE-STOCK.                           REORDLST
008110*                                                         REORDLST
008120     ADD BF-ON-HAND BF-ON-ORDER                           REORDLST
008130         GIVING AVAILABLE-STOCK                           REORDLST
008140         ON SIZE ERROR                                    REORDLST
008150             DISPLAY 'REORDLST  A  2  CALCULATION ERROR FOR ITEM 'REORDLST
008160                 'NO. ' BF-ITEM-NO '--CARD IGNORED'       REORDLST
008170             MOVE 99999 TO AVAILABLE-STOCK.               REORDLST
008180*                                                         REORDLST
009010 130-PRINT-REORDER-LINE.                                  REORDLST
009020*                                                         REORDLST
009030     IF LINE-COUNT IS GREATER THAN LINES-ON-PAGE          REORDLST
009040         PERFORM 140-PRINT-HEADING-LINES.                 REORDLST
009050     MOVE BF-ITEM-NO       TO RL-ITEM-NO.                 REORDLST
009060     MOVE BF-ITEM-DESC     TO RL-ITEM-DESC.               REORDLST
009070     MOVE BF-UNIT-PRICE    TO RL-UNIT-PRICE.              REORDLST
009080     MOVE AVAILABLE-STOCK  TO RL-AVAILABLE-STOCK.         REORDLST
009090     MOVE BF-REORDER-POINT TO RL-REORDER-POINT.           REORDLST
009100     MOVE REORDER-LINE     TO PRINT-AREA.                 REORDLST
009110     PERFORM 150-WRITE-REPORT-LINE.                       REORDLST
009120     MOVE 1 TO SPACE-CONTROL.                             REORDLST
009130*                                                         REORDLST
```

Figure 2-24   The refined reorder-listing program (part 3 of 4)

that will contain the results of calculations done by the program; PRINT-FIELDS for the fields that control the printing of the output report; and COUNT-FIELDS for the fields that contain a running tally of certain records in the program. These fields are then followed by the descriptions of the printer work areas. Note that there is a different work area for each line that will be printed on the report.

```
009140 140-PRINT-HEADING-LINES.                             REORDLST
009150*                                                     REORDLST
009160      MOVE HDG-LINE-1 TO PRINT-AREA.                  REORDLST
009170      PERFORM 160-WRITE-PAGE-TOP-LINE.                REORDLST
009180      MOVE HDG-LINE-2 TO PRINT-AREA.                  REORDLST
009190      MOVE 2 TO SPACE-CONTROL.                        REORDLST
010010      PERFORM 150-WRITE-REPORT-LINE.                  REORDLST
010020      MOVE HDG-LINE-3 TO PRINT-AREA.                  REORDLST
010030      MOVE 1 TO SPACE-CONTROL.                        REORDLST
010040      PERFORM 150-WRITE-REPORT-LINE.                  REORDLST
010050      MOVE 2 TO SPACE-CONTROL.                        REORDLST
010060*                                                     REORDLST
010070 150-WRITE-REPORT-LINE.                               REORDLST
010080*                                                     REORDLST
010090      WRITE PRINT-AREA                                REORDLST
010100          AFTER ADVANCING SPACE-CONTROL LINES.        REORDLST
010110      ADD SPACE-CONTROL TO LINE-COUNT.                REORDLST
010120*                                                     REORDLST
010130 160-WRITE-PAGE-TOP-LINE.                             REORDLST
010140*                                                     REORDLST
010150      WRITE PRINT-AREA                                REORDLST
010160          AFTER ADVANCING PAGE-TOP.                   REORDLST
010170      MOVE ZERO TO LINE-COUNT.                        REORDLST
010180*                                                     REORDLST
011010 200-PRINT-TOTAL-LINE.                                REORDLST
011020*                                                     REORDLST
011030      MOVE CARD-COUNT TO TL-CARD-COUNT.               REORDLST
011040      MOVE TOTAL-LINE TO PRINT-AREA.                  REORDLST
011050      MOVE 3 TO SPACE-CONTROL.                        REORDLST
011060      PERFORM 150-WRITE-REPORT-LINE.                  REORDLST
```

Figure 2-24   The refined reorder-listing program (part 4 of 4)

6. CARD-EOF-SWITCH is set to an initial value of N in working storage rather than in module 000.

7. AVAILABLE-STOCK and CARD-COUNT are both defined in working storage as signed (S) COMP-3 fields. COMP-3 is the most efficient usage for these fields since they are involved in arithmetic operations in the program.

8. The PRINT-FIELDS in working storage are assigned synchronized COMP usage at the 01 (or group) level. This means that all three of the elementary items will be COMP SYNC fields. On an OS system, COMP is the most efficient usage for these fields because they are all involved in arithmetic operations or comparisons with SPACE-CONTROL, and SPACE-CONTROL is used in the WRITE AFTER statement. On a DOS system, the most efficient usage would be COMP-3 because DOS doesn't require that the SPACE-CONTROL field be converted to COMP usage before the WRITE AFTER statement can be executed.

Whenever a USAGE clause is given at the group level, it applies to all the elementary items within the group. In contrast, if you assign SYNC at the group level, it applies only to those elementary items with COMP usage.

9. LINES-ON-PAGE, the field that specifies how many lines can be printed on a page of the output report, is given a starting literal value of +57. Later on, if the programmer wants to adjust the number of lines per page, he can simply change the value of this field. Note that the literal has a plus sign, since the PICTURE for the field is signed.

10. Because all print lines are constructed in working storage and all FILLER areas are given a starting value of SPACE, the print area doesn't have to be cleared to spaces before constructing each output line. In other words,

```
MOVE SPACE TO PRINT-AREA
```

isn't needed before moving the working-storage areas to the print area. In your programs, too, all output records should be constructed in working storage.

11. Because AFTER ADVANCING is used in the WRITE statements for this program, all printer work areas as well as the print area itself are given a length of 133 characters.

12. In module 000, one OPEN statement is used to open both files. Also, the DISPLAY statement is used to print an end-of-job message when the program reaches its normal conclusion. Notice that this message is in the form recommended for operational messages (see the writeup on the DISPLAY statement earlier in this topic).

13. Module 100, the module that drives the subordinate modules, is unchanged.

14. In module 110, an ADD statement adds one to CARD-COUNT for each input card. Note that CARD-COUNT was given a starting value of zero in working storage, so it will represent the total number of data cards read when the program ends.

15. In module 120, the ON SIZE ERROR clause is used when calculating AVAILABLE-STOCK. If a size error occurs, a message is printed in the recommended form and a value of 99999 is moved into AVAILABLE-STOCK. As a result, no reorder line will be printed for a card with a size error.

16. Module 130 gives the logic for printing heading and reorder lines. If LINE-COUNT is greater than LINES-ON-PAGE, the heading lines are printed. Then, whether heading lines have been printed or not, a reorder line is formatted and printed and a spacing value of 1 is moved into SPACE-CONTROL. Since

LINE-COUNT is given a starting value of +99 and LINES-ON-PAGE has a value of +57, heading lines will be printed before the first reorder line. LINE-COUNT is given a value of +99 so that if LINES-ON-PAGE is ever increased, the logic for printing the heading lines on the first page will still work without changing the initial value of LINE-COUNT.

17. Module 140 prints the first heading line by performing module 160, which contains one of the two WRITE statements used for the printer file. The second and third heading lines are printed by performing module 150, which contains the second WRITE statement. After each heading line is printed, a spacing value is moved to SPACE-CONTROL.

18. Module 150 contains the primary WRITE statement of the program. It is called by modules 130, 140, and 200. If the program wasn't coded in this fashion, three more WRITE statements would be required. This module also keeps track of the number of lines that have been printed on a page by adding the SPACE-CONTROL value to LINE-COUNT after printing each line.

19. Module 160 prints the first line on each page of the report. It does this by executing a WRITE statement that causes a skip to PAGE-TOP (a channel-1 punch in the carriage-control tape) before printing. After the line is printed, the module resets LINE-COUNT to zero.

20. Module 200 moves the output data to the printer output area and performs module 150. Once again, module 150 causes the output line to be printed.

Conclusion

If you understand the refined reorder-listing program, you should now be able to begin writing programs of your own. However, you will probably have difficulty in creating proper structure charts. After all, this book has given only superficial treatment to structured design thus far. In the next chapter, then, structured design and documentation will be covered in detail.

Terminology

comment card

comment

mnemonic name

implementor name

elementary item

group item

numeric literal

non-numeric literal

forms overflow

external decimal

packed decimal

internal decimal

storage boundary

editing

stroke

Input record layout:

Field Name	Item No.	Item Description	Unit Cost	Unit Price	Reorder Point	On Hand	On Order	Unused
Characteristics	9(5)	X(20)	999V99	999V99	9(5)	9(5)	9(5)	X(30)
Usage								
Position	1-5	6-25	26-30	31-35	36-40	41-45	46-50	51-80

Print chart:

Record Name		
	1	
HDG-LINE	2	ITEM NO. COST ON HAND $ VALUE
	3	
INVESTMENT-LINE	4	99999 999.99 99999 9,999,999.99
	5	99999 999.99 99999 9,999,999.99
	6	99999 999.99 99999 9,999,999.99
	7	
TOTAL-LINE	8	99999 INPUT RECORDS....... 9,999,999.99 * *
	9	
	10	INVSTLST I I NORMAL EOJ
	11	
	12	
	13	
	14	
	15	
	16	

Narrative:

1. Amount invested = on-hand × unit-cost.
2. Forms overflow should be provided for and headings should be printed on each overflow page.
3. Do not suppress lead zeros on the item-number field; on other numeric fields, use zero suppression.

Figure 2-25   The investment-listing problem

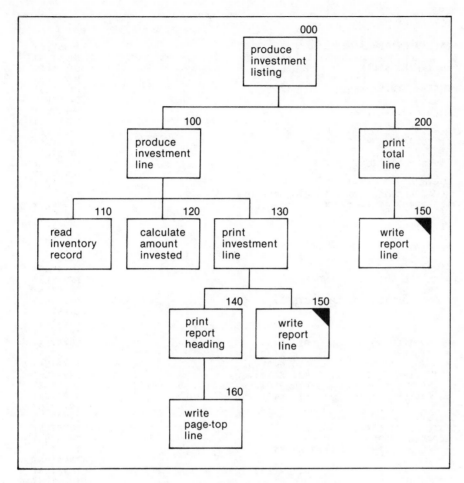

Figure 2-26   Structure chart for the investment-listing program

Objectives

1. Given a programming problem and a structure chart for its solution, code a program for its solution in COBOL. The problem will have card input and printer output and may require any functions described in this chapter.

Problems

1. Figure 2-25 defines a problem that consists of printing an investment report from a deck of inventory cards like those used for the reorder-listing program. At the end of the report, a total line consisting of a count of the number of input cards and a total of the amounts invested is to be printed. Using the structure chart in figure 2-26 for this program, code a COBOL solution. You don't have to provide for size errors in the calculations.

```
001010 IDENTIFICATION DIVISION.                                    INVSTLST
001020*                                                            INVSTLST
001030 PROGRAM-ID. INVSTLST.                                       INVSTLST
001040*                                                            INVSTLST
001050 ENVIRONMENT DIVISION.                                       INVSTLST
001060*                                                            INVSTLST
001070 CONFIGURATION SECTION.                                      INVSTLST
001080*                                                            INVSTLST
001090 SPECIAL-NAMES.                                              INVSTLST
001100     C01 IS PAGE-TOP.                                        INVSTLST
001110*                                                            INVSTLST
001120 INPUT-OUTPUT SECTION.                                       INVSTLST
001130*                                                            INVSTLST
001140 FILE-CONTROL.                                               INVSTLST
001150     SELECT BFCRDS ASSIGN TO UT-S-BFCRDS.                    INVSTLST
001160     SELECT INVLST ASSIGN TO UT-S-INVLST.                    INVSTLST
001170*                                                            INVSTLST
002010 DATA DIVISION.                                              INVSTLST
002020*                                                            INVSTLST
002030 FILE SECTION.                                               INVSTLST
002040*                                                            INVSTLST
002050 FD  BFCRDS                                                  INVSTLST
002060     LABEL RECORDS ARE STANDARD                              INVSTLST
002070     RECORDING MODE IS F                                     INVSTLST
002080     RECORD CONTAINS 80 CHARACTERS.                          INVSTLST
002090*                                                            INVSTLST
002100 01  BF-CARD.                                                INVSTLST
002110*                                                            INVSTLST
002120     05  BF-ITEM-NO        PIC 9(5).                         INVSTLST
002130     05  FILLER            PIC X(20).                        INVSTLST
002140     05  BF-UNIT-COST      PIC 999V99.                       INVSTLST
002150     05  FILLER            PIC X(10).                        INVSTLST
002160     05  BF-ON-HAND        PIC 9(5).                         INVSTLST
002170     05  FILLER            PIC X(35).                        INVSTLST
002180*                                                            INVSTLST
003010 FD  INVLST                                                  INVSTLST
003020     LABEL RECORDS ARE STANDARD                              INVSTLST
003030     RECORDING MODE IS F                                     INVSTLST
003040     RECORD CONTAINS 133 CHARACTERS.                         INVSTLST
003050*                                                            INVSTLST
003060 01  PRINT-AREA            PIC X(133).                       INVSTLST
003070*                                                            INVSTLST
003080 WORKING-STORAGE SECTION.                                    INVSTLST
003090*                                                            INVSTLST
003100 01  SWITCHES.                                               INVSTLST
003110*                                                            INVSTLST
003120     05  CARD-EOF-SWITCH   PIC X          VALUE 'N'.         INVSTLST
003130*                                                            INVSTLST
```

Figure 2-27   The investment-listing program (part 1 of 4)

2.   Figure 2-27 is a listing of a solution for problem 1 above; included are the sequence numbers in columns 1-6 of the source cards. Suppose there is a request for an extra total line that gives the average amount invested in inventory for each item, using this format:

```
AVERAGE INVESTMENT PER ITEM IS XX,XXX.XX
```

```
003140 01  WORK-FIELDS.                                              INVSTLST
003150*                                                             INVSTLST
003160     05  ITEM-INVESTMENT     PIC S9(7)V99      COMP-3.        INVSTLST
003170*                                                             INVSTLST
004010 01  PRINT-FIELDS           COMP            SYNC.             INVSTLST
004020*                                                             INVSTLST
004030     05  LINE-COUNT          PIC S99          VALUE +99.       INVSTLST
004040     05  LINES-ON-PAGE       PIC S99          VALUE +57.       INVSTLST
004050     05  SPACE-CONTROL       PIC S9.                          INVSTLST
004060*                                                             INVSTLST
004070 01  COUNT-FIELDS.                                            INVSTLST
004080*                                                             INVSTLST
004090     05  CARD-COUNT          PIC S9(5)        VALUE ZERO COMP-3. INVSTLST
004100*                                                             INVSTLST
004110 01  TOTAL-FIELDS.                                            INVSTLST
004120*                                                             INVSTLST
004130     05  TOTAL-INVESTMENT    PIC S9(7)V99     VALUE ZERO COMP-3. INVSTLST
004140*                                                             INVSTLST
004150 01  HDG-LINE.                                                INVSTLST
004160*                                                             INVSTLST
004170     05  HL-CC               PIC X.                           INVSTLST
004180     05  FILLER              PIC X(37)                        INVSTLST
004190         VALUE 'ITEM NO.   COST   ON HAND    $ VALUE'.         INVSTLST
004200     05  FILLER              PIC X(95)        VALUE SPACE.     INVSTLST
005010*                                                             INVSTLST
005020 01  INVESTMENT-LINE.                                         INVSTLST
005030*                                                             INVSTLST
005040     05  IL-CC               PIC X.                           INVSTLST
005050     05  FILLER              PIC X(2)         VALUE SPACE.     INVSTLST
005060     05  IL-ITEM-NO          PIC 9(5).                        INVSTLST
005070     05  FILLER              PIC X(3)         VALUE SPACE.     INVSTLST
005080     05  IL-UNIT-COST        PIC Z(3).99.                     INVSTLST
005090     05  FILLER              PIC X(3)         VALUE SPACE.     INVSTLST
005100     05  IL-ON-HAND          PIC Z(5).                        INVSTLST
005110     05  FILLER              PIC X(3)         VALUE SPACE.     INVSTLST
005120     05  IL-ITEM-INVESTMENT  PIC Z,ZZZ,ZZZ.99.               INVSTLST
005130     05  FILLER              PIC X(93)        VALUE SPACE.     INVSTLST
005140*                                                             INVSTLST
005150 01  TOTAL-LINE.                                              INVSTLST
005160*                                                             INVSTLST
005170     05  TL-CC               PIC X.                           INVSTLST
005180     05  FILLER              PIC X            VALUE SPACE.     INVSTLST
005190     05  TL-CARD-COUNT       PIC Z(5).                        INVSTLST
006010     05  FILLER              PIC X(21)                        INVSTLST
006020         VALUE ' INPUT RECORDS...... '.                       INVSTLST
006030     05  TL-TOTAL-INVESTMENT PIC Z,ZZZ,ZZZ.99.               INVSTLST
006040     05  FILLER              PIC X(4)         VALUE ' * *'.    INVSTLST
006050     05  FILLER              PIC X(89)        VALUE SPACE.     INVSTLST
```

Figure 2-27   The investment-listing program (part 2 of 4)

Code the changes that would have to be made to the original program to cause the new total line to print on the line immediately after the original total line. Use appropriate sequence numbers.

```
006060*                                                    INVSTLST
006070 PROCEDURE DIVISION.                                 INVSTLST
006080*                                                    INVSTLST
006090 000-PRODUCE-INVESTMENT-LISTING.                     INVSTLST
006100*                                                    INVSTLST
006110     OPEN INPUT  BFCRDS                              INVSTLST
006120         OUTPUT INVLST.                              INVSTLST
006130     PERFORM 100-PRODUCE-INVESTMENT-LINE             INVSTLST
006140         UNTIL CARD-EOF-SWITCH IS EQUAL TO 'Y'.      INVSTLST
006150     PERFORM 200-PRINT-TOTAL-LINE.                   INVSTLST
006160     CLOSE BFCRDS                                    INVSTLST
006170         INVLST.                                     INVSTLST
006180     DISPLAY 'INVSTLST  I  1   NORMAL EOJ'.          INVSTLST
006190     STOP RUN.                                       INVSTLST
006200*                                                    INVSTLST
007010 100-PRODUCE-INVESTMENT-LINE.                        INVSTLST
007020*                                                    INVSTLST
007030     PERFORM 110-READ-INVENTORY-RECORD.              INVSTLST
007040     IF CARD-EOF-SWITCH IS NOT EQUAL TO 'Y'          INVSTLST
007050         PERFORM 120-CALCULATE-AMOUNT-INVESTED       INVSTLST
007060         PERFORM 130-PRINT-INVESTMENT-LINE.          INVSTLST
007070*                                                    INVSTLST
007080 110-READ-INVENTORY-RECORD.                          INVSTLST
007090*                                                    INVSTLST
007100     READ BFCRDS                                     INVSTLST
007110         AT END                                      INVSTLST
007120             MOVE 'Y' TO CARD-EOF-SWITCH.            INVSTLST
007130     IF CARD-EOF-SWITCH IS NOT EQUAL TO 'Y'          INVSTLST
007140         ADD 1 TO CARD-COUNT.                        INVSTLST
007150*                                                    INVSTLST
007160 120-CALCULATE-AMOUNT-INVESTED.                      INVSTLST
007170*                                                    INVSTLST
007180     MULTIPLY BF-UNIT-COST BY BF-ON-HAND             INVSTLST
007190         GIVING ITEM-INVESTMENT.                     INVSTLST
007200     ADD ITEM-INVESTMENT TO TOTAL-INVESTMENT.        INVSTLST
008010*                                                    INVSTLST
```

Figure 2-27   The investment-listing program (part 3 of 4)

Solutions

1.   Figure 2-27 is an acceptable solution for an OS system. If you weren't able to code a solution by yourself, be sure to study this one until you're confident you understand how it works.

```
008020 130-PRINT-INVESTMENT-LINE.                                INVSTLST
008030*                                                          INVSTLST
008040     IF LINE-COUNT IS GREATER THAN LINES-ON-PAGE           INVSTLST
008050        PERFORM 140-PRINT-REPORT-HEADING.                  INVSTLST
008060     MOVE BF-ITEM-NO          TO IL-ITEM-NO.               INVSTLST
008070     MOVE BF-UNIT-COST        TO IL-UNIT-COST.             INVSTLST
008080     MOVE BF-ON-HAND          TO IL-ON-HAND.               INVSTLST
008090     MOVE ITEM-INVESTMENT     TO IL-ITEM-INVESTMENT.       INVSTLST
008100     MOVE INVESTMENT-LINE     TO PRINT-AREA.               INVSTLST
008110     PERFORM 150-WRITE-REPORT-LINE.                        INVSTLST
008120     MOVE 1 TO SPACE-CONTROL.                              INVSTLST
008130*                                                          INVSTLST
008140 140-PRINT-REPORT-HEADING.                                 INVSTLST
008150*                                                          INVSTLST
008160     MOVE HDG-LINE TO PRINT-AREA.                          INVSTLST
008170     PERFORM 160-WRITE-PAGE-TOP-LINE.                      INVSTLST
008180     MOVE 2 TO SPACE-CONTROL.                              INVSTLST
008190*                                                          INVSTLST
009010 150-WRITE-REPORT-LINE.                                    INVSTLST
009020*                                                          INVSTLST
009030     WRITE PRINT-AREA                                      INVSTLST
009040         AFTER ADVANCING SPACE-CONTROL LINES.              INVSTLST
009050     ADD SPACE-CONTROL TO LINE-COUNT.                      INVSTLST
009060*                                                          INVSTLST
009070 160-WRITE-PAGE-TOP-LINE.                                  INVSTLST
009080*                                                          INVSTLST
009090     WRITE PRINT-AREA                                      INVSTLST
009100         AFTER ADVANCING PAGE-TOP.                         INVSTLST
009110     MOVE ZERO TO LINE-COUNT.                              INVSTLST
009120*                                                          INVSTLST
009130 200-PRINT-TOTAL-LINE.                                     INVSTLST
009140*                                                          INVSTLST
009150     MOVE CARD-COUNT          TO TL-CARD-COUNT.            INVSTLST
009160     MOVE TOTAL-INVESTMENT TO TL-TOTAL-INVESTMENT.         INVSTLST
009170     MOVE TOTAL-LINE          TO PRINT-AREA.               INVSTLST
009180     MOVE 2 TO SPACE-CONTROL.                              INVSTLST
009190     PERFORM 150-WRITE-REPORT-LINE.                        INVSTLST
```

Figure 2-27   The investment-listing program (part 4 of 4)

2. The coding form in figure 2-28 gives an example of acceptable changes, including sequence numbers. Note that the DIVIDE statement puts the result in a numeric edited field, TL2-AVG-INVESTMENT. This illustrates that the data name used in a GIVING clause can be either numeric or numeric edited. Note also that the result is rounded.

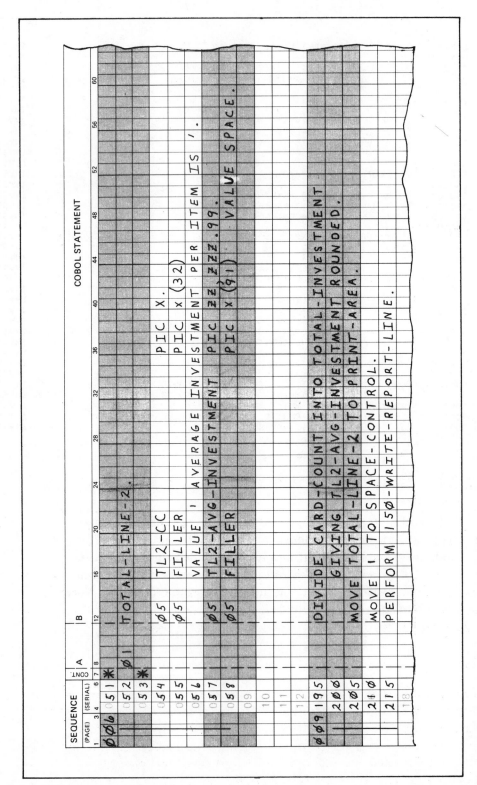

Figure 2-28 Modifications to the investment-listing program

3

The Principles of Structured Programming

This chapter is divided into four topics. The first introduces the theory of structured programming. The next three use typical business programs to give specific guidelines for structured design and module documentation.

TOPIC 1   An Introduction to Structured Programming

To appreciate structured programming, you almost have to have written and tested unstructured programs. If you are new to programming, of course, it's impractical to have you write programs the wrong way just so you'll understand the mistakes of the past. So let me simply describe the old methods of program development. Then, I think you'll be able to understand some of their pitfalls.

Traditional Methods of Program Development

Although it's a simple example, suppose the refined reorder-listing program shown in figure 2-24 were developed in an unstructured fashion. After the programmer had the problem definition clearly in mind, he would probably draw a *program flowchart* for its solution . . . something like the one in figure 3-1. A flowchart like this is supposed to show the sequence of instructions to be used for the

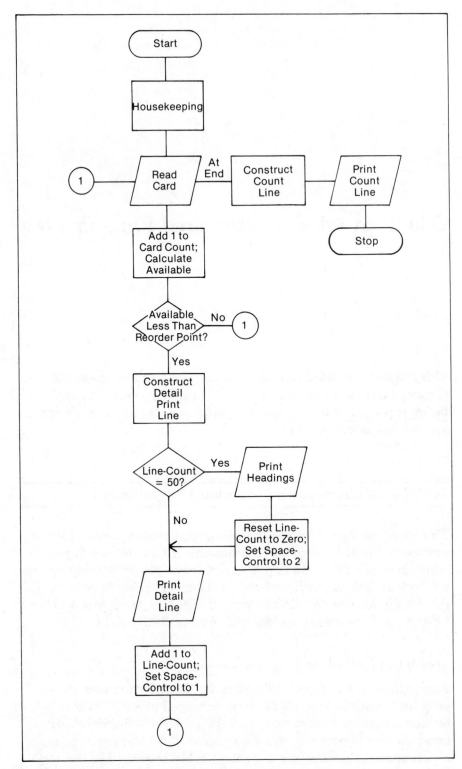

Figure 3-1   Flowchart for the refined reorder-listing program

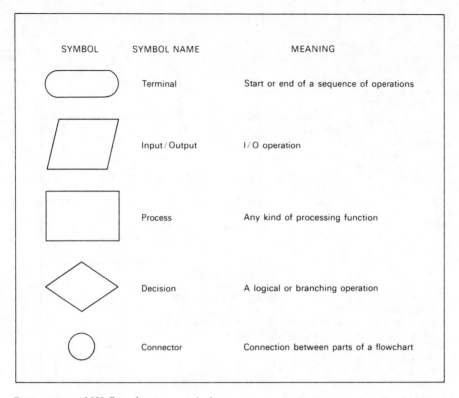

Figure 3-2   ANSI flowcharting symbols

program and the logic required to derive the output from the input. The meanings of the symbols used in this flowchart are shown in figure 3-2.

To follow a flowchart like the one in figure 3-1, you start at the top and read down and to the right unless arrows indicate otherwise. When you come to a connector circle with a number in it, you continue at a connector circle containing the same number. For example, after calculating the available stock, the program reaches a connector circle with a 1 in it if the available stock is *not* less than the reorder point. This means that the flow of the program continues at the connector circle leading into the Read Card symbol. If the available stock is less than the reorder point, the program continues by constructing a detail print line for the output report.

After the programmer finished the program flowchart, he would code the unstructured program using the flowchart as a guide. Although the first three divisions of this solution would be much like those of the structured version, the Procedure Division would be significantly different . . . something like the one in figure 3-3.

If you check the code in figure 3-3, you will see the *GO TO statement* is used in seven different places. The GO TO statement

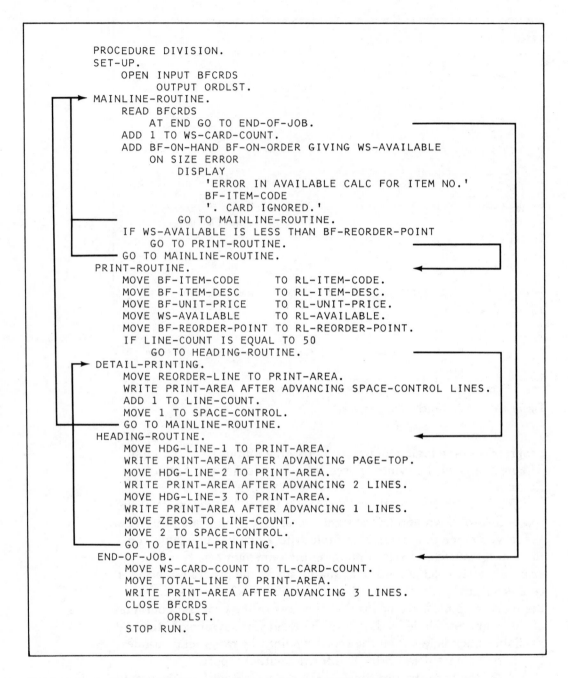

```
        PROCEDURE DIVISION.
        SET-UP.
            OPEN INPUT BFCRDS
                 OUTPUT ORDLST.
        MAINLINE-ROUTINE.
            READ BFCRDS
                AT END GO TO END-OF-JOB.
            ADD 1 TO WS-CARD-COUNT.
            ADD BF-ON-HAND BF-ON-ORDER GIVING WS-AVAILABLE
                ON SIZE ERROR
                    DISPLAY
                        'ERROR IN AVAILABLE CALC FOR ITEM NO.'
                        BF-ITEM-CODE
                        '. CARD IGNORED.'
                    GO TO MAINLINE-ROUTINE.
            IF WS-AVAILABLE IS LESS THAN BF-REORDER-POINT
                GO TO PRINT-ROUTINE.
            GO TO MAINLINE-ROUTINE.
        PRINT-ROUTINE.
            MOVE BF-ITEM-CODE     TO RL-ITEM-CODE.
            MOVE BF-ITEM-DESC     TO RL-ITEM-DESC.
            MOVE BF-UNIT-PRICE    TO RL-UNIT-PRICE.
            MOVE WS-AVAILABLE     TO RL-AVAILABLE.
            MOVE BF-REORDER-POINT TO RL-REORDER-POINT.
            IF LINE-COUNT IS EQUAL TO 50
                GO TO HEADING-ROUTINE.
        DETAIL-PRINTING.
            MOVE REORDER-LINE TO PRINT-AREA.
            WRITE PRINT-AREA AFTER ADVANCING SPACE-CONTROL LINES.
            ADD 1 TO LINE-COUNT.
            MOVE 1 TO SPACE-CONTROL.
            GO TO MAINLINE-ROUTINE.
        HEADING-ROUTINE.
            MOVE HDG-LINE-1 TO PRINT-AREA.
            WRITE PRINT-AREA AFTER ADVANCING PAGE-TOP.
            MOVE HDG-LINE-2 TO PRINT-AREA.
            WRITE PRINT-AREA AFTER ADVANCING 2 LINES.
            MOVE HDG-LINE-3 TO PRINT-AREA.
            WRITE PRINT-AREA AFTER ADVANCING 1 LINES.
            MOVE ZEROS TO LINE-COUNT.
            MOVE 2 TO SPACE-CONTROL.
            GO TO DETAIL-PRINTING.
        END-OF-JOB.
            MOVE WS-CARD-COUNT TO TL-CARD-COUNT.
            MOVE TOTAL-LINE TO PRINT-AREA.
            WRITE PRINT-AREA AFTER ADVANCING 3 LINES.
            CLOSE BFCRDS
                  ORDLST.
            STOP RUN.
```

Figure 3-3   An unstructured Procedure Division for the reorder-listing program

causes an unconditional branch to the paragraph named in the statement. Thus,

```
        READ BFCRDS
            AT END GO TO END-OF-JOB
```

causes an unconditional branch to the last paragraph of the program when there are no more cards to be read. Similarly, the last statement in the paragraph named MAINLINE-ROUTINE causes a branch to the start of the paragraph:

```
GO TO MAINLINE-ROUTINE
```

In other words, the program repeatedly executes the MAINLINE-ROUTINE paragraph.

Since this program is short, its flowchart and its Procedure Division are relatively easy to follow. But what if the program required several thousand instructions? What if the program had extensive logical requirements? Then, the program might require hundreds of GO TO statements, and its logic would be as difficult to follow as the pieces of pasta in a plate of spaghetti. In fact, unstructured code is often referred to as "spaghetti coding."

In brief, traditional methods of program development had shortcomings in the areas of design, coding, and testing. In the design stage, the flowchart was difficult to create and once created was difficult to change. Furthermore, it was easy to leave out important details of the program when creating the flowchart. Most damning of all, however, the flowchart didn't help simplify large or complex programs. As a result, the flowchart was a poor guide for coding and was usually incomplete as documentation.

In the coding stage, unstructured coding was just that . . . unstructured. The programmer was free to determine in what sequence he would code paragraphs and in what sequence they would be placed in the program. Using the flowchart in figure 3-1, for example, the programmer might code the end-of-job routine right after coding the READ statement for the card file. Or he might code the entire mainline routine and then code all other paragraphs required by that routine. As he coded, he would have to create paragraph names and be sure that he included these paragraphs in the program later on. Is it any wonder that important details were frequently overlooked and required paragraphs were missing?

As for testing, it was far too often a nightmare. In this stage, all of the mistakes made in design and coding come back to haunt you. When a bug is detected, you have to locate it. But if the program lacks structure, how do you know where to look? Using traditional techniques, then, a program of several thousand source cards might contain hundreds of errors and take months to debug.

The ultimate criticism of the traditional methods, however, can be stated in terms of programmer productivity. In a study done in 1965, the average COBOL programmer was found to produce only ten lines of tested code per day. A study done in 1975 showed no improvement. Since this lack of productivity was a significant problem for the computer industry, it was clear that new methods of program development were needed.

The Theory of Structured Programming

In the mid-1960s, various computer scientists began to give rigid definitions for the structure of a *proper program*. These efforts led to a discipline known as *structured programming*. This discipline is intended to improve program clarity, simplify debugging, and increase programmer productivity.

The basic assumption in structured programming is that any program can be written using only three logical structures. These structures are summarized in figure 3-4. They are called the sequence, selection, and iteration structures.

The *sequence structure* is simply the idea that imperative program statements are executed in sequence. For instance, if the COBOL MOVE, ADD and SUBTRACT statements are coded in sequence in a program, they are executed one after the other. As a result, a sequence box can consist of one imperative statement or many. And two sequence boxes can be combined into one without changing the basic sequential structure.

The *selection structure* is a choice between two and only two actions based on a condition. If the condition is true, one function is done; if false, the other is done. Either one of the two actions may be null, or not expressly stated; in other words, an action may be specified for only one result of the condition test. Then, when the other result occurs, the program continues by executing the next statement in sequence. This structure is often referred to as the IF-THEN-ELSE structure, and many programming languages have code that closely approximates it.

The *iteration structure*, often called the DO-WHILE structure, provides for doing a function as long as a condition is true. When the condition is no longer true, the program continues with the next structure. A common alternate structure for iteration is the fourth one shown in figure 3-4, the DO-UNTIL structure. Logically related to the DO-WHILE, the DO-UNTIL does a function *until* a condition becomes true.

Although COBOL doesn't directly provide for either the DO-WHILE or DO-UNTIL structure, it does offer the PERFORM-UNTIL structure. This is the third iteration structure shown in figure 3-4. As you can see, it is closely related to the DO-UNTIL structure. In fact, it differs from the DO-UNTIL only in that the condition is tested *before* the function is done rather than after.

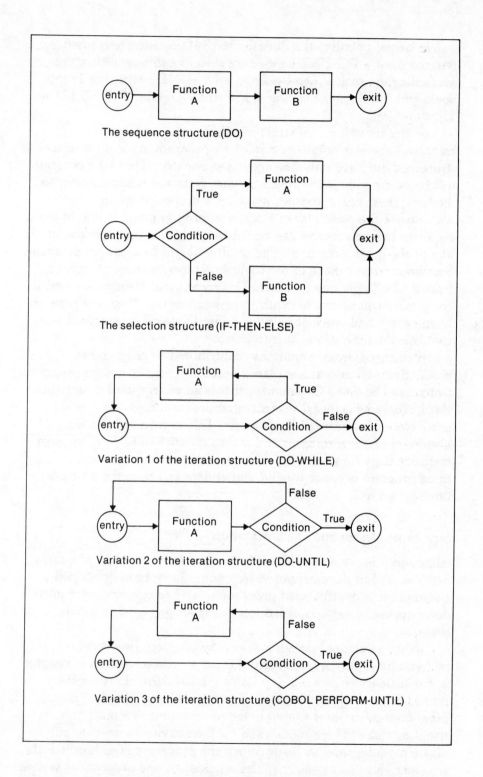

The sequence structure (DO)

The selection structure (IF-THEN-ELSE)

Variation 1 of the iteration structure (DO-WHILE)

Variation 2 of the iteration structure (DO-UNTIL)

Variation 3 of the iteration structure (COBOL PERFORM-UNTIL)

Figure 3-4   The basic structures of structured programming

In actual practice, the PERFORM-UNTIL structure is often referred to as a DO-UNTIL structure since the difference is more academic than real. When I refer to a DO-UNTIL structure in this book, you can imagine coding it with the COBOL PERFORM UNTIL statement.

Notice that all of the structures in figure 3-4 have only one entry and one exit point. As a result, a program made up of these structures will have only one entry and one exit. Thus, the program will be executed in a controlled manner from the first statement to the last. These characteristics make up a proper program.

One of the principles of structured programming is that any of the three basic structures can be substituted for a function box in any of the other structures. The result will still be a proper program. Similarly, two or more of the basic structures in sequence can be treated as a single function box. This means that structures of great complexity can be created with the assurance that they will have only one entry and one exit point and that they will be executed in a controlled manner from start to finish.

Structured programming has contributed to programmer productivity because it has placed necessary restrictions on program structure. The GO TO statement that is so widely used in unstructured programs is illegal in structured programming. As a result, uncontrolled branching is impossible. This in turn reduces the likelihood of program bugs and makes it easier to find errors when there are bugs. In addition, when handled correctly, the structured program is easier to read and understand than the unstructured program.

Structured Design and Documentation

Although it is possible to draw flowcharts for structured programs, new design and documentation techniques have been developed in conjunction with structured programming. The one you were introduced to in chapter 1 is called *top-down design*, or *structured design*.

When structured design is used, the program flowchart is replaced by some sort of structure chart as you have seen in chapter 2. For instance, figure 3-5 duplicates the structure chart for the refined reorder-listing program. To create a chart like this, the programmer first tries to divide the program into its major functional modules. These modules in turn are divided into their subordinate modules, and so forth. When the programmer is finished, the structure chart shows all modules required by the program as well as

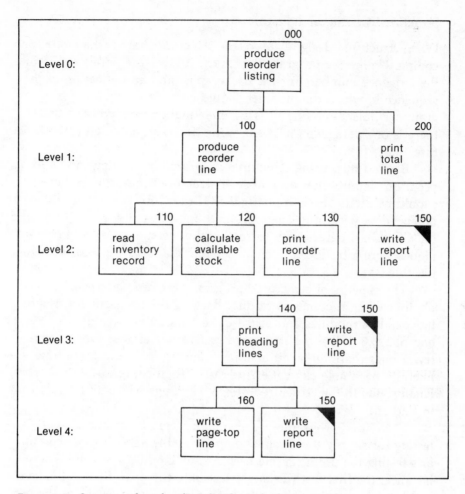

Figure 3-5 Structure chart for the refined reorder-listing program

the relationships between these modules. Later on, these modules can be coded with one entry and one exit point using only the sequence, selection, and iteration structures. Thus, the complete program is a proper program. In topic 2 of this chapter, you will learn how to create structure charts of your own.

After the programmer creates the structure chart, he documents each of the modules in the chart before coding them. It is only at this stage that the programmer concerns himself with the detailed specifications required by the program. Although a program flowchart can be used to document each of the modules, new methods of documentation are rapidly replacing the flowchart, even for this purpose. In topic 3, you will be taught how to use the most common form of structured module documentation, the HIPO diagram.

Structured Coding and Testing

When structured design is used, the structure chart is the guide for coding. Unlike the program flowchart, it gives the paragraph names, the sequence numbers for the paragraphs, and an indication of the sequence in which the modules should be coded. When the programmer finishes coding, it is a simple matter to make sure that there is one paragraph in the program for each module in the structure chart.

Beyond this, using structured programming to develop COBOL programs implies that a number of structured coding techniques should be used. These are designed (1) to insure that the modules are independent with only one entry and one exit point and (2) to make the COBOL program easy to read and understand. These techniques were introduced in chapter 2 and will be expanded throughout this text.

The benefits of structured programming are perhaps most obvious when it comes to testing. Because the program consists of independent modules and because these modules have only one entry and one exit point, the structured program is almost sure to have fewer bugs than the traditional program. In addition, these bugs are likely to be simple clerical errors rather than complex logical errors. Finally, due to the structured design, the bugs will be relatively easy to find and correct.

Structured programming also makes *top-down coding and testing* (or simply *top-down testing*) possible. This implies coding and testing the program one level or one module at a time. For instance, the first test run might test only the operation of the level-0 and level-1 modules. Then, depending on the complexity of the program, all of the level-2 modules or only a few of the level-2 modules can be added to the program for the next test run. Eventually, the lowest-level modules will be tested in combination with all the other modules of the program.

The advantage of top-down testing is that testing is controlled. If a bug is detected when using the same test data as in the previous test run, it is clearly the result of the module or modules added since that run. Since these modules are independent, it is relatively easy to find the cause of the bug and correct it. Top-down testing sharply contrasts traditional test methods in which the entire program with its dozens or hundreds of bugs is tested at once.

To use top-down testing, the programmer uses *dummy modules*, or *program stubs*, for those modules that aren't ready to be tested. For instance, modules 100 and 200 would be dummy modules when testing module 000 in figure 3-5. In this case, the modules would receive control from module 000, print a message saying that they have received control, and pass control back to module 000. Module 100 would also set CARD-EOF-SWITCH to Y as required by the COBOL code so that module 000 could run to completion.

Since top-down testing is more helpful in testing large programs than small ones, you probably won't need it for any of the programs you'll write in this course. However, chapter 10 explains this technique in detail and shows you when and how to use it for production programs.

Discussion

Although the term *structured programming* originally meant creating programs consisting of only the three proper structures (sequence, selection, and iteration), it has now come to mean far more. Today, it is used to refer to a collection of techniques that includes structured design, module documentation, and top-down coding and testing along with several others. All of these techniques depend on the notion of independent modules with only one entry and one exit point. And all of them are designed to increase programmer productivity.

At present, the techniques of structured programming are by no means standard. Structure charts are done in a variety of ways throughout the computer industry, and module documentation is done in many different ways. There is even debate as to the proper techniques for coding and testing structured programs. Nevertheless, structured programming is here to stay. It is simply a more efficient way to design, document, code and test programs.

Terminology

program flowchart

GO TO statement

proper program

structured programming

sequence structure

selection structure

iteration structure

top-down design

structured design

top-down coding and testing

top-down testing

dummy module

program stub

Objectives

1. Explain the theory of structured programming.
2. Name and describe the three valid structures that make up a proper program.

TOPIC 2   Structured Design

Structured design (or top-down design) sharply contrasts traditional methods of program design. Instead of worrying about programming details, the top-down designer tries to focus on the overall structure of the program. After the major modules have been designed, the designer works on the design of the next level down. He continues this process until the entire program is divided into functional modules that can be coded with limited difficulty.

When structured design is used, the program designer creates some sort of structure chart like the one in figure 3-5. Although there are many different forms of structure charts, this book uses a standard form called a *visual table of contents*, or a *VTOC* (pronounced VEE-tock). The VTOC is part of a method of documentation called *HIPO* (Hierarchy plus Input-Process-Output). As a result, you will sometimes hear the VTOC referred to as a *hierarchy chart*. In topic 3, you will learn how to create HIPO diagrams, which are used to document the functions of the individual program modules.

We recommend HIPO documentation because we believe it is the most practical technique for documenting structured programs that is currently available. It is also one of the most widely used methods for documenting structured programs, and, in our opinion, it is the one that has the best chance of becoming an industry standard.

Step 1—Create the First Draft of the VTOC

To illustrate the procedure for creating VTOCs, take a minute and study the problem specifications in figure 3-6. This program is supposed to read a file of inventory transaction records and check (or

System flowchart:

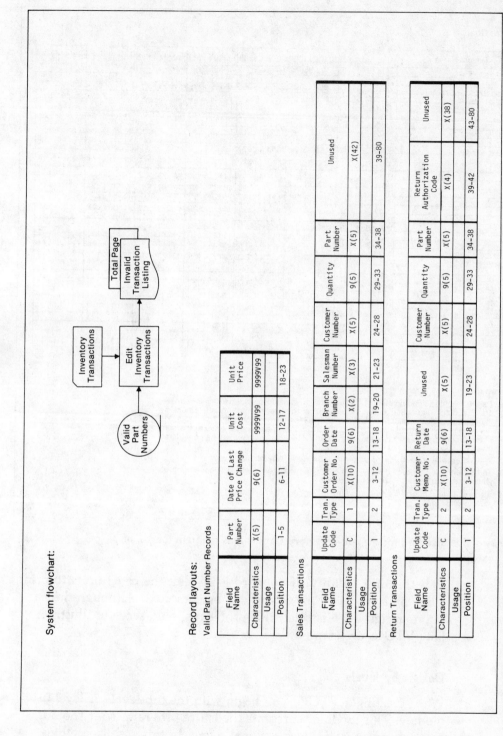

Record layouts:

Valid Part Number Records

Field Name	Part Number	Date of Last Price Change	Unit Cost	Unit Price
Characteristics	X(5)	9(6)	9999V99	9999V99
Usage				
Position	1-5	6-11	12-17	18-23

Sales Transactions

Field Name	Update Code	Tran. Type	Customer Order No.	Order Date	Branch Number	Salesman Number	Customer Number	Quantity	Part Number	Unused
Characteristics	C	1	X(10)	9(6)	X(2)	X(3)	X(5)	9(5)	X(5)	X(42)
Usage										
Position		1	3-12	13-18	19-20	21-23	24-28	29-33	34-38	39-80

Return Transactions

Field Name	Update Code	Tran. Type	Customer Memo No.	Return Date	Unused	Customer Number	Quantity	Part Number	Return Authorization Code	Unused
Characteristics	C	2	X(10)	9(6)	X(5)	X(5)	9(5)	X(5)	X(4)	X(38)
Usage										
Position		2	3-12	13-18	19-23	24-28	29-33	34-38	39-42	43-80

Figure 3-6 Specifications for the edit-inventory-transactions program (part 1 of 2)

Print Chart:

Record Name		Line
HDG-LINE-1	1	INVALID SALES AND RETURN TRANSACTIONS
	2	
HDG-LINE-2	3	TRAN ----------------- * INDICATES ERROR FIELDS ----------------
HDG-LINE-3	4	CODE REF NO DATE BR SLSMN CUST QTY PART AUTH
	5	
ITL-LINE	6	*X1 *XXXXXXXXXX *999999 *XX *XXX *XXXXX *99999 *XXXXX
	7	
ITL-LINE	8	*X2 *XXXXXXXXXX, *999999 *XXXXX *99999 *XXXXX *XXXX
	9	
ITL-LINE	10	*XX XXXXXXXXXX 999999 XX XXX XXXXX 99999 XXXXX XXXX
	11	
	12	
	13	
	14	
	15	
	16	
	17	
	18	
TOTAL-LINE-1	19	SUMMARY FOR SALES-RETURN VERIFICATION RUN
	20	
TOTAL-LINE-2	21	VALID SALES 99,999
TOTAL-LINE-3	22	RETURNS 99,999
TOTAL-LINE-4	23	TOTAL 99,999 *
	24	
TOTAL-LINE-5	25	INVALID SALES 99,999
TOTAL-LINE-6	26	RETURNS 99,999
TOTAL-LINE-7	27	TOTAL 99,999 *
	28	
TOTAL-LINE-8	29	INVALID TRAN CODES 99,999 *
	30	
TOTAL-LINE-9	31	TRANSACTIONS PROCESSED 99,999 * *
	32	
	33	
	34	

Narrative:

1. Detailed editing specifications for each type of transaction will be developed later on. For both transaction types, however, the transaction part number must be matched against the valid part numbers in the valid part-number file. To do this, the file of valid part numbers must be read and stored in a part-number table at the start of the program. If no match is found, the transaction part number will be considered invalid.

2. The transaction code should be a 1 (sale) or 2 (return). Anything else is an error.

3. The size and location of the fields in a transaction record will vary depending on whether the transaction is a sale or a return.

4. All invalid transactions are printed on the listing. An asterisk should be used to mark each invalid field.

Figure 3-6   Specifications for the edit-inventory-transactions program (part 2 of 2)

edit) them for validity. If a record is invalid, the program is to print a line on a report so the record can be corrected. Although the narrative in figure 3-6 is brief, this problem should serve to illustrate how VTOCs are created.

Design by levels

When creating a VTOC, you begin with the top-level, or level-0, module. This module represents the entire program, so it should be given an appropriate functional name. In this case, something like "verify inventory transactions" or "edit inventory transactions" is appropriate.

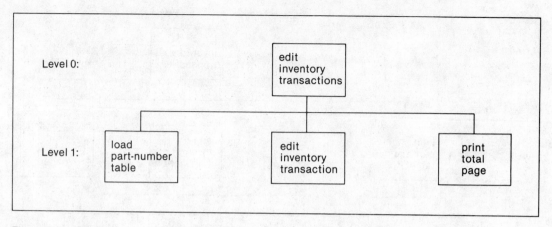

Figure 3-7   The first two levels of the VTOC for the edit-inventory-transactions program

To name a module, you should use one verb, one or at most two adjectives, and one object. Although this may seem limiting, you will find that it will be all that you need. As you will see, all of the structure charts in this book use this naming technique.

After the top-level module has been named and a block drawn for it at the top of the VTOC, the program designer tries to determine what functions (modules) the top-level module consists of. For instance, a simple report-printing program like the reorder-listing program consists of a module that produces the body lines of the report and a module that produces the total lines.

For the edit-inventory-transactions program, the designer has decided upon the level-1 modules shown in figure 3-7. As you can see, the entire program consists of three major modules: (1) a module that loads the part-number table into storage at the start of the program, (2) a module that edits one inventory transaction, and (3) a module that prints the total page of the report after all transactions have been edited.

In order to create the level-1 modules in a VTOC, you should begin by deciding upon one primary functional module that will be performed repeatedly during the execution of the program. In figure 3-7, this is the edit-inventory-transaction module. In other words, the level-0 module represents the processing for all input records; the primary level-1 module represents processing for only one input record (or set of records).

After you have decided upon the primary level-1 module, you should think about functional modules that need to be performed before the primary module. In figure 3-7, this is the load-part-number-table module, because the part-number table must be loaded before any of the transactions can be checked for validity. Then,

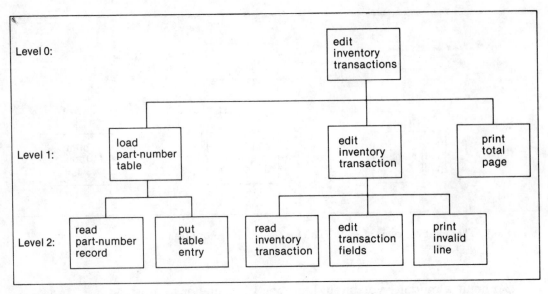

Figure 3-8   The first three levels of the VTOC for the edit-inventory-transactions
program

you should think of functional modules that need to be performed
after the primary module. In figure 3-7, this is the print-total-page
module. In other words, after all transaction records have been processed by the primary module, the total page should be printed.

In general, the left-to-right placement of modules in the VTOC
indicates the probable sequence of module execution. This is cer-
tainly true for the level-1 modules in figure 3-7. However, this isn't
always the case. In many instances, subordinate modules will be
executed in a sequence that isn't apparent at the time the VTOC
is created.

After the level-1 modules have been created, the program
designer tries to decide whether any of these consist of subordinate
functions. If so, subordinate modules should be created. Here, the
designer is thinking in terms of clearly defined functions.

For the edit-inventory-transactions program, the designer has
decided upon the level-2 modules shown in the VTOC in figure 3-8.
Thus, the load-part-number-table module has been broken down
into two subordinate modules: one for reading the part-number
records and one for putting the records into the part-number table.
These are clearly defined functions and both are required if the table
is to be stored properly.

Similarly, the edit-inventory-transaction module is subdivided
into three subordinate modules: one will read a transaction record,
one will edit the individual fields in the record, and one will print a
line on the report for each invalid transaction. As you might guess,
the read-inventory-transaction and edit-transaction-fields modules

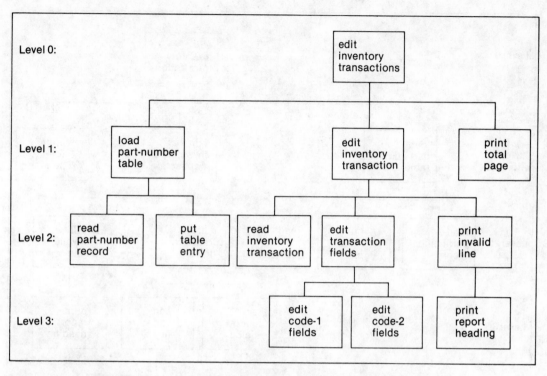

Figure 3-9   The first four levels of the VTOC for the edit-inventory-transactions program

will be performed once for each transaction record. However, the print-invalid-line module will only be executed when the transaction record is invalid.

As for the print-total-page module, it isn't subdivided any further. The designer feels that it is a clearly defined function that needs no more simplification.

The programmer next decides whether any of the level-2 modules can be subdivided into clearly defined functions. Thus, the edit-inventory-transactions program can be further subdivided as shown in figure 3-9. Here, the edit-transaction-fields module is broken down into two modules that edit the fields in the transaction records—one module for each of the two types of transactions. Here too, the print-invalid-line module is given a subordinate module that will print a heading on each page of the report. In this case, then, a single subordinate module is broken out of a higher-level module.

When the designer decides upon the modules for editing the fields in each of the two record types, he realizes that the part-number field must be edited by searching the part-number table for an equal comparison. He also realizes that this module must be subordinate to each of the edit-fields modules. Thus, he adds one

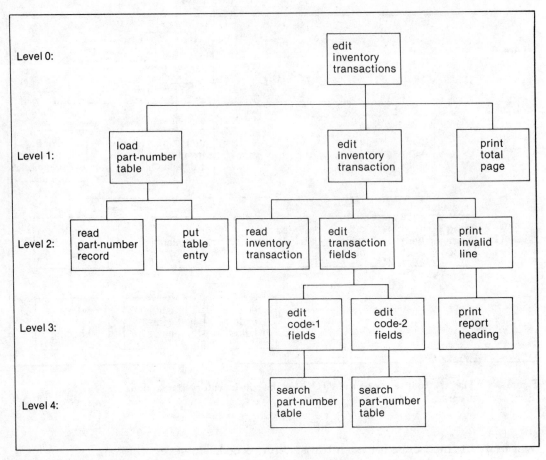

Figure 3-10 The first five levels of the VTOC for the edit-inventory-transactions
program

more level to the VTOC as shown in figure 3-10. As you can see,
the search-part-number-table module is subordinate to the edit-
code-1-fields module as well as to the edit-code-2-fields module.

At this stage, the VTOC in figure 3-10 is logically complete; all
modules have been broken down into their functional components.
Note, however, that you do *not* need to concern yourself with the
details of the program to create a VTOC like this. For instance, the
designer has created the edit modules without even knowing what
the editing rules are going to be. All he knows is that the rules will
probably be different for each type of transaction, so he has provided a separate module for each.

Whether you are given all specifications or not, you should
make every effort to avoid the details of a program when you're
designing the VTOC. Once you have convinced yourself that the
function of any given module can be programmed, forget the details.

You shouldn't have to confront them again until you are called upon to document or code the module.

Add one read or write module for each file

After the VTOC is logically complete as in figure 3-10, the designer adds read and write modules that are specific to each physical file required by the program. The idea here is that there should only be one READ statement in the program for each file read by the program. Similarly, there should only be one WRITE statement for each output file.

It isn't always possible, however, to have only one WRITE statement for each output file. For instance, as we saw in chapter 2, COBOL print files usually require one WRITE statement that skips to the top of a page as well as one WRITE statement that spaces one or more lines based on the value in a space-control field. Similarly, files with variable-length records often require several WRITE statements, one for each record size. (You will learn how to work with such files in chapter 7.) In all other cases, however, you should be able to follow the rule of one READ or WRITE statement per file.

In order to limit the number of READ and WRITE statements for each file, the READ and WRITE statements must be coded in separate read and write modules. These modules can then be performed whenever a record needs to be read or written. By isolating the READ and WRITE statements in this way, you end up with a more efficient program and one that is easy to modify.

Because there are already two read modules in figure 3-10, one for each of the input files, the designer doesn't have to add any other specific read modules. However, since the printer file needs both page-top and body lines, specific write modules should be added subordinate to the three print modules. These write modules are shown in the VTOC for the edit-inventory-transactions program in figure 3-11. One of them will write a line after skipping to the top of the next page (module 290); the other will write a line after spacing one or more lines as determined by a space-control field (module 270). You have seen this use of write modules in the refined reorder-listing program in figure 2-24.

Although the read and write modules will often consist of only one COBOL statement, it is worthwhile to isolate the statements. Later on, if you want to count the number of records read or the number of lines printed, the code can easily be added to these modules. The alternative in a large program is to have several READ or WRITE statements for each file dispersed in many different modules, an inefficient and confusing practice.

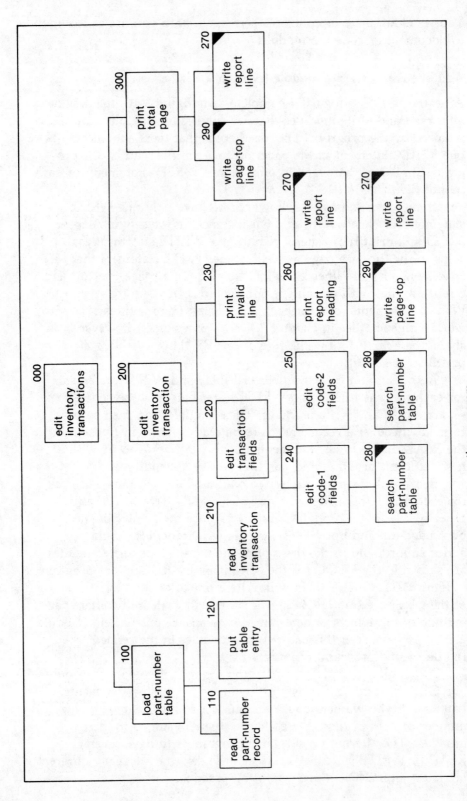

Figure 3-11 Complete VTOC for the edit-inventory-transactions program

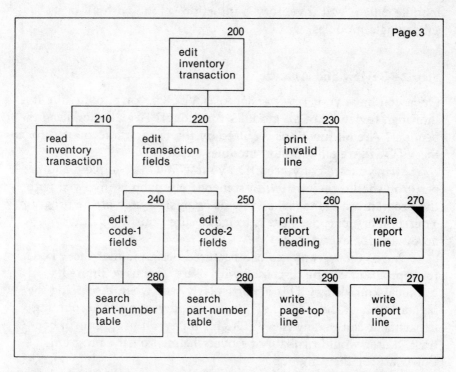

Figure 3-12   Page 3 of the VTOC for the edit-inventory-transactions program: the edit-inventory-transaction branch

Shade common modules

Because the search and write modules in figure 3-11 are subordinate to more than one module, they are called *common modules*. As a result, the upper righthand corner of these blocks is shaded. This simply shows that the modules are used in more than one place in the VTOC. Thus, module 280 is common to modules 240 and 250; module 270 is common to modules 230, 260, and 300; and module 290 is common to modules 260 and 300.

Use more than one page for large charts

If a structure chart is so large that it is difficult to get it on a single page, it should extend to two or more pages. To do this, the first page should contain the top-level module and the level-1 modules, such as those shown in figure 3-7. Then, subsequent pages will start with one of the level-1 modules: page 2 will contain the first level-1 module and all its subordinates; page 3 will contain the second level-1 module and its subordinates; and so on. If, for example, the edit-inventory-transactions program were larger, page 3 of the structure chart might be as shown in figure 3-12. This is the level-1 module called "edit inventory transaction" along with all of its subordinate modules.

Step 2—Review and Analyze

Once you have your first version of a VTOC, you should give it a thorough review. Are all modules functional? Are all modules independent? Are all functions required by the program accounted for by the VTOC? Are all common modules shaded?

After you are convinced that your VTOC is complete and proper, you should review it with someone else who is involved with the program—a manager, a systems analyst, a user of the program. Your primary purpose here is to make sure your VTOC has accounted for everything.

One of the advantages of structured design is that the VTOC for a program can be discussed with users who have limited technical knowledge. This is particularly true when discussing the higher levels of the VTOC. Thus, an employee in the accounting department can review the VTOC for a payroll program. In contrast, a user would probably be overwhelmed by the program flowchart for the same job.

Some companies have specific requirements for VTOC reviews. For instance, a programmer may be required to review each VTOC with the systems analyst who created the specifications for the program. In other words, the programmer can't continue the program development until the VTOC has been okayed by the systems analyst. Requirements like this can increase the productivity of a programming department because many errors can be caught and corrected before the testing phase is even begun.

Based on your review, you are likely to change your VTOC. Sometimes this means changing or moving only a block or two. Sometimes this means redrawing the entire chart. Later on, as you document the individual modules, you may decide that other changes are also needed. These changes, however, are usually minor.

What to look for when reviewing the VTOC

When you review your VTOC, there are a number of things you should watch for. Above all, you should ask yourself (1) whether all the modules are functional and (2) whether the VTOC is complete. After that, you should consider verb consistency, module independence, proper subordination, span of control, and module size.

Are all the modules functional?   Perhaps you've noticed the emphasis on function as I described how VTOCs are created. This emphasis, as you might guess, is one of the important principles of effective top-down design. In brief, *all* modules should represent one and only one program function.

You can be sure your modules are functional if you can describe them in a single imperative sentence such as "print the heading lines," "update the records in the master file," or "search the customer table." This, of course, is what you do when you name the module by using one verb, one or two adjectives, and an object. If you can't describe your modules in this way, they probably aren't functional and your program design is probably faulty.

One type of module that isn't functional is a module that refers to time. Thus "perform end-of-file processing" isn't a functional description. The elements in a module like this are only related by the fact that they are done *after* all records have been processed. Similary, "perform initialization" modules aren't functional. Their elements are only related because they are done *before* the main processing routines. They too are related by time.

Another type of module description to watch out for is one that refers to a class of data. Traditionally, for example, programs contained "process input data" modules. The elements in these modules were only related insofar as they operated upon the same type of data (input data). In other words, these modules were simply a conglomeration of all the functions that had to do with any part of the input data. Thus, the modules weren't functional and were indicative of faulty program design. So watch out for modules built around classes of data—they aren't likely to be functional.

If your module description requires the use of the word *and* or *or*, it is a good indication that the module contains more than one function. Thus, a "read and store table records" module should be divided into two functional modules. And a "print valid or invalid message" module should be two modules.

In any event, strive for functional modules. Test all of them to see whether they can be described in a single imperative sentence. Test all of these sentences to see whether they represent a function rather than a collection of elements related by time or class of data. If your modules are functional, they will be relatively easy to document, code, and test. If they aren't functional, you will run into problems as you develop the program.

Is the VTOC complete?   When you're sure that each module represents one function, your next question should be this: Does the

VTOC provide for all functions that must be done by the program? When a VTOC consists of a hundred or more modules, however, this can be a difficult question to answer.

The way to approach this question is one level at a time, from the top down. In figure 3-11, for example, you should first ask whether the three level-1 modules do everything implied by their boss, module 000. In other words, does editing the inventory transactions consist only of loading the part-number table (module 100), editing the individual transactions (module 200), and printing the total page (module 300)? Or should there be other level-1 functions (modules)? In my opinion, level 1 is complete as shown.

After you have analyzed one level for completeness, you continue with the next level down. For instance, do modules 110 and 120 provide for everything that module 100 implies? Do modules 210, 220, and 230 provide for everything module 200 implies? And do modules 290 and 270 provide for everything module 300 implies?

Since this analysis seems to give a lot of people trouble, I often tell my students to jot down what they mean by a certain module description on a piece of scratch paper. In figure 3-11, for example, what does load part-number table (module 100) mean to you? To me it means (1) reading the table records and (2) loading the records into a working-storage area. As a result, level-2 beneath module 100 seems to be complete.

You can use this scratch-pad idea whenever you have doubts about completeness. It is particularly useful when reviewing a VTOC with another person. As questions arise, you can list the functions that you think a boss module implies. Then, you can discuss the items on the list to determine (1) whether all functions are accounted for and (2) whether all functions contribute to the objective of the boss module. If you decide that all functions are *not* accounted for, you simply add the required modules and continue your analysis.

When you do a scratch-pad analysis, you will often discover problems with the verbs used in module descriptions. The major problem seems to be using verbs that are too general. For example, it's tempting to name a module "process sales record" when you're not sure what it's going to require. What you really mean is that the module should do everything that is required—but you don't know what that is—or that the module should do everything that isn't done by other modules at that level. In either case, you will *not* be able to list the functions required by the module. So avoid using a general verb like "process"; whenever possible, find a more precise verb to use in the module description. Only after you have a clear idea of what the module must do will you be able to continue your analysis.

Are the verbs consistent?   Besides using precise verbs in your module descriptions, you should try to be consistent in their use. In other words, one verb should mean the same thing throughout a VTOC and, if possible, throughout a programming department. For instance, I use the word *print* to mean at the least (1) formatting the output record in storage (if necessary) and (2) writing the record on the printer; I use the word *write* to mean physically placing the record on the output device (as in the COBOL WRITE statement). Similarly, I use the word *get* to mean (1) reading a record, (2) checking the record for validity, and (3) doing something with the invalid records; I use the word *read* to mean physically reading the record from the input device (as in the COBOL READ statement).

Quite frankly, the way I use these words can be debated. However, I am consistent in my use of verbs throughout this book. So once you understand what I mean by the verbs I use, you will be able to understand the module descriptions in figure 3-11 as well as in all of the other VTOCs in this book.

The important thing, then, is consistency. As you review your VTOCs for completeness, you should keep a close eye on the verbs you use. Whenever you see the same verb used in more than one way, you should change the VTOC so the verbs are consistent.

Are the modules independent?   Structured programming depends on the use of independent modules. This means a module should only be *called* by the module above it in the VTOC. Thus, module 220 in figure 3-11 (the *called module)* should only be called by module 200 (the *calling module).*

To maintain independence, control codes created in a called module should only be used by the calling module. To say it another way, codes created in the subordinate module should only be *passed* to the calling module. For example, the end-of-file code that must be created by module 210 in figure 3-11 should only be passed to module 200. If the code is required by the print-invalid-line module, module 230, this latter module isn't properly independent.

Although a code should only be required by the calling module, it is okay to pass a code from one calling module to another. For example, the end-of-file switch created by module 210 is passed to and tested by module 200, which is module 210's calling module. Module 200 in turn passes the code up to the next calling module, module 000, which also tests the code. In other words, it's okay to pass a code up the line, from one calling module to another. But a code created in one module should *not* be required by modules at the same level or at lower levels in the VTOC; if it is, it indicates that the modules aren't independent.

Note here that I said *control codes* shouldn't be passed erratically from one module to another. I said nothing about data. On the contrary, it is perfectly all right for data that is created in one module to be used in modules other than the calling module. In figure 3-11, for example, data read by the read-inventory-transaction module (module 210) is used in modules 220, 230, 240, 250, and 280. And these modules are at the same or lower levels as module 210. Similarly, data created in a computational module is likely to be used in print modules at the same or lower levels.

In some cases, it is difficult or impossible to decide whether a module is independent by looking at a VTOC. If the modules are functional, there is a good chance that they will be properly independent. Nevertheless, the programmer should keep the goal of module independence in mind. This is important when creating the VTOC, and it is important when creating the HIPO diagrams for the individual modules.

Is proper subordination shown?   When we refer to *proper subordination*, it means that called modules are related to the correct calling module. Since the program designer has many options when creating a VTOC, it is not always easy to achieve proper subordination. To some extent, at least, it is only achieved after a program designer has gained some experience with the techniques of structured design and documentation.

To illustrate, look at the VTOC in figure 3-13. It is for the edit-inventory-transactions program that is charted in figure 3-11. Here, the program designer has decided on five level-1 modules. Now the question is: Why is this improper subordination and why do the three level-1 modules in figure 3-11 represent proper subordination?

As I said, the ability to answer this question depends to some extent on experience. In brief, however, you won't be able to code the VTOC in figure 3-13 in structured code. Specifically, the top-level module in a structured program must repeatedly execute the major level-1 module using a DO-UNTIL structure. This level-1 module in turn must control the major functions of the program. Since the VTOC in figure 3-13 doesn't provide for this level-1 control module, it doesn't represent proper subordination.

Although you may not be able to detect improper subordination at this point, it will show up when you document the modules. As a result, you will be better able to detect improper subordination after you learn how to document the modules in topic 3. For now, though, try to use this guideline: Use level-1 for the one major function of the program, for functions that must be done before the major function, and for functions that must be done after the major function.

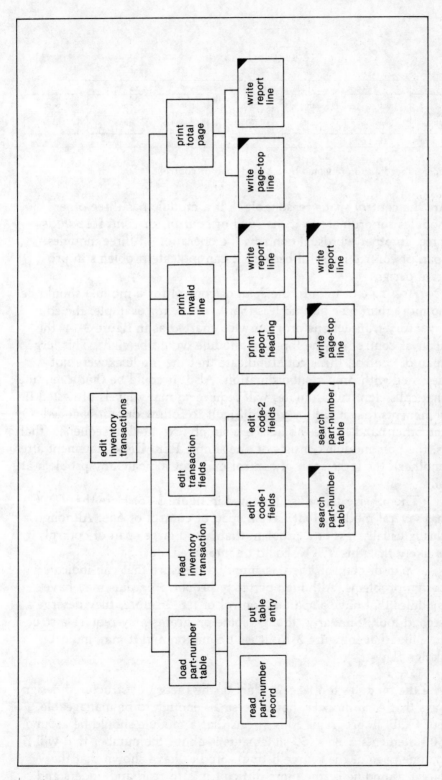

Figure 3-13   Improper subordination for the edit-inventory-transactions program

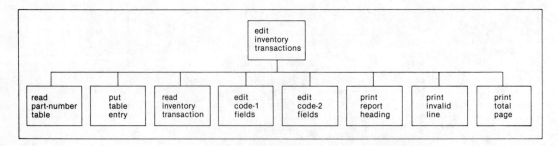

Figure 3-14   Improper subordination reflected by a broad span of control

Are the control spans reasonable?   If a module has three other modules subordinate to it, its *span of control*, or *control span*, is three. In other words, it controls the operation of three modules. Span of control is useful because it can indicate problems in program design.

As a rule of thumb, the span of control for a module should be no more than nine and no less than two. If, for example, the edit-inventory-transactions program was charted as in figure 3-14, the span of control for the top-level module would be eight. This large span of control, then, could indicate that the modules were not designed with proper subordination. Also, it could be that a module that calls eight subordinates will require so many levels of nested IF statements that it will be very difficult to follow once it is coded. On the other hand, if the modules are simply executed in sequence (that is, the boss module consists of one simple PERFORM statement after another), the large span of control may not indicate any problem at all.

The other extreme is illustrated in figure 3-15. Here the VTOC has several modules that have a span of control of one. Although this is usually less of a problem than a too-large span of control, it is likely that this VTOC could be improved.

Span of control, then, is simply a measure that can indicate design problems. Although perfectly proper programs may have modules that have a span of control of ten or more, they deserve a second look. Similarly, though some programs may require a structure like that in figure 3-15, it isn't common and it may indicate design flaws.

Are the modules too large?   Part of the theory of structured design says that each module should be small enough to be manageable. For COBOL programs, this means that a module should be around 50 statements or less (50 statements is about the number that will fit on one page of the source listing). Studies have shown that the larger a module is, the more difficult it is to read and understand.

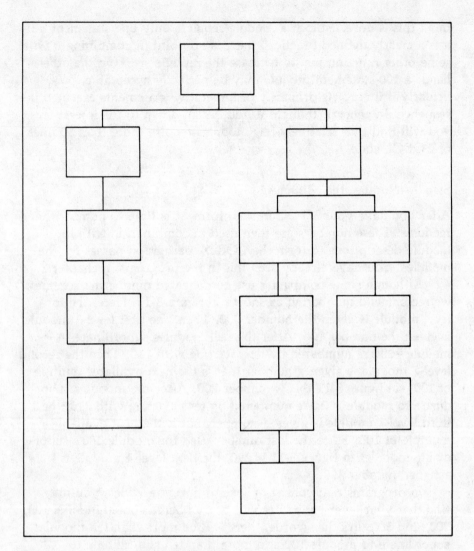

Figure 3-15   Questionable control spans

Furthermore, the difficulty does not increase in direct proportion to the size of the module. For example, a 100-statement module is often three or four times as difficult to read and understand as a 50-statement module, rather than being only twice as troublesome.

Needless to say, you can't tell how large a module will be by looking at a VTOC. As a result, you may have to make changes to the VTOC when coding the program. If, for example, you code a module that requires 500 statements, you should attempt to divide it into smaller component parts.

The simplest rule to go by is to develop your VTOC down to the lowest functional level. Although some books on structured design recommend that modules range from 10 to 50 statements, I think this is unrealistic. If a module requires only one statement but it is a clearly defined function, there is no point in combining it with some other function just to increase the module size. On the other hand, a 100-statement module may be perfectly acceptable, particularly if it consists primarily of imperative statements executed in sequence. In general, though, if you design down to the lowest level, you will find that relatively few modules require more than 50 lines of COBOL code.

Step 3—Number the Modules

After you have your VTOC in final form, it is time to number the modules. These numbers are then used in combination with the module descriptions to form the COBOL paragraph names for the modules. You have already seen this in the programs in chapter 2.

Although some companies use complicated numbering schemes, we recommend numbering as shown in figure 3-11. Here, the top-level module is given the number 000. Then, the first level-1 module is given the number 100. After this, all modules subordinate to module 100 are numbered by tens starting with 110. Then the second level-1 module is given a number that is the next available multiple of 100—in figure 3-11 this is number 200. After the modules subordinate to module 200 are numbered by tens starting with 210, the third level-1 module is given a number that is the next available multiple of 100. Since the last number used for module 200's subordinate modules in figure 3-11 is 290, the next level-1 module is assigned number 300.

In programs that consist of several dozen modules, you may find that your level-1 modules will be numbered something like 100, 300, and 500. In other words, there will be more than ten modules subordinate to module 100 and more than ten subordinate to module 300.

In this numbering scheme, the numbers do *not* indicate at what level the module can be found. This means that changes can be made to the VTOC without changing module numbers. In contrast, when more complex numbering systems are used, a change to the VTOC usually means a change to the module number, which in turn means a change to the module documentation, which in turn means a change in the COBOL source code.

For instance, some numbering systems use a number like 1.2.4 to indicate the fourth block under block number 1.2, which is the second block under block number 1.0. If the chart is changed so block 1.2.4 should be the first block under block 3.1, its number must be changed to 3.1.1. In brief, you can easily become a slave to a numbering system like this.

Numbering by hundreds and tens also allows for great flexibility if additional blocks must be added to the VTOC after the programmer thinks it is complete. For example, if another module must be added subordinate to module 100 in figure 3-11, it can be numbered 130 without having to change any other module number. Likewise, if a programmer finds he needs two subordinate modules for module 210, he can easily and logically number them 211 and 212 without affecting the rest of the VTOC.

Incidentally, in some systems the numbers are placed inside the blocks themselves, in the lower righthand corner. However, by placing them outside the boxes as in figure 3-11, you have more room for the module description, and the numbers are easier to locate.

Step 4—If Necessary, Shorten Module Names

When you document each of the modules in your VTOC as described in topic 3, you will create the actual COBOL paragraph names for each of the modules. To create the COBOL name, you will use the module number followed by the module description with the number and words separated by hyphens. Thus, module 000 in figure 3-11 will be coded in the paragraph named

```
000-EDIT-INVENTORY-TRANSACTIONS
```

Unfortunately, however, this name is invalid since it has more than 30 characters.

After you number the modules, then, you should inspect the module names to make sure they're not too long. In general, you will only have to be careful when two of the words in the module description are long, like *inventory* and *transaction*, or when a four-word module description is used. Then, if the paragraph name will be over 30 characters, you should shorten the description by abbreviating one or more words. Make every effort, however, to keep the module name on the VTOC meaningful. In figure 3-11, the module descriptions for modules 000, 200, and 210 were too long or on the borderline, so I shortened them as shown in figure 3-16. I simply changed the words *transactions* and *transaction* to *trans* and *tran*. Figure 3-16, then, represents the final VTOC for the edit-inventory-transactions program.

Discussion

As I mentioned at the start of this topic, there are other forms of structure charts besides the VTOC. Some of these use arrows and

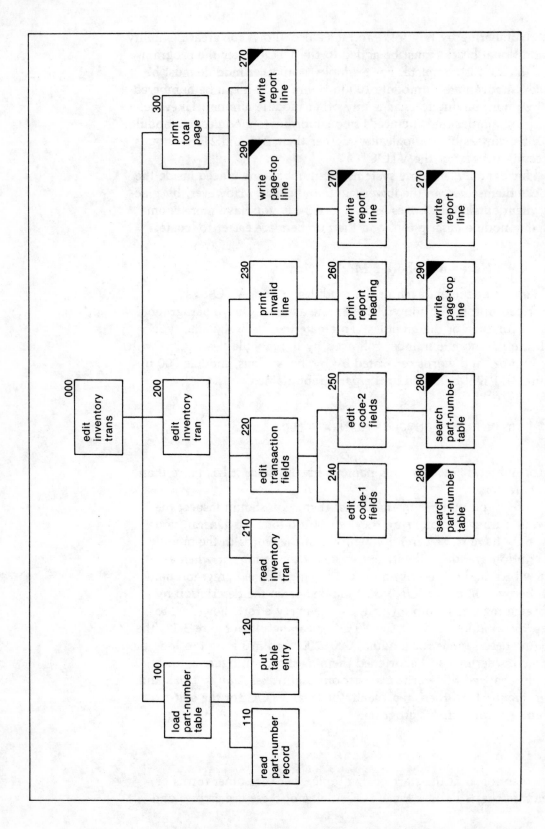

Figure 3-16 Complete VTOC for the edit-inventory-transactions program after the module descriptions have been shortened

other symbols to indicate the data and codes that are passed from one module to another. Other types of charts indicate whether a module is always executed or whether it depends upon a condition that varies during processing.

In my opinion, this type of information is best omitted from the structure chart. Not only does it make the structure chart more difficult to create, it makes it more difficult to change. Furthermore, some of this information is difficult to develop without actually documenting the modules. Finally, it forces the programmer to think in terms of procedure and details . . . just the type of thinking you should try to avoid during design. I recommend, therefore, that this information be recorded only as part of the module documentation.

In summary, then, the purpose of the structure chart is to show the relationships of the modules required by the program. Once created, it is a guide for program development. The module documentation will follow this guide. The program itself will follow this guide. As for the detailed processing specifications, including the codes and data required by each module, they are documented by HIPO diagrams or pseudocode as you will see in the next topic.

Terminology

visual table of contents

VTOC

HIPO

hierarchy chart

common module

module independence

calling a module

called module

calling module

passing a control code

proper subordination

span of control

control span

Objectives

1. List the four steps you should follow when creating a VTOC.
2. Explain how you can tell when a module is *functional*.

3. List and describe seven characteristics you should analyze when you review a VTOC.

Note: If you are new to programming, you will probably have difficulty creating your own VTOCs at this time. After all, many new ideas have been presented in just three chapters. That's why being able to create your own VTOCs isn't one of the objectives of this topic, though it will be one after topic 4.

TOPIC 3   Structured Module Documentation

After the structure chart or VTOC is created, the programmer documents the processing required by the individual modules. In other words, the documentation for a structured program before coding consists of (1) the VTOC and (2) module documentation. Now that you have learned how to create VTOCs, this topic will concentrate on module documentation.

Although it is possible to use traditional program flowcharts for module documentation, the trend in industry is to avoid program flowcharts altogether. As mentioned before, flowcharts are difficult to create and maintain, and they don't represent a problem solution in a form that is an efficient guide for coding. Worst of all, they force you to focus on how the processing can be done before you have documented what it is that must be done.

Although many different techniques are currently being used for structured module documentation, all of the techniques attempt to do the same thing. For each module, they try to show the required input files and data, the required output files and data, and the required processing. Or, briefly stated, they show input, output, and processing.

In this book, we recommend that all module documentation be done using *HIPO diagrams* (also known as *IPO diagrams* or simply *IPOs*). They are part of the HIPO (Hierarchy plus Input-Process-Output) system of documentation developed and promoted by IBM. In our opinion, this is the most widely used technique for structured program documentation, and it stands the best chance of becoming an industry standard. Complete HIPO documentation for a program consists of the VTOC and one HIPO or IPO diagram for each module in the VTOC.

HIPO Diagrams

Figure 3-17 is a HIPO diagram for the top-level module in figure 3-16, the edit-inventory-transactions program. Below the heading,

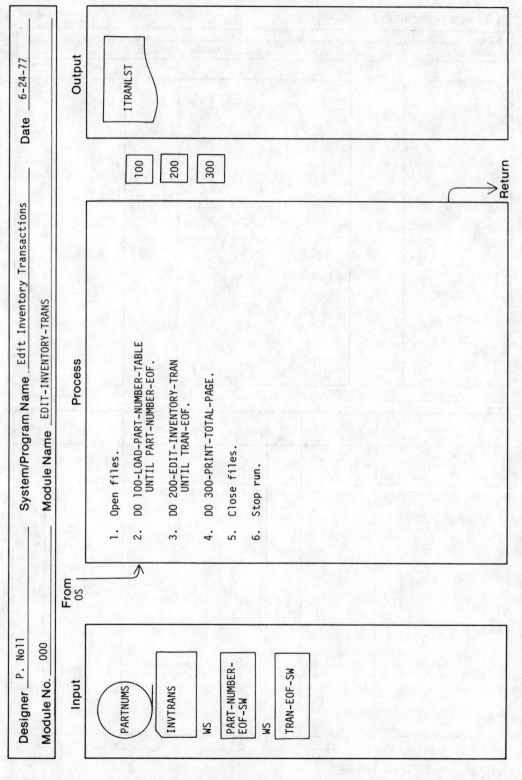

Figure 3-17 HIPO diagram for module 000 of the edit-inventory-transactions program

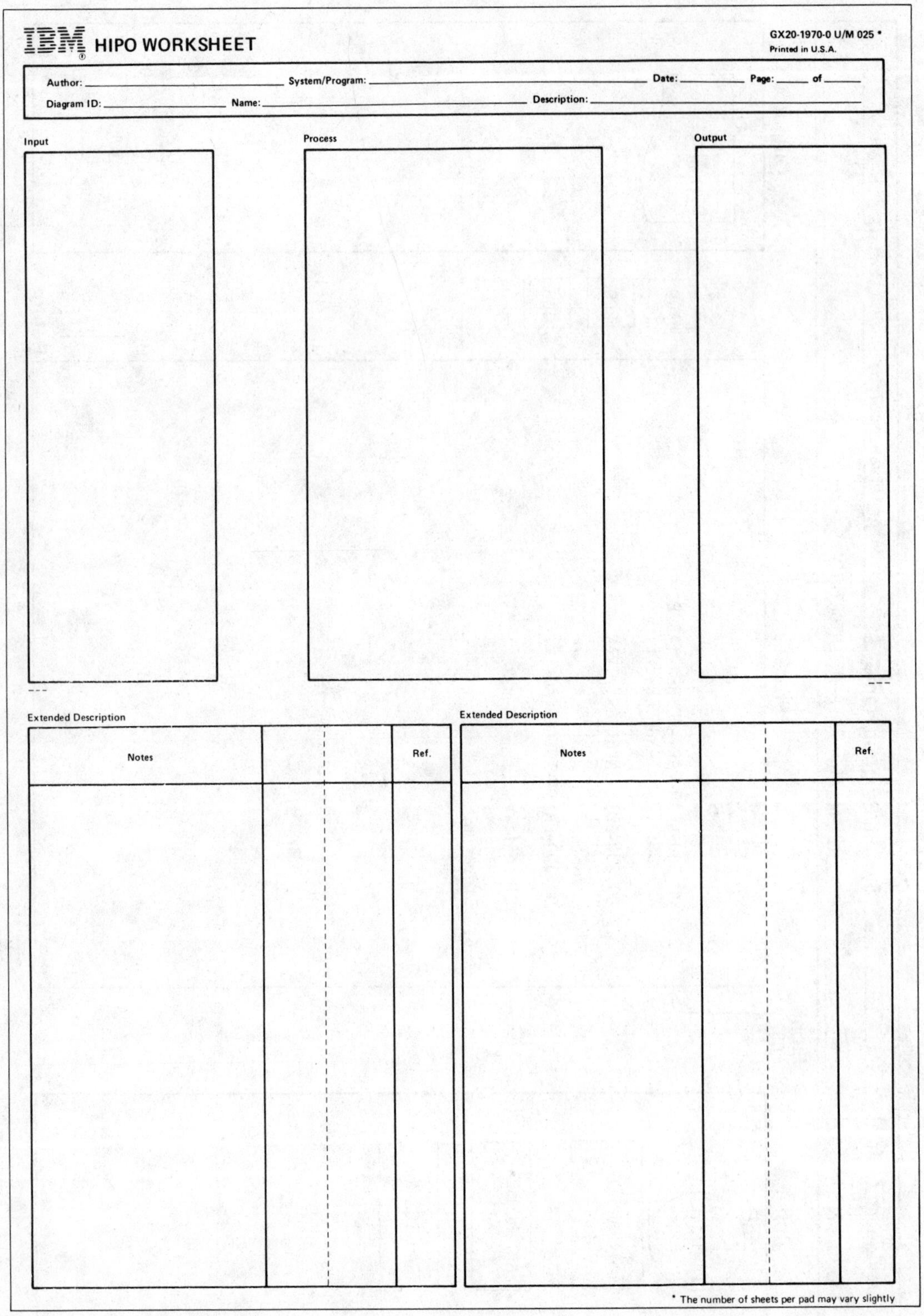

IBM HIPO WORKSHEET

GX20-1970-0 U/M 025 *
Printed in U.S.A.

Author: _____ System/Program: _____ Date: _____ Page: _____ of _____

Diagram ID: _____ Name: _____ Description: _____

Input

Process

Output

Extended Description

Notes		Ref.

Extended Description

Notes		Ref.

* The number of sheets per pad may vary slightly

Figure 3-18 The HIPO worksheet

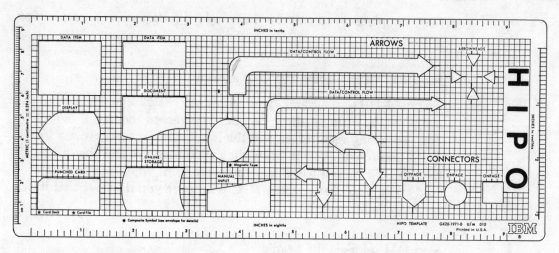

Figure 3-19   The HIPO template

there are three boxes on the HIPO diagram: the left box for describing input, the right box for describing output, and the middle box for describing processing. For this module, there are four different input requirements: a tape file of valid-part-number records, a card file of transaction records, one working-storage field called PART-NUMBER-EOF-SW, and another called TRAN-EOF-SW. The only output of this module is the listing of invalid transactions. As for processing, six steps are documented.

To create HIPO diagrams, most programmers use a printed form like the one in figure 3-18. This is IBM form GX20-1970; it comes in pads and can be purchased through any IBM office. As you can see, the top portion of the form has the input, process, and output boxes. The bottom portion of the form allows additional processing specifications (extended descriptions) to be documented. The use of extended descriptions will be illustrated later in this topic.

Because the IBM form is large (11 × 16½), we recommend two 8½ × 11 forms in its place. The first form should be used for all HIPO diagrams; the second form should be used whenever extended descriptions are required. Because 8½ × 11 forms can be filed in standard file folders without folding, they are more efficient than the larger IBM forms, and they will be illustrated throughout this text. You should realize, though, that they are modifications of the IBM form.

As the documentation is recorded on the HIPO forms, various boxes and symbols are required. For this purpose, the plastic HIPO template shown in figure 3-19 can be useful. It is IBM's GX20-1971, and it can be purchased in packages of ten through any IBM office. By placing a pen or pencil inside the symbols, you can draw more precise symbols than you can do freehand. If you don't have one of these templates, you can use the standard programmer's template of years past.

Six Steps for Preparing HIPO Diagrams

To create HIPO diagrams, you follow six basic steps. First, you complete the form heading. Second, you record the input, output, and processing requirements in the input, output, and process boxes. Third and fourth, you indicate the called modules and the calling modules. Fifth, you use extended descriptions whenever necessary. And sixth, you change the VTOC whenever you discover that it can be improved.

Step 1—Complete the heading

In the heading of the HIPO form, you record your name, the program name, and the date. If your form has room for page numbers, I suggest leaving them blank since the module numbers will be used to keep the HIPO diagrams in order. Then, for the module number (or ID), you use the module number from the VTOC. Similarly, for the module name you use the name given in the VTOC with the words separated by hyphens. Thus, the module name for module 000 in the VTOC in figure 3-16 and in the HIPO diagram in figure 3-17 is

```
EDIT-INVENTORY-TRANS
```

Since the module number and the module name combine to form the paragraph name in the actual COBOL program, this numbering and naming technique relates the VTOC with the module documentation and the COBOL program. As a result, you should make every effort to be precise when recording the numbers and names at all three levels.

Step 2—Record the input, output, and processing requirements

When the heading is complete, you begin the actual module documentation. Whether you begin by recording the I/O requirements or the processing steps depends on which you know the most about. In the higher-level modules, when the I/O requirements are clear, you will probably record the input and output requirements first. Then, you can finish up by listing the processing steps that are required. In the lower-level modules, however, the input and output requirements usually aren't so clear, so it is best to start by listing the processing steps. Then you can record the input or output files, records, or fields as you find that you need them. As a general guideline, begin by recording the processing steps whenever you are in doubt about the detailed I/O requirements.

I/O requirements In a top-level module like the one in figure 3-17, you can start by recording the input and output files since you know what they are. For the edit-inventory-transactions program, the input files are a card file of inventory transactions and a tape file of part-number records. The only output file is a printed listing of inventory transactions. Inside the input and output symbols for the files in figure 3-17, I have recorded the actual file names that I will use in my COBOL code later on.

In addition to files, the input and output boxes for a top-level module should show any data fields required by the module. Thus the IPO in figure 3-17 shows two input fields, both of which are switches (SW is a shortened form of SWITCH that I will use from now on in this book). One switch will be used to indicate the end-of-file (EOF) condition for the PARTNUMS file; the other will indicate EOF for the INVTRANS file.

Because switches are common in structured programming, they should always be used in a standard way. So here are the standards used in this book. First, all switch-field names end in SW. Second, the condition represented by the switch is self-explanatory if you drop the SW. Thus, TRAN-EOF means the end of the transaction file, and PART-NUMBER-EOF means the end of the part-number file. Similarly, a switch named VALID-TRAN-SW can be used to indicate a valid transaction. And NOT before a condition—as in NOT TRAN-EOF—means the condition isn't true. (In chapter 5, you will learn how to code these conditions using condition names.) Third, a switch is off if it contains a value of N (for "no") and on if it contains a value of Y (for "yes"). Finally, all switches are initialized to their proper starting values in working storage. This use of switches was illustrated in COBOL in chapter 2 and will be followed in the programs and HIPO diagrams throughout the rest of this book.

To record I/O requirements, you will use the symbols on the left side of the HIPO template in figure 3-19. For card files, you will use the card symbol; for print files, the document symbol; for direct-access files, the online storage symbol; and for tape files, the magnetic tape symbol.

For records and fields in storage, you will use data-item symbols (rectangles) like those in the upper lefthand corner of the HIPO template. These boxes can be as large or as small as needed to record the data names that are required by the module. Above each of these boxes, you should indicate where these data items can be found in the COBOL program. Use WS for working-storage items and FD for items described in the Input-Output Section.

Processing requirements   When you record the processing steps, you have considerable leeway as to the language you use. Sometimes just plain English is used, sometimes a special documentation language called *pseudocode* is used, and sometimes COBOL itself is used. In figure 3-17, I have used a form of pseudocode that is explained later in detail. Briefly, though, all of the structured programming words like DO, UNTIL, IF, THEN, and ELSE are capitalized, and all COBOL names are capitalized. Otherwise, English is used in lower-case letters to indicate the processing functions.

Can you follow the processing steps in figure 3-17? First, the files are opened. Second, module 100 is repeatedly executed until the end of the part-number file has been reached. Third, module 200 is repeatedly executed until the end of the transaction file has been reached. Then in the last three steps, module 300 is executed, the files are closed, and the program ends.

Although the processing in figure 3-17 is quite limited, the requirements for other modules may be extensive. In that case, it may be difficult or impossible to list all of the required steps in the processing box. If so, it is a good indication that the module will require more than 50 COBOL statements, and you should consider dividing it into two or more subordinate modules. After analysis, however, if you feel that the module size will be acceptable, you can use a second form to finish off the list of processing steps.

Step 3—Set off the numbers of the called modules

In figure 3-17, the module numbers for all modules called by module 000 are recorded between the process and the output boxes to the right of the step that called each module. As a result, it is easy to see that module 000 calls three other modules. You can record the module numbers for the called modules as you record the processing steps, or you can record them in a separate step after all processing steps have been recorded. I usually put boxes around the numbers as in figure 3-17 to distinguish them from the processing steps in case the steps overrun the process box. But boxing the numbers is optional.

Why list the numbers of the called modules? Because it makes them easy to find. Then, you can check them against the VTOC to make sure that all subordinate modules have been called. And you can easily refer to the documentation for any of the called modules without referring back to the VTOC.

Step 4—List the calling modules

Figure 3-20 is another example of a HIPO diagram. It is for module 200 in the VTOC for the edit-inventory-transactions program. It

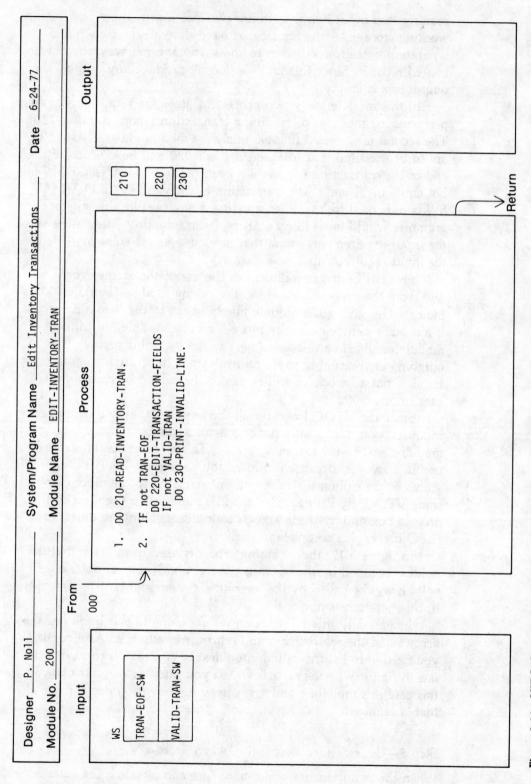

Figure 3-20 HIPO diagram for module 200 of the edit-inventory-transactions program

Designer ___P. Noll___   System/Program Name ___Edit Inventory Transactions___   Date ___6-24-77___

Module No. ___200___   Module Name ___EDIT-INVENTORY-TRAN___

Input

WS

| TRAN-EOF-SW |
| VALID-TRAN-SW |

From
000

Process

1. DO 210-READ-INVENTORY-TRAN.

2. IF not TRAN-EOF
        DO 220-EDIT-TRANSACTION-FIELDS
        IF not VALID-TRAN
            DO 230-PRINT-INVALID-LINE.

Output

210

220

230

Return

requires two input items; both are switches that will be described in working storage. Although I could have shown each switch in a separate box, I grouped them to show you another way of recording related records. Since this module doesn't produce any output, the output box is empty.

In this module, only two processing steps are required. The first performs the module for reading a transaction record (module 210). The second uses nested IF logic to show when modules 220 and 230 are to be executed. For instance, module 230 will be executed if the end of the transaction file has *not* been reached (TRAN-EOF-SW is not equal to Y) and if the transaction is *not* valid (VALID-TRAN-SW is not equal to Y). When creating a module like this, the programmer would most likely start by listing the processing steps since the input requirements aren't that obvious. As the steps are listed, the input requirements become clear.

This HIPO diagram illustrates the use of the arrows going to and from the process box. Here, the calling module (module 000) is indicated by giving the module number next to the incoming arrow. If a module can be called by more than one module, all calling module numbers can be listed next to the incoming arrow. The outgoing arrow simply says "return," since structured programming implies that all modules will return to the calling module, in this case, module 000.

Since the VTOC indicates all the modules that will call other modules, you don't really have to list the numbers of the calling modules next to the incoming arrow. This documentation can be useful, however, because it allows you to refer to the HIPO diagrams of the calling modules without referring to the more cumbersome VTOC. By listing called module numbers to the right of the process box and by using arrows to indicate calling modules, each HIPO diagram is complete in itself.

In figure 3-17, the incoming arrow is used to indicate that the module is called by the operating system (OS). Since module zero will always be called by the operating system and return control to it, this notation is optional.

Incidentally, the HIPO form we are using in this book has the arrows and the words *from* and *return* printed on it. As a result, you need only list the calling modules. In contrast, a form like the one in figure 3-18 has no arrows, so you must draw your own. In this case, a simple line and arrowhead as shown on our form is all that is required.

Step 5—Use extended description when necessary

When the requirements of a module are complicated, the *extended description* form is useful. In this case, the HIPO diagram should indicate the overall logic of the module, and the extended description form should be used to document the details.

To illustrate, consider the HIPO diagram in figure 3-21. It is part of the documentation for module 240 taken from the VTOC in figure 3-16. Basically, it says to move N into VALID-TRAN-SW if any field in the transaction record is invalid. It also says to move an asterisk (*) into the output record (ITL-LINE) to mark each invalid field. But what determines whether a field is valid or invalid?

This information is given by the extended description shown in figure 3-22. For instance, ITR-BRANCH-NO should be numeric and less than 25, and ITR-SALESMAN-NO should be numeric. In the reference column for these items, 3 is specified, meaning that this information pertains to step 3 in the process box of the HIPO diagram. Similarly, step 1 is specified next to the information for the part-number field. By using reference numbers, it is easy to relate the extended descriptions to the steps in the HIPO diagram.

As you can see from figure 3-22, the extended description form consists of areas for notes and areas for reference numbers. As a result, you can use it for whatever you want. Sometimes you will give a narrative description of processing requirements. Sometimes you will use it to record a table or to refer to a table. For instance, you might say, "Refer to the decision table labelled 'Credit Rules' for detailed logical requirements." In short, you can use this form to record or refer to any documentation that will help clarify the requirements of the module.

Step 6—Adjust the VTOC when necessary

As you document the modules of a program, you may find that there are problems with the VTOC. For instance, you may find that a module doesn't really require the subordinate modules shown on the VTOC. Or you may find that a module actually consists of two or more functions so it should be divided into two or more modules. Or you may find that it is impossible to document a module because it isn't really functional; that is, its processing requirements are unclear.

In cases like these, the programmer must modify the VTOC. Sometimes, this may mean an extensive modification. Sometimes it may be a simple matter of adding a few modules to the VTOC. In any case, the numbering scheme we use in this text will make it possible to change the VTOC without changing the names or numbers of other modules.

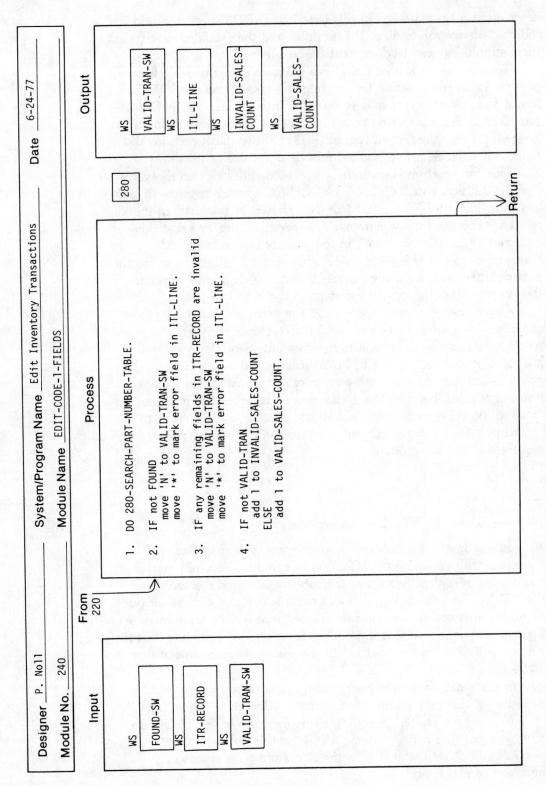

Figure 3-21 HIPO diagram for module 240 of the edit-inventory-transactions program

Designer	P. Noll	System/Program Name	Edit Inventory Transactions	Date	6-24-77
Module No.	240	Module Name	EDIT-CODE-1-FIELDS		

Notes	Ref.
Validity is:	
ITR-UPDATE-CODE — Must be 'C'	3
ITR-CUST-ORDER-NO — Any data	3
ITR-ORDER-DATE — Numeric with	3
ITR-ORDER-DAY — day less than 32	
ITR-ORDER-MONTH — month less than 13	
ITR-ORDER-YEAR — year = current year or current year - 1	
ITR-BRANCH-NO — Numeric and less than 25	3
ITR-SALESMAN-NO — Numeric	3
ITR-CUST-NO — Numeric	3
ITR-QUANTITY — Numeric	3
ITR-PART-NUMBER — Numeric with match in the valid-part-number file	1
NOTES:	
All numeric fields must be greater than zero.	

Notes	Ref.

Figure 3-22 Extended description for module 240 of the edit-inventory-transactions program

Chapter 3

```
1.  Open files.

2.  DO module-100
        UNTIL no more table records.

3.  DO module-200
        UNTIL no more transaction records.

4.  DO module-300.

5.  Close files.

6.  Stop run.
```

Figure 3-23   Strict pseudocode for module 000 of the edit-inventory-transactions program

Some Guidelines for Preparing HIPO Diagrams

When you start to prepare HIPO diagrams for your own programs, you'll probably find that a number of minor questions are raised. For instance, what level of detail should be shown in the process box? Or, in which module should a subfunction be placed if it could logically be placed in two or more different modules? The four subtopics that follow will give you some ideas that I hope will help you answer many of the questions that do come up.

Use pseudocode plus COBOL in the process box

In all of the HIPO diagrams shown so far, I have used a form of pseudocode in the process boxes. I say a form of pseudocode because COBOL names are used in these examples. In strict pseudocode, there would be no COBOL words, so the processing specifications for module 000 of the edit program would be something like what is shown in figure 3-23. If you compare this with the processing steps shown in figure 3-17, you can see that no COBOL words are used, so the pseudocode is not related to any one programming language.

To use strict pseudocode, you capitalize all structure words such as DO, UNTIL, IF, THEN, and ELSE. These words indicate the logical structure of the module. In contrast, all functions required by the module are described as clearly as possible in English. These words are written in lowercase letters.

Although some companies go out of their way to avoid the use of COBOL words in their HIPO diagrams, I think there is little point in this. If a program is definitely going to be written in COBOL, why not use COBOL data names and even COBOL verbs? In fact, in short modules, there is nothing wrong with using COBOL itself within the process box. Be careful, though. One thing you don't want to do is code the program twice, once in the HIPO diagram and again on the coding forms. So in general, resist the urge to code.

In most cases, I find that the combination of pseudocode and COBOL shown in figures 3-17, 3-20, and 3-21 is the most efficient. Here, the important file, record, and data names are created as part of the HIPO diagram. In particular, the actual COBOL names for files, control fields and switches are used. Also, the name of any module called by another module is quoted verbatim. This combination of pseudocode and COBOL will be used throughout the remainder of this book.

As in COBOL, indentation is used to make pseudocode easy to read and understand. For instance, the clauses in nested IF structures should be indented and aligned as shown in the examples in figures 3-20 and 3-21. Similarly, the UNTIL phrase should be indented from the start of the DO phrase as shown in figure 3-17. This corresponds closely to the proper use of indentation for COBOL code, as shown throughout this text.

Although we've shown how to mix capital and lowercase words, in practice, many programmers prefer to use all capitals in the process box of the HIPO diagram. In general, this causes no confusion. For instance,

```
1.   OPEN FILES.

2.   DO 100-LOAD-PART-NUMBER-TABLE
        UNTIL PART-NUMBER-EOF.

3.   DO 200-EDIT-INVENTORY-TRAN
        UNTIL TRAN-EOF.
```

is as easy to understand as the pseudocode in figure 3-17. So feel free to use all capitals if you prefer them to a combination of capital and lowercase words.

One question that comes up when using pseudocode in the process box is this: To what level should the logical details be recorded? For instance, figure 3-21 uses one search-table step and three IF structures to indicate the editing requirements of the entire module. When actually coding this module, however, many IF statements are likely to be required. As a result, the pseudocode could be taken to another level of detail as shown in figure 3-24.

```
1.  DO 280-SEARCH-PART-NUMBER-TABLE.

2.  IF not FOUND
        move 'N' to VALID-TRAN-SW
        move '*' to mark error field in ITL-LINE.

3.  IF ITR-UPDATE-CODE is invalid
        move 'N' to VALID-TRAN-SW
        move '*' to mark error field.

4.  IF ITR-ORDER-DATE is invalid
        move 'N' to VALID-TRAN-SW
        move '*' to mark error field.

5.  IF ITR-BRANCH-NO is invalid
        move 'N' to VALID-TRAN-SW
        move '*' to mark error field.

6.  IF ITR-SALESMAN-NO is invalid
        move 'N' to VALID-TRAN-SW
        move '*' to mark error field.

7.  IF ITR-CUST-NO is invalid
        move 'N' to VALID-TRAN-SW
        move '*' to mark error field.

8.  IF ITR-QUANTITY is invalid
        move 'N' to VALID-TRAN-SW
        move '*' to mark error field.

9.  IF not VALID-TRAN
        add 1 to INVALID-SALES-COUNT
    ELSE
        add 1 to VALID-SALES-COUNT.
```

Figure 3-24   Expanded pseudocode for module 240 of the edit-inventory-
transactions program

Is this documentation better than that of figure 3-21? I think the
answer is debatable. Both are acceptable because they clearly indicate the processing requirements for the module. Yet some would
argue that version 1 is better because it's simpler, while others would
argue that version 2 is better because it's a better guide for COBOL
coding. In practice, you, the programmer, must make these decisions. I think you'll find that in most cases you'll use pseudocode
that's closer to COBOL in the higher-level modules; in the lower-
level modules, you'll find it easier to summarize what processing

must be done. However, if you ever feel you need to refine the processing steps in order to better understand the processing requirements, by all means go to whatever level of detail you feel is required for clarity. Remember, clarity is the goal.

Keep the modules independent

As you create your HIPO diagrams, remember that the modules of a structured program must be independent. In theory, then, you should be able to document one module without referring to the HIPO diagrams for other modules. In other words, you shouldn't need to know what is happening in any of the other modules.

In practice, however, you will need to refer to other HIPO diagrams for the proper names of files, records, and fields. Also, you may want to check another module to see whether you remembered to set a switch or move a field or something like that. But that's all. If you find that you continually need to refer to the processing steps in one HIPO diagram in order to create another HIPO diagram, something's wrong. Either your modules aren't independent or your functions aren't clearly defined.

Move subfunctions down the line

Perhaps the most difficult task when creating HIPO diagrams is deciding in which module a subfunction should be placed. For instance, you know that a report-printing program like the reorder-listing program must count lines and reset the LINE-COUNT field to zero after page overflow. But subfunctions like these don't really require their own separate modules since they are not major functions and usually consist of just a line or two of code. So how do you decide in which existing module to place them?

Whenever you are in doubt as to the proper placement of a subfunction, I suggest moving the subfunction down the line in the VTOC. In figure 3-16, for example, you could count the number of valid and invalid transactions in either module 220 or in modules 240 and 250. Using the down-the-line guideline, modules 240 and 250 will be responsible for these subfunctions. Similarly, you should move subfunctions like resetting total fields down the line whenever you're in doubt about where they should go.

Remember, however, that decisions like these are debatable. So the main thing is to strive for consistency. If you develop a pattern for your decisions, like always moving subfunctions down the line, you will minimize clerical errors and simplify debugging. And remember, too, that this applies only to *subfunctions*; a major function should always have its own module, regardless of how few lines of coding it will require.

Document only the function named

Another point that should be emphasized is this: Only document the function described by the module name. In other words, never place a subfunction in a module where it doesn't belong just because you can't find a good place for it. It is better to add another module to the VTOC for a subfunction like this, even if it is only a few coding lines long, than to place it where you won't be able to find it later on.

With this in mind, you might object to the down-the-line guideline I just recommended. For example, since the program in figure 3-16 is supposed to count the number of input transactions read, the down-the-line rule will place the counting statement in module 210, the read-inventory-tran module. But doesn't this violate the principle of documenting only the function specified in the module name?

My answer here is to think of it as a convention. Whenever input or output records must be counted, it will be done in the associated read or write module. In other words, we'll agree that counting is included in the notion of reading or writing. In the long run, this convention will simplify module design, documentation, and coding.

Similarly, as you will see in topic 4, a report-printing program that prints group summary lines will often require subfunctions that (1) reset the total field to zero after printing, (2) set up fields for the first record of the next group, (3) increase the LINE-COUNT field as lines are printed, etc. Because it is usually hard to decide in which module these subfunctions should be placed, you should use the down-the-line principle. But this usually means that these subfunctions will end up in print or write modules. And isn't this misleading?

Again I say, think of it as a convention. Specifically, let's agree that a print module can include code that (1) formats the output line, (2) moves a proper spacing value into a space-control field, (3) calls a module to physically print a line, (4) increases the line-count field, (5) resets total fields to zero in preparation for the next group of records, and (6) sets up control or data fields in preparation for the next group of records. In some cases, you may even allow your print module to add totals for a group just printed to total fields for a group at a higher level. In other words, by convention we will allow a print module to do far more than its name implies.

Fortunately, the two conventions just discussed will help you decide where to place many common subfunctions. In addition, you may want to develop other conventions either on your own or in conjunction with other members in your programming group. In the absence of conventions, however, don't be misleading: only document the function named in the VTOC.

Understanding the Edit Program

In general, all structured programs are made up of two types of modules. The lower-level modules do most of the actual work required by the program such as reading input records, performing calculations, and formatting output records. So I call these *work modules*. In contrast, the upper-level modules that call two or more subordinate modules do little work. Their primary job is to control the execution of their subordinates. As a result, I call them *control modules*. Although a control module may do some work, it will be incidental to its control function.

In the VTOC in figure 3-16, modules 000, 100, 200, and 220 are the primary control modules. The other modules do most of the work. Module 230, as you will see, is primarily a work module even though it does control the execution of two subordinate I/O modules.

In some books, you will see control modules called *branch modules* because they are always part of a branchlike structure. Similarly, you will see work modules called *leaf modules* since they can be compared to leaves on the branches. Use whichever terminology you prefer, but be aware of the distinction between control and work modules since it is a useful one.

In general, you should be able to understand the operation of a structured program if you have the problem specifications, the VTOC, and the HIPO diagrams for the primary control modules. You shouldn't need to know much about the work modules since each one should represent a single, clearly defined function. Because I want you to understand the operation and documentation of the edit-inventory-transactions program, I'm now going to show you the HIPO diagrams for a few more of the key modules.

As you have seen in the HIPO diagram in figure 3-17, module 000 of the edit program performs module 100 until all part-number records have been read, performs module 200 until all transaction records have been read, and performs module 300 to print the total page. As you have seen in the HIPO diagram in figure 3-20, module 200 performs module 210 to read one transaction, performs module 220 to edit the transaction, and performs module 230 *if the transaction is not valid*. So now let's look at modules 210, 220, and 230.

The HIPO diagram for module 210 is shown in figure 3-25. It reads one transaction record and moves the value Y into TRAN-EOF-SW if the end-of-file record is read. This switch in turn is tested by module 200 before processing continues and by module 000 after

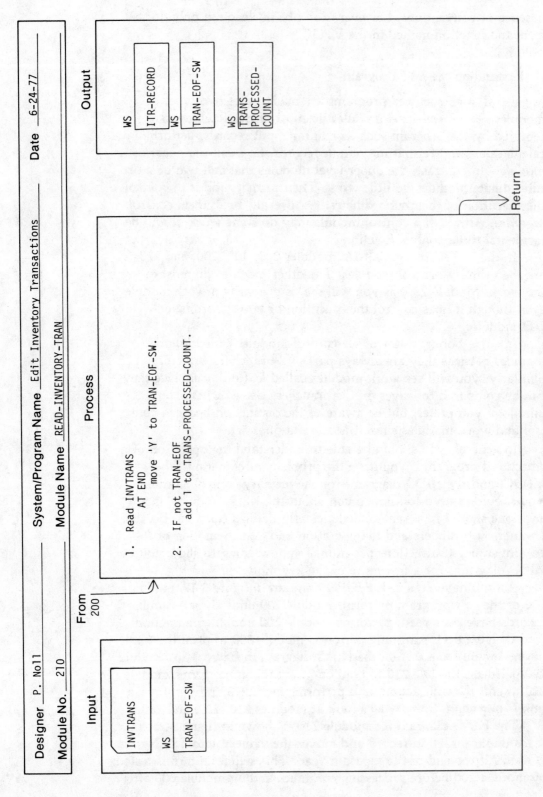

Figure 3-25 HIPO diagram for module 210 of the edit-inventory-transactions program

each execution of module 200. If the end-of-file record isn't read, module 210 adds one to TRANS-PROCESSED-COUNT for use by module 300.

The HIPO diagram for module 220 is shown in figure 3-26. In step 1, the value Y is moved to VALID-TRAN-SW. This means that module 220, 240 or 250 must change the switch to N if an invalid field is detected. In step 2, the invalid-transaction-line record (ITL-LINE) in working storage is cleared to spaces. In step 3, nested IF statements are used to determine whether module 240 or 250 is to be performed or whether the transaction code itself is invalid.

The HIPO diagram for module 230 is shown in figure 3-27. As I said, this is more of a work module than a control module. In step 1, it prepares the invalid-transaction-line record in working storage. In step 2, it performs module 260 if the output page is full. Then, in steps 3 and 4, the invalid-transaction-line record is moved to the print area and module 270 is performed. This causes the invalid-transaction line to be printed. Although a value could be added to LINE-COUNT in this module to keep track of the number of lines printed, I would move this subfunction down the line to the write-report-line module.

Can you understand the operation of the edit program now that you have seen the documentation for the primary modules? Because the HIPO diagrams are spread all over this topic, I have duplicated the processing steps for the major modules in figure 3-28. I hope this will make the documentation easier to follow.

If you are reviewing the documentation for someone else's program, a pseudocode summary of the control modules like the one in figure 3-28 is sometimes an aid to understanding. Similarly, if you are having trouble doing a VTOC design because you can't visualize how the control modules will work, a pseudocode summary on scratch paper can be helpful. In any event, studying figure 3-28 should help you understand the major processing done by the edit program. All modules not shown are simple control modules or straightforward work modules.

Discussion

I hope by now you can see the advantage of HIPO documentation over flowcharting. Without question, the HIPO diagram is much easier to create and maintain than a flowchart. And it is a much better guide to coding the program.

One criticism of HIPO documentation is that it is cumbersome. If you have a VTOC consisting of 20 modules, you will end up with at least 21 pages of documentation (1 VTOC and 20 IPOs). And if extended descriptions are used, it may be many more pages.

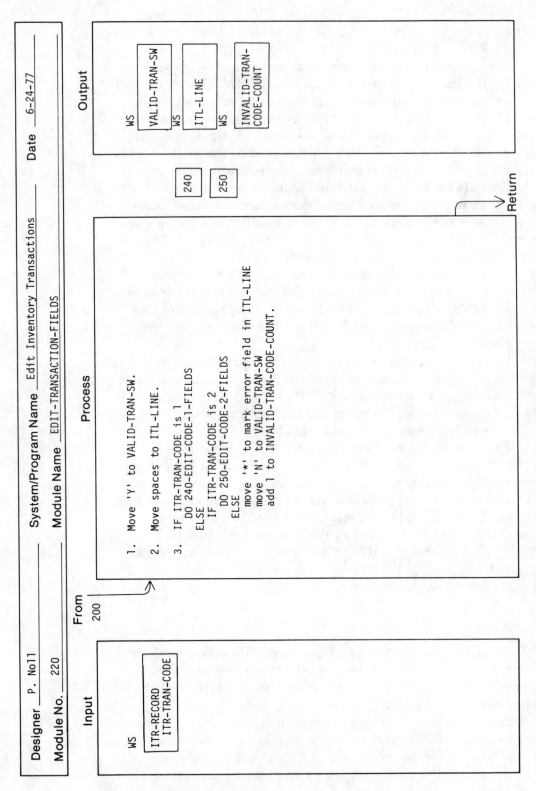

Figure 3-26 HIPO diagram for module 220 of the edit-inventory-transactions program

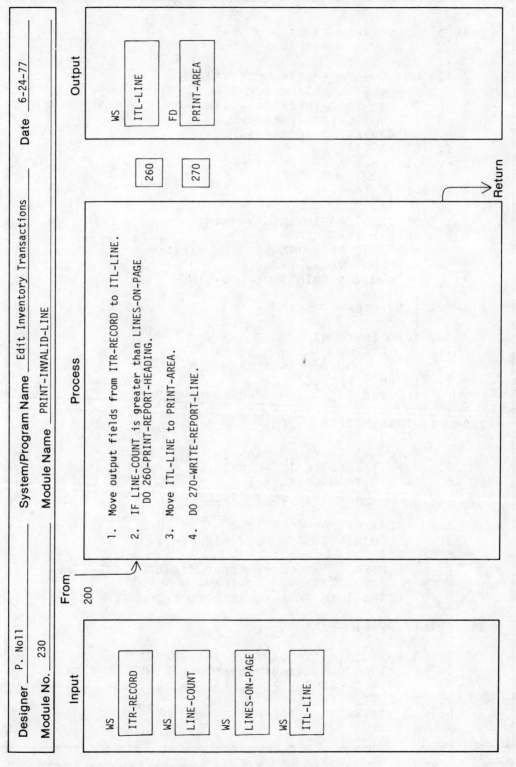

Figure 3-27 HIPO diagram for module 230 of the edit-inventory-transactions program

```
000-EDIT-INVENTORY-TRANS

    1.  Open files.
    2.  DO 100-LOAD-PART-NUMBER-TABLE
            UNTIL PART-NUMBER-EOF.
    3.  DO 200-EDIT-INVENTORY-TRAN
            UNTIL TRAN-EOF.
    4.  DO 300-PRINT-TOTAL-PAGE.
    5.  Close files.
    6.  Stop run.

200-EDIT-INVENTORY-TRAN

    1.  DO 210-READ-INVENTORY-TRAN.
    2.  IF not TRAN-EOF
            DO 220-EDIT-TRANSACTION-FIELDS
            IF not VALID-TRAN
                DO 230-PRINT-INVALID-LINE.

210-READ-INVENTORY-TRAN

    1.  Read INVTRANS
            AT END
                move 'Y' to TRAN-EOF-SW.
    2.  IF not TRAN-EOF
            add 1 to TRANS-PROCESSED-COUNT.

220-EDIT-TRANSACTION-FIELDS

    1.  Move 'Y' to VALID-TRAN-SW.
    2.  Move spaces to ITL-LINE.
    3.  IF ITR-TRAN-CODE is 1
            DO 240-EDIT-CODE-1-FIELDS
        ELSE
            IF ITR-TRAN-CODE is 2
                DO 250-EDIT-CODE-2-FIELDS
            ELSE
                move '*' to mark error field in ITL-LINE
                move 'N' to VALID-TRAN-SW
                add 1 to INVALID-TRAN-CODE-COUNT.

230-PRINT-INVALID-LINE

    1.  Move output fields from ITR-RECORD to ITL-LINE.
    2.  IF LINE-COUNT is greater than LINES-ON-PAGE
            DO 260-PRINT-REPORT-HEADING.
    3.  Move ITL-LINE to PRINT-AREA.
    4.  DO 270-WRITE-REPORT-LINE.
```

Figure 3-28 Pseudocode summary of key modules in the edit-inventory-transactions program

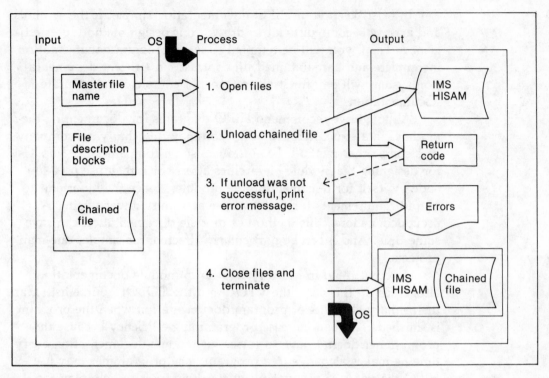

Figure 3-29   HIPO diagram with emphasis on graphics

Another criticism is directed at the detail shown on the diagrams. For instance, some HIPO courses recommend that arrows be used to show the relationships between the processing steps and input and output data. Thus, a HIPO chart may look like the one in figure 3-29. Here, black arrows are used to indicate calling modules, and white arrows are used to show the relationships between I/O and processing steps. Furthermore, additional boxes may be placed around two or more data items to show that a single arrow relates them to some processing step.

If you go to this level of detail on the HIPO diagram, I agree that HIPO is too cumbersome to be practical. By using the fancy arrows and additional boxes, the HIPO diagram is that much more difficult to create and that much more difficult to change. In addition, the extra detail doesn't make the diagram easier to understand; and it doesn't make the diagram a better guide for coding.

What I have presented in this topic, then, is a subset of HIPO documentation, a subset that is easy to create and maintain. So don't use arrows to show data relationships unless the module is unusually complex and you think the arrows will help you better understand the processing requirements. And then only use single line arrows, ones that are easy to draw and erase.

In brief, keep your HIPO documentation simple. If the symbols and arrows become difficult to draw, your design method loses efficiency. Then, you will be tempted to leave program documentation incomplete and unmaintained. In contrast, an efficient documentation system will pay for itself in terms of complete and accurate documentation.

Although we recommend HIPO diagrams for documenting the modules in a structured program, you may find that your company uses some other method. For instance, some companies use VTOCs for designing the module hierarchies after which they use pseudocode by itself for documenting the modules. Since the input and output requirements for each module are omitted when using pseudocode alone, this method of module documentation can save some time. And it can be particularly effective for simple, one-man projects.

A recent trend in industry is to drop module documentation altogether. In this case, the VTOC and the COBOL source listing are the primary elements of program documentation when the program is finished. This can increase programming efficiency because the programmer doesn't have to revise his module documentation every time he makes a change to a program. The programmer may use HIPO diagrams or pseudocode as working tools to help plan the coding that must be done. But after coding, these working tools are thrown away, and the COBOL code becomes the final module documentation—module documentation that is always up-to-date.

In any event, this book will teach you structured design and coding regardless of the method of module documentation that you end up using. In general, the principles you have just learned about recording input, output, and processing requirements and about using pseudocode will apply to any effective method of module documentation that you may come in contact with. So if you can create and use HIPO diagrams, you will have no trouble transferring this skill to other methods of module documentation.

Terminology

HIPO diagram
IPO diagram
IPO
pseudocode
extended description
work module
control module

branch module

leaf module

Objective

Given the problem definition for a program and the VTOC for its program design, create a HIPO diagram for any of the modules. If necessary, use the extended description form to document details.

Problems

1. Refer to the VTOC in figure 3-16 and the problem definition in figure 3-6.

    a. Document module 260.

    b. Document module 270.

    c. Document module 290.

    d. Document module 300.

Solutions

1. a. Figure 3-30 is an acceptable solution. Here FD is used to show that PRINT-AREA can be found in the Input-Output Section of the Data Division.

    b. Figure 3-31 is an acceptable solution. Note that the SPACE-CONTROL value is added to LINE-COUNT to keep track of the number of lines that have been printed on a page. Also notice that I have used COBOL itself to document this short module.

    c. Figure 3-32 is an acceptable solution. Here again, COBOL itself is used to describe the processing. Also note that resetting LINE-COUNT to zero has been moved down the line into this module.

    d. My documentation for module 300 is shown in figure 3-33. Because there are nine different print lines, I have summarized the pseudocode for the last eight lines in steps 5 and 6. Remember, you don't want to code the module twice. If it's straightforward, simplify. Step 5 means that for each output line, the output area must be formatted and a proper character must be moved into the SPACE-CONTROL field. Step 6 means that module 270 should be executed after the preparation of each output line.

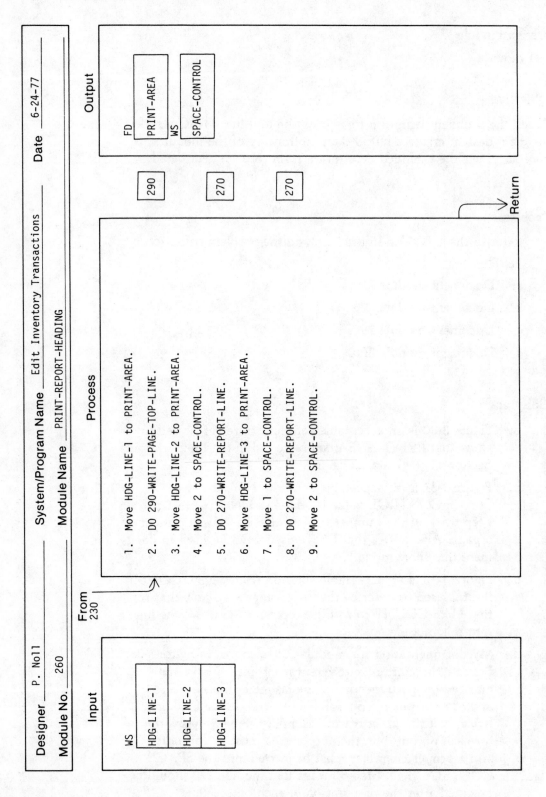

Figure 3-30 HIPO diagram for module 260 of the edit-inventory-transactions program

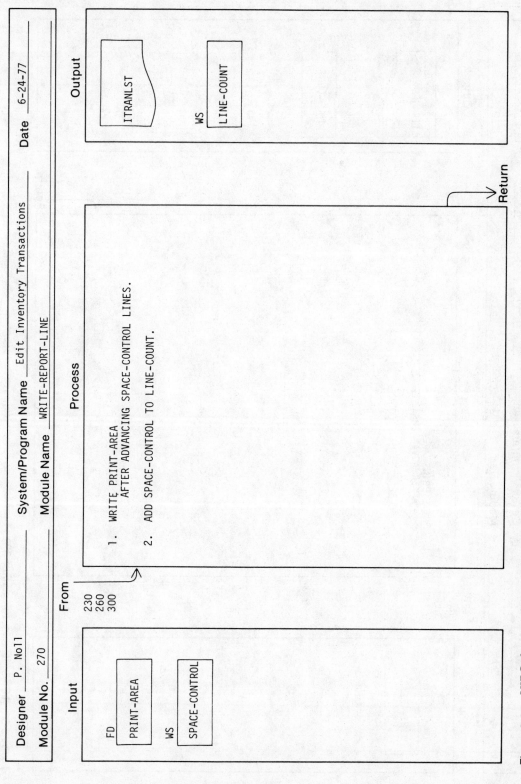

Figure 3-31 HIPO diagram for module 270 of the edit-inventory-transactions program

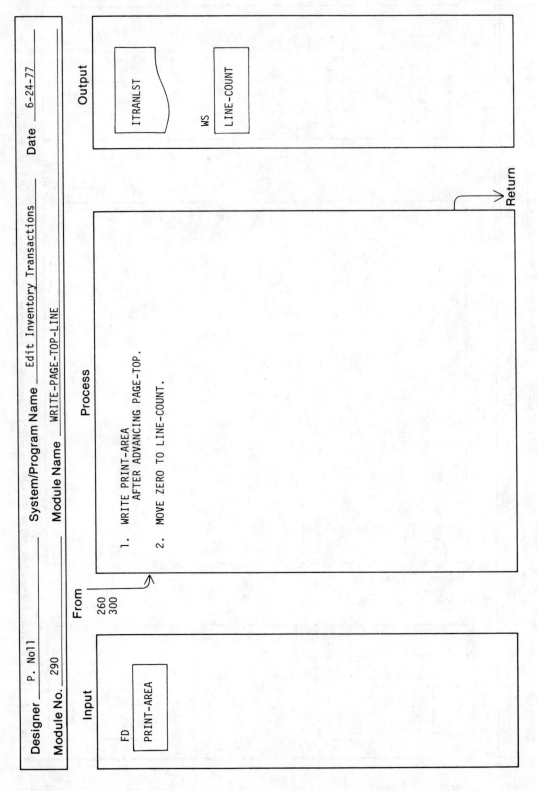

Figure 3-32 HIPO diagram for module 290 of the edit-inventory-transactions program

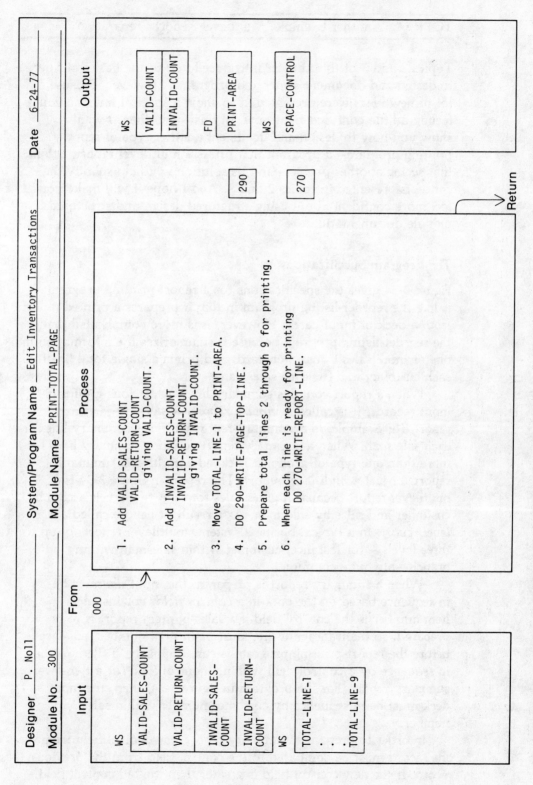

Figure 3-33 HIPO diagram for module 300 of the edit-inventory-transactions program

---

TOPIC 4   Another Example: Multilevel Report Preparation

Topics 2 and 3 of this chapter introduced you to the basics of how
to design and document structured programs. However, because a
lot of new ideas were presented in so short a space, I imagine you're
feeling a little confused right now. In this topic, then, I want to
show you how to design and document another type of report-
printing program—a program that prints a multilevel report. I think
that seeing another problem and its solution will help solidify the
concepts presented in topics 2 and 3. And I hope it will make you
feel more confident about using structured design and structured
module documentation.

The Program Specifications

Figure 3-34 gives the specifications for a report-printing program. It
is like the reorder-listing program in that it prepares a printed report
from a deck of input cards. However, it is more complicated than
the reorder-listing program because it summarizes the information in
one or more sales transaction cards and prints a single total line for
each customer and for each salesman.

When a report contains summary lines for various groups of
input records, it is called *summary report*. A sales-by-salesman
report, for example, is a summary report with one summary line for
each salesman. When a summary report contains summary lines for
more than one type of group, it is called a multilevel summary
report, or just a *multilevel report*. The report in figure 3-34 is a
multilevel report because it gives sales totals at two levels—sales by
customer and sales by salesman. As a result, it can be called a *two-
level report*. In a typical business system, multilevel reports of up to
three levels— for instance, customer within salesman within
branch—are quite common.

When a summary report is prepared, the input file must be
in sequence based on the data in a *control field*. For instance,
item number is the control field if a sales-by-item report is to be
prepared, so the transaction file must be in item-number sequence
before the report-printing program is run. Similarly, a file must be
in sequence by a control field within a control field for a two-level
summary report. For the program in figure 3-34, then, the input
deck must be in sequence by customer number within salesman
number.

In order to prepare a summary report, the control field from
one record must be compared to the control field from the previous
record. If the new control field is greater than the old control field,

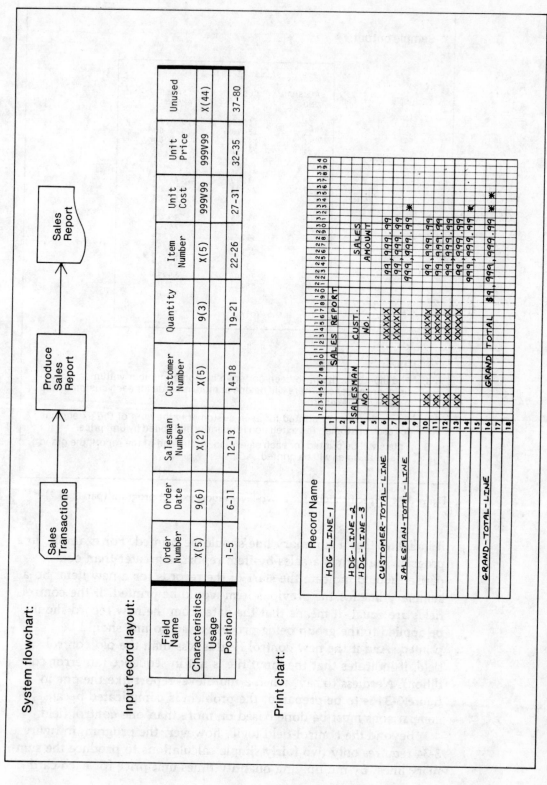

Figure 3-34 Specifications for a two-level report extract program (part 1 of 2)

Sample output:

```
                    SALES  REPORT

   SALESMAN      CUST.            SALES
   NO.           NO.              AMOUNT

      31          1052         1,376.75
      31         13498         1,024.00
      31         19763         4,875.00
      31         24291           188.75
                              7,464.50 ※

      37          1940         1,125.00
      37         22341           913.00
                              2,038.00 ※

      44         26888           295.25
      44         27430           175.43
      44         31284         2,257.39
      44         32290           874.50
      44         32292         1,573.20
      44         33480           985.20
      44         49200         1,354.95
      44         58111           540.75
                              8,056.67 ※

         GRAND  TOTAL     $17,559.17 ※ ※
```

Narrative:

1. The input records have been sorted in customer-number within salesman-number sequence. There will be one or more records for each customer line printed on the report.

2. The sales amount printed for each customer is the sum of the extensions for each customer; the extension is quantity multiplied by unit price.

3. Totals will be printed for each salesman. At the end of the report, the grand total of all sales will be printed.

Figure 3-34 Specifications for a two-level report extract program (part 2 of 2)

it indicates that a summary line should be printed. For example, in a program that prints a sales-by-item report, a greater-than comparison would indicate the start of the records for a new item. So a summary line for the previous item would be printed. If the control fields are equal, it means that the data from the new record should be applied to the group being processed, so no line should be printed. And if the new control field is less than the old control field, it indicates that the input file is not in sequence (an error condition). Needless to say, when a multilevel report like the one in figure 3-34 is to be prepared, the problem is complicated because comparisons must be done based on more than one control field.

Beyond the control-field logic, however, the program in figure 3-34 requires only two fairly simple calculations to produce the summary lines. By multiplying quantity times unit price for each card

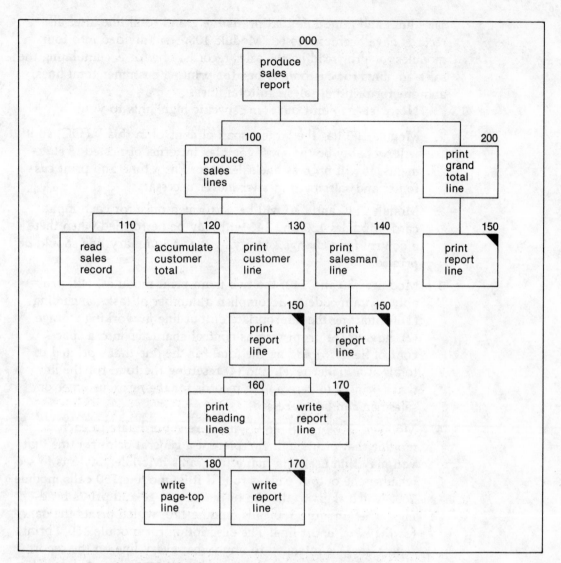

Figure 3-35 Complete VTOC for the two-level report extract program

and accumulating the total sales amount for each customer, the customer lines can be printed. By accumulating the customer totals for each salesman, the salesman total lines can be printed. Keep in mind that only one line is printed for each customer or salesman, regardless of the number of input cards for that customer or salesman.

The VTOC

Figure 3-35 shows a VTOC for the sales-report program. At level 1, it requires only two modules: the main module that produces the sales lines and a module that prints the grand total line after all records have been processed. Module 100 is subdivided into four modules: one for reading the sales records, one for accumulating the sales amounts for customers, one for printing customer total lines, and one for printing salesman total lines.

Now, let me point out some specific highlights to you:

1. Module 100 has the largest span of control in this VTOC, so it will probably be the most complex in terms of nested IF statements. It will process one sales record at a time and print customer and salesman lines whenever necessary.

2. Modules 110 and 120 will be performed once for each input card. Modules 130 and 140 will only be performed when there's a control-field change, signifying that a summary line should be printed.

3. Modules 130 and 140, the two main print modules, will probably contain code to accomplish a number of tasks, including (1) formatting the appropriate output line in working storage, (2) moving the proper forms-control character into a space-control field, (3) adding the total for the line that's printed to totals at a higher level, and (4) resetting the total for the line that's printed to zero so the records for the next customer or salesman can be processed.

4. Modules 150 through 180, which are subordinate to each module that prints a line, represent a general print routine that you may find useful in many programs. Module 150 tests to see whether the output page is full. If it is, module 150 calls module 160, which skips to the top of the next page and prints headings. Then module 150 calls module 170, which prints the data for the next report line. The description for module 150, "print report line," is intended to imply that every line on the report will be physically printed by the execution of this module. This module is particularly useful in programs that print many different types of lines.

5. Rather than show modules 160, 170, and 180 every time I use module 150, I omit module 150's subordinates after I've shown them once. This makes the VTOC easier to read and change. Understand, however, that module 150 will always have modules 160 and 170 subordinate to it even when they're not shown. And module 160 will always call modules 180 and 170.

Another solution

A workable VTOC for a program usually won't spring fullblown into your mind; it will be the result of thought, time, and expe-

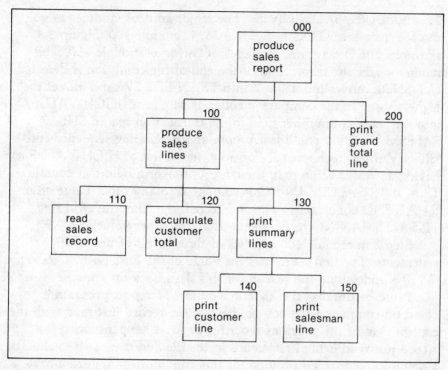

Figure 3-36   An acceptable structure for the extract program

rience. Furthermore, you'll usually be able to come up with more than one workable VTOC for any program you design. For example, figure 3-36 shows the basic structure of another solution to the problem in figure 3-34. Here, module 130 controls the printing of the detail lines. Again, a general print routine (modules 150 through 180 in figure 3-35) would be used subordinate to modules 140, 150, and 200.

For a simple two-level report, the extra control level in figure 3-36 isn't really necessary. After all, the control span of module 100 in figure 3-35 is only four. However, as you go on to more complicated problems that print totals at three or more levels, you might find the VTOC in figure 3-36 much easier to work with. To adapt it to more complex problems, you would simply put one module subordinate to module 130 for each different type of body line (not heading or total lines) that is to be printed.

The IPOs

In order to understand the logic needed to code a multilevel-report program, you must study the IPOs. So let's look now at the IPOs for the control modules in the sales-report program.

100-PRODUCE-SALES-LINES   The major control module, as you can see from the VTOC in figure 3-35, is module 100. Figure 3-37 shows its HIPO diagram. In step 1, it performs module 110. This module reads one record and, if the end-of-file condition is detected (AT END), moves the value Y into TRAN-EOF-SW and moves the highest value in the computer's collating sequence (HIGH-VALUE) into the salesman-number field in the transaction record (TR-SALESMAN-NO). You'll learn more about collating sequence and HIGH-VALUE in chapter 5. For now, just think of HIGH-VALUE as having a greater value than the largest number a field can contain. Thus, if TR-SALESMAN-NO is compared to any other value after the AT END condition has been detected, the computer will find TR-SALESMAN-NO to be greater than the other value.

Step 2 in module 100 consists of three levels of nested IF statements. The first level tests the value of the FIRST-RECORD-SW. To understand the reason for this, let's back up a moment.

I said before that the logic in a summary report program is based on comparing the control field of the record just read with the control field of the previous record. But what happens when the record just read is the first record in the file and there is no value for a previous record? To provide for this condition, you need a first-record switch. As you can see from the IPO, when the switch is on, the control-field values in the transaction (TR-SALESMAN-NO and TR-CUSTOMER-NO) are moved to two working-storage fields (OLD-SALESMAN-NO and OLD-CUSTOMER-NO). These working-storage fields, or holding fields, always contain the values of the control fields of the previous record. Thus, these are the fields that are compared to the control fields in the transaction just read to determine what further processing should be done.

If the first-record switch is on, it is turned off after the holding fields are set up and step 2 is finished. Otherwise, the program executes the ELSE portion of the first IF statement in step 2. In this case, if TR-SALESMAN-NO is greater than OLD-SALESMAN-NO, the transaction marks both a new salesman and a new customer. So customer and salesman total lines are printed for the previous customer and salesman by modules 130 and 140, and the holding fields in working-storage are adjusted. If TR-CUSTOMER-NO is greater than OLD-CUSTOMER-NO, the total line for the previous customer is printed by module 130, and only the customer holding field is adjusted. This ends step 2.

You may have noticed that step 2 doesn't indicate what should be done if the transaction control fields are equal to the holding fields. This is taken care of in step 3 when module 120 is executed. In addition, step 2 doesn't indicate what should be done if the transaction control fields are less than the holding fields, thus indicating

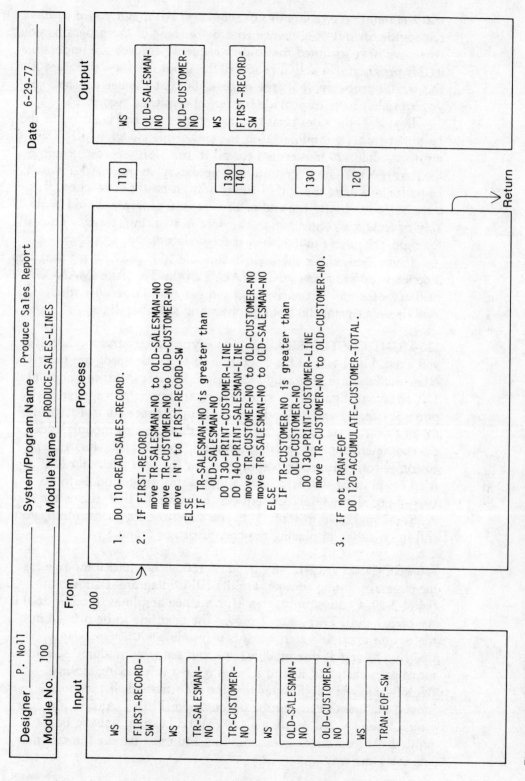

Figure 3-37 HIPO diagram for module 100 of the produce-sales-report program

that the input records are out of sequence. Although you may have
to provide for out-of-sequence records in some of the programs you
write, we have assumed that out-of-sequence records are impossible
in this program. (In actual practice, the input file for a program like
this would probably be a tape or disk file that has been sorted, so
you wouldn't have to provide for out-of-sequence records.)

In step 3, the sales total for the record just read is added to the
customer total by module 120 if the end-of-file switch is off. This
means module 120 is executed for all transaction records including
the first record. The IF condition is necessary so module 120 won't
be performed after the end-of-file condition has been reached. If it
were performed after the end of the file, the program would probably operate a second time on the data in working storage. Thus,
the report wouldn't match the expected output.

If you desk check the logic in module 100, you will see that step
2 depends upon having HIGH-VALUE in the TR-SALESMAN-NO
field after the end of the file has been reached. Otherwise, this
module won't print the last customer and salesman lines.

130-PRINT-CUSTOMER-LINE   Once you understand module 100,
you should understand the operation of the entire program since the
other modules are primarily work modules. For instance, module
130, shown in figure 3-38, simply formats the output line (step 1),
prints it (steps 2 and 3), and sets the proper space-control value for
the next line to be printed (step 4). In addition, this module adds
the customer total to the salesman total (step 5) and returns the
customer total to zero in preparation for the next customer line
(step 6). In other words, I have allowed this print module to do
everything remotely associated with printing the line; this is the convention I suggested in topic 3. If you don't use this convention, you
will have difficulty placing the code for steps 5 and 6.

150-PRINT-REPORT-LINE   Module 150 is the control module for
the general printing routine, and its HIPO diagram is shown in
figure 3-39. Quite simply, step 1 prints heading lines (module 160) if
the page is full. Then, step 2 moves the next line to be printed into
the output area, and step 3 prints it (module 170).

By looking at this module, you can see why module 130 must
move each customer line to a holding area in working storage
(NEXT-REPORT-LINE) after the line is formatted. If the module
moved the line directly to the output area (PRINT-AREA), the line
would be destroyed if module 150 caused heading lines to be
printed. As you might guess, module 140 must handle the salesman
line the same way.

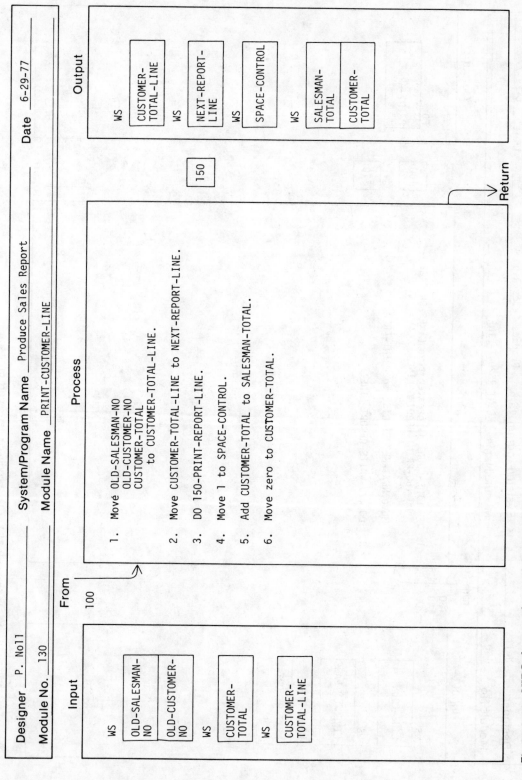

Designer P. Noll

Module No. 130

System/Program Name Produce Sales Report

Module Name PRINT-CUSTOMER-LINE

Date 6-29-77

Input

WS

| OLD-SALESMAN-NO |
| OLD-CUSTOMER-NO |

WS

| CUSTOMER-TOTAL |

WS

| CUSTOMER-TOTAL-LINE |

From

100

Process

1. Move OLD-SALESMAN-NO
   OLD-CUSTOMER-NO
   CUSTOMER-TOTAL
       to CUSTOMER-TOTAL-LINE.

2. Move CUSTOMER-TOTAL-LINE to NEXT-REPORT-LINE.

3. DO 150-PRINT-REPORT-LINE.

4. Move 1 to SPACE-CONTROL.

5. Add CUSTOMER-TOTAL to SALESMAN-TOTAL.

6. Move zero to CUSTOMER-TOTAL.

150

Return

Output

WS

| CUSTOMER-TOTAL-LINE |

WS

| NEXT-REPORT-LINE |

WS

| SPACE-CONTROL |

WS

| SALESMAN-TOTAL |
| CUSTOMER-TOTAL |

Figure 3-38 HIPO diagram for module 130 of the produce-sales-report program

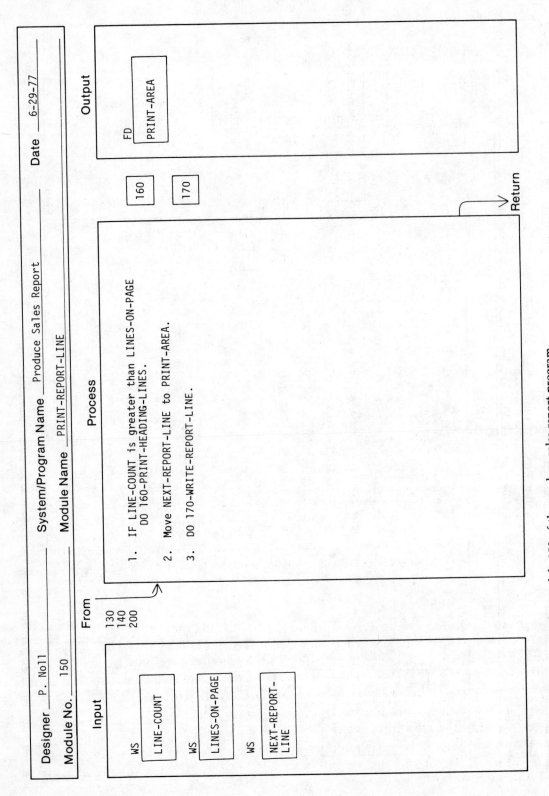

Figure 3-39 HIPO diagram for module 150 of the produce-sales-report program

```
000-PRODUCE-SALES-REPORT

   1.  Open files.
   2.  DO 100-PRODUCE-SALES-LINE
          UNTIL TRAN-EOF.
   3.  DO 200-PRINT-GRAND-TOTAL-LINE.
   4.  Close files.
   5.  Stop run.

100-PRODUCE-SALES-LINE

   1.  DO 110-READ-SALES-RECORD.
   2.  IF FIRST-RECORD
          move TR-SALESMAN-NO to OLD-SALESMAN-NO
          move TR-CUSTOMER-NO to OLD-CUSTOMER-NO
          move 'N' to FIRST-RECORD-SW
       ELSE
          IF TR-SALESMAN-NO is greater than OLD-SALESMAN-NO
             DO 130-PRINT-CUSTOMER-LINE
             DO 140-PRINT-SALESMAN-LINE
             move TR-CUSTOMER-NO to OLD-CUSTOMER-NO
             move TR-SALESMAN-NO to OLD-SALESMAN-NO
          ELSE
             IF TR-CUSTOMER-NO is greater than OLD-CUSTOMER-NO
                DO 130-PRINT-CUSTOMER-LINE
                move TR-CUSTOMER-NO to OLD-CUSTOMER-NO.
   3.  IF not TRAN-EOF
          DO 120-ACCUMULATE-CUSTOMER-TOTAL.

110-READ-SALES-RECORD

   1.  Read TRANFILE
          AT END
             move 'Y' to TRAN-EOF-SW
             move HIGH-VALUE to TR-SALESMAN-NO.
```

Figure 3-40 Pseudocode summary of key modules in the produce-sales-report program

Pseudocode summary

To help you understand the overall operation of this program, I
have isolated the pseudocode for modules 000, 100, and 110 in
figure 3-40. These three modules contain all of the control code and
they take care of all necessary changes in control fields and switches.
As I've mentioned before, a pseudocode summary of key modules
can help you understand someone else's program and can help you
check out the flow of control between modules in your own programs. In addition, many programming shops don't use HIPO
diagrams, but they are almost certain to use pseudocode in some
form or another.

Discussion

Now that you have seen the VTOC and IPOs for another typical business program, I hope you feel more confident of your own ability to design and document structured programs. Maybe it will help you to know that you can adapt the VTOCs and IPOs you've seen in the last three topics to a wide range of report-preparation programs. For example, all single-level report-printing programs will have a basic structure like the one for the reorder-listing program in figure 3-5. And all multilevel report-printing programs will have a structure similar to that in figure 3-35 or 3-36. Likewise, the control logic for all summary report-printing programs will be similar to that in the sales-report program. In fact, in some cases the logic may be so similar that you'll be able to transfer the IPOs for the control modules from one program to another simply by changing procedure and data names.

This, then, is a major advantage of structured programming. Because all programs are made up of independent modules, you don't have to start every new program from scratch. Instead, you can begin by asking yourself how it is like other programs you have written and go on from there. Although all the VTOCs and IPOs you've seen thus far have been for report-printing programs, chapter 7 will present programs for sequential tape and disk files, including file-creation and update programs. So by the time you finish this book, you will have a number of sample programs you can use as models when you design and document programs of your own.

Although I realize that this is a difficult chapter for the novice programmer, you should now be able to start to use the important techniques of structured design and documentation. If you have any doubts, I think the problems for this topic will give you more confidence. Then, as you get more experience and as you learn more about COBOL coding, you will gain proficiency in structured design and documentation. By the time you complete this book, you should be able to create VTOCs and IPOs for a wide range of programming problems.

Terminology

summary report

multilevel report

two-level report

control field

Objectives

1. Given the specifications for a programming problem, create an acceptable VTOC for it.

2. Given the problem definition for a program and the VTOC for its program design, create a HIPO diagram for any of the modules. If necessary, use the extended description form to document the details. (This is the same objective given for topic 3 of this chapter. But you should now be able to document the modules for a wider range of programs.)

Problems

1. (Objective 1) Figure 3-41 presents a programming problem. This program is supposed to print an aged trial balance from a file of unpaid invoice cards. Each card represents one unpaid invoice. The main problem of the program is determining the age of each unpaid invoice; that is, whether it is current (less than 30 days old), over 30 days old, over 60 days old, or over 90 days old.
   Create a VTOC for this program.

2. (Objective 2) Figure 3-42 is a VTOC for problem 1 above. Using this VTOC and the program specifications in figure 3-41, document the following modules using pseudocode:

   a. Module 000
   b. Module 200
   c. Module 210
   d. Module 220
   e. Module 230
   f. Module 240

Solutions

1. Figure 3-42 is an acceptable solution. Before the customer lines can be written, there must be a module that finds out what the current date is. After the customer lines have been written, there must be a module to print the total line. (Did you use the refined reorder-listing VTOC and the two-level-report VTOC as models for creating this VTOC?)

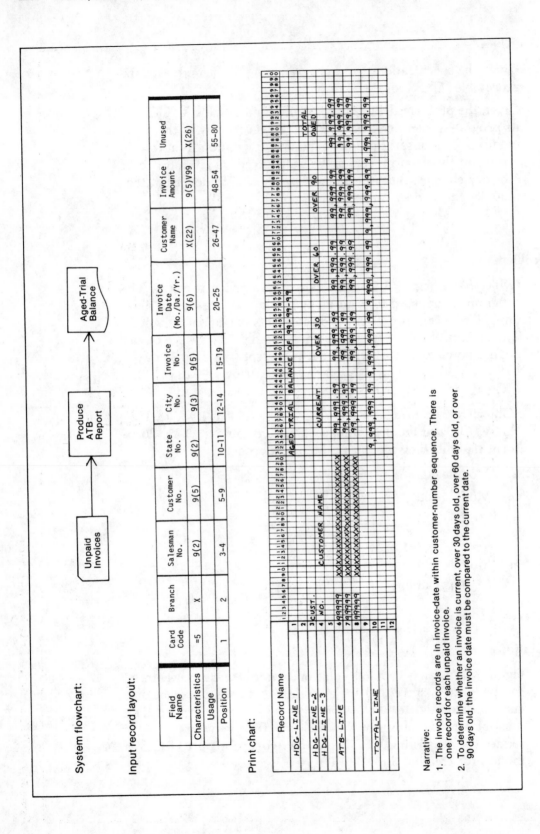

System flowchart:

Input record layout:

Print chart:

Narrative:

1. The invoice records are in invoice-date within customer-number sequence. There is one record for each unpaid invoice.

2. To determine whether an invoice is current, over 30 days old, over 60 days old, or over 90 days old, the invoice date must be compared to the current date.

Figure 3-41   Specifications for the aged-trial-balance program

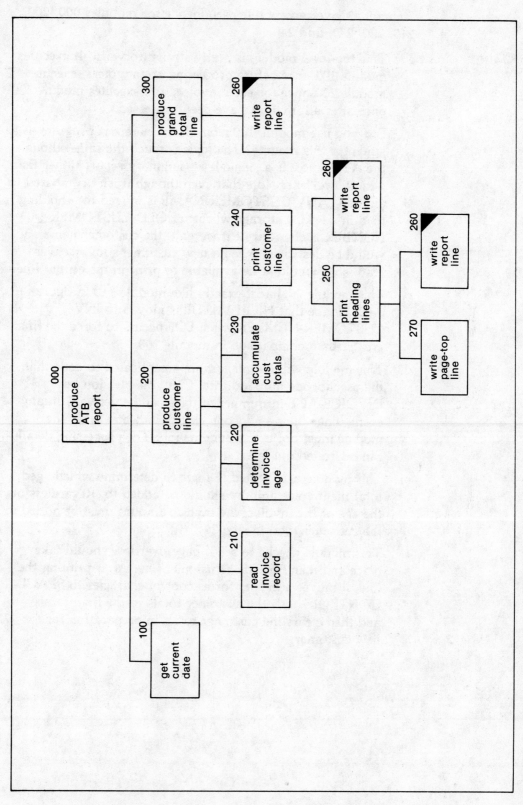

Figure 3-42 VTOC for the aged-trial-balance program

2. Figure 3-43 gives acceptable pseudocode for modules 000, 200, 210, 220, 230, and 240.

   a. This top-level module is pretty straightforward. It executes module 100 once before processing any invoices, executes module 200 once for each invoice, and executes module 300 once after all invoices have been processed.

   b. Did you use module 100 from the sales-report program as a guide for this module? The logic is much the same, though the ATB report is a single-level summary report rather than a multilevel one. Note that even though it isn't compared to anything, INV-CUSTOMER-NAME is moved to a holding field in working storage whenever OLD-CUSTOMER-NUMBER is changed. If it weren't, the customer name would be destroyed when a new customer's invoice was read, so it wouldn't be available to print in the output line.

   c. This module is almost exactly like module 110 in figure 3-40. Notice that HIGH-VALUE is moved to INV-CUSTOMER-NUMBER when EOF occurs to force the final greater-than comparison in module 200.

   d. This module will be much more complicated to code than the pseudocode may indicate. Can you envision how INVOICE-AGE in number of days can be derived? In any event, since the pseudocode clearly indicates what the module must do, it has done its job. The processing details can be ironed out later.

   e. This module uses nested IF logic to determine which aged total the invoice amount should be added to. Regardless of the age of the invoice, the invoice amount must be added to the customer total in step 2.

   f. This module checks to see if page overflow should take place and then formats a customer line. After printing the line, it moves a proper forms-control character to SPACE-CONTROL, adds the customer totals to the final totals, and then clears the customer totals in preparation for the new customer.

```
000-PRODUCE-ATB-REPORT

    1.  Open files.
    2.  DO 100-GET-CURRENT-DATE.
    3.  DO 200-PRODUCE-CUSTOMER-LINE
            UNTIL INVOICE-EOF.
    4.  DO 300-PRODUCE-GRAND-TOTAL-LINE.
    5.  Close files.
    6.  Stop run.

200-PRODUCE-CUSTOMER-LINE

    1.  DO 210-READ-INVOICE-RECORD.
    2.  IF FIRST-RECORD
            move INV-CUSTOMER-NUMBER to OLD-CUSTOMER-NUMBER
            move INV-CUSTOMER-NAME   to OLD-CUSTOMER-NAME
            move 'N' to FIRST-RECORD-SW
        ELSE
            IF INV-CUSTOMER-NUMBER is greater than OLD-CUSTOMER-NUMBER
                DO 240-PRINT-CUSTOMER-LINE
                move INV-CUSTOMER-NUMBER to OLD-CUSTOMER-NUMBER
                move INV-CUSTOMER-NAME   to OLD-CUSTOMER-NAME.
    3.  IF not INVOICE-EOF
            DO 220-DETERMINE-INVOICE-AGE
            DO 230-ACCUMULATE-CUSTOMER-TOTALS.

210-READ-INVOICE-RECORD

    1.  Read INVFILE
            AT END
                move 'Y' to INVOICE-EOF-SW
                move HIGH-VALUE to INV-CUSTOMER-NUMBER.

220-DETERMINE-INVOICE-AGE

    1.  Determine INVOICE-AGE in number of days based on the current
            date and INV-DATE.

230-ACCUMULATE-CUST-TOTALS

    1.  IF INVOICE-AGE is less than 31
            add INV-AMOUNT to CUST-CURRENT-TOTAL
        ELSE
            IF INVOICE-AGE is less than 61
                add INV-AMOUNT to CUST-OVER-30-TOTAL
            ELSE
                IF INVOICE-AGE is less than 91
                    add INV-AMOUNT to CUST-OVER-60-TOTAL
                ELSE
                    add INV-AMOUNT to CUST-OVER-90-TOTAL.
    2.  Add INV-AMOUNT to CUST-TOTAL-OWED.

240-PRINT-CUSTOMER-LINE

    1.  IF LINE-COUNT is greater than LINES-ON-PAGE
            DO 250-PRINT-HEADING-LINES.
    2.  Move OLD-CUSTOMER-NUMBER to ATB-CUSTOMER-NUMBER.
    3.  Move OLD-CUSTOMER-NAME   to ATB-CUSTOMER-NAME.
    4.  Move the customer totals to the proper positions in the ATB line.
    5.  Move ATB-LINE to PRINT-AREA.
    6.  DO 260-WRITE-REPORT-LINE.
    7.  Move 1 to SPACE-CONTROL.
    8.  Add the customer totals to the corresponding final totals.
    9.  Move zero to the customer totals.
```

Figure 3-43   Pseudocode for modules 000, 200, 210, 220, 230, and 240 of the ATB
program

4

Diagnostics and Debugging

Although the emphasis thus far has been on design and coding, these are only two parts of the programmer's job. Before a program is ready for use, the source code must be keypunched into a source deck, the source deck must be compiled without errors, thus creating an object program, and the object program must be tested to make sure it does what is intended. In actual practice, a programmer usually desk checks his program before it is keypunched. Then, he corrects diagnostic messages until the compilation process detects no errors. Finally, he tests the program on data that has been prepared earlier. If any problems (bugs) are detected, he debugs the program until no more errors can be found.

In chapter 10, you will learn about the eight phases that a programmer goes through in developing a program. Right now, though, you need to know more about desk checking, correcting diagnostics, testing, and debugging. As a result, topic 1 of this chapter covers desk checking and diagnostics; topic 2 covers testing and debugging.

TOPIC 1 Desk Checking and Diagnostics

A programmer normally *desk checks* his program before keypunching. This saves computer time and programmer time because desk

225

checking almost always catches an error or two and thus saves a compilation or a test run.

Before you have your program keypunched, then, you should go over your coding forms several times, desk checking them for a different type of error each time through. Here are some guidelines on what to look for:

1. Check for completeness and the spelling of reserved words. Are all required division, section, and paragraph names present, and are they spelled correctly? A misspelled division name (such as ENVIROMNENT DIVISION), a missing section name (such as FILE SECTION), or a missing dash in a paragraph name (such as 150-WRITE REPORT-LINE) can lead to dozens of diagnostics in a long program. Likewise, misspelling a reserved word like STANDARD in the LABEL RECORDS clause will lead to a program bug.

2. Check each statement for punctuation and spacing. Is the end of each statement or series of statements marked by a period? Are there spaces between data names, literals, and reserved words? Is every non-numeric literal enclosed in quotation marks?

3. Check all file, record, data, and procedure names used in the statements of the Procedure Division to be sure they are defined elsewhere in the program. You can often catch a misspelled name this way.

4. Sketch record layouts as described by the PICTUREs of your program and compare them to the layouts given in the problem definition. Be sure the I/O work areas are the proper size for the actual records.

5. The initial data in your working-storage fields, print line areas, and so on, may be important. If so, you must define them with an initial value or else code instructions to set or reset the values in these areas. Check to make sure that these values are properly established.

6. Check column 7 of each statement to make sure it is blank or contains an asterisk. If any other character is punched in this column, it can lead to diagnostics.

7. If you want the keypuncher to punch the same data in the same columns of several statements (such as punching PIC in columns 32-34 of each data description line), be sure to indicate it clearly on your coding forms. Otherwise, you may end up with a stack of cards that have blanks where data should be punched.

8. Although you should have used your HIPO diagrams or pseudocode summaries as guides for your coding, this is a good time to compare your code with your module documentation.

You may find that you overlooked something. Maybe you've left out a step. Maybe your code doesn't correspond to the processing intended by your pseudocode. In any event, if you've taken the time to prepare complete module documentation, it's worth double-checking to make sure that your coding follows it.

When you have checked for errors in this manner, your program is ready for keypunching. Unfortunately, keypunching provides another opportunity for errors to be entered into the source code, even when the cards are key verified after they are punched. For instance, you may discover later that your Us look like Vs to the keypunch and verifier operators or that the way you write a 5 is mistaken for an S. Rather than try to detect errors like these before compilation, however, most programmers let the compiler do this kind of checking for them.

Compiler Output

When a program is compiled, a number of different types of output can be printed as part of the *compiler output*. Three of the most common types are illustrated in figure 4-1 (parts 1-6). They are (1) the source listing, (2) the cross-reference listing, and (3) the diagnostic listing. Figure 4-1 illustrates the output from an OS System/360-370 compiler, but the DOS output is almost identical to that shown.

The *source listing* is shown in parts 1-4. This is primarily a listing of the source deck. On the far left of the listing is a column of statement numbers generated by the compiler. Thus, each source statement of the program can be referred to by a statement number from 1 through 202.

Between the statement number column and the program listing are three spaces. If a card is out of sequence, two asterisks print in this area. For instance, there is one sequence error (indicated in statement number 188) in part 4 of the listing.

The *cross-reference listing* (part 5) is a listing of all names created by the programmer. The DEFN column gives the number of the statement in which each name is defined. For example, BF-ITEM-NO is defined in statement 29. Then, the REFERENCE column gives the numbers of the statements that refer to each name. If necessary, multiple lines are used for the reference numbers. In a long program, this listing is a handy reference when correcting diagnostics and debugging.

The last page of the compiler output is the *diagnostic listing* (part 6). In the CARD column, the statement number of the card in error is given. Then, the ERROR MESSAGE column gives an error code and the *diagnostic message* itself.

```
PP 5734-CB1 V3 RELEASE 3.2 30APR74     IBM OS AMERICAN NATIONAL STANDARD COBOL          DATE JUL 29,1978

  1

00001  001010 IDENTIFICATION DIVISION.                              REORDLST
00002  001020*                                                      REORDLST
00003  001030 PROGRAM-ID. REORDLST.                                 REORDLST
00004  001040*                                                      REORDLST
00005  001050 ENVIRONMENT DIVISION.                                 REORDLST
00006  001060*                                                      REORDLST
00007  001070 CONFIGURATION SECTION.                                REORDLST
00008  001080*                                                      REORDLST
00009  001090 SPECIAL-NAMES.                                        REORDLST
00010  001100     C01 IS PAGE-TOP.                                  REORDLST
00011  001110*                                                      REORDLST
00012  001120 INPUT-OUTPUT SECTION.                                 REORDLST
00013  001130*                                                      REORDLST
00014  001140 FILE-CONTROL.                                         REORDLST
00015  001150     SELECT BFCRDS ASSIGN TO UT-S-BFCRDS.              REORDLST
00016  001160     SELECT ORDLST ASSIGN TO UT-S-ORDLST.              REORDLST
00017  001170*                                                      REORDLST
00018  002010 DATA DIVISION.                                        REORDLST
00019  002020*                                                      REORDLST
00020  002030 FILE SECTION.                                         REORDLST
00021  002040*                                                      REORDLST
00022  002050 FD  BFCRDS                                            REORDLST
00023  002060     LABEL RECORDS ARE STANDARD                        REORDLST
00024  002070     RECORDING MODE IS F                               REORDLST
00025  002080     RECORD CONTAINS 80 CHARACTERS.                    REORDLST
00026  002090*                                                      REORDLST
00027  002100 01  BAL-FWD-CARD.                                     REORDLST
00028  002110*                                                      REORDLST
00029  002120     05  BF-ITEM-NO        PIC 9(5).                   REORDLST
00030  002130     05  BF-ITEM-DESC      PIC X(24)                   REORDLST
00031  002140     05  FILLER            PIC X(5).                   REORDLST
00032  002150     05  BF-UNIT-PRICE     PIC 999V99.                 REORDLST
00033  002160     05  BF-REORDER-POINT  PIC 9(5).                   REORDLST
00034  002170     05  BF-ON-HAND        PIC 9(5).                   REORDLST
00035  002180     05  BF-ON-ORDER       PIC 9(5).                   REORDLST
00036  002190     05  FILLER            PIC X(30).                  REORDLST
00037  002200*                                                      REORDLST
00038  003010 FD  ORDLST                                            REORDLST
00039  003020     LABEL RECORDS ARE STANDARD                        REORDLST
00040  003030     RECORDING MODE IS F                               REORDLST
00041  003040     RECORD CONTAINS 133 CHARACTERS.                   REORDLST
00042  003050*                                                      REORDLST
00043  003060 01  PRINT-AREA           PIC X(133).                  REORDLST
00044  003070*                                                      REORDLST
00045  003080 WORKING-STORAGE SECTION.                              REORDLST
00046  003090*                                                      REORDLST
00047  003100 01  SWITCHES.                                         REORDLST
00048  003110*                                                      REORDLST
```

Figure 4-1 Source listing (part 1 of 6)

```
 2

00049 003120      05  CARD-EOF-SWITCH      PIC X            VALUE "N".                REORDLST
00050 003130*                                                                        REORDLST
00051 003140 01  WORK-FIELDS.                                                         REORDLST
00052 003150*                                                                        REORDLST
00053 003160      05  AVAILABLE-STOCK      PIC S9(5)        COMP-3.                   REORDLST
00054 003170*                                                                        REORDLST
00055 003180 01  PRINT-FIELDS            COMP   SYNC.                                 REORDLST
00056 003190*                                                                        REORDLST
00057 003200      05  LINE-COUNTER         PIC S99          VALUE +99.                REORDLST
00058 003210      05  LINES-ON-PAGE        PIC S99          VALUE +57.                REORDLST
00059 003220      05  SPACE-CONTROL        PIC X.                                     REORDLST
00060 004010*                                                                        REORDLST
00061 004020 01  COUNT-FIELDS.                                                        REORDLST
00062 004030*                                                                        REORDLST
00063 004040      05  CARD-COUNT           PIC S9(5)   COMP-3   VALUE ZERO.           REORDLST
00064 004050*                                                                        REORDLST
00065 004060 01  HDG-LINE-1.                                                          REORDLST
00066 004070*                                                                        REORDLST
00067 004080      05  HDG1-CC              PIC X.                                     REORDLST
00068 004090      05  FILLER               PIC 9(23)        VALUE SPACE.              REORDLST
00069 004100      05  FILLER               PIC X(15)        VALUE 'REORDER LISTING'.  REORDLST
00070 004110      05  FILLER               PIC X(94)        VALUE SPACE.              REORDLST
00071 004120*                                                                        REORDLST
00072 004130 01  HDG-LINE-2.                                                          REORDLST
00073 004140*                                                                        REORDLST
00074 004150      05  HDG2-CC              PIC X.                                     REORDLST
00075 004160      05  FILLER               PIC X(4)         VALUE 'ITEM'.             REORDLST
00076 004170      05  FILLER               PIC X(12)        VALUE SPACE.              REORDLST
00077 004180      05  FILLER               PIC X(4)         VALUE 'ITEM'.             REORDLST
00078 004190      05  FILLER               PIC X(16)        VALUE SPACE.              REORDLST
00079 004200      05  FILLER               PIC X(4)         VALUE 'UNIT'.             REORDLST
00080 005010      05  FILLER               PIC X(15)        VALUE SPACE.              REORDLST
00081 005020      05  FILLER               PIC X(7)         VALUE 'REORDER'.          REORDLST
00082 005030      05  FILLER               PIC X(70)        VALUE SPACE.              REORDLST
00083 005040*                                                                        REORDLST
00084 005050 01  HDG-LINE-3.                                                          REORDLST
00085 005060*                                                                        REORDLST
00086 005070      05  HDG3-CC              PIC X.                                     REORDLST
00087 005080      05  FILLER               PIC X(3)         VALUE SPACE.              REORDLST
00088 005090      05  FILLER               PIC X(3)         VALUE 'NO.'.              REORDLST
00089 005100      05  FILLER               PIC X(9)         VALUE SPACE.              REORDLST
00090 005110      05  FILLER               PIC X(11)        VALUE 'DESCRIPTION'.      REORDLST
00091 005120      05  FILLER               PIC X(11)        VALUE SPACE.              REORDLST
00092 005130      05  FILLER               PIC X(5)         VALUE 'PRICE'.            REORDLST
00093 005140      05  FILLER               PIC X(4)         VALUE SPACE.              REORDLST
00094 005150      05  FILLER               PIC X(9)         VALUE 'AVAILABLE'.        REORDLST
00095 005160      05  FILLER               PIC X(3)         VALUE SPACE.              REORDLST
00096 005170      05  FILLER               PIC X(5)         VALUE 'POINT'.            REORDLST
00097 005180      05  FILLER               PIC X(71)        VALUE SPACE.              REORDLST
00098 005190*                                                                        REORDLST
00099 006010 01  REORDER-LINE.                                                        REORDLST
```

Figure 4-1 Source listing (continued) (part 2 of 6)

```
3

00100  006020*
00101  006030         05  RL-CC               PIC X.
00102  006040         05  RL-ITEM-NO          PIC Z(5).
00103  006050         05  FILLER              PIC X(5).
00104  006060         05  RL-ITEM-DESC        PIC X(20).
00105  006070         05  FILLER              PIC X(5)   VALUE SPACE.
00106  006080         05  RL-UNIT-PRICE       PIC ZZZ.99.
00107  006090         05  FILLER              PIC X(5).
00108  006100         05  RL-AVAILABLE-STOCK  PIC Z(5).
00109  006110         05  FILLER              PIC X(5)   VALUE SPACE.
00110  006120         05  RL-REORDER-POINT    PIC Z(5).
00111  006130         05  FILLER              PIC X(71)  VALUE SPACE.
00112  006140*
00113  006150     01  TOTAL-LINE.
00114  006160*
00115  006170         05  TL-CC               PIC X.
00116  006180         05  TL-CARD-COUNT       PIC ZZ,ZZZ.
00117  006190         05  FILLER              PIC X(24)
00118  006200               VALUE ' CARDS IN THE INPUT DECK'.
00119  006210         05  FILLER              PIC X(102) VALUE SPACE.
00120  006220*
00121  007010     PROCEDURE DIVISION.
00122  007020*
00123  007030     000-PRODUCE-REORDER-LISTING.
00124  007040*
00125  007050         OPEN INPUT BFCRDS
00126  007060              OUTPUT ORDLST.
00127  007070         PERFORM 100-PRODUCE-REORDER-LINE
00128  007080             UNTIL CARD-EOF-SWITCH IS EQUAL TO 'Y'.
00129  007090         PERFORM 200-PRINT-TOTAL-LINE.
00130  007100         CLOSE BFCRDS
00131  007110               ORDLST.
00132  007120         DISPLAY 'REORDLST  I  1  NORMAL EOJ'.
00133  007130         STOP RUN.
00134  007140*
00135  007150     100-PRODUCE-REORDER-LINE.
00136  007160*
00137  007170         PERFORM 110-READ-INVENTORY-RECORD.
00138  007180         IF CARD-EOF-SWITCH IS NOT EQUAL TO 'Y'
00139  007190             PERFORM 120-CALCULATE-AVAILABLE-STOCK
00140  007200             IF AVAILABLE-STOCK IS LESS THAN BF-REORDER-POINT
00141  007210                 DO 130-PRINT-REORDER-LINE.
00142  008010*
00143  008020     110-READ-INVENTORY-RECORD.
00144  008030*
00145  008040         READ BFCRDS
00146  008050             AT END
00147  008060                 MOVE 'Y' TO CARD-EOF-SWITCH.
00148  008070         IF CARD-EOF-SWITCH IS NOT EQUAL TO 'Y'
00149  008080             ADD 1 TO CARD-COUNT.
00150  008090*
```

(REORDLST appears in the identification area of each source line.)

Figure 4-1 Source listing (continued) (part 3 of 6)

```
00151  008100  120-CALCULATE-AVAILABLE-STOCK.                                          REORDLST
00152  008110*                                                                         REORDLST
00153  008120      ADD BF-ON-HAND BF-ON-ORDER                                          REORDLST
00154  008130          GIVING AVAILABLE-STOCK                                          REORDLST
00155  008140          ON SIZE ERROR                                                   REORDLST
00156  008150              DISPLAY 'REORDLST A    2    CALCULATION ERROR FOR ITEM '     REORDLST
00157  008160              'NO. ' BF-ITEM-NO '--CARD IGNORED'                          REORDLST
00158  008170              MOVE 99999 TO AVAILABLE-STOCK.                              REORDLST
00159  008180*                                                                         REORDLST
00160  009010  130-PRINT-REORDER-LINE.                                                 REORDLST
00161  009020*                                                                         REORDLST
00162  009030      IF LINE-COUNT IS GREATER THAN LINES-ON-PAGE                         REORDLST
00163  009040          PERFORM 140-PRINT-HEADING-LINES.                                REORDLST
00164  009050      MOVE BF-ITEM-NO         TO RL-ITEM-NO.                              REORDLST
00165  009060      MOVE BF-ITEM-DESC       TO RL-ITEM-DESC.                            REORDLST
00166  009070      MOVE BF-UNIT-PRICE      TO RL-UNIT-PRICE.                           REORDLST
00167  009080      MOVE AVAILABLE-STOCK    TO RL-AVAILABLE-STOCK.                      REORDLST
00168  009090      MOVE BF-REORDER-POINT   TO RL-REORDER-POINT.                        REORDLST
00169  009100      MOVE REORDER-LINE       TO PRINT-AREA.                              REORDLST
00170  009110      PERFORM 150-WRITE-REPORT-LINE.                                      REORDLST
00171  009120      MOVE 1 TO SPACE-CONTROL.                                            REORDLST
00172  009130*                                                                         REORDLST
00173  009140  140-PRINT-HEADING-LINES.                                                REORDLST
00174  009150*                                                                         REORDLST
00175  009160      MOVE HDG-LINE-1 TO PRINT AREA.                                      REORDLST
00176  009170      PERFORM 160-WRITE-PAGE-TOP-LINE.                                    REORDLST
00177  009180      MOVE HDG-LINE-2 TO PRINT-AREA.                                      REORDLST
00178  009190      MOVE 2 TO SPACE-CONTROL.                                            REORDLST
00179  010010      PERFORM 150-WRITE-REPORT-LINE.                                      REORDLST
00180  010020      MOVE HDG-LINE-3 TO PRINT-AREA.                                      REORDLST
00181  010030      MOVE 1 TO SPACE-CONTROL.                                            REORDLST
00182  010040      PERFORM 150-WRITE-REPORT-LINE.                                      REORDLST
00183  010050      MOVE 2 TO SPACE-CONTROL.                                            REORDLST
00184  010060*                                                                         REORDLST
00185  010070  150-WRITE-REPORT-LINE.                                                  REORDLST
00186  010080*                                                                         REORDLST
00187  010090      ADD SPACE-CONTROL TO LINE-COUNT.                                    REORDLST
00188 **010090      WRITE PRINT-AREA                                                   REORDLST
00189  010100          AFTER ADVANCING SPACE-CONTROL LINES.                            REORDLST
00190  010120*                                                                         REORDLST
00191  010130  160-WRITE-PAGE-TOP-LINE.                                                REORDLST
00192  010140*                                                                         REORDLST
00193  010150      WRITE PRINT-AREA                                                    REORDLST
00194  010160          AFTER ADVANCING PAGE-TOP.                                       REORDLST
00195  010170      MOVE ZERO TO LINE-COUNT.                                            REORDLST
00196  010180*                                                                         REORDLST
00197  011010  200-PRINT-TOTAL-LINE.                                                   REORDLST
00198  011020*                                                                         REORDLST
00199  011030      MOVE WS-CARD-COUNT TO TL-CARD-COUNT.                                REORDLST
00200  011040      MOVE TOTAL-LINE TO PRINT-AREA.                                      REORDLST
00201  011050      MOVE 3 TO SPACE-CONTROL.                                            REORDLST
00202  011060      PERFORM 150-WRITE-REPORT-LINE.                                      REORDLST
```

4

Figure 4-1   Source listing (continued) (part 4 of 6)

12

CROSS-REFERENCE DICTIONARY

DATA NAMES	DEFN	REFERENCE					
AVAILABLE-STOCK	000053	000140	000153	000158	000167		
BAL-FWD-CARD	000027	000156	000164				
BF-ITEM-NO	000029	000153					
BF-ON-HAND	000034	000153					
BF-ON-ORDER	000035	000140	000168				
BF-REORDER-POINT	000033	000166					
BF-UNIT-PRICE	000032	000125	000130	000145			
BFCRDS	000015						
BL-ITEM-DESC	000030						
CARD-COUNT	000063	000149					
CARD-EOF-SWITCH	000049	000127	000138	000147	000148		
COUNT-FIELDS	000061						
HDG-LINE-1	000065						
HDG-LINE-2	000072	000177					
HDG-LINE-3	000084	000180					
HDG1-CC	000067						
HDG2-CC	000074						
HDG3-CC	000086						
LINES-ON-PAGE	000058						
ORDLST	000016	000125	000130	000188	000193		
PRINT-AREA	000043	000169	000177	000180	000188		
PRINT-FIELDS	000055						
REORDER-LINE	000099	000169					
RL-AVAILABLE-STOCK	000108	000167					
RL-CC	000101						
RL-ITEM-DESC	000104						
RL-ITEM-NO	000107	000164					
RL-REORDER-POINT	000110	000168					
RL-UNIT-PRICE	000106	000166					
SPACE-CONTROL	000059	000171	000178	000181	000183	000187	000188 000193 000200 000201
SWITCHES	000047						
TL-CARD-COUNT	000116						
TL-CC	000115						
TOTAL-LINE	000113	000200					
WORK-FIELDS	000051						

Figure 4-1 Cross-reference listing (part 5 of 6)

```
                    14

                    ERROR MESSAGE

                    IKF6006I-E    SUPMAP SPECIFIED AND E-LEVEL DIAGNOSTIC HAS OCCURRED. PMAP CLIST LOAD DECK STATE FLOW IGNORED
CARD                ERROR MESSAGE

 31                 IKF1100I-W    1 SEQUENCE ERROR IN SOURCE PROGRAM.
 15                 IKF1043I-W    END OF SENTENCE SHOULD PRECEDE 05 . ASSUMED PRESENT.
                    IKF2146I-C    RECORD SIZE IN RECORD-CONTAINS CLAUSE DISAGREES WITH COMPUTED RECORD SIZE. USING
                                  MAXIMUM COMPUTED SIZE.
 57                 IKF1001I-C    NUMERIC LITERAL NOT RECOGNIZED AS LEVEL NUMBER BECAUSE LINE-COUNTER ILLEGAL AS
                                  USED. SKIPPING TO NEXT LEVEL, SECTION OR DIVISION.
 59                 IKF2142I-E    ALPHABETIC OR ALPHANUMERIC ITEM HAS ILLEGAL USAGE. PICTURE CHANGED TO 9.
 68                 IKF2075I-C    NUMERIC PICTURE - DIGIT LENGTH GT 18. PICTURE REPLACED BY 9(1).
 68                 IKF2129I-C    VALUE CLAUSE LITERAL DOES NOT CONFORM TO PICTURE. CHANGED TO ZERO.
 83                 IKF1004I-E    INVALID WORD ASTERISK . SKIPPING TO NEXT RECOGNIZABLE WORD.
103                 IKF1004I-E    INVALID WORD VALUE . SKIPPING TO NEXT RECOGNIZABLE WORD.
119                 IKF2039I-C    PICTURE CONFIGURATION ILLEGAL. PICTURE CHANGED TO 9 UNLESS USAGE IS 'DISPLAY-ST',
                                  THEN L(6)BDZ9BDZ9.
119                 IKF2129I-C    VALUE CLAUSE LITERAL DOES NOT CONFORM TO PICTURE. CHANGED TO ZERO.
137                 IKF1087I-W    ' PERFORM ' SHOULD NOT BEGIN A-MARGIN.
140                 IKF3001I-E    DO NOT DEFINED. DELETING TILL LEGAL ELEMENT FOUND.
140                 IKF4032I-C    NO ACTION INDICATED IF PRECEDING CONDITION IS TRUE. NEXT SENTENCE ASSUMED.
149                 IKF4072I-W    EXIT FROM PERFORMED PROCEDURE ASSUMED BEFORE PROCEDURE-NAME .
158                 IKF4072I-W    EXIT FROM PERFORMED PROCEDURE ASSUMED BEFORE PROCEDURE-NAME .
162                 IKF3001I-E    LINE-COUNT NOT DEFINED. TEST DISCARDED.
165                 IKF3001I-E    BF-ITEM-DESC NOT DEFINED. DISCARDED.
175                 IKF3001I-E    PRINT NOT DEFINED. DISCARDED.
175                 IKF4052I-E    AREA  MAY NOT BE TARGET FIELD FOR DNM=2-269  (GRF) IN MOVE STATEMENT, AND IS
                                  DISCARDED.
187                 IKF3001I-E    LINE-COUNT NOT DEFINED. SUBSTITUTING TALLY .
195                 IKF3001I-E    LINE-COUNT NOT DEFINED. DISCARDED.
199                 IKF3001I-E    WS-CARD-COUNT NOT DEFINED. DISCARDED.
```

Figure 4-1 Diagnostic listing (part 6 of 6)

To get a complete listing of messages on the System/360-370, you can run a COBOL program (*any* COBOL program) using a PROGRAM-ID of ERRMSG. This will list all of the diagnostic messages that are used by your compiler. In general, however, you shouldn't need the ERRMSG listing.

The letter following the error code indicates what action the compiler will take in response to the error. On the System/360-370, there are four action codes: W for warning, C for conditional, E for error, and D for disaster.

When a *warning diagnostic* occurs, the program is compiled without any changes being made to it. In other words, the compiler simply ignores the error for the time being.

The program is also compiled when a *conditional diagnostic* occurs, but only after the compiler has made some assumption to correct the error. Unfortunately, the assumption made usually isn't the one you want, so the error still exists.

The compiler doesn't even attempt to correct an *error diagnostic*. It simply drops the statement that caused the diagnostic from the program and then finishes the compilation.

When a *disaster diagnostic* occurs, the compiler can't complete the compilation. Unlike the other types of diagnostics, about 90% of all disaster diagnostics result from a single cause: the use of continuation cards. A continuation card has a hyphen in column 7, which tells the compiler that the card contains a continuation of the statement in the previous card. This allows a programmer to divide a COBOL statement in the middle and to continue it on the continuation card. However, because these cards are the major source of disaster diagnostics, you should never use them. In other words, column 7 should always be blank or contain an asterisk. And a COBOL statement should only be broken up at the end of a full word that completes a phrase.

Correcting Diagnostics

To correct diagnostics, you should normally take them in sequence and correct each statement as needed. If you come to a message you can't figure out, skip over it since one of the later diagnostics may indicate its cause. After going through all the diagnostics, if there are still a few you can't figure out, you might try recompiling the program with all other errors corrected. Sometimes, this will solve your problem because the problem diagnostics are caused by errors you have already corrected.

The first diagnostic in figure 4-1 lets you know that the program contains at least one E-level diagnostic. The rest of the message has to do with system parameters, which you will learn more about in chapters 8 and 9. Thus, while this diagnostic gives some information, it doesn't point to any specific errors that should be corrected, as the rest of the diagnostic messages do.

The second diagnostic in figure 4-1 points to a specific source-deck error; however, it doesn't have a card number because it concerns itself with the number of out-of-sequence cards in the source deck. It is a warning diagnostic because a sequence error may cause a logic error in the object program, but it may also be harmless. In this case, the program isn't affected by the single sequence error, but you should switch the source cards anyway (sequence code 10110 comes after 10090 and 10100) so the program will read more consistently. (LINE-COUNT won't be increased until the reorder line has actually been printed.)

The third diagnostic is a warning and refers to card 31. It indicates that a period is missing before card 31 and that one is assumed by the compiler. This is the actual problem, so the missing period of card 30 won't affect the object program.

The fourth diagnostic is conditional and refers to card 15, the SELECT statement for the card file. The error message says the program has tried to describe a record that doesn't have the same number of characters given in the RECORD CONTAINS clause of the file description (card 25). In this case, the PICTUREs of the record description add up to eighty-four characters because the PICTURE for BF-ITEM-DESC is X(24) when it should be X(20). According to the diagnostic, the compiler will treat the input record as though it had 84 characters. As a result, this error must be corrected before the program is tested.

The next diagnostic refers to card 57. It says that this card is skipped because LINE-COUNTER is "illegal as used." The problem is that LINE-COUNTER is a COBOL reserved word. As a result, the programmer can't use it as the name of one of his fields. In this case, the programmer meant to use LINE-COUNT but it was either coded or keypunched incorrectly. In any event, this error must be corrected before testing.

Note that this error is also the cause of three other errors—cards 162, 187, and 195. These statements refer to LINE-COUNT, which has never been properly defined. By correcting card 57, these diagnostics will also be corrected.

One diagnostic that you'll see quite frequently in structured programs is the one listed for cards 140, 149, and 158:

```
EXIT FROM PERFORMED PROCEDURE ASSUMED BEFORE PROCEDURE-NAME
```

This diagnostic occurs when a performed paragraph ends in a conditional statement. For example, card 149 is the last statement in the paragraph named 110-READ-INVENTORY-RECORD, and it's part of the IF statement that specifies what to do if CARD-EOF-SWITCH is not equal to Y. Normally, if the condition was not met, the program would continue with the next statement of the program, the first statement of the next paragraph. Fortunately, however, the compiler realizes that this is a performed paragraph and assumes a proper paragraph exit (that is, it returns to the statement following the PERFORM statement that called 110-READ-INVENTORY-RECORD).

As the programmer goes down the list of diagnostics, he marks all required changes on the source listing, usually in red so they are easy to spot. Then, he either (1) keypunches the corrections from the listing, (2) marks the source cards themselves and keypunches using them as a guide, or (3) codes the corrections on a coding form so they can be submitted for keypunching. When the cards are corrected, the source deck is adjusted as necessary.

One final thought: Should warning messages be corrected? We say, yes, whenever possible. Otherwise, it is too easy to overlook E- and C-level diagnostics in a maze of W diagnostics. As a result, when a program is submitted for testing, the only diagnostic messages that remain should be:

```
EXIT FROM PERFORMED PROCEDURE ASSUMED BEFORE PROCEDURE-NAME
```

And in some shops, this warning message has been deleted from the compiler so all compilations can be perfectly clean (no diagnostic messages at all).

Terminology

desk checking

compiler output

source listing

cross-reference listing

diagnostic listing

diagnostic message

warning diagnostic

conditional diagnostic

error diagnostic

disaster diagnostic

Objectives

1. Given typical output of a COBOL compilation including the diagnostic listing, correct the COBOL source deck.

Problems

1. Refer to the diagnostics in figure 4-1.

   a. How should card 59 be corrected?

   b. How should card 68 be corrected?

   c. How should card 83 be corrected?

   d. How should card 103 be corrected?

   e. How should card 119 be corrected?

   f. How should card 137 be corrected?

   g. What's wrong with card 140 and how should it be corrected?

   h. How should the error in card 165 be corrected?

   i. How should card 175 be corrected?

   j. How should card 199 be corrected?

Solutions

1. a. This diagnostic says in effect that the USAGE and the PIC-TURE for the field don't agree. This is because SPACE-CONTROL is defined in card 55 as a COMP field; if you check IBM's COBOL manual, you'll find that a COMP field cannot have a PICTURE of X or A. So card 59 should be changed to PIC S9.

   b. The PICTURE should be X(23).

   c. The asterisk should be in column 7, not column 8.

   d. There shouldn't be a period after the PICTURE clause.

   e. The PICTURE should be X(102).

   f. The statement should begin in the B, not the A, margin.

   g. The error, which is actually in card 141, is that the programmer has carried over the pseudocode from his module documentation and coded DO rather than PERFORM. So card 141 must be changed to PERFORM 130-PRINT-REORDER-LINE.

   h. To find the source of this diagnostic, you have to look back to the description of the input record. There you'll find the programmer accidentally coded BL-ITEM-DESC rather than BF-ITEM-DESC. So card 30 must be changed to BF-ITEM-DESC.

i. Insert a hyphen between PRINT and AREA.

j. The statement should read

```
MOVE CARD-COUNT TO TL-CARD-COUNT.
```

Sometimes in a case like this, it's tempting to correct the diagnostic by changing the data name in the Data Division (for example, changing the name in statement 63 to WS-CARD-COUNT). Though this may seem like the easy way out at first, it will cause E-level diagnostics in any statement that references the field correctly (by the name CARD-COUNT). So always change the faulty statement instead of the data description.

TOPIC 2   Testing and Debugging

Testing and debugging refer to the process of executing the object program to see if it works as intended, finding errors, correcting them, and trying again. More specifically, the object of testing is to find errors, while the object of debugging is to remove them.

One of the major pitfalls in the process of programming is inadequate testing. In other words, a program is not tried on enough combinations of input data to be sure all of its routines work. Nevertheless, it is considered to be tested and is put into production. Then, when actual data causes inaccurate output to be produced or causes program cancellation, a crisis often occurs. Imagine the scurrying that goes on when a program that prints payroll checks is cancelled prematurely. Or when a payroll check for double the amount owed to an employee is discovered.

Testing

To guard against inadequate testing, a program is usually tested in three phases: unit test, systems test, and acceptance test. The *unit test* is the programmer test in which the programmer tries to make sure that all modules in his program are adequately tested. The *systems test* is designed to test the relationships between the programs within a system; if, for example, the output from one program in a system is input to another program, the systems test helps determine whether the programs are properly coordinated. Finally, the *acceptance test* is designed to determine whether the instructions to the operations department are clear enough that the program can be run without any help from the program developers.

To prepare for the unit test, you should develop a *test plan*. To do this, you first make a list of all of the conditions that should be tested in each module. Then, you decide in what sequence the conditions should be tested. In general, you want to discover the major problems first, so you start by using only valid data to see whether the major modules are entered properly and whether control passes from one major module to another as intended. Then you can test for independent errors, after which you can test for errors that result when one condition has an effect on another condition. Finally, you can test conditions that depend upon volume; to test a page overflow routine, for example, you need enough data to force 60 or more print lines.

Once you have a test plan, you create data that will test the conditions specified in your plan. As you create the data, you also determine what output to expect.

After a test run is made, you compare the actual output with the expected output. If the program involves tape or disk input or output, listings of the contents of these files must be made before and after the test run. In a disk update run, for example, the contents of the disk file must be printed before and after testing to determine what changes were made in the file during the test run.

In order to get a listing of a file's contents, you may have to write your own programs or you may use *utility programs* that are supplied with an operating system. In any event, if the actual output disagrees with the expected output, you must find the cause of the error, change the source code, recompile, and test again.

After you make a test run, you should document it. The documentation for each test run should include the following:

1. The compiler output for the run

2. Listings of each input file used

3. Listings of each output file created during the test run

In addition, you should mark any output errors on the output listing, and, on the source listing, you should mark what changes you made to correct these errors. Since a programmer in a typical data-processing department is frequently coding, testing, and debugging several programs at one time, this documentation can save backtracking and confusion.

Because creating the test plan and test data are essential to the success of a testing effort, they are covered in detail in chapter 10. As a result, you are not expected to create test plans and test data

right now. For any programs that you write before you study
chapter 10, you can assume that test data will be supplied with the
program specifications.

In chapter 10, you will also see where test-plan and test-data
creation fit into the overall scheme of program development.
Although these phases have traditionally been done after a program
has been coded and just prior to testing, we recommend that they be
done before a program is coded.

Debugging

Debugging is one of the most challenging jobs of a programmer. In a
large, complex program, debugging an error can be much like solving a mystery. To determine what happened, you begin with clues
and trace backward until you find the culprit: a coding error or
input error.

When a program is tested, there are two possible outcomes: (1)
it can run to completion (STOP RUN), or (2) it can be abnormally
terminated or cancelled. If a program runs to completion, the programmer discovers any errors or bugs by comparing actual output
with expected output. If a program is abnormally terminated, the
programmer must discover the cause of the termination, correct it,
and test again.

Normal termination (end of job)

To illustrate debugging after normal termination of a test run, I will
use the reorder-listing program. I have included in the source code of
this program some minor errors that will cause defective output. Of
the several test cases that I would design to fully test the program,
let me select two basic ones for this illustration:

	Case 1	Case 2
Item number	00101	00103
Description	GENERATOR	HEATER SOLENOID
On-hand quantity	00070	00034
On-order quantity	00050	00000
Reorder point	00100	00050

The first item does not require reordering so it should not appear on
the report; the second item should appear on the report.

Figure 4-2 gives the output of the test run. Parts 1-4 show the
source listing that resulted from the compilation step; part 5 is the
DISPLAY output resulting from the execute step (remember that
DISPLAY output is printed separately from printer output when
spooling is used); and part 6 is the printer output that resulted from

```
PP 5734-CB1 V3 RELEASE 3.2 30APR74     IBM OS AMERICAN NATIONAL STANDARD COBOL      DATE JUL 29,1978

  1

00001   001010 IDENTIFICATION DIVISION.                                REORDLST
00002   001020*                                                        REORDLST
00003   001030 PROGRAM-ID. REORDLST.                                   REORDLST
00004   001040*                                                        REORDLST
00005   001050 ENVIRONMENT DIVISION.                                   REORDLST
00006   001060*                                                        REORDLST
00007   001070 CONFIGURATION SECTION.                                  REORDLST
00008   001080*                                                        REORDLST
00009   001090 SPECIAL-NAMES.                                          REORDLST
00010   001100     C01 IS PAGE-TOP.                                    REORDLST
00011   001110*                                                        REORDLST
00012   001120 INPUT-OUTPUT SECTION.                                   REORDLST
00013   001130*                                                        REORDLST
00014   001140 FILE-CONTROL.                                           REORDLST
00015   001150     SELECT BFCRDS ASSIGN TO UT-S-BFCRDS.                REORDLST
00016   001160     SELECT ORDLST ASSIGN TO UT-S-ORDLST.                REORDLST
00017   001170*                                                        REORDLST
00018   002010 DATA DIVISION.                                          REORDLST
00019   002020*                                                        REORDLST
00020   002030 FILE SECTION.                                           REORDLST
00021   002040*                                                        REORDLST
00022   002050 FD BFCRDS                                               REORDLST
00023   002060     LABEL RECORDS ARE STANDARD                          REORDLST
00024   002070     RECORDING MODE IS F                                 REORDLST
00025   002080     RECORD CONTAINS 80 CHARACTERS.                      REORDLST
00026   002090*                                                        REORDLST
00027   002100 01 BAL-FWD-CARD.                                        REORDLST
00028   002110*                                                        REORDLST
00029   002120     05 BF-ITEM-NO        PIC 9(5).                      REORDLST
00030   002130     05 BF-ITEM-DESC      PIC X(20).                     REORDLST
00031   002140     05 FILLER            PIC X(5).                      REORDLST
00032   002150     05 BF-UNIT-PRICE     PIC 999V99.                    REORDLST
00033   002160     05 BF-REORDER-POINT  PIC 9(5).                      REORDLST
00034   002170     05 BF-ON-HAND        PIC 9(5).                      REORDLST
00035   002180     05 BF-ON-ORDER       PIC 9(5).                      REORDLST
00036   002190     05 FILLER            PIC X(30).                     REORDLST
00037   002200*                                                        REORDLST
00038   003010 FD ORDLST                                               REORDLST
00039   003020     LABEL RECORDS ARE STANDARD                          REORDLST
00040   003030     RECORDING MODE IS F                                 REORDLST
00041   003040     RECORD CONTAINS 133 CHARACTERS.                     REORDLST
00042   003050*                                                        REORDLST
00043   003060 01 PRINT-AREA           PIC X(133).                     REORDLST
00044   003070*                                                        REORDLST
00045   003080 WORKING-STORAGE SECTION.                                REORDLST
00046   003090*                                                        REORDLST
00047   003100 01 SWITCHES.                                            REORDLST
00048   003110*                                                        REORDLST
```

Figure 4-2 Source listing (part 1 of 6)

```
2

00049 003120    05  CARD-EOF-SWITCH   PIC X        VALUE 'N'.               REORDLST
00050 003130*                                                              REORDLST
00051 003140 01 WORK-FIELDS.                                               REORDLST
00052 003150*                                                              REORDLST
00053 003160    05  AVAILABLE-STOCK   PIC S9(5)    COMP-3.                 REORDLST
00054 003170*                                                              REORDLST
00055 003180 01 PRINT-FIELDS          COMP         SYNC.                   REORDLST
00056 003190*                                                              REORDLST
00057 003200    05  LINE-COUNT        PIC S99      VALUE +99.              REORDLST
00058 003210    05  LINES-ON-PAGE     PIC S99      VALUE +57.              REORDLST
00059 003220    05  SPACE-CONTROL     PIC S9.                              REORDLST
00060 004010*                                                              REORDLST
00061 004020 01 COUNT-FIELDS.                                              REORDLST
00062 004030*                                                              REORDLST
00063 004040    05  CARD-COUNT        PIC S9(5)    COMP-3  VALUE ZERO.     REORDLST
00064 004050*                                                              REORDLST
00065 004060 01 HDG-LINE-1.                                                REORDLST
00066 004070*                                                              REORDLST
00067 004080    05  HDG1-CC           PIC X.                               REORDLST
00068 004090    05  FILLER            PIC X(23)    VALUE SPACE.            REORDLST
00069 004100    05  FILLER            PIC X(15)    VALUE 'REORDER LISTING'. REORDLST
00070 004110    05  FILLER            PIC X(94).                           REORDLST
00071 004120*                                                              REORDLST
00072 004130 01 HDG-LINE-2.                                                REORDLST
00073 004140*                                                              REORDLST
00074 004150    05  HDG2-CC           PIC X.                               REORDLST
00075 004160    05  FILLER            PIC X(4)     VALUE 'ITEM'.           REORDLST
00076 004170    05  FILLER            PIC X(12)    VALUE SPACE.            REORDLST
00077 004180    05  FILLER            PIC X(4)     VALUE 'ITEM'.           REORDLST
00078 004190    05  FILLER            PIC X(16)    VALUE SPACE.            REORDLST
00079 004200    05  FILLER            PIC X(4)     VALUE 'UNIT'.           REORDLST
00080 005010    05  FILLER            PIC X(5)     VALUE SPACE.            REORDLST
00081 005020    05  FILLER            PIC X(7)     VALUE 'REORDER'.        REORDLST
00082 005030    05  FILLER            PIC X(70)    VALUE SPACE.            REORDLST
00083 005040*                                                              REORDLST
00084 005050 01 HDG-LINE-3.                                                REORDLST
00085 005060*                                                              REORDLST
00086 005070    05  HDG3-CC           PIC X.                               REORDLST
00087 005080    05  FILLER            PIC X        VALUE SPACE.            REORDLST
00088 005090    05  FILLER            PIC X(3)     VALUE 'NO.'.            REORDLST
00089 005100    05  FILLER            PIC X(9)     VALUE SPACE.            REORDLST
00090 005110    05  FILLER            PIC X(11)    VALUE 'DESCRIPTION'.    REORDLST
00091 005120    05  FILLER            PIC X(11)    VALUE SPACE.            REORDLST
00092 005130    05  FILLER            PIC X(5)     VALUE 'PRICE'.          REORDLST
00093 005140    05  FILLER            PIC X(4)     VALUE SPACE.            REORDLST
00094 005150    05  FILLER            PIC X(9)     VALUE 'AVAILABLE'.      REORDLST
00095 005160    05  FILLER            PIC X(3)     VALUE SPACE.            REORDLST
00096 005170    05  FILLER            PIC X(5)     VALUE 'POINT'.          REORDLST
00097 005180    05  FILLER            PIC X(71)    VALUE SPACE.            REORDLST
00098 005190*                                                              REORDLST
00099 006010 01 REORDER-LINE.                                              REORDLST
```

Figure 4-2 Source listing (continued) (part 2 of 6)

```
3
00100  006020*                                                        REORDLST
00101  006030      05  RL-CC             PIC X.                        REORDLST
00102  006040      05  RL-ITEM-NO        PIC Z(5).                     REORDLST
00103  006050      05  FILLER            PIC X(5)     VALUE SPACE.     REORDLST
00104  006060      05  RL-ITEM-DESC      PIC X(20).                    REORDLST
00105  006070      05  FILLER            PIC X(5)     VALUE SPACE.     REORDLST
00106  006080      05  RL-UNIT-PRICE     PIC ZZZ.99.                  REORDLST
00107  006090      05  FILLER            PIC X(5)     VALUE SPACE.     REORDLST
00108  006100      05  RL-AVAILABLE-STOCK PIC Z(5).                   REORDLST
00109  006110      05  FILLER            PIC X(5)     VALUE SPACE.     REORDLST
00110  006120      05  RL-REORDER-POINT  PIC Z(5).                     REORDLST
00111  006130      05  FILLER            PIC X(7l)    VALUE SPACE.     REORDLST
00112  006140*                                                        REORDLST
00113  006150  01  TOTAL-LINE.                                        REORDLST
00114  006160*                                                        REORDLST
00115  006170      05  TL-CC             PIC X.                        REORDLST
00116  006180      05  TL-CARD-COUNT     PIC ZZ,ZZZ.                  REORDLST
00117  006190      05  FILLER            PIC X(24)                     REORDLST
00118  006200                            VALUE ' CARDS IN THE INPUT DECK'. REORDLST
00119  006210      05  FILLER            PIC X(102)   VALUE SPACE.     REORDLST
00120  006220*                                                        REORDLST
00121  007010  PROCEDURE DIVISION.                                    REORDLST
00122  007020*                                                        REORDLST
00123  007030  000-PRODUCE-REORDER-LISTING.                           REORDLST
00124  007040*                                                        REORDLST
00125  007050      OPEN INPUT BFCRDS                                  REORDLST
00126  007060           OUTPUT ORDLST.                                REORDLST
00127  007070      PERFORM 100-PRODUCE-REORDER-LINE                   REORDLST
00128  007080          UNTIL CARD-EOF-SWITCH IS EQUAL TO 'Y'.         REORDLST
00129  007090      PERFORM 200-PRINT-TOTAL-LINE.                      REORDLST
00130  007100      CLOSE BFCRDS                                       REORDLST
00131  007110           ORDLST.                                       REORDLST
00132  007120      DISPLAY 'REORDLST I  1 NORMAL EOJ'.                REORDLST
00133  007130      STOP RUN.                                          REORDLST
00134  007140*                                                        REORDLST
00135  007150  100-PRODUCE-REORDER-LINE.                              REORDLST
00136  007160*                                                        REORDLST
00137  007170      PERFORM 110-READ-INVENTORY-RECORD.                 REORDLST
00138  007180      IF CARD-EOF-SWITCH IS NOT EQUAL TO 'Y'             REORDLST
00139  007190          PERFORM 120-CALCULATE-AVAILABLE-STOCK          REORDLST
00140  007200          IF AVAILABLE-STOCK IS LESS THAN BF-REORDER-POINT REORDLST
00141  007210              PERFORM 130-PRINT-REORDER-LINE.            REORDLST
00142  008010*                                                        REORDLST
00143  008020  110-READ-INVENTORY-RECORD.                             REORDLST
00144  008030*                                                        REORDLST
00145  008040      READ BFCRDS                                        REORDLST
00146  008050          AT END                                         REORDLST
00147  008060              MOVE 'Y' TO CARD-EOF-SWITCH.               REORDLST
00148  008070      IF CARD-EOF-SWITCH IS NOT EQUAL TO 'Y'             REORDLST
00149  008080          ADD 1 TO CARD-COUNT.                           REORDLST
00150  008090*                                                        REORDLST
```

Figure 4-2   Source listing (continued) (part 3 of 6)

```
00151  008100 120-CALCULATE-AVAILABLE-STOCK.                                      REORDLST
00152  008110*                                                                    REORDLST
00153  008120     ADD BF-ON-HAND BF-ON-ORDER                                      REORDLST
00154  008130        GIVING AVAILABLE-STOCK                                       REORDLST
00155  008140     ON SIZE ERROR                                                   REORDLST
00156  008150        DISPLAY 'REORDLST A  2   CALCULATION ERROR FOR ITEM'REORDLST
00157  008160               'NO. ' BF-ITEM-NO '--CARD IGNORED'                    REORDLST
00158  008170        MOVE 99999 TO AVAILABLE-STOCK.                               REORDLST
00159  008180*                                                                    REORDLST
00160  009010 130-PRINT-REORDER-LINE.                                             REORDLST
00161  009020*                                                                    REORDLST
00162  009030     IF LINE-COUNT IS GREATER THAN LINES-ON-PAGE                     REORDLST
00163  009040        PERFORM 140-PRINT-HEADING-LINES.                             REORDLST
00164  009050     MOVE BF-ITEM-NO       TO RL-ITEM-NO.                            REORDLST
00165  009060     MOVE BF-ITEM-DESC     TO RL-ITEM-DESC.                          REORDLST
00166  009070     MOVE BF-UNIT-PRICE    TO RL-UNIT-PRICE.                         REORDLST
00167  009080     MOVE AVAILABLE-STOCK  TO RL-AVAILABLE-STOCK.                    REORDLST
00168  009090     MOVE BF-REORDER-POINT TO RL-REORDER-POINT.                      REORDLST
00169  009100     MOVE REORDER-LINE     TO PRINT-AREA.                            REORDLST
00170  009110     MOVE 1 TO SPACE-CONTROL.                                        REORDLST
00171  009120     PERFORM 150-WRITE-REPORT-LINE.                                  REORDLST
00172  009130*                                                                    REORDLST
00173  009140 140-PRINT-HEADING-LINES.                                            REORDLST
00174  009150*                                                                    REORDLST
00175  009160     MOVE HDG-LINE-1 TO PRINT-AREA.                                  REORDLST
00176  009170     PERFORM 160-WRITE-PAGE-TOP-LINE.                                REORDLST
00177  009180     MOVE HDG-LINE-2 TO PRINT-AREA.                                  REORDLST
00178  009190     MOVE 2 TO SPACE-CONTROL.                                        REORDLST
00179  010010     PERFORM 150-WRITE-REPORT-LINE.                                  REORDLST
00180  010020     MOVE HDG-LINE-3 TO PRINT-AREA.                                  REORDLST
00181  010030     MOVE 1 TO SPACE-CONTROL.                                        REORDLST
00182  010040     PERFORM 150-WRITE-REPORT-LINE.                                  REORDLST
00183  010050     MOVE 2 TO SPACE-CONTROL.                                        REORDLST
00184  010060*                                                                    REORDLST
00185  010070 150-WRITE-REPORT-LINE.                                              REORDLST
00186  010080*                                                                    REORDLST
00187  010090     WRITE PRINT-AREA                                                REORDLST
00188  010100        AFTER ADVANCING SPACE-CONTROL LINES.                         REORDLST
00189  010110     ADD SPACE-CONTROL TO LINE-COUNT.                                REORDLST
00190  010120*                                                                    REORDLST
00191  010130 160-WRITE-PAGE-TOP-LINE.                                            REORDLST
00192  010140*                                                                    REORDLST
00193  010150     WRITE PRINT-AREA                                                REORDLST
00194  010160        AFTER ADVANCING PAGE-TOP.                                    REORDLST
00195  010170     MOVE ZERO TO LINE-COUNT.                                        REORDLST
00196  010180*                                                                    REORDLST
00197  011010 200-PRINT-TOTAL-LINE.                                               REORDLST
00198  011020*                                                                    REORDLST
00199  011030     MOVE CARD-COUNT TO TL-CARD-COUNT.                               REORDLST
00200  011040     MOVE TOTAL-LINE TO PRINT-AREA.                                  REORDLST
00201  011050     MOVE 3 TO SPACE-CONTROL.                                        REORDLST
       011060     PERFORM 150-WRITE-REPORT-LINE.                                  REORDLST
```

Figure 4-2   Source listing (continued) (part 4 of 6)

```
REORDLST  I  1  NORMAL EOJ
```

Figure 4-2 DISPLAY output (part 5 of 6)

```
                  REORDER LISTING9& 1   & 1              K 1     0 &     1 K 1 1  1 K 1 1   1 1    9  H  B  0 1 K 1
ITEM          ITEM               UNIT     REORDER
 NO.       DESCRIPTION          PRICE   AVAILABLE   POINT

   2 CARDS IN THE INPUT DECK
```

Figure 4-2 Test run output (part 6 of 6)

the execute step. As you can see, there are three different errors in the printer output: (1) there is some unexpected data (garbage) in the first heading line; (2) in the second heading line, REORDER is printed over AVAILABLE instead of over POINT; and (3) the detail line for the second input card did not print.

Can you determine the cause of these errors? Those in the heading lines are fairly easy to debug. Quite simply, statement 70 doesn't give an initial value of SPACE to the last 94 positions of the work area. As a result, data from the previous program prints in the last 94 print positions. As for the misplacement of REORDER, statement 80 should have a PICTURE of X(15), not X(5).

But why didn't the detail line print? There are several possibilities. The second data card could be punched incorrectly so no line was supposed to print. The statements for calculating available could be in error so available was considered to be larger than reorder point. The IF statement that determines whether available is less than the reorder point could be worded wrong so the PERFORM statement wasn't executed as intended. The paragraph that prints the detail line could be incomplete so that the reorder line never reached the PRINT-AREA or was never actually written. Or perhaps the program ended before the second card was completely processed. By checking out each of these possibilities, you should be able to determine that a PERFORM statement is missing near the end of the paragraph named 130-PRINT-REORDER-LINE. Thus, the program never reached paragraph 150-WRITE-REPORT-LINE, and the reorder line wasn't printed.

How to use DISPLAY statements for debugging Since this program is short, debugging is relatively simple. However, if a program is long or the calculations are complex, it may be very difficult to determine why the output is not as expected. In this case, you may want to use debugging statements (such as DISPLAY statements) to print messages as the program executes. These statements are inserted in your program during testing, and they are removed after the errors are corrected. The messages printed by these statements can show the contents of selected storage fields or they can indicate which modules were executed. They can thus help you find the bugs. After the errors are corrected, the statements are removed from the source deck, the program is recompiled, and a final test run is made.

To illustrate the use of DISPLAY statements for debugging, suppose you couldn't figure out why the reorder line wasn't printed during the test run that is documented in figure 4-2. You might then insert the DISPLAY statements shown in figure 4-3 at the end of module 120 (line numbers 8171–8174). This time when the program is tested using the two cards given earlier, you will have the addi-

```
DISPLAY statements inserted in module 120:

008171      DISPLAY 'BF-ON-HAND        = ' BF-ON-HAND.              DEBUG
008172      DISPLAY 'BF-ON-ORDER       = ' BF-ON-ORDER.             DEBUG
008173      DISPLAY 'AVAILABLE-STOCK   = ' AVAILABLE-STOCK.         DEBUG
008174      DISPLAY 'BF-REORDER-POINT  = ' BF-REORDER-POINT.        DEBUG




OS DISPLAY statement output:

BF-ON-HAND        = 00070
BF-ON-ORDER       = 00050
AVAILABLE-STOCK   = 0012
BF-REORDER-POINT  = 00100
BF-ON-HAND        = 00034
BF-ON-ORDER       = 00000
AVAILABLE-STOCK   = 0003D
BF-REORDER-POINT  = 00050
REORDLST   I   1   NORMAL EOJ
```

Figure 4-3   Using DISPLAY statements to print the contents of selected fields during the execution of a test run

tional output shown in figure 4-3. By analyzing this output, you can see that the input data and available-stock calculation are correct, so you must check out other possibilities. Remember here that the rightmost digit of a numeric field will be displayed as a letter or special character if the field carries a sign, as long as the combination of digit and zone punches represents a printable EBCDIC character. Otherwise, the position will be blank (look at the rightmost position in the first value for AVAILABLE-STOCK). Also, notice that I coded DEBUG in columns 73–80 of the source cards so they will be easy to remove from the deck at the end of the test run.

If you still couldn't figure out why the reorder line wasn't printed, you might use DISPLAY statements to show the sequence in which the modules of the program were executed. For instance, you could take out the DISPLAY statements of figure 4-3 (since you know the data values are correct) and insert the DISPLAY statements of figure 4-4 into the reorder-listing program. If you check the line numbers of these statements, you can see that one DISPLAY statement is inserted into each paragraph of the program to print the module number of the paragraph. As a result, the output from these statements, as shown in figure 4-4, clearly indicates that module 150 was executed only twice. By checking the HIPO diagrams, you can see that this module should be called twice by module 140 and once by module 130, so the problem is probably within module 130.

```
DISPLAY statements inserted in modules 100 through 200:

007161        DISPLAY 100.                              DEBUG
008031        DISPLAY 110.                              DEBUG
008111        DISPLAY 120.                              DEBUG
009021        DISPLAY 130.                              DEBUG
009051        DISPLAY 140.                              DEBUG
010081        DISPLAY 150.                              DEBUG
010141        DISPLAY 160.                              DEBUG
011021        DISPLAY 200.                              DEBUG



OS DISPLAY statement output:

100
110
120
100
110
120
130
140
160
150
150
100
110
200
REORDLST   I   1   NORMAL EOJ
```

Figure 4-4   Using DISPLAY statements to list the modules that are executed
              during a test run

In book two of this series, you will learn more sophisticated
ways to trace the execution of a program and to find out the values
of certain fields during a test run. For now, though, the DISPLAY
statement will help you get the information you need to debug a
program that ran to completion.

Abnormal termination

If a program is *abnormally terminated*, it is referred to as a *program
check*. This means the object program tried to do something
impossible—such as trying to operate arithmetically on non-numeric
data. When a program check occurs, an error message is printed and
the program is cancelled. If the dump option is on at the time of the
program check (the option is set by the job-control language), a
storage dump, or *storage printout*, is also printed. This dump is a
listing of the contents of a computer's storage at the time of the program check.

```
0S03I   PROGRAM CHECK INTERRUPTION - HEX LOCATION 00689A - CONDITION CODE 2 - DATA EXCEPTION
0S00I   JOB ORDERLST CANCELLED
```

Figure 4-5   DOS message indicating a program check due to data exception

On a DOS system, the program-check message will follow the output that has been printed prior to the program check. If, for example, a blank card is accidentally put into the input deck for the reorder-listing program, a message like the one in figure 4-5 will be printed following the output that was printed before the blank card was processed. These two lines indicate that the program has been cancelled, that the instruction starting at storage location 00689A was the next instruction to be executed at the time of the program check, and that the cause of the program check is data exception.

On an OS system, the program-check message can be found on the first page of your output as shown in figure 4-6. This page gives the job-control statements supplied by the programmer (beginning with //), the job-control statements taken from the procedure library (beginning with XX), and various OS messages that give information about each of the steps within the job. Near the end of this output, you will find the program-check message if your program terminated abnormally (the message is shaded in part 1 of figure 4-6). Here, the second line of the message says that the instruction starting at storage location 4BODC2 was the next instruction to be executed at the time of the program check. The first line of the message specifies the cause of the program check by giving the system *completion code* OC7.

The number of system completion codes and their system messages is large; in fact, an entire IBM manual is devoted to their explanation. Some of the codes relate to system functions over which you have no control, some indicate certain types of I/O errors that are beyond the control of your program, and a small subset identifies program-check interruptions that are caused by errors in your program or its input data. It's this latter group that you should become familiar with since these codes point to bugs in your program.

The program-check completion codes all have the form OCX, where X can have a value of 1, 2, 3, 4, 5, 6, 7, 8, 9, A, B, C, D, E, or F to indicate one of the 15 types of program checks. All you need to be familiar with for now, however, are the most common causes of program checks, which are listed in figure 4-7. By using this table, you can deduce that the program in figure 4-6 ended because of data exception.

In a later book in this series, you will learn how to use certain pieces of optional compiler output to help you in debugging. For

```
//MMA$REF   JOB  (048-9038,COBOL),'MMA-LOWE',MSGLEVEL=(1,1),CLASS=N
LOG IEF403I MMA$REF  STARTED TIME=13.59.42                                          00001
LOG IEF450I MMA$REF  .GO         .       ABEND SOC7    TIME=14.00.11                 00002
LOG IEF404I MMA$REF  ENDED    TIME=14.00.12                                          00003
//          EXEC COBUCG,                                                             00004
//          PARM.COB=(CLIST,$XREF,NODECK,NOSTATE,NOFLOW)                             00005
XXCOB EXEC PGM=IKFCBL00,PARM='LOAD',REGION=86K                                       00006
***                                                                                  00007
***                                                                                  00008
XXSYSPRINT DD SYSOUT=A                                                               00009
XXSYSUT1   DD UNIT=DISK,SPACE=(460,(700,100)),DSN=&&SYSUT1                           00010
XXSYSUT2   DD UNIT=DISK,SPACE=(460,(700,100)),DSN=&&SYSUT2                           00011
XXSYSUT3   DD UNIT=DISK,SPACE=(460,(700,100)),DSN=&&SYSUT3                           00012
XXSYSUT4   DD UNIT=DISK,SPACE=(460,(700,100)),DSN=&&SYSUT4                           00013
XXSYSLIN   DD DSN=&LOADSET,DISP=(MOD,PASS),                                          00014
XX            UNIT=DISK,SPACE=(80,(500,100))                                         00015
***
***
***
//COB.SYSIN     DD  *
IEF236I ALLOC. FOR MMA$REF  COB
IEF237I 47A    ALLOCATED TO SYSUT1
IEF237I 47B    ALLOCATED TO SYSUT2
IEF237I 475    ALLOCATED TO SYSUT3
IEF237I 47A    ALLOCATED TO SYSUT4
IEF237I 47B    ALLOCATED TO SYSLIN
IEF142I - STEP WAS EXECUTED - COND CODE 0004
IEF285I    SYS78210.T135941.RF108.MMA$REF.SYSUT1          DELETED
IEF285I    VOL SER NOS= PUB001.
IEF285I    SYS78210.T135941.RF108.MMA$REF.SYSUT2          DELETED
IEF285I    VOL SER NOS= PUB002.
IEF285I    SYS78210.T135941.RF108.MMA$REF.SYSUT3          DELETED
IEF285I    VOL SER NOS= PUB003.
IEF285I    SYS78210.T135941.RF108.MMA$REF.SYSUT4          DELETED
IEF285I    VOL SER NOS= PUB001.
IEF285I    SYS78210.T135941.RF108.MMA$REF.LOADSET         PASSED
IEF285I    VOL SER NOS= PUB002.
IEF373I STEP /COB     / START 78210.1359
IEF374I STEP /COB     / STOP  78210.1400 CPU    0MIN 03.78SEC STOR VIRT 164K
ESS220 - B158-BSY606-01  7/29/78
XXGO       EXEC  PGM=LOADER,PARM=(LIST,MAP),COND=(5,LT,COB)                          00016
XXSYSLIN DD DSN=*.COB,SYSLIN,DISP=(OLD,DELETE)                                       00017
XXSYSLOUT DD SYSOUT=A                                                                00018
XXSYSLIB DD DSN=SYS1.COBLIB,DISP=SHR                                                 00019
//GO.SYSOUT    DD  SYSOUT=A
//GO.ORDLST    DD  SYSOUT=A
//GO.BFCRDS    DD  *
IEF236I ALLOC. FOR MMA$REF  GO
IEF237I 47B    ALLOCATED TO SYSLIN
IEF237I 258    ALLOCATED TO SYSLIB
```

COMPLETION CODE - SYSTEM=0C7 USER=0000

INTERRUPT AT 480DC2

```
FL.PT.REGS 0-6    00.000000 00000000    00.000000 00000000    00.000000 00000000    00.000000 00000000
```

Figure 4-6 OS JCL and message listing indicating a program check due to data exception (part 1 of 2)

```
ACTIVE RBS

PRB    4FFE10  NM LOADER    SZ/STAB 000400C2  USE/EP 004B0000  PSW 07R01000    00480DC2    Q    4FFDCO   WT/LNK 00018818

SVRB   4FFCBO  NM SVC-801C  SZ/STAB 0016D062  USE/EP 00FEC000  PSW 070C0000  C0E4864E  004BOD9A  Q    00C273   WT/LNK 0044FFE10
               RG 0-7  00480038  004B0DBO  00480070  0000005  004B0288         004B0530  0044FF760
               RG 8-15  004B04A8  004B1060  00480288  004B0A70  004807F8         50480D88  12ED1D44

IEF285I   SYS78210.T135941.RFI08.MMA$REF.LOADSET       DELETED
IEF285I   VOL SER NOS= PUB002.
IEF285I   SYS1.COBLIB                                  KEPT
IEF285I   VOL SER NOS= LIB001.
IEF373I   STEP /GO      / START 78210.1400
IEF374I   STEP /GO      / STOP  78210.1400 CPU    OMIN 00.78SEC STOR VIRT 320K
IEF298I   MMA$REF  SYSOUT=A.
IEF375I   JOB /MMA$REF / START 78210.1359
IEF376I   JOB /MMA$REF / STOP  78210.1400 CPU    OMIN 04.56SFC
```

Figure 4-6 OS JCL and message listing indicating a program check due to data exception (part 2 of 2)

Code	Exception Type	Explanation
OC1	Operation	The computer has tried to execute a machine-language code that it is unable to interpret. This is often caused by a file-handling error.
OC7	Data	Data that is invalid for the statement being executed has been found. This is usually caused by faulty data, faulty data descriptions, or improperly initialized values.
OC8 OCA	Overflow	An add, subtract, or multiply statement has resulted in a value that is too large for the receiving field. This is often caused by bad input data. To avoid it, check your input data to make sure the fields are a size that's reasonable for your program before you operate on them arithmetically.
OC9 OCB	Divide	The quotient resulting from a divide statement is too large for the quotient field. This is usually caused by dividing by zero.

Figure 4-7   Common program checks

instance, you will learn how to use the Procedure Division map to find the statement that was last to be executed before the program check. In most cases, this information will be all that you will need to debug the problem. You will also learn how to use the Data Division map and the storage dump as tools for debugging. Right now, however, I want to show you that you can debug many program checks by using the clues that are available to you without getting into the Procedure Division map, the Data Division map, and the storage dump.

In many cases, you will be able to tell which record was last to be processed before the program check occurred. This is your first debugging clue. If, for example, the program prints one line for each input record, you can tell which record was last to be processed by analyzing the printed output up to the time of the program check. Similarly, if a program prints one line for each group of input records, you will be able to narrow the problem down to a group of records by analyzing the output that was printed before the program check occurred. Then, by analyzing the record that was being processed at the time of the program check, you can often find something unusual that is likely to have caused the program check.

A second debugging clue is the cause of the program check given in the program-check message. As I mentioned before, a vast majority of all program checks result from a relatively limited number of causes. So here are descriptions of the four common causes listed in figure 4-7.

Data exception   The most common type of program check is called *data exception*. It occurs when an arithmetic statement tries to operate on non-numeric data. In general, there are two cases in which data exception occurs in COBOL programs.

In the first case, the input data doesn't conform to the input descriptions in the Data Division. If, for example, blanks are read into a storage field with a picture of 9(3), data exception will result when the field is operated upon by an ADD statement. This type of error is caused either by faulty input data or by faulty data descriptions.

In the second case, a field in working storage isn't initialized properly. If, for example, a field is supposed to have a starting value of zero but is given no starting value, data exception will occur when an ADD statement tries to add a number to it.

If you can figure out which record was being processed at the time of the program check, it's usually rather easy to debug a program that was ended because of data exception. If the program check occurs during the processing of the first input record, it's likely that some field in working storage wasn't initialized properly or that a field description in the Data Division is wrong. If the program check occurs during the processing of a later record, it's likely that one of the input fields contains invalid data.

Divide exception   When a program tries to divide a field by zero, a *divide exception* occurs. In this case, you should be able to locate the bug by checking the DIVIDE statements in your program along with the data in the record that was being processed at the time of the program check. As a good programming practice, your programs should always check to make sure that the divisor isn't zero before executing a DIVIDE statement; then the divide exception should never occur.

Overflow exception   When the execution of an arithmetic statement leads to a result that is larger than the receiving field can hold and the ON SIZE ERROR clause hasn't been used, an *overflow exception* can occur. Here again, you should be able to find the bug by analyzing the data in the record that was being processed at the time of the program check. If you follow this data through your program, you should reach a set of arithmetic instructions in which the result exceeds the size of the receiving field. This in turn means that either your size specifications in the Data Division are inaccurate or the data exceeds its expected limits. As a good programming practice, whenever possible your program should check the input data to make sure it's a reasonable size; then the overflow exception should never occur.

Operation exception   When the computer tries to execute an invalid machine-language operation code, an *operation exception* occurs. In a COBOL program, this often means a file-handling problem. For example, the following may indicate the cause of an operation exception in COBOL:

1.   Did a READ statement attempt to read a file before it was opened?
2.   Did a READ or WRITE statement try to operate on a file after it was closed?
3.   Did a statement refer to a field in the input area of storage after the AT END clause for the file had been executed?
4.   Did a statement attempt to operate on a field in the input area before the first READ statement was executed for the file?
5.   Did SPACE-CONTROL have an invalid value at the time a WRITE statement was executed? In other words, was it left blank or did it contain some value other than a positive integer?
6.   Was a STOP RUN statement executed before all files were closed?

All of these errors are common causes of operation exceptions on the System/360-370.

Although this book isn't intended to teach you how to debug all types of program checks, this introduction to program checks should help you debug most of the abnormal terminations you will run into using the COBOL elements presented in this book. Then, in a later book, you will learn more sophisticated methods of debugging abnormal terminations. Even then, however, you should always look for the obvious bug first.

Discussion

The benefits of structured programming are perhaps most obvious when it comes to testing. Because the structured program consists of independent modules and because these modules have only one entry and one exit point, the structured program is almost sure to have fewer bugs than the traditional program. In addition, these bugs are likely to be simple clerical errors rather than complex logical errors. Finally, due to the structured design, the bugs will be relatively easy to find and correct.

Because testing and debugging is so critical to the development of a successful program, later books in this series will cover debugging in more detail. First, they will show you how to use the COBOL debugging statements to help you isolate bugs at the COBOL level. Second, they will show you how to debug at the assembler-language level by using Data Division maps, Procedure Division maps, and storage dumps. For now, however, remember that the debugging techniques presented here should help you debug most of the problems you will encounter.

Terminology

unit test	storage dump
systems test	storage printout
acceptance test	completion code
test plan	data exception
utility program	divide exception
abnormal termination	overflow exception
program check	operation exception

Objectives

1. Given test data, expected output, compiler output, and test run output, debug any program ending in normal termination.

Problems

1. Figure 4-8 gives the output for a test run made on the reorder-listing program. It includes (1) a listing of the test data, (2) the source listing, (3) the DISPLAY statement output, and (4) the printer output. However, reorder lines have printed for all five input cards when they should have only printed for two of the cards. In addition, the amounts in the AVAILABLE column aren't correct. How should these errors be corrected?

Solutions

1. BF-ON-HAND in statement 34 should have a PICTURE of 9(5).

Card Columns	1-5	6-25	26-30	31-35	36-40	41-45	46-50
	00101	GENERATOR	04000	04900	00100	00070	00050
	00103	HEATER SOLENOID	00330	00440	00050	00034	00000
	03244	GEAR HOUSING	06500	07900	00010	00012	00000
	03981	PLUMB LINE	00210	00240	00015	00035	00000
	04638	STARTER SWITCH	00900	00980	00030	00016	00000

Figure 4-8   Test data listing (part 1 of 7)

```
PP 5734-CB1 V3 RELEASE 3.2 30APR74      IBM OS AMERICAN NATIONAL STANDARD COBOL              DATE JUL 29,1978

 1

00001   001010 IDENTIFICATION DIVISION.                                          REORDLST
00002   001020*                                                                  REORDLST
00003   001030 PROGRAM-ID. REORDLST.                                             REORDLST
00004   001040*                                                                  REORDLST
00005   001050 ENVIRONMENT DIVISION.                                            REORDLST
00006   001060*                                                                  REORDLST
00007   001070 CONFIGURATION SECTION.                                           REORDLST
00008   001080*                                                                  REORDLST
00009   001090 SPECIAL-NAMES.                                                   REORDLST
00010   001100        C01 IS PAGE-TOP.                                          REORDLST
00011   001110*                                                                  REORDLST
00012   001120 INPUT-OUTPUT SECTION.                                            REORDLST
00013   001130*                                                                  REORDLST
00014   001140 FILE-CONTROL.                                                    REORDLST
00015   001150      SELECT BFCRDS ASSIGN TO UT-S-BFCRDS.                        REORDLST
00016   001160      SELECT ORDLST ASSIGN TO UT-S-ORDLST.                        REORDLST
00017   001170*                                                                  REORDLST
00018   002010 DATA DIVISION.                                                   REORDLST
00019   002020*                                                                  REORDLST
00020   002030 FILE SECTION.                                                    REORDLST
00021   002040*                                                                  REORDLST
00022   002050 FD  BFCRDS                                                       REORDLST
00023   002060     LABEL RECORDS ARE STANDARD                                   REORDLST
00024   002070     RECORDING MODE IS F                                          RFORDLST
00025   002080     RECORD CONTAINS 80 CHARACTERS.                               REORDLST
00026   002090*                                                                  REORDLST
00027   002100 01  BAL-FWD-CARD.                                                REORDLST
00028   002110*                                                                  REORDLST
00029   002120     05  BF-ITEM-NO        PIC 9(5).                              REORDLST
00030   002130     05  BF-ITEM-DESC      PIC X(20).                             REORDLST
00031   002140     05  FILLER            PIC X(5).                              REORDLST
00032   002150     05  BF-UNIT-PRICE     PIC 999V99.                            REORDLST
00033   002160     05  BF-REORDER-POINT  PIC 9(5).                              REORDLST
00034   002170     05  BF-ON-HAND        PIC 999V99.                            REORDLST
00035   002180     05  BF-ON-ORDER       PIC 9(5).                              REORDLST
00036   002190     05  FILLER            PIC X(30).                             REORDLST
00037   002200*                                                                  REORDLST
00038   003010 FD  ORDLST                                                       REORDLST
00039   003020     LABEL RECORDS ARE STANDARD                                   REORDLST
00040   003030     RECORDING MODE IS F                                          REORDLST
00041   003040     RECORD CONTAINS 133 CHARACTERS.                              REORDLST
00042   003050*                                                                  REORDLST
00043   003060 01  PRINT-AREA            PIC X(133).                            REORDLST
00044   003070*                                                                  REORDLST
00045   003080 WORKING-STORAGE SECTION.                                         REORDLST
00046   003090*                                                                  REORDLST
00047   003100 01  SWITCHES.                                                    REORDLST
00048   003110*                                                                  REORDLST
```

Figure 4-8   Source listing (part 2 of 7)

```
2

00049 003120           05  CARD-EOF-SWITCH      PIC X       VALUE 'N'.            REORDLST
00050 003130*                                                                    REORDLST
00051 003140 01  WORK-FIELDS.                                                     REORDLST
00052 003150*                                                                     REORDLST
00053 003160     05  AVAILABLE-STOCK     PIC S9(5)   COMP-3.                      REORDLST
00054 003170*                                                                     REORDLST
00055 003180 01  PRINT-FIELDS            COMP        SYNC.                        REORDLST
00056 003190*                                                                     REORDLST
00057 003200     05  LINE-COUNT          PIC S99     VALUE +99.                   REORDLST
00058 003210     05  LINES-ON-PAGE       PIC S99     VALUE +57.                   REORDLST
00059 003220     05  SPACE-CONTROL       PIC S9.                                  REORDLST
00060 004010*                                                                     REORDLST
00061 004020 01  COUNT-FIELDS.                                                    REORDLST
00062 004030*                                                                     REORDLST
00063 004040     05  CARD-COUNT          PIC S9(5)   COMP-3   VALUE ZERO.         REORDLST
00064 004050*                                                                     REORDLST
00065 004060 01  HDG-LINE-1.                                                      REORDLST
00066 004070*                                                                     REORDLST
00067 004080     05  HDG1-CC             PIC X.                                   REORDLST
00068 004090     05  FILLER              PIC X(23)   VALUE SPACE.                 REORDLST
00069 004100     05  FILLER              PIC X(15)   VALUE 'REORDER LISTING'.     REORDLST
00070 004110     05  FILLER              PIC X(94)   VALUE SPACE.                 REORDLST
00071 004120*                                                                     REORDLST
00072 004130 01  HDG-LINE-2.                                                      REORDLST
00073 004140*                                                                     REORDLST
00074 004150     05  HDG2-CC             PIC X.                                   REORDLST
00075 004160     05  FILLER              PIC X(4)    VALUE 'ITEM'.                REORDLST
00076 004170     05  FILLER              PIC X(12)   VALUE SPACE.                 REORDLST
00077 004180     05  FILLER              PIC X(4)    VALUE 'ITEM'.                REORDLST
00078 004190     05  FILLER              PIC X(16)   VALUE SPACE.                 REORDLST
00079 004200     05  FILLER              PIC X(4)    VALUE 'UNIT'.                REORDLST
00080 005010     05  FILLER              PIC X(15)   VALUE SPACE.                 REORDLST
00081 005020     05  FILLER              PIC X(7)    VALUE 'REORDER'.             REORDLST
00082 005030     05  FILLER              PIC X(70)   VALUE SPACE.                 REORDLST
00083 005040*                                                                     REORDLST
00084 005050 01  HDG-LINE-3.                                                      REORDLST
00085 005060*                                                                     REORDLST
00086 005070     05  HDG3-CC             PIC X.                                   REORDLST
00087 005080     05  FILLER              PIC X       VALUE SPACE.                 REORDLST
00088 005090     05  FILLER              PIC X(3)    VALUE 'NO.'.                 REORDLST
00089 005100     05  FILLER              PIC X(9)    VALUE SPACE.                 REORDLST
00090 005110     05  FILLER              PIC X(11)   VALUE 'DESCRIPTION'.         REORDLST
00091 005120     05  FILLER              PIC X(5)    VALUE SPACE.                 REORDLST
00092 005130     05  FILLER              PIC X(5)    VALUE 'PRICE'.               REORDLST
00093 005140     05  FILLER              PIC X(4)    VALUE SPACE.                 REORDLST
00094 005150     05  FILLER              PIC X(9)    VALUE 'AVAILABLE'.           REORDLST
00095 005160     05  FILLER              PIC X(3)    VALUE SPACE.                 REORDLST
00096 005170     05  FILLER              PIC X(5)    VALUE 'POINT'.               REORDLST
00097 005180     05  FILLER              PIC X(71)   VALUE SPACE.                 REORDLST
00098 005190*                                                                     REORDLST
00099 006010 01  REORDER-LINE.                                                    REORDLST
```

Figure 4-8   Source listing (continued) (part 3 of 7)

```
3
00100  006020*                                                           REORDLST
00101  006030      05  RL-CC              PIC X.                         REORDLST
00102  006040      05  RL-ITEM-NO         PIC Z(5).                      REORDLST
00103  006050      05  FILLER             PIC X(5).     VALUE SPACE.     REORDLST
00104  006060      05  RL-ITEM-DESC       PIC X(20).                     REORDLST
00105  006070      05  FILLER             PIC X(5).     VALUE SPACE.     REORDLST
00106  006080      05  RL-UNIT-PRICE      PIC ZZZ.99.                    REORDLST
00107  006090      05  FILLER             PIC X(5).     VALUE SPACE.     REORDLST
00108  006100      05  RL-AVAILABLE-STOCK PIC Z(5).                      REORDLST
00109  006110      05  FILLER             PIC X(5).     VALUE SPACE.     REORDLST
00110  006120      05  RL-REORDER-POINT   PIC Z(5).                      REORDLST
00111  006130      05  FILLER             PIC X(71)     VALUE SPACE.     REORDLST
00112  006140*                                                          REORDLST
00113  006150  01  TOTAL-LINE.                                          REORDLST
00114  006160*                                                          REORDLST
00115  006170      05  TL-CC              PIC X.                         REORDLST
00116  006180      05  TL-CARD-COUNT      PIC ZZ,ZZZ.                    REORDLST
00117  006190      05  FILLER             PIC X(24)                      REORDLST
00118  006200             VALUE ' CARDS IN THE INPUT DECK'.             REORDLST
00119  006210      05  FILLER             PIC X(102) VALUE SPACE.        REORDLST
00120  006220*                                                          REORDLST
00121  007010  PROCEDURE DIVISION.                                      REORDLST
00172  007020*                                                          REORDLST
00123  007030  000-PRODUCE-REORDER-LISTING.                             REORDLST
00124  007040*                                                          REORDLST
00125  007050      OPEN INPUT BFCRDS                                    REORDLST
00126  007060           OUTPUT ORDLST.                                  REORDLST
00127  007070      PERFORM 100-PRODUCE-REORDER-LINE                     REORDLST
00128  007080           UNTIL CARD-EOF-SWITCH IS EQUAL TO 'Y'.          REORDLST
00129  007090      PERFORM 200-PRINT-TOTAL-LINE.                        REORDLST
00130  007100      CLOSE BFCRDS                                         REORDLST
00131  007110            ORDLST.                                        REORDLST
00132  007120      DISPLAY 'REORDLST   I   1   NORMAL EOJ'.             REORDLST
00133  007130      STOP RUN.                                            REORDLST
00134  007140*                                                          REORDLST
00135  007150  100-PRODUCE-REORDER-LINE.                                REORDLST
00136  007160*                                                          REORDLST
00137  007170      PERFORM 110-READ-INVENTORY-RECORD.                   REORDLST
00138  007180      IF CARD-EOF-SWITCH IS NOT EQUAL TO 'Y'               REORDLST
00139  007190      PERFORM 120-CALCULATE-AVAILABLE-STOCK                REORDLST
00140  007200           IF AVAILABLE-STOCK IS LESS THAN BF-REORDER-POINT REORDLST
00141  007210               PERFORM 130-PRINT-REORDER-LINE.             REORDLST
00142  008010*                                                          REORDLST
00143  008020  110-READ-INVENTORY-RECORD.                               REORDLST
00144  008030*                                                          REORDLST
00145  008040      READ BFCRDS                                          REORDLST
00146  008050          AT END                                           REORDLST
00147  008060              MOVE 'Y' TO CARD-EOF-SWITCH.                 REORDLST
00148  008070      IF CARD-EOF-SWITCH IS NOT EQUAL TO 'Y'               REORDLST
00149  008080          ADD 1 TO CARD-COUNT.                             REORDLST
00150  008090*                                                          REORDLST
```

Figure 4-8   Source listing (continued) (part 4 of 7)

```
4
00151 008100 120-CALCULATE-AVAILABLE-STOCK.                                 REORDLST
00152 008110*                                                               REORDLST
00153 008120     ADD BF-ON-HAND BF-ON-ORDER                                 REORDLST
00154 008130         GIVING AVAILABLE-STOCK                                 REORDLST
00155 008140         ON SIZE ERROR                                          REORDLST
00156 008150             DISPLAY 'REORDLST A  2   CALCULAT ON ERROR FOR ITEM 'REORDLST
00157 008160                 'NO. ' BF-ITEM-NO '--CARD IGNORED'             REORDLST
00158 008170             MOVE 99999 TO AVAILABLE-STOCK.                     REORDLST
00159 008180*                                                               REORDLST
00160 009010 130-PRINT-REORDER-LINE.                                        REORDLST
00161 009020*                                                               REORDLST
00162 009030     IF LINE-COUNT IS GREATER THAN LINES-ON-PAGE                REORDLST
00163 009040         PERFORM 140-PRINT-HEADING-LINES.                       REORDLST
00164 009050     MOVE BF-ITEM-NO       TO RL-ITEM-NO.                       REORDLST
00165 009060     MOVE BF-ITEM-DESC     TO RL-ITEM-DESC.                     REORDLST
00166 009070     MOVE BF-UNIT-PRICE    TO RL-UNIT-PRICE.                    REORDLST
00167 009080     MOVE AVAILABLE-STOCK  TO RL-AVAILABLE-STOCK.               REORDLST
00168 009090     MOVE BF-REORDER-POINT TO RL-REORDER-POINT.                 REORDLST
00169 009100     MOVE REORDER-LINE TO PRINT-AREA.                           REORDLST
00170 009110     PERFORM 150-WRITE-REPORT-LINE.                             REORDLST
00171 009120     MOVE 1 TO SPACE-CONTROL.                                   REORDLST
00172 009130*                                                               REORDLST
00173 009140 140-PRINT-HEADING-LINES.                                       REORDLST
00174 009150*                                                               REORDLST
00175 009160     MOVE HDG-LINE-1 TO PRINT-AREA.                             REORDLST
00176 009170     PERFORM 160-WRITE-PAGE-TOP-LINE.                           REORDLST
00177 009180     MOVE HDG-LINE-2 TO PRINT-AREA.                             REORDLST
00178 009190     MOVE 2 TO SPACE-CONTROL.                                   REORDLST
00179 010010     PERFORM 150-WRITE-REPORT-LINE.                             REORDLST
00180 010020     MOVE HDG-LINE-3 TO PRINT-AREA.                             REORDLST
00181 010030     MOVE 1 TO SPACE-CONTROL.                                   REORDLST
00182 010040     PERFORM 150-WRITE-REPORT-LINE.                             REORDLST
00183 010050     MOVE 2 TO SPACE-CONTROL.                                   REORDLST
00184 010060*                                                               REORDLST
00185 010070 150-WRITE-REPORT-LINE.                                         REORDLST
00186 010080*                                                               REORDLST
00187 010090     WRITE PRINT-AREA                                           REORDLST
00188 010100         AFTER ADVANCING SPACE-CONTROL LINES.                   REORDLST
00189 010110     ADD SPACE-CONTROL TO LINE-COUNT.                           REORDLST
00190 010120*                                                               REORDLST
00191 010130 160-WRITE-PAGE-TOP-LINE.                                       REORDLST
00192 010140*                                                               REORDLST
00193 010150     WRITE PRINT-AREA                                           REORDLST
00194 010160         AFTER ADVANCING PAGE-TOP.                              REORDLST
00195 010170     MOVE ZERO TO LINE-COUNT.                                   REORDLST
00196 010180*                                                               REORDLST
00197 011010 200-PRINT-TOTAL-LINE.                                          REORDLST
00198 011020*                                                               REORDLST
00199 011030     MOVE CARD-COUNT TO TL-CARD-COUNT.                          REORDLST
00200 011040     MOVE TOTAL-LINE TO PRINT-AREA.                             REORDLST
00201 011050     MOVE 3 TO SPACE-CONTROL.                                   REORDLST
00202 011060     PERFORM 150-WRITE-REPORT-LINE.                             REORDLST
```

Figure 4-8 Source listing (continued) (part 5 of 7)

```
REORDLST  I   1   NORMAL EOJ
```

Figure 4-8   DISPLAY statement output (part 6 of 7)

```
                REORDER LISTING

ITEM              UNIT                REORDER
NO.  DESCRIPTION  PRICE    AVAILABLE  POINT

101  GENERATOR        49.00     50      100
103  HEATER SOLENOID   4.40             50
3244 GEAR HOUSING     79.00             10
3981 PLUMB LINE        2.40             15
4638 STARTER SWITCH    9.80             30

      5 CARDS IN THE INPUT DECK
```

Figure 4-8   Test run output (part 7 of 7)

5

A Professional Subset of COBOL

This chapter expands the basic COBOL subset presented in chapter 2 by introducing some material that should prove helpful to the professional COBOL programmer. Some elements and techniques commonly used by professional programmers are discussed in topic 1. Although these elements don't involve any additional computing functions, they do make it possible for you to code more efficiently. Then, topic 2 provides some conceptual background to the execution of I/O operations. When you have completed this topic, you should understand why it is necessary to clear I/O areas more than once of data from a previous program. Finally, in topic 3, techniques for performing repetitive operations are illustrated.

TOPIC 1 COBOL Elements by Division

Once you have an overall understanding of the COBOL language, it is relatively easy to learn additional COBOL elements. Remember, however, that these advanced elements will not allow you to do much more than you can do with the basic elements already presented. In most cases, they will simply allow you to code in a more efficient and less time-consuming manner.

Identification Division Elements

Although the division name and PROGRAM-ID are the only lines
required in the Identification Division, other identifying information
can be given using the formats shown in the first part of figure
5-1. When these optional paragraphs are used, they must be written
in the sequence shown. Then, when the program is compiled, the
statements are listed on the program listing; however, no object code
is created for them.

   The second part of figure 5-1 illustrates a listing of an Identification Division that uses the optional paragraphs. Most of the
statements are self-explanatory; however, you may be wondering
why the DATE-COMPILED statement isn't followed by a comment.
When this paragraph is used, the compiler substitutes the current
date for whatever comment the programmer has written. Thus, it is
usually coded with no comment following. Since the compiler prints
the date-compiled on the top of the first page of each source listing,
this paragraph isn't really necessary. However, most programmers
include it in the Identification Division.

   In the 1968 ANS standards, a REMARKS paragraph was
another option in the Identification Division. However, this
paragraph has been dropped in the 1974 standards. If you are using
a 1968 ANS compiler, then, you should stop coding the REMARKS
paragraph so it will be easier for you to convert your programs to
future compilers. In the second part of figure 5-1, I've coded a
REMARKS paragraph, but I've preceded the lines in the paragraph
with asterisks in column 7 so the entire paragraph is treated as comments. As a result, the paragraph will be compiled properly by
either a 1968 or a 1974 compiler.

   The third part of figure 5-1 shows an Identification Division in
which the author, installation, date-written, and security paragraphs
are also coded as comments. Although these paragraphs are part of
the 1974 standards, it has been recommended that they be dropped
from the next set of standards (due sometime in the 1980s). So to
allow for future changes, you should use only the PROGRAM-ID
and DATE-COMPILED paragraphs in the Identification Division;
code anything else as a comment.

Data Division Elements

The REDEFINES clause

In some cases, one type of record may differ from another in only a
minor way. For instance, two transaction records may differ depending on whether the transaction is an issue from or a receipt to inven-

```
                 Identification Division Elements

IDENTIFICATION DIVISION.
PROGRAM-ID.  program-name.
[AUTHOR.  [comment-entry]   ...]
[INSTALLATION.  [comment-entry]   ...]
[DATE-WRITTEN.  [comment-entry]   ...]
[DATE-COMPILED.  [comment-entry]  ...]
[SECURITY.  [comment-entry]  ...]

            Sample Identification Division (1974 standards)

   IDENTIFICATION DIVISION.
   PROGRAM-ID.    REVSSPL.
   AUTHOR.        PAUL NOLL  BILL GRAHAM.
   INSTALLATION.  PTT.
   DATE-WRITTEN.  JULY 10, 1978.
   DATE-COMPILED.
   SECURITY.      THIS PROGRAM MAY NOT BE SHOWN TO ANYONE OUTSIDE
                  THE BELL SYSTEM.
  *REMARKS.       THIS PROGRAM PRODUCES THE DIVISION OF REVENUE
  *               REPORTS FOR SPECIAL SERVICE PRIVATE LINES.

             Sample Identification Division using comments

   IDENTIFICATION DIVISION.
   PROGRAM-ID.    REVSSPL.
   DATE-COMPILED.
  *AUTHORS.       PAUL NOLL AND BILL GRAHAM.
  *INSTALLATION.  PTT.
  *DATE-WRITTEN.  JULY 10, 1978.
  *SECURITY.      THIS PROGRAM MAY NOT BE SHOWN TO ANYONE OUTSIDE
  *               THE BELL SYSTEM.
  *REMARKS.       THIS PROGRAM PRODUCES THE DIVISION OF REVENUE
  *               REPORTS FOR SPECIAL SERVICE PRIVATE LINES.
```

Figure 5-1   The Identification Division

tory. In the first case, the reference number may be a six-column numeric field representing the invoice number; in the second case, it may be a six-column alphanumeric field representing the order number. To describe the same six columns in both ways, REDE-FINES may be used as follows:

```
01   TRAN-CARD.
     05   TR-TRAN-CODE        PIC X.
     05   TR-DATE             PIC 9(6).
     05   TR-ITEM-NO          PIC 9(6).
     05   TR-QUANTITY         PIC 9(5).
     05   TR-INVOICE-NO       PIC 9(6).
     05   TR-ORDER-NO         REDEFINES TR-INVOICE-NO
                              PIC X(6).
     05   FILLER              PIC X(56).
```

Thereafter in the program, the field that is punched in columns 19–24 of the transaction cards may be called TR-INVOICE-NO, in which case the data is treated as numeric, or TR-ORDER-NO, in which case the data is treated as alphanumeric.

If order number was a five-column numeric field in columns 19–23 and invoice number was a six-column numeric field in columns 19–24, REDEFINES could be used in this way:

```
05   TR-INVOICE-NO          PIC 9(6).
05   TR-ORDER-NO-X          REDEFINES TR-INVOICE-NO.
     10   TR-ORDER-NO       PIC 9(5).
     10   FILLER            PIC X.
```

Thus, REDEFINEᴐ can be used in a group item.

You may also redefine a data area more than once. For instance, suppose that in the second example above, there can be a third type of transaction: a return from a customer. In this case, columns 19–24 of the transaction card will contain alphanumeric data. Then, the field could be described like this:

```
05   TR-INVOICE-NO          PIC 9(6).
05   TR-ORDER-NO-X          REDEFINES TR-INVOICE-NO.
     10 TR-ORDER-NO         PIC 9(5).
     10  FILLER             PIC X.
05   TR-RETURN-NO           REDEFINES TR-INVOICE-NO
                            PIC X(6).
```

Because each of the three fields is just a different form of the reference number, you could call the area TR-REFERENCE-NO. Then, the fields which REDEFINE it could be indented like this:

```
05   TR-REFERENCE-NO        PIC X(6).
     05   TR-INVOICE-NO     REDEFINES TR-REFERENCE-NO
                               PIC 9(6).
     05   TR-ORDER-NO-X     REDEFINES TR-REFERENCE-NO.
          10   TR-ORDER-NO  PIC 9(5).
          10   FILLER       PIC X.
     05   TR-RETURN-NO      REDEFINES TR-REFERENCE-NO
                               PIC X(6).
```

This clearly shows that each of the fields is a redefinition of the reference number.

The format of the REDEFINES clause is this:

```
level-number data-name-1 REDEFINES data-name-2
```

When it is used, it must be the first clause following data-name-1 and must have the same level number as the data name it is redefining (data-name-2). Also, because two or more data names are assigned to the same storage area when REDEFINES is used, VALUE clauses cannot be used *after* the REDEFINES clause. As a result, the following code is illegal:

```
WORKING-STORAGE SECTION.
01  EXAMPLES.
    05  WS-EXAMPLE-1      PIC X(4)      VALUE 'ABCD'.
    05  WS-EXAMPLE-2      REDEFINES WS-EXAMPLE-1
                          PIC 9(4)    VALUE 100.
```

(It is also illogical and impossible, since two different values cannot be stored in the same storage positions.) A VALUE clause can be used on the field that is being redefined, however. So the following code is legal:

```
WORKING-STORAGE SECTION.
01  EXAMPLES.
    05  WS-EXAMPLE-1      PIC X(4)     VALUE 'ABCD'.
    05  WS-EXAMPLE-2      REDEFINES WS-EXAMPLE-1
                          PIC 9(4).
```

The REDEFINES clause has two main uses. One, as we have already seen, is to allow a single field to contain two or more types of data. The second is to get around some kind of technical limitation. You'll see an example of this second use later in this topic, in the discussion of the IF statement.

Condition names

The 88 level in the Data Division can be used to give *condition names* to various values that a field may contain. Suppose, for example, that an input transaction code (TR-TRAN-CODE) may be a 1, 2, or R, depending on whether the transaction is an issue from inventory, a receipt to inventory, or a return of merchandise from a customer. Figure 5-2 shows how a condition name can be assigned to each of these values in the input area. (RETURNS is used as one of the condition names because RETURN is a COBOL reserved word.)

To understand how these condition names are used in the Procedure Division, look at paragraph 100-PREPARE-SALES-LINE in figure 5-2. As you can see, the conditions in the IF statements of

```
 DATA DIVISION.
::
 FILE SECTION.
::      .
        .
        .
     05  TR-TRAN-CODE            PIC X.
         88  ISSUE                         VALUE '1'.
         88  RECEIPT                       VALUE '2'.
         88  RETURNS                       VALUE 'R'.
        .
        .
::      .

 WORKING-STORAGE SECTION.
::
 01  SWITCHES.
::
     05  CARD-EOF-SW            PIC X    VALUE 'N'.
         88  CARD-EOF                   VALUE 'Y'.
::
 01  FLAGS.
::
     05  COMMISSION-LEVEL-FLAG   PIC X.
         88  LEVEL-1                       VALUE '1'.
         88  LEVEL-2                       VALUE '2'.
         88  LEVEL-3                       VALUE '3'.
         88  LEVEL-4                       VALUES '4' 'D' THRU 'F'.
        .
        .
::      .
```

Figure 5-2 Using condition names (part 1 of 2)

this paragraph are simply the condition names assigned to the field
TR-TRAN-CODE. As a result, this statement

```
IF ISSUE
    PERFORM 150-PROCESS-INV-ISSUE
```

is saying, in effect, that if TR-TRAN-CODE contains a 1, the program should perform 150-PROCESS-INV-ISSUE. Though all the
conditions in this paragraph are positive, the word NOT can be used
to form a negative condition, as in this example:

```
IF NOT ISSUE
    ADD TR-QUANTITY TO WS-ON-HAND
```

Then, as long as TR-TRAN-CODE does *not* contain a value of 1,
TR-QUANTITY will be added to WS-ON-HAND.

```
      PROCEDURE DIVISION.
:c
      000-PRODUCE-SALES-SUMMARY.
:c
          .
          .
          PERFORM 100-PREPARE-SALES-LINE
              UNTIL CARD-EOF.
          .
          .
:c
      100-PREPARE-SALES-LINE.
:c
          PERFORM 110-READ-INPUT-RECORD.
          .
          .
          IF ISSUE
              PERFORM 150-PROCESS-INV-ISSUE
          ELSE
              IF RECEIPT
                  PERFORM 160-PROCESS-INV-RECEIPT
              ELSE
                  IF RETURNS
                      PERFORM 170-PROCESS-INV-RETURN
                  ELSE
                      PERFORM 180-PRINT-INVALID-CODE-MSGE.
          .
          .
:c
      110-READ-INPUT-RECORD.
:c
          READ INVCDS
              AT END
                  MOVE 'Y' TO CARD-EOF-SW.
          .
          .
:c
      190-DETERMINE-SALES-COMMISSION.
:c
          IF LEVEL-1
              MOVE L1-PCT TO COMMISSION-PCT
          ELSE
              IF LEVEL-2
                  MOVE L2-PCT TO COMMISSION-PCT
              ELSE
                  IF LEVEL-3
                      MOVE L3-PCT TO COMMISSION-PCT
                  ELSE
                      IF LEVEL-4
                          MOVE L4-PCT TO COMMISSION-PCT.
```

Figure 5-2 Using condition names (part 2 of 2)

You'll discover how valuable condition names are when you have to change a program because the codes in it have been changed. Without condition names, you have to change every statement in the Procedure Division that refers to the codes. With condition names, only the 88-level statements in the Data Division need to be changed.

Condition names are also useful for setting and testing switches and flags in a program. (In this book, the difference between a switch and a *flag* is that a switch has only two possible values, while a flag has more than two.) For example, in figure 5-2, CARD-EOF is the condition name given to the end-of-file switch (CARD-EOF-SW) when the switch has a value of Y. The switch is set to this value in paragraph 110-READ-INPUT-RECORD when there are no more input records to be read. The value of the switch is tested by the PERFORM UNTIL statement in 000-PRODUCE-SALES-SUMMARY. Thus, this procedure will perform paragraph 100-PREPARE-SALES-LINE until CARD-EOF (that is, until CARD-EOF-SW equals Y.)

As illustrated in figure 5-2, condition names can be used in either the File Section or the Working-Storage Section of the Data Division. Also, the field being described can be numeric or alphanumeric. Note that it is the field itself that has the PICTURE clause, while VALUE clauses are given at the 88-level. Moreover, a single condition name can have more than one value, as does LEVEL-4 under COMMISSION-LEVEL-FLAG. Then, if the field contains any of the values, the condition is true. In other words,

```
IF LEVEL-4
```

in figure 5-2 is the same as

```
IF COMMISSION-LEVEL-FLAG IS EQUAL TO
    '4' OR 'D' OR 'E' OR 'F'
```

Note that THRU includes the beginning and ending literal values along with all values in between. It can be used with numeric, as well as non-numeric, literals.

To keep the names consistent, the condition names should be related to the data names whenever practical. For a switch, the condition name should be meaningful like CARD-EOF, which stands for the card end-of-file. And the switch name should be the condition name followed by SWITCH or just SW. Thus, the switch name for the CARD-EOF condition should be CARD-EOF-SWITCH or CARD-EOF-SW. (We will always use SW in this book.)

For a flag, the condition names may or may not be closely related to the flag name. For a flag like COMMISSION-LEVEL-FLAG in figure 5-2, it makes sense to relate the names as shown. For

Constant	Represents
ZERO ZEROS ZEROES	One or more zeros
SPACE SPACES	One or more blanks (spaces)
ALL 'character'	One or more occurrences of the character within quotation marks
QUOTE QUOTES	One or more occurrences of the quotation mark (" or ')
HIGH-VALUE HIGH-VALUES	One or more occurrences of the highest value that can be placed in a storage position of a specific computer
LOW-VALUE LOW-VALUES	One or more occurrences of the lowest value that can be placed in a storage position of a specific computer

Figure 5-3   Figurative constants

other types of flags, it makes more sense to give meaningful condition names like TRAINEE, ASSOCIATE, SENIOR-ASSOCIATE, and MANAGER and to use a general flag name like SALESMAN-STATUS-FLAG.

Because condition names are valuable in programs that have code fields or various types of switches or flags, you should use them often. As a result, you will see them frequently in the programs in the rest of this book.

Figurative constants

The COBOL words ZERO and SPACE are called *figurative constants*. The complete list of figurative constants for ANS COBOL is given in figure 5-3. Except for the words ZERO, ZEROS, and ZEROES, these figurative constants act as if they were non-numeric literals. If, for example, a field is described as

```
05  FILLER  PIC  X(5)  VALUE ALL'-'.
```

the effect is the same as if it were described as

```
05  FILLER  PIC  X(5)  VALUE '-----'.
```

Similarly,

```
05  QUOTE-EXAMPLE  PIC X  VALUE QUOTE.
```

describes a field of one byte that contains one quotation mark. Because quotation marks are used to enclose non-numeric literals in COBOL, using the word QUOTE is the only way you can store a quotation mark.

The figurative constants HIGH-VALUE and LOW-VALUE represent the highest and lowest values in a computer's collating sequence. This means that a field that is given a value of HIGH-VALUE contains the highest possible value that can be stored in a field of that size. Similarly, a field with a value of LOW-VALUE is given the lowest possible value that can be stored in a field of that size. In general, these figurative constants are used when you want to force an unequal comparison (HIGH-VALUE will never be less than another value, and LOW-VALUE will never be more). You saw this use in the module documentation for the report extract program in figure 3-40. And you will see it again in chapter 7.

Although you can use either the singular or plural forms of figurative constants, we suggest you stick to the singular forms (SPACE, ZERO, etc.). Because both the singular and plural forms mean the same thing, the plurals are unnecessary. And the plural forms allow a greater chance of misspelling with resulting diagnostics.

Indentation

Indentation should be used in the Data Division to show the structure of related data items and to make the code easier to read, as shown in figure 5-2. As you can see, there should always be two spaces between the level number and the data name, and each successive level should be indented four spaces from the preceding level. Whenever possible, I like to see PICTURE clauses starting in column 32 and VALUE clauses in column 44. Wherever they begin, though, these clauses as well as USAGE and SYNC clauses should be vertically aligned within 01-level items.

The sequence of elements

To make it easy to locate file or data descriptions in the Data Division, I recommend that standard coding sequences be used. For example, the FD statements in the File Section should be coded in the same sequence as the SELECT statements in the Environment Division. Then, the SELECT statements are a directory for finding the FD statements.

Furthermore, the record descriptions in the Working-Storage Section should be coded in the same sequence each time. For instance, you might use a standard sequence like this: (1) switches, (2) flags, (3) work fields, (4) control fields, (5) print fields like LINE-COUNT and SPACE-CONTROL, (6) counters, (7) total fields, (8) subscripts, (9) tables, (10) input or output record descriptions in the same order as the related files are listed in the SELECT statements. (Numbers 8 and 9 have to do with repetitive processing, so don't worry about them for now.) When you code the working-storage areas for lines that are associated with print files, you can code them in the same sequence that they are shown on the print chart: (1) heading lines, (2) body lines, and (3) total lines. If you use standard coding sequences like these throughout your shop, it is easier for one programmer to locate code within another programmer's program. And it is easier for you to locate your own code as you go from one of your programs to another.

Procedure Division Elements

Section names

The Procedure Division of a program can be divided into sections made up of one or more paragraphs by using *section names*. A section name is any valid procedure name followed by the word SECTION and a period. It must appear on a coding line by itself. When a section name is referred to in a PERFORM statement, the word SECTION isn't used—that is, you code PERFORM MAINLINE, not PERFORM MAINLINE SECTION. A section continues until the next section name or the end of the program is reached.

In unstructured programs, sections were often used. In structured programs, however, there are only three instances in which it is necessary to use them. Two of these—declaratives and the sort feature—are not covered in this book. The third is the case structure, which you will see later in this topic.

Figurative constants

Figurative constants may be used in the Procedure Division as well as in the Data Division. These COBOL words have the same meaning in either division. The following are some examples of their use in the Procedure Division:

```
1.   MOVE ZERO TO WS-CUSTOMER-TOTAL.

2.   MOVE ALL '*' TO PRINT-AREA.

3.   MOVE HIGH-VALUE TO TR-CUSTOMER-NO.
```

In example 1, the value of WS-CUSTOMER-TOTAL is set to zero. In example 2, one asterisk is moved to each storage position in PRINT-AREA. And in example 3, the highest value possible in the computer's collating sequence is moved to TR-CUSTOMER-NO.

The READ INTO option

The READ INTO option of the READ statement reads a record and moves it into an area of working storage. It is thus the equivalent of a READ statement followed by a MOVE. Its format is this:

```
READ file-name RECORD INTO data-name
     AT END imperative-statement.
```

When it is used, the individual fields of the input record are normally defined in the Working-Storage Section rather than in the File Section of the Data Division. This is illustrated in figure 5-4.

The INTO clause of the READ statement can also specify an output area of another file. Then, input data can be moved directly into an output area by the READ statement. This is often done when processing tape or disk files.

The main reason for using the INTO option is that the data from the last record in a file is available after the AT END clause for that file has been executed. This is often valuable when preparing summary reports or when processing tape or disk files. In contrast, when the data for the last input record hasn't been moved to working storage, its data is not available to the program after the end-of-file has been reached. In general, then, you should use the INTO option and process input records in the Working-Storage Section.

The WRITE FROM option

The WRITE FROM option of the WRITE statement is comparable to the READ INTO option of the READ statement. Its format is this:

```
WRITE record-name FROM data-name

    [ {BEFORE}   ADVANCING  {integer LINES    } ]
    [ {AFTER }              {data-name LINES   } ]
    [                       {mnemonic-name     } ]
```

If the FROM option is used, an output record is moved from an area in working storage to an output area described in the File Section, and then it is printed.

The FROM option is useful when a file has only one record format and the record is described and developed in working storage.

```
        DATA DIVISION.
x
        FILE SECTION.
x
        FD   CARDFILE
             LABEL RECORDS ARE STANDARD
             RECORDING MODE IS F
             RECORD CONTAINS 80 CHARACTERS.
x
        01  CARD-AREA              PIC X(80).
x
        FD   PRINTFLE
              .
              .
x
        WORKING-STORAGE SECTION.
x
              .
              .
x
        01  CARD-RECORD.
x
            05  CR-ITEM-CODE    PIC X(5).
            05  CR-REF-NO       PIC X(6).
              .
              .
x
        PROCEDURE DIVISION.
x
              .
              .
        READ CARDFILE INTO CARD-RECORD
             AT END
                 MOVE 'Y' TO CARD-EOF-SW.
              .
              .
```

Figure 5-4   The READ INTO statement

Then, the WRITE FROM statement can be used to move the record into the output area and to write it. When a file consists of records with more than one record format, however, using the FROM option results in more than one WRITE statement for the file (one for each record format). And this conflicts with our structured-programming goal of one WRITE statement per file. So if you have a file consisting of more than one record format (most print files are that way), don't use the FROM option of the WRITE statement.

Getting the current date

In general, whenever an operating system is used, the current date is stored somewhere in the supervisor area of storage at the start of the day's processing. This date is commonly printed in report headings and on other documents such as invoices or payroll checks.

Unfortunately, the ANS 68 COBOL specifications didn't provide any language for getting the date into the user's program area, so individual manufacturers had to extend the specifications. Thus, on the System/360-370 compilers that operate under the 68 standards, the current date is available through the use of a CURRENT-DATE field. Later, the ANS 74 specifications corrected the 68 omission by providing the ACCEPT statement for getting the date, day, or time from the supervisor area. So some System/360-370 compilers allow you to get the date either way.

The CURRENT-DATE field   To get the date under the IBM extension to the ANS 68 standards, CURRENT-DATE is used as the sending field in a MOVE statement, as shown in the top part of figure 5-5:

```
MOVE CURRENT-DATE TO USER-DATE.
```

When executed, the date is moved from the supervisor area to any eight-position field in the user's program (in figure 5-5, USER-DATE). The date is in the form of MM/DD/YY where MM is a two-digit number indicating the month, DD is a two-digit number indicating the day, and YY is a two-digit number indicating the year. For example, if the date is April 30, 1979 when the MOVE statement in figure 5-5 is executed, UD-MONTH will contain 04, UD-DAY will contain 30, and UD-YEAR will contain 79. The FILLER fields will contain slashes (/).

The ACCEPT statement   Under the ANS 74 specifications, the standard statement for getting the date, day, or time from the supervisor area has this format:

$$\underline{ACCEPT} \text{ data-name } \underline{FROM} \left\{ \begin{array}{l} \underline{DATE} \\ \underline{DAY} \\ \underline{TIME} \end{array} \right\}$$

When executed, date, day, or time is moved to a field described in the user's program, and the receiving field can be numeric or numeric edited. At this writing, this statement is available on two System/360-370 compilers: the Version 4 and OS/VS compilers.

The form of the standard DATE field is an unedited YYMMDD (two-digit year, month, and day), so July 1, 1978 is stored as 780701. Similarly, the form of the standard DAY field is YYDDD,

```
                    The MOVE CURRENT-DATE statement:
                      DATA DIVISION.
                         .
                         .
                      WORKING-STORAGE SECTION.
                         .
                         .
              ::
              01    DATE-FIELDS.
              ::
                      05    USER-DATE.
                            10    UD-MONTH     PIC 99.
                            10    FILLER       PIC X.
                            10    UD-DAY       PIC 99.
                            10    FILLER       PIC X.
                            10    UD-YEAR      PIC 99.
                         .
                         .
                      PROCEDURE DIVISION.
                         .
                         .
                            MOVE CURRENT-DATE TO USER-DATE.
                         .
                         .


                    The ACCEPT statement:
                      DATA DIVISION.
                         .
                         .
                      WORKING-STORAGE SECTION.
                         .
                         .
              ::
              01    DATE-FIELDS.
              ::
                      05    PRESENT-DATE.
                            10    PD-YEAR      PIC 99.
                            10    PD-MONTH     PIC 99.
                            10    PD-DAY       PIC 99.
                      05    PRESENT-DAY.
                            10    FILLER       PIC XX.
                            10    PD-DAY-NO    PIC 999.
                      05    EDITED-DATE.
                            10    ED-MONTH     PIC 99.
                            10    FILLER       PIC X       VALUE '/'.
                            10    ED-DAY       PIC 99.
                            10    FILLER       PIC X       VALUE '/'.
                            10    ED-YEAR      PIC 99.
                         .
                         .
                      PROCEDURE DIVISION.
                         .
                         .
              ::
              100-GET-CURRENT-DATE.
              ::
                      ACCEPT PRESENT-DATE FROM DATE.
                      MOVE PD-MONTH TO ED-MONTH.
                      MOVE PD-DAY    TO ED-DAY.
                      MOVE PD-YEAR   TO ED-YEAR.
                      ACCEPT PRESENT-DAY FROM DAY.
                         .
                         .
```

Figure 5-5   Getting the current date

where DDD represents three digits that indicate what number day in the year it is. Thus, July 1, 1978 is stored as 78182 (the 182nd day of 1978). The second part of figure 5-5 illustrates how these fields can be moved into the Working-Storage Section of a user's program. In this example, the date is edited after it is moved, so EDITED-DATE will print July 1, 1978 as 7/01/78.

Although TIME isn't used very often, its standard form is HHMMSSHH (two-digit hours, minutes, seconds, and hundredths of seconds). This assumes a 24-hour clock, so 2:00 P.M. is hour 14. As a result, 2:41 P.M. is stored as 14410000. The minimum value of TIME is 00000000; the maximum is 23595999.

The COMPUTE statement

The format of the COMPUTE statement is this:

```
COMPUTE data-name [ROUNDED] = arithmetic-expression
     [ON SIZE ERROR statement-1 ...]
```

It can be used to express arithmetic calculations in a form that is reasonably close to normal arithmetic notation. For example,

```
COMPUTE NET-PAY ROUNDED = HOURS * RATE - DEDUCTIONS
```

can be used to indicate the contents of the field named HOURS should be multiplied (*) by the contents of the field named RATE and the contents of the field named DEDUCTIONS should be subtracted ($-$) from the product. The result should be rounded and placed in the field named NET-PAY.

To form an arithmetic expression in COBOL, the following symbols can be used:

Symbol	Meaning
+	Addition
−	Subtraction
*	Multiplication
/	Division
**	Exponentiation

Since exponentiation means "raising to the power of," the COBOL expression X ** 2 is equivalent to the arithmetic expression X^2. And the COBOL expression X ** .5 is equivalent to the arithmetic expression $X^{1/2}$, or $\sqrt{X}$ (the square root of X). Exponentiation is a slow process in COBOL, though, so whenever practical, you should use multiplication instead. For example, X ** 2 would execute more quickly if you coded it as X * X. When the arithmetic symbols are

used to indicate an operation, they must be preceded and followed
by one or more spaces.

Sequence of operations   When a series of arithmetic operations is
expressed in a single COMPUTE statement, it is important to know
the order in which the operations will be executed. The expression
H * R − D, for example, can have different values depending on
whether the multiplication or the subtraction is done first. If H =
40, R = 2, and D = 5.00, the value of the expression is 75.00 if the
multiplication is done first or −120.00 if the subtraction is done first
(2 − 5.00 = −3.00; −3.00 * 40 = −120.00).

In COBOL, the order in which arithmetic operations are executed is this: (1) exponentiation, (2) multiplication and division, (3)
addition and subtraction. If the same type of operation is used more
than once in an expression, the sequence is from left to right for
each type. For example, in the statement

```
COMPUTE N = H * R - D
```

multiplication takes place first. In the expression A * B + C * D,
first A and B are multiplied, then C and D are multiplied, and then
the two products are added together to give the final result.

Sometimes an expression is so complex that it's hard to keep
track of which part is evaluated first by the compiler. In such a case,
you should use parentheses to indicate the sequence in which the
operations will be done. Operations within parentheses are performed before operations outside parentheses. When there are parentheses within parentheses, the operations in the innermost set of
parentheses are performed first. Thus, in the expression

```
A + B ** 3 / C - D * E * F
```

parentheses would be used as follows:

```
A + ((B ** 3) / C) - (D * E * F)
```

As you can see, this reflects the compiler's sequence of evaluation:
exponentiation will be done first, followed by multiplication and
division from left to right, and finally addition and subtraction from
left to right.

Now suppose that you want to add two values and then cube
the sum. How do you make the compiler change its normal sequence
of evaluation? Again, you use parentheses. And again, whatever is
in the innermost set of parentheses will be evaluated first, followed
by the next set of parentheses, and so on. To illustrate, suppose the
expression above were written like this:

```
((A + B) ** 3) / ((C - D) * E) * F
```

In this case, the expressions (A + B) and (C − D) would be
evaluated first; then the cube of (A + B) would be taken and (C −
D) would be multiplied by E; next the result of ((A + B) * * 3)
would be divided by the result of ((C − D) * E); and finally, the
quotient would be multiplied by F. In short, parentheses can dictate
as well as clarify the order in which an expression will be evaluated.
So use them frequently to improve the clarity of your COMPUTE
statements.

Result fields   Since intermediate fields in a COMPUTE statement
are given the same size as the final result field and since the ON
SIZE ERROR clause applies only to final results, errors will occur if
intermediate results are larger than the final result field. In the statement

```
COMPUTE RESULT = A * B / C
     ON SIZE ERROR
          PERFORM 170-PRINT-ERROR-MESSAGE.
```

an error will result if A * B is greater than can be stored in the final
result field—even if A * B / C is not larger than the result field. As
a result, it is the programmer's responsiblity to make the result field
large enough for any intermediate results. The result field may be
described as a numeric item of any USAGE or as a numeric edited
item. If it is a numeric edited item, the result is edited as it is moved
to this field.

In the 1974 ANS specifications, a minor change was made to the
format of the COMPUTE statement. Where formerly only one result
field was allowable, a series of result fields is now acceptable. For
instance,

```
COMPUTE FIELD-A FIELD-B ROUNDED =
     1.23 * FIELD-X + (FIELD-Y - FIELD-Z)
```

is acceptable under the revised specifications. Here, the result of the
arithmetic expression is moved to FIELD-A and FIELD-B, but only
FIELD-B is rounded. A statement such as this would be useful for
calculating something like interest where you need a rounded result
for the current amount as well as an unrounded result for ongoing
calculations. At present, this feature is available on only one
System/360-370 compiler, the OS/VS compiler.

Advanced IF statements

You are already familiar with simple IF statements and with IF
statements that have ELSE clauses. You are also familiar with nested
IF statements. Now, you will get additional information about the
operation and coding of the IF statement.

Collating sequence Perhaps the most important yet most difficult aspect of the IF statement is determining when a condition is true or false. In a simple *relation test* between two numeric fields—such as IF HOURS-WORKED IS LESS THAN FORTY—the fields are evaluated based on their numeric value; the size or USAGE of the fields does not affect the results. Thus, 30.5 is less than 40 and 58 is greater than 40.00.

When a relation test compares alphanumeric data, the evaluation is made in a different way. The fields are evaluated character by character, from left to right. Since the computer considers A to have the least value and Z to have the greatest, it's fairly easy to compare purely alphabetic fields—for example, JONES comes before (IS LESS THAN) THOMAS. However, it is hard to say whether X-12-13 is less than or greater than X1213. In fact, it depends on the *collating sequence* of a computer and varies by computer model. On the System/360-370, the hyphen (-) comes before the digits in the collating sequence, so X-12-13 is less than X1213.

The following is the collating sequence of some commonly used System/360-370 characters (from lowest to highest):

> LOW-VALUE
> the blank
>
> .
>
> (
>
> &
>
>)
>
> -
>
> /
>
> , (comma)
>
> #
>
> ' (apostrophe)
>
> "
>
> the letters A–Z
> the numbers 0–9
> HIGH-VALUE

The complete collating sequence is given in the green and yellow reference cards for the System/360 and 370 (forms X20-1703 and GX20-1850). Based on this collating sequence, T. S. is less than TOM, H&R is less than H-R, and T2S is less than T29.

One thing to remember when coding relation tests is to compare numeric items with numeric items and non-numeric with non-numeric items. It is illegal to compare an alphabetic item with a numeric item, and, although an alphanumeric item can be compared with a numeric item of DISPLAY usage, the comparison takes place based on collating sequence instead of on the numeric value of the fields. For object program efficiency, numeric items that are compared should have the same number of decimal places. And alphanumeric items should be the same size.

Using relational symbols Whenever you need the *relational operators* LESS THAN, EQUAL TO, and GREATER THAN in relation tests, you can code them in a couple of different ways. You can use the shorter forms LESS, EQUAL, and GREATER. Or you can use the symbols <, =, and >. The following are examples of the second usage:

```
1.   IF CR-CUST-ORDER > 200
         PERFORM 430-LIST-SIZE-ERROR.

2.   IF TR-CODE-2 = 'C'
         PERFORM 180-CALCULATE-CALIF-TAX.
```

Before you start using these symbols, though, check and make sure they're available on all your printers. Since some print chains don't have the "less than" and "greater than" symbols, A < B can come out looking like A (B on your source listing. Naturally, this can be confusing. So check the printer before you use the symbols. And if you're interested in maintaining the transferability of your programs from one computer to another, don't use the symbols at all. In fact, we recommend that you use the words rather than the symbols in all your programs.

Using arithmetic expressions Arithmetic expressions such as those in COMPUTE statements may also be used in relation tests. Some examples follow:

```
1.   IF X + Y EQUAL TO 200
         PERFORM 430-LIST-SIZE-ERROR.

2.   IF .5 * G / T ** 2 NOT LESS THAN 4
         MOVE 'Y' TO INVALID-RESULT-SW
         PERFORM 140-PROCESS-INVALID-RESULT
     ELSE
         PERFORM 130-CALCULATE-INT-PAYMENT.
```

If necessary, parentheses can be used within the expression to dictate the order of operations. And they should always be used if they make the expression easier to understand.

In general, though, you should avoid using arithmetic expressions in relation tests. Instead, you should do the calculation in one statement and the relation test in a second statement. For instance, example 2 above can be coded like this:

```
COMPUTE RESULT = .5 * G / T ** 2.
IF RESULT NOT LESS THAN 4
    MOVE 'Y' TO INVALID-RESULT-SW
    PERFORM 140-PROCESS-INVALID-RESULT
ELSE
    PERFORM 130-CALCULATE-INT-PAYMENT.
```

Then, if the program specifications change and the result of the calculation is needed in another part of the program, you don't have to repeat the calculation. You can simply reference the field named RESULT because it already contains the answer.

Sign tests   Although relation tests are the most common, sign and class tests can also be used in COBOL. The format for a sign test is this:

$$\begin{Bmatrix} \text{data-name} \\ \text{arithmetic-expression} \end{Bmatrix} \quad \text{IS} \quad [\underline{\text{NOT}}] \quad \begin{Bmatrix} \underline{\text{POSITIVE}} \\ \underline{\text{ZERO}} \\ \underline{\text{NEGATIVE}} \end{Bmatrix}$$

It simply tests whether a numeric item is greater than, equal to, or less than zero. Zero is considered neither positive nor negative. Here are some examples:

```
1.   IF FIELD-1 IS POSITIVE
         PERFORM 210-CALCULATE-PAY-RATE.

2.   IF FIELD-2 IS NOT NEGATIVE
         PERFORM 350-PRINT-TOTAL-LINE-INVEST.
```

The sign test can only be used on numeric data items.

Class tests   Besides sign and relation tests, you can also code class tests. The class test format is this:

$$\text{data-name} \quad \text{IS} \quad [\underline{\text{NOT}}] \quad \begin{Bmatrix} \underline{\text{NUMERIC}} \\ \underline{\text{ALPHABETIC}} \end{Bmatrix}$$

The alphabetic form of this test can be performed on an alphabetic or alphanumeric field. If the field consists entirely of the letters A through Z and blanks (SPACE), the field is considered to be alphabetic.

The numeric test can be performed on an elementary item that is (1) an alphanumeric field, (2) a numeric field with DISPLAY usage, or (3) a numeric field with COMP-3 usage. An alphanumeric field is considered numeric if all bytes consist of the digits 0 through 9. Likewise, an *unsigned* numeric field of DISPLAY or COMP-3 usage is considered numeric if it contains only digits and does not contain a sign.

In a *signed* numeric field, however, the rightmost byte carries the sign of the field. As a result, a field like this is considered numeric if it contains all digits with a valid sign in the rightmost byte. More specifically, a three-byte DISPLAY field on the System/360-370 must have this form:

FD	FD	SD

Here, FD represents a digit in DISPLAY form and SD represents a signed digit. Similarly, a three-byte COMP-3 field must have this form:

DD	DD	DS

Here, the first two bytes contain two digits each and the rightmost byte contains one digit and a valid sign. If you're familiar with hex notation on the System/360-370, a valid sign is hex F (positive), hex D (negative), or hex C (positive).

The numeric test points up one instance in which you may have to use the REDEFINES clause to get around a technical problem. For example, suppose you describe a date field like this:

```
05   INV-DATE.
     10   INV-MONTH        PIC 99.
     10   INV-DAY          PIC 99.
     10   INV-YEAR         PIC 99.
```

If you want to check the date field to make sure it contains numeric data, you will have to check the month, day, and year fields individually because the numeric test cannot be made on a group item. However, suppose you describe the date field like this:

```
05   INV-DATE                 PIC X(6).
     05   INV-DATE-GROUP       REDEFINES INV-DATE.
          10   INV-MONTH            PIC 99.
          10   INV-DAY              PIC 99.
          10   INV-YEAR             PIC 99.
     05   INV-DATE-ELEM        REDEFINES INV-DATE
                                   PIC X(6).
```

Then, you can use this statement:

```
IF INV-DATE-ELEM IS NUMERIC
```

to check that the date field contains numeric data because INV-DATE-ELEM is an elementary item.

Compound conditions   A *compound condition* is created by using the words AND and OR, as these examples:

```
1.  IF ER-HOURS IS NUMERIC AND ER-RATE IS NUMERIC
        PERFORM 120-CALCULATE-EMPLOYEE-PAY.

2.  IF AP-AGE LESS THAN 18 OR AP-CODE-A EQUAL TO 1
        PERFORM 180-PRINT-ERROR-MESSAGE
    ELSE
        PERFORM 130-LOOKUP-INSURANCE-RATE.
```

In these statements, AND means "both" and OR means "either or both." In other words, when using AND, both conditions must be true before the compound condition is true; when using OR, the compound condition is true if either condition or both conditions are true. In example 1, both ER-HOURS and ER-RATE must be numeric for the program to perform 120-CALCULATE-EMPLOYEE-PAY. In example 2, the program will perform 180-PRINT-ERROR-MESSAGE if AP-AGE is less than 18, if AP-CODE-A is equal to 1, or if AP-AGE is less than 18 and AP-CODE-A is equal to 1.

When more than two conditions are linked in a compound condition, the NOT conditions are evaluated first, followed by the AND conditions and then the OR conditions. Because compound conditions can be very confusing, however, parentheses should be used to make these statements more understandable. For example,

```
A GREATER THAN B OR A EQUAL TO C AND D NOT POSITIVE
```

is confusing, while

```
(A GREATER THAN B) OR (A EQUAL TO C AND D NOT POSITIVE)
```

is less confusing. As in arithmetic expressions, conditions within parentheses are evaluated first. And parentheses can be used to override the compiler's normal sequence of evaluation.

Although COBOL allows compound conditions of great complexity, it is best to keep them relatively simple. Then programming errors are less likely to occur and program changes can be made more easily. Remember that the goal of structured COBOL is program clarity.

As an aid to clarity, indentation should be used for each of the conditions within a compound condition. For instance, figure 5-6 illustrates a two-level nested IF statement with compound conditions at both levels. Because of the use of indentation and parentheses, however, the statement can be understood with relative ease.

```
General form:

IF        condition-1
      OR condition-2
      AND condition-3
    statement-group-1
ELSE
    statement-group-2.




Example:

IF        (CM-TIMES-DUNNED LESS THAN 4
          AND CM-CUST-YEARS GREATER THAN 2)
       AND CM-OVER-60-BAL-OWED EQUAL TO ZERO
    PERFORM 550-PREPARE-SHIPPING ORDER
ELSE
    IF        (CM-TIMES-DUNNED GREATER THAN 3
              OR CM-CUST-YEARS NOT GREATER THAN 2)
           AND CM-OVER-60-BAL-OWED GREATER THAN ZERO
        PERFORM 560-PRINT-REFUSE-CREDIT-LINE
    ELSE
        PERFORM 570-PRINT-REFER-TO-MGR-LINE.
```

Figure 5-6 Indentation in compound conditions

Implied subjects and relational operators   If you want to compare a single field to two or more fields in a condition, you can code the comparison like this:

```
AP-AGE LESS THAN 60 AND AP-AGE GREATER THAN 18
```

Or you can write it this way:

```
AP-AGE LESS THAN 60 AND GREATER THAN 18
```

In the second half of this comparison, AP-AGE is the *implied subject*, since it's not written out twice. In other words, it's simply implied that AP-AGE is to be compared to 18 because AP-AGE is the most recently stated subject.

Relational operators can also be implied. For example,

```
    AP-AGE LESS THAN 60
AND AP-AGE GREATER THAN 18
AND AP-AGE GREATER THAN PREVIOUS-AGE
```

can be written

```
AP-AGE LESS THAN 60 AND AP-AGE GREATER THAN 18 AND PREVIOUS-AGE
```

This means that besides being compared to 60, AP-AGE must be tested for being both greater than 18 and greater than PREVIOUS-AGE. In other words, since there is no relational operator given immediately before PREVIOUS-AGE, the last-stated operator is assumed to still be in effect. And, as seen before, AP-AGE doesn't have to be repeated either:

```
AP-AGE LESS THAN 60 AND GREATER THAN 18 AND PREVIOUS-AGE
```

This statement would be true if (1) AP-AGE is less than 60, (2) AP-AGE is greater than 18, and (3) AP-AGE is greater than PREVIOUS-AGE.

The word NOT can also be used in conjunction with implied subjects and relational operators. In the 1974 standards, if NOT precedes the operator, it's considered to be part of the operator. Thus,

```
    AP-AGE NOT EQUAL TO 60 AND GREATER THAN 18
```

is equivalent to

```
    AP-AGE NOT EQUAL TO 60 AND AP-AGE GREATER THAN 18
```

And

```
    AP-AGE NOT GREATER THAN 18 OR PREVIOUS-AGE
```

is equivalent to

```
        AP-AGE NOT GREATER THAN 18
    OR AP-AGE NOT GREATER THAN PREVIOUS-AGE
```

However, under the 1968 standards, the meaning of NOT in a condition with implied subjects and relational operators varies according to (1) the operating system (DOS or OS) and (2) whether it's the subject or the operator that's being implied.

How often should you use implied subjects and relational operators? That depends on you. If you find them easy to work with, you may use them as long as the conditional statements are understandable. However, once it becomes unclear what the implied subjects or operators are, you should state the complete condition. This is particularly true when you're operating under the 68 standards and have to use NOT in a condition. In fact, even when you're working under the 74 standards, you should state the complete condition whenever you use NOT. This will contribute to the clarity and readability of your programs.

```
      PROCEDURE DIVISION.
   .
          .
          .
      IF TR-ACTIVITY-CODE EQUAL TO 1
          PERFORM CODE-1-FUNCTION
      ELSE IF TR-ACTIVITY-CODE EQUAL TO 2
          PERFORM CODE-2-FUNCTION
      ELSE IF TR-ACTIVITY-CODE EQUAL TO 3
          PERFORM CODE-3-FUNCTION
      ELSE IF TR-ACTIVITY-CODE EQUAL TO 4
          PERFORM CODE-4-FUNCTION
      ELSE IF TR-ACTIVITY-CODE EQUAL TO 5
          PERFORM CODE-5-FUNCTION
      ELSE IF TR-ACTIVITY-CODE EQUAL TO 6
          PERFORM CODE-6-FUNCTION
      ELSE IF TR-ACTIVITY-CODE EQUAL TO 7
          PERFORM CODE-7-FUNCTION
      ELSE IF TR-ACTIVITY-CODE EQUAL TO 8
          PERFORM CODE-8-FUNCTION
      ELSE IF TR-ACTIVITY-CODE EQUAL TO 9
          PERFORM CODE-9-FUNCTION
      ELSE
          MOVE 'Y' TO INVALID-ACTIVITY-CODE-SW.
```

Figure 5-7 Nested IF statements in linear form (the recommended alternative to the case structure)

Linear nesting   In chapter 2, you saw how to use indentation to make nested IF statements easy to read and understand. However, if a string of nested IF statements merely checks a single field for a succession of independent values, the IF statements can be written without indentation as shown in figure 5-7. As you can see, this code performs one module if the activity code is equal to 1, performs another module if it is equal to 2, and so on for seven more values. If the activity code isn't equal to a value from 1 to 9, some default code is executed. I hope you will agree that this code is at least as clear as it would be with indentation.

This method of coding IF statements is sometimes referred to as *linear nesting* since the IF conditions are tested one right after the other. But note that you should only use linear nesting when a single item is being tested and when each IF statement is contained in the ELSE clause of the IF statement that precedes it. Furthermore, you shouldn't use linear nesting within another IF nest. In other words, the use of linear nesting must be limited as illustrated in this book or it doesn't work toward the goal of clarity. In a few moments, you will see linear nesting used to implement the case structure of structured programming.

The TIMES option in the PERFORM statement

You have already seen how the simple PERFORM and the PER-
FORM UNTIL statements work in examples like these:

```
1.   PERFORM 300-PRINT-TOTAL-PAGE.

2.   PERFORM 100-PRODUCE-REPORT-LINE
          UNTIL CARD-EOF.
```

In the first statement, the program will branch to the procedure
named 300-PRINT-TOTAL-PAGE and execute the procedure one
time. In the second example, the program will repeatedly execute the
procedure named 100-PRODUCE-REPORT-LINE until the condition
assigned to the condition name CARD-EOF is true. In both cases,
when the procedures have been executed the required number of
times, the program returns to the statement following the PERFORM
statement and continues from there.

A third format for the PERFORM statement is this:

$$\underline{\text{PERFORM}} \text{ procedure-name-1} \left\{ \begin{matrix} \text{data-name} \\ \text{integer} \end{matrix} \right\} \underline{\text{TIMES}}.$$

Here, the procedure named is executed as many times as indicated.
For example,

```
PERFORM 140-CALCULATE-MONTHLY-PAYMENT 12 TIMES
```

causes the procedure named 140-CALCULATE-MONTHLY-
PAYMENT to be executed twelve times before returning to the statement following the PERFORM. If a data name is used, it must be
described as an integer, and the procedure named is executed as
many times as the value of the data name at the time of execution.
Thus, if MONTH-NO has a value of 4 at the time this statement is
executed

```
PERFORM 140-CALCULATE-MONTHLY-PAYMENT MONTH-NO TIMES
```

procedure 140-CALCULATE-MONTHLY-PAYMENT will be performed four times. This format of the PERFORM statement is not
too useful, though, so you won't use it very often.

The GO TO DEPENDING statement and the case structure

The GO TO DEPENDING statement has this format:

```
GO TO procedure-1 [procedure-2] ...
     DEPENDING ON data-name
```

It is used to branch to two or more different procedures based on
the value in the field named in the DEPENDING ON clause. This
field cannot have decimal positions and for the sake of efficiency

should be described as a signed, COMP SYNC field. If the value of the field is 1, the program branches to the first procedure named; if the value is 2, the program branches to the second procedure named; and so on. If the value is something other than an integer from 1 through the number of procedures named, the program continues with the next statement in sequence.

In structured programming, the GO TO DEPENDING statement should only be used in a series of procedures that is executed by a PERFORM statement. In other words, the entire series makes up a single structure with only one entry and one exit point. This is called the *case structure*. A flowchart for the case structure is given in the top portion of figure 5-8.

To provide for the exit from the case structure, you have to use the simple GO TO statement (this is one of only two times it's used in structured programming) and the EXIT statement. The EXIT statement is a one-word statement that does not cause any processing to take place. Its format is this:

```
paragraph-name.   EXIT.
```

No other statements are allowed in the paragraph.

To see how these statements work together in the case structure, look at figure 5-8. Here, TR-ACTIVITY-CODE is used in the GO TO DEPENDING statement and can have a value from 1 through 9. If, for example, its value is 2, the program will branch to 320-CASE-2-FUNCTION, the second procedure named in the statement. If the value of TR-ACTIVITY-CODE is other than an integer between 1 and 9, the program continues with the next statement in sequence and moves Y to the field named INVALID-ACTIVITY-CODE-SW. It then reaches the GO TO statement and branches to the paragraph named 400-CASE-STRUCTURE-EXIT, which marks the end of the case structure and a return to the statement following the original PERFORM statement in paragraph 000. Note that all of the other GO TO statements also branch to the EXIT statement. They would be used illegally if they branched out of the structure.

Because it forces sections, EXITs, and GOTOs on a structured program, we recommend that you do *not* use the GO TO DEPENDING statement to implement the case structure. Instead, we recommend that the case structure be implemented as shown in figure 5-7. This nest of linear IF statements has the same effect as the coding in figure 5-8. Although the GO TO DEPENDING implementation may be somewhat more effective in terms of object program efficiency, the nested IF statements are much better in terms of program clarity and programmer productivity.

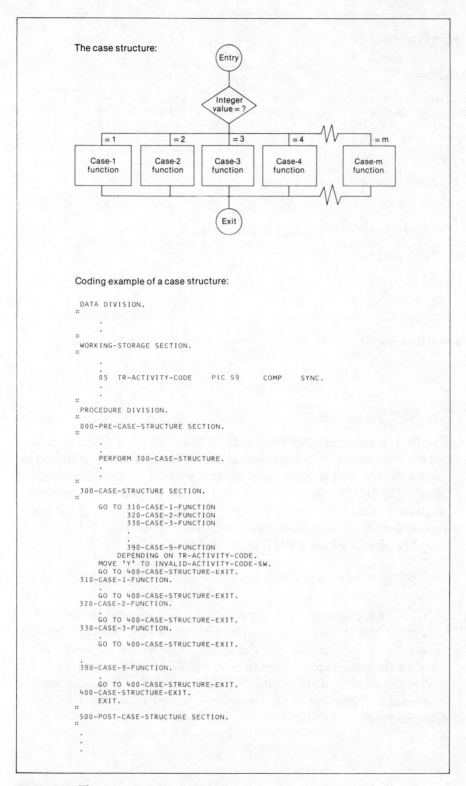

The case structure:

Entry

Integer
value = ?

= 1   = 2   = 3   = 4   = m

Case-1
function

Case-2
function

Case-3
function

Case-4
function

Case-m
function

Exit

Coding example of a case structure:

```
DATA DIVISION.
::
    .
    .
::
WORKING-STORAGE SECTION.
::
    .
    .
    05  TR-ACTIVITY-CODE    PIC S9    COMP    SYNC.
    .
    .
::
PROCEDURE DIVISION.
::
000-PRE-CASE-STRUCTURE SECTION.
::
    .
    .
    PERFORM 300-CASE-STRUCTURE.
    .
    .
::
300-CASE-STRUCTURE SECTION.
::
    GO TO 310-CASE-1-FUNCTION
          320-CASE-2-FUNCTION
          330-CASE-3-FUNCTION
          .
          .
          390-CASE-9-FUNCTION
       DEPENDING ON TR-ACTIVITY-CODE.
    MOVE 'Y' TO INVALID-ACTIVITY-CODE-SW.
    GO TO 400-CASE-STRUCTURE-EXIT.
310-CASE-1-FUNCTION.
    .
    GO TO 400-CASE-STRUCTURE-EXIT.
320-CASE-2-FUNCTION.
    .
    GO TO 400-CASE-STRUCTURE-EXIT.
330-CASE-3-FUNCTION.
    .
    GO TO 400-CASE-STRUCTURE-EXIT.
    .
    .
390-CASE-9-FUNCTION.
    .
    GO TO 400-CASE-STRUCTURE-EXIT.
400-CASE-STRUCTURE-EXIT.
    EXIT.
::
500-POST-CASE-STRUCTURE SECTION.
::
    .
    .
    .
```

Figure 5-8   The case structure in COBOL

```
     PROCEDURE DIVISION.
         .
         .
     NOTE-PARAGRAPH.
   ::
         NOTE THAT IF NOTE IS THE FIRST WORD OF A PARAGRAPH, THE ENTIRE
         PARAGRAPH IS TREATED BY THE COMPILER AS A SERIES OF EXPLANATORY
         COMMENTS.  REMEMBER, THOUGH, THAT THE NOTE STATEMENT IS NO
         LONGER USED IN COBOL PROGRAMS.
   ::
     130-CALCULATE-GROSS-PAY.
   ::
         IF EMP-HOURS GREATER THAN 40
             COMPUTE GROSS-PAY ROUNDED =
                 (1.5 :: PAY-RATE :: (EMP-HOURS - 40)) + (40 :: PAY-RATE)
         ELSE
             COMPUTE GROSS-PAY ROUNDED = EMP-HOURS :: PAY-RATE.
         NOTE THAT AN EMPLOYEE IS PAID TIME AND A HALF FOR ANY WORK
         HOURS OVER FORTY.
         .
         .
         .
```

Figure 5-9   The NOTE statement

The NOTE statement

The NOTE statement has been deleted from the 1974 COBOL standards. As a result, this statement is primarily of interest to programmers who will be maintaining programs written on the older compilers. The NOTE statement was used to make clarifying comments
anywhere within the Procedure Division of a program and has been
replaced by the more general comment card (asterisk in column 7).

The format of the NOTE statement is this:

NOTE comment ...

If NOTE is the first word of a paragraph, all sentences in the
paragraph are treated as comments. Otherwise, the NOTE comment
ends with the first period and the compiler looks for the next statement of the paragraph. In figure 5–9, NOTE is used to indicate a
paragraph of comments in NOTE-PARAGRAPH and to indicate a
one-sentence comment in the paragraph named 130-CALCULATE-
GROSS-PAY.

If you are maintaining old programs, you should prepare for 1974 ANS compilers by placing an asterisk in column 7 of all NOTE statements. At the same time, you should check to make sure that the note is the only thing coded in each NOTE statement. If any other COBOL statement is begun at the end of a NOTE statement, it should be transferred to a new line. Once you've made these changes, the code will present no problems when NOTE is dropped from some compiler of the future.

Indentation

You have already seen how indentation should be used to clarify the intent of nested IF statements, statements with conditional clauses, and statements with compound conditions. Figure 5-10 shows in more detail how indentation should be used throughout the Procedure Division to show the relationships between the phrases and clauses within a statement.

In general, start the first word of each Procedure Division statement in column 12 of the coding form. If a statement is too long for one coding line, break it up at the start of a clause or phrase and indent the succeeding lines four spaces. In statements like the OPEN, CLOSE, and MOVE (examples 1, 2, and 3), align similar elements like file and data names. Indent conditional clauses, such as AT END and ON SIZE ERROR, by four spaces. If one or more statements are part of the conditional clause of another statement, indent the conditional statements four spaces from their conditional clause. For instance, the two statements following the AT END condition in example 4 of figure 5–10 are indented four more spaces to show they're part of the AT END condition.

In general, nested IF statements are indented by four spaces for each level as shown in example 8 in figure 5-10. However, if several levels of nesting are used, you may run out of coding space. In this case, you can indent by only two spaces for each level. Furthermore, related IF and ELSE clauses should be aligned, unless you're using a linear nest as in example 9. In either case, the imperative statements that are to be executed if the condition is met are indented.

Since you will undoubtedly encounter statements that are not covered by this simple set of rules, always remember that the goal of indentation is clarity. If you encounter a special situation, code it in the way that is most understandable and most consistent with the rest of your code.

```
Example 1:
OPEN INPUT   TRANSACTION-FILE
             OLD-MASTER-FILE
     OUTPUT  NEW-MASTER-FILE
             REPORT-FILE
             ERROR-FILE.

Example 2:
CLOSE TRANSACTION-FILE
      OLD-MASTER-FILE
      NEW-MASTER-FILE
      REPORT-FILE
      ERROR-FILE.

Example 3:
MOVE SPACE        TO PR-RECORD.
MOVE TP-ITEM-NO   TO PR-ITEM-NO.
MOVE TP-ITEM-DESC TO PR-ITEM-DESC.

Example 4:
READ TRANSACTION-FILE INTO TR-INPUT-AREA
     AT END
          MOVE 'Y' TO TRAN-EOF-SW
          MOVE HIGH-VALUE TO TR-ITEM-NO.

Example 5:
WRITE PR-OUTPUT-AREA
     AFTER ADVANCING SPACE-CONTROL LINES.

Example 6:
PERFORM 110-READ-ITEM-CODE-TABLE
     UNTIL TABLE-EOF.

Example 7:
MULTIPLY TR-QUANTITY BY TB-UNIT-PRICE
     GIVING IL-SALES-AMOUNT
     ON SIZE ERROR
          PERFORM 360-PROCESS-INVALID-TRAN.

Example 8:
IF CR-CUST-CODE EQUAL TO 1
     MOVE .050 TO DISCOUNT-PERCENT
ELSE
     IF CR-CUST-CODE EQUAL TO 2
          MOVE .020 TO DISCOUNT-PERCENT
     ELSE
          MOVE .000 TO DISCOUNT-PERCENT.

Example 9:
IF CR-CUST-CODE EQUAL TO 1
     MOVE .050 TO DISCOUNT-PERCENT
ELSE IF CR-CUST-CODE EQUAL TO 2
     MOVE .020 TO DISCOUNT-PERCENT
ELSE
     MOVE .000 TO DISCOUNT-PERCENT.
```

Figure 5-10   Proper use of indentation in the Procedure Division

Terminology

condition name

flag

figurative constant

section name

relation test

collating sequence

relational operator

compound condition

implied subject

implied relational operator

linear nesting

case structure

Objectives

1. Apply the COBOL elements described in this topic to appropriate aspects of programming problems.

Problems

1. An investment-listing program is shown in figure 2-27. Modify this program using either the ACCEPT or the MOVE CURRENT-DATE statement (depending on your compiler) so that a new first heading line including the current date will print as follows:

    ```
    INVESTMENT LISTING OF XX/XX/XX
    ```

    Add whatever descriptions are needed to the Working-Storage Section, and rewrite the paragraph named 140-PRINT-REPORT-HEADING entirely. Add the ACCEPT or MOVE statement to paragraph 000-PRODUCE-INVESTMENT-LISTING, not to module 140. (It's more efficient to execute the statement only once rather than each time headings are printed.) The second heading line should print two lines after the first one.

2. Code one COMPUTE statement for each of the following calculations. Use the ROUNDED option as you think necessary.

    a. Gross profit (GROSS-PROFIT) should be calculated by multiplying sales (IR-QTY) by unit cost (IR-UNIT- COST) and subtracting it from sales multiplied by unit price (IR-UNIT-PRICE).

```
    DATA DIVISION.
 ::
    FILE SECTION.
 ::
    FD   TRANFILE
         LABEL RECORDS ARE STANDARD
         RECORDING MODE IS F
         RECORD CONTAINS 80 CHARACTERS.
 ::
    01   TR-CARD.
 ::
         05   TR-CARD-CODE          PIC X.
         05   TR-TRAN-CODE          PIC X.
              88   ISSUE                          VALUE '1'.
              88   RECEIPT                        VALUE '2'.
         05   TR-REFERENCE-NO       PIC X(6).
              05   TR-CUST-NO       REDEFINES TR-REFERENCE-NO
                                        PIC 9(6).
                   05   TR-VEND-NO-X   REDEFINES TR-REFERENCE-NO.
                        10   TR-VEND-NO    PIC 9(5).
                        10   TR-BLANK      PIC X.
         05   TR-ITEM-NO            PIC X(5).
         05   TR-QUANTITY           PIC 9(5).
         05   TR-UNIT-PRICE         PIC 9(3)V99.
         05   FILLER                PIC X(57).
 ::
```

Figure 5-11   Use of REDEFINES in a record description

b. Calculate the new principal on an investment after one compounding period using this formula:

$$\text{NEW PRINCIPAL} = \text{OLD-PRINCIPAL} \left(1 + \frac{\text{INTEREST-RATE}}{\text{TIMES-COMPOUNDED}}\right)$$

3. Figure 5-11 shows a portion of the File Section of the Data Division for a program that edits input records to make sure they contain valid data. If the transaction code (TR-TRAN-CODE) is a 1, the input record represents an issue transaction, and the reference number field should contain a six-digit positive numeric customer number. If TR-TRAN-CODE is a 2, the input record represents a receipt transaction, and the reference number should contain a five-digit positive numeric vendor number followed by a blank.

In the Procedure Division, write a procedure that checks the transaction code of each input record and then performs procedures that check the reference number field for valid data. If the data is not valid, you should move an N into VALID-TRANSACTION-SW and your program should not check the remaining fields in the record. If the transaction code is neither a 1 or 2, the program should move N into VALID-TRAN-CODE-SW and end the editing function. Assume that the portion of the VTOC that represents the editing procedure looks like this:

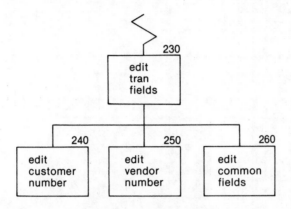

Now code modules 230, 240, and 250.

Solutions

1. Figure 5-12 shows acceptable modifications using the MOVE CURRENT-DATE statement; figure 5-13 shows the modifications using the ACCEPT statement (the sequence numbers for HDG-LINE would also have to be changed to something like 4190–4240).

2. a. Here's an acceptable COMPUTE statement:

```
COMPUTE GROSS-PROFIT =
    (IR-QTY * IR-UNIT-PRICE) - (IR-QTY * IR-UNIT-COST).
```

   b. Here's an acceptable COMPUTE statement:

```
COMPUTE NEW-PRINCIPAL ROUNDED =
    OLD-PRINCIPAL * (1 + (INTEREST-RATE / TIMES-COMPOUNDED)).
```

3. Figure 5-14 is an acceptable solution. Note that the tests for valid data only check that the data in the field is numeric and not equal to zero. Since the card input fields aren't signed, their values will be considered positive.

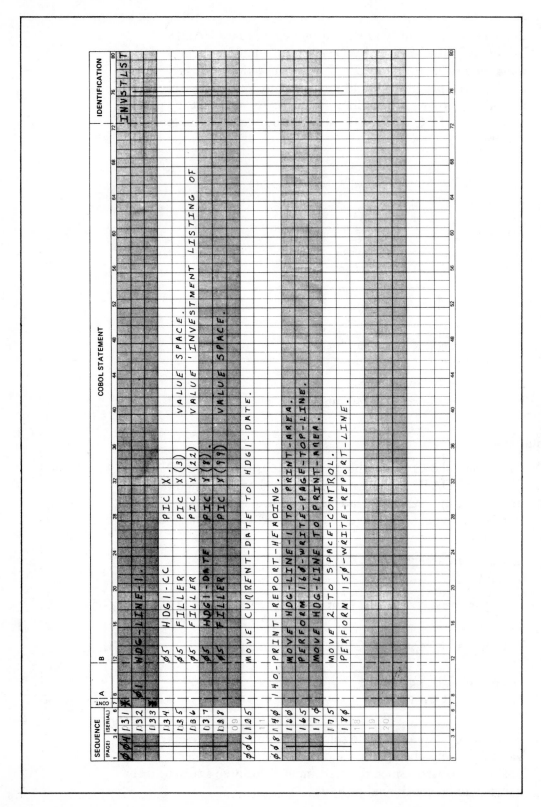

Figure 5-12 Modifications to the investment-listing program using CURRENT-DATE

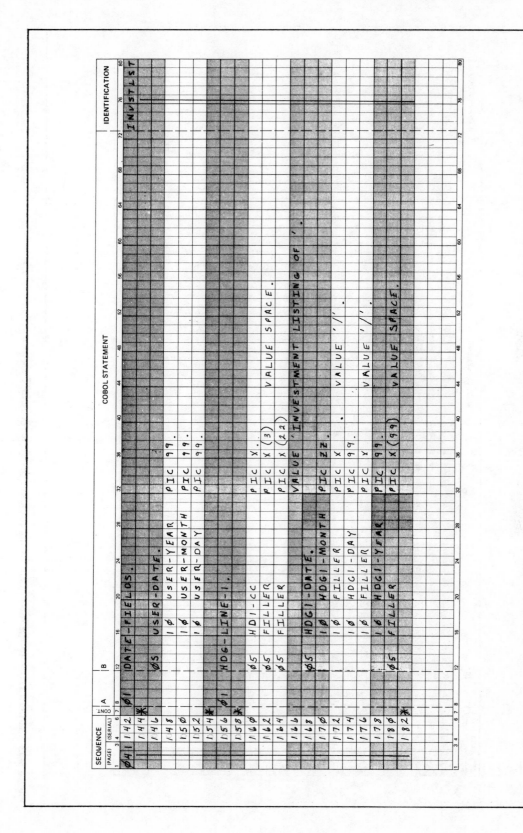

Figure 5-13   Modifications to the investment-listing program using the ACCEPT statement (part 1 of 2)

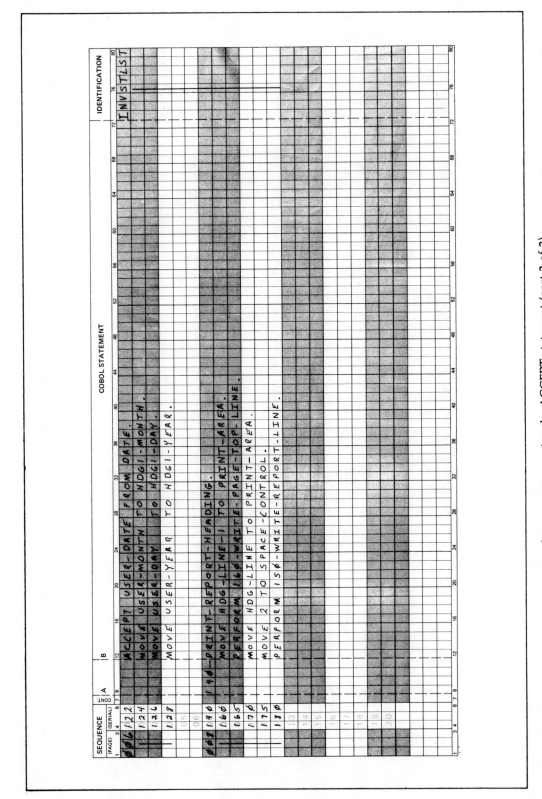

Figure 5-13   Modifications to the investment-listing program using the ACCEPT statement (part 2 of 2)

```
   230-EDIT-TRAN-FIELDS.
*
       MOVE 'Y' TO VALID-TRANSACTION-SW.
       IF ISSUE
           PERFORM 240-EDIT-CUSTOMER-NUMBER
       ELSE IF RECEIPT
           PERFORM 250-EDIT-VENDOR-NUMBER
       ELSE
           MOVE 'N' TO VALID-TRAN-CODE-SW.
       IF          VALID-TRANSACTION
             AND VALID-TRAN-CODE
           PERFORM 260-EDIT-COMMON-FIELDS.
*
   240-EDIT-CUSTOMER-NUMBER.
*
       IF          TR-CUST-NO NOT NUMERIC
             OR TR-CUST-NO = ZERO
           MOVE 'N' TO VALID-TRANSACTION-SW.
*
   250-EDIT-VENDOR-NUMBER.
*
       IF          TR-VEND-NO NOT NUMERIC
             OR TR-VEND-NO = ZERO
             OR TR-BLANK NOT = SPACE
           MOVE 'N' TO VALID-TRANSACTION-SW.
*
```

Figure 5-14   An editing routine

TOPIC 2   Overlap and I/O Operations

Until the mid-1960s, most computer systems could perform only one operation at a time. For instance, a typical small system read a card, processed it, and printed an output line on the printer. This sequence was then repeated for the next card record. Similarly, a typical tape system read input, processed it, and gave output—but only one operation at a time. The problem with this method of processing was that most of the components of the computer system were idle, even though the system was running.

To illustrate, suppose a tape system executes a program that reads a tape record, processes it, and writes a tape record. Figure 5-15 might then represent the relative amounts of time that the CPU and the tape drives would be busy during execution of the program. (These percentages, of course, would vary depending on the speed of the components.) In this example, the CPU is busy 44 percent of the time that the system is running, while each tape drive is busy only 28 percent of the time.

To overcome this problem of idle components, systems were developed to *overlap* I/O operations with CPU processing. The difference between nonoverlapped and overlapped processing is illustrated in figure 5-16. On system A, the nonoverlapped system, nine time intervals are required to read, process, and write three records. On system B, the overlapped system, nine records have been read, eight have been processed, and seven have been written at the end of nine time intervals. Although this example is based on the unlikely assumption that reading, processing, and writing take equal amounts of time, the message is clear: overlap can significantly increase the amount of work that a computer system can do.

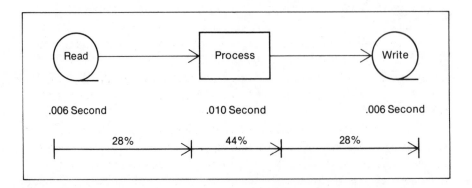

Figure 5-15   The problem of idle computer components

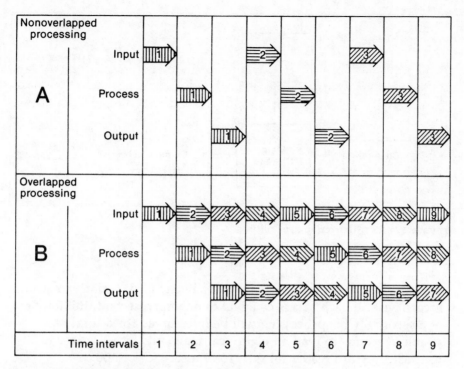

Figure 5-16   Overlapped and nonoverlapped processing

Channels   One reason earlier computers weren't able to overlap operations is that the CPU executed all of the instructions of a program, one after the other. In contrast, the CPU of an overlapped system like the System/360-370 doesn't execute I/O instructions. Instead, *channels* are used to execute the I/O instructions, while the CPU executes the arithmetic, logical, and data-movement instructions. The I/O instructions executed by the channels are called *channel commands*. Figure 5-17 illustrates the components of an overlapped system: one channel executes an input command, a second channel executes an output command, and the CPU executes other instructions of the program—all at the same time. (Although the CPU is generally considered to consist of storage and control circuitry, the CPU and storage are shown separately in the illustration to indicate that both CPU and channels can access data from storage.)

Whenever data is transferred from a channel to storage or from storage to a channel, CPU processing is interrupted for one *storage access cycle* (or just *access cycle*). Because of the tremendous difference between access-cycle speeds and I/O speeds, however, this is a minor interruption. To illustrate, suppose cards read by a 600-card-per-minute card reader are being processed by a computer

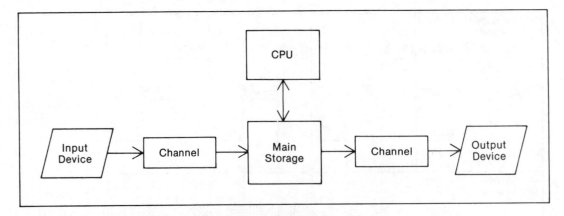

Figure 5-17   A computer system with overlap capability

that transfers two storage positions (or bytes) of data during each access cycle. If each access cycle takes one microsecond (millionths of a second), CPU processing will be interrupted for a total of 40 microseconds to read all eighty card columns into storage. In contrast, the card reader takes 1/10 of a second, or 100,000 microseconds to read all eighty card columns. This means that while each card is read, the CPU can spend over 99 percent of its time—99,960 seconds out of 100,000 to be exact—executing other instructions of the program.

Although tape and disk devices are many times faster than card readers and printers, this same type of inequality is likely to exist between the speeds of these I/O devices and the access-cycle speeds. For example, a tape drive with a 50,000 byte-per-second transfer rate reads or writes one byte of data every 20 microseconds. If the CPU requires one-half microsecond to transfer the byte to or from storage, 19.5 microseconds per byte are available for other processing. In other words, because of the overlap capability, the CPU can spend 97.5 percent of its time executing other instructions.

Since a channel, like a CPU, can execute only one operation at a time, the number of overlapping operations that a system can have is limited by the number of channels on the system. For instance, a one-channel system can overlap one I/O operation with CPU processing, and a three-channel system can overlap three I/O operations with CPU processing. The one exception to this is the *multiplexor channel*, which can read or write on two or more slow-speed I/O devices at one time.

The multiplexor channel has the ability to alternate between several I/O devices. For example, if a card reader, card punch, and printer are attached to a multiplexor channel, the channel can accept

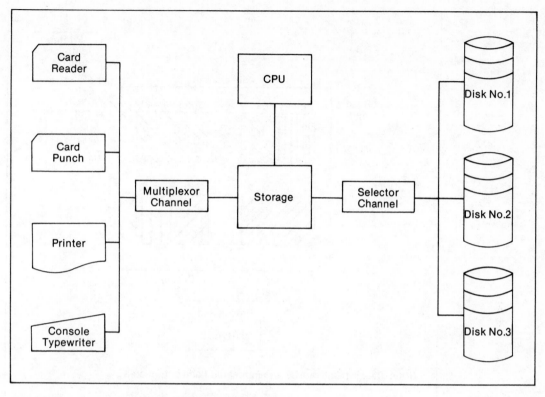

Figure 5-18   A typical small System/370 configuration

one byte of data from the card reader, send one byte to the card
punch, send one byte to the printer, and then accept another byte
from the card reader. By switching from one device to another, this
single channel can overlap several different devices. Here again, the
extreme difference in speeds between I/O devices and access cycles
makes this possible.

Figure 5-18 shows a typical configuration of a small System/370
with three disk drives. All of its slow-speed devices—the card
reader, card punch, printer, and console typewriter—are attached to
a multiplexor channel, while the disk drives are attached to the other
type of channel—a *selector channel.* This system, then, can overlap
card reading, printing, punching, console-typewriter operations, and
reading or writing on one of the disk drives. Because a selector
channel can perform only one operation at a time, however, reading
from disk drive 1 and writing on disk drive 2 cannot be overlapped.
Since disk drives are considerably faster than the slow-speed devices,
it is more important that slow-speed operations be overlapped than
disk operations. In general, a System/360-370 consists of one
multiplexor channel and one or more selector channels.

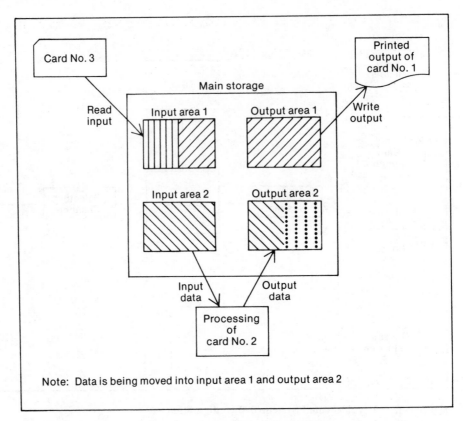

Figure 5-19 Use of dual I/O areas for overlapped processing

Dual I/O areas   One programming complexity resulting from overlap is that two I/O areas in storage must be used for each I/O operation. If only one input area of storage was used for a card-reading operation, for example, the second card would be read into the input area while the first card was being processed—thus destroying the data from the first card. Instead, the second card must be read into a second input area of storage while the first card is being processed in the first input area. Then, the third card is read into the first input area, while the second card is processed in the second input area. This switching from one input area to the other, which is shown schematically in figure 5-19, must be continued throughout the program. Similarly, dual I/O areas must be used for all other I/O operations that are overlapped.

COBOL implications

Fortunately, the COBOL programmer doesn't have to be concerned much with overlap. In fact, all of the COBOL programs illustrated so far have used overlap although the programmer has done nothing to provide for dual I/O areas or switching from one I/O area to another. In general, the COBOL compiler in conjunction with the operating system automatically provides for overlap.

Perhaps the main reason for presenting the concept of overlap is that it explains why the I/O area of an output file (as described by the COBOL program) must be cleared more than once to blanks. In many COBOL programs, for example, you will find a statement such as

```
MOVE SPACE TO OUTPUT-AREA
```

at the start of a routine that constructs an output record for a file. You should now understand that the first time the statement is executed, it clears the first output area for the file; the second time it is executed, it clears the second output area. If both areas aren't cleared, data from a previous program or record might be written in an output record.

Figure 5-20 presents two different ways of removing foreign data from all output records when using a compiler that automatically provides two output areas for each output file. Example 1 illustrates the method just described in which SPACE is moved to the output area before each output record is constructed. Thus, both output areas are cleared before an output record is written. This method is used in the reorder-listing program in figure 2-5.

In example 2, all output data, with all required areas set to blanks, is moved from working storage to the output area and then the line is printed. This is accomplished by a MOVE statement coupled with a statement that performs a write procedure. This is the method most commonly used in structured programs. And it is the one used in the refined reorder-listing program in figure 2-24.

Terminology

overlap

channel

channel command

storage access cycle

access cycle

multiplexor channel

selector channel

```
Example 1:                                      Example 2:

        •                                               •
        •                                               •
        SELECT PRINTFLE ASSIGN TO UT-S-PRINTFLE.        SELECT PRINTFLE ASSIGN TO UT-S-PRINTFLE.
        •                                               •
        •                                               •
 ⸭                                               ⸭
 DATA DIVISION.                                  DATA DIVISION.
 ⸭                                               ⸭
        •                                               •
        •                                               •
 ⸭                                               ⸭
 FD  PRINTFLE                                    FD  PRINTFLE
     LABEL RECORDS ARE STANDARD                      LABEL RECORDS ARE STANDARD
     RECORDING MODE IS F                             RECORDING MODE IS F
     RECORD CONTAINS 133 CHARACTERS.                 RECORD CONTAINS 133 CHARACTERS.
 ⸭                                               ⸭
 01  PR-RECORD.                                  01  PRINT-AREA        PIC X(133).
 ⸭                                               ⸭
     05  PR-CC         PIC X.                            •
 ⸭                                                      •
        •                                        ⸭
        •                                        WORKING-STORAGE SECTION.
 ⸭                                               ⸭
 PROCEDURE DIVISION.                                    •
 ⸭                                                      •
 000-PREPARE-PRINTED-OUTPUT.                      ⸭
 ⸭                                               01  PR-RECORD.
     OPEN INPUT  ...                              ⸭
          OUTPUT PRINTFLE.                            05  PR-CC          PIC X.
        •                                            05  PR-FIELD-1     PIC Z(5).
        •                                            05  FILLER         PIC X(4)      VALUE SPACE.
 ⸭                                                   05  PR-FIELD-2     PIC ZZZ.99.
 130-PRINT-OUTPUT-LINE.                              05  FILLER         PIC X(4)      VALUE SPACE.
 ⸭                                                   05  PR-FIELD-3     PIC Z(3).
     MOVE SPACE TO PR-RECORD.                        05  FILLER         PIC X(110)    VALUE SPACE.
        •                                               •
        •                                               •
     PERFORM 140-WRITE-OUTPUT-LINE.              ⸭
 ⸭                                               PROCEDURE DIVISION.
 140-WRITE-OUTPUT-LINE.                          000-PREPARE-PRINTED-OUTPUT.
 ⸭                                               ⸭
     WRITE PR-RECORD                                  OPEN INPUT  ...
          AFTER ADVANCING SPACE-CONTROL LINES.            OUTPUT PRINTFLE.
                                                        •
                                                        •
                                                 130-PRINT-OUTPUT-LINE.
                                                 ⸭
                                                        •
                                                        •
                                                     MOVE PR-RECORD TO PRINT-AREA.
                                                     PERFORM 140-WRITE-OUTPUT-LINE.
                                                 ⸭
                                                 140-WRITE-OUTPUT-LINE.
                                                 ⸭
                                                     WRITE PRINT-AREA
                                                          AFTER ADVANCING SPACE-CONTROL LINES.
```

Figure 5-20 Two ways to clear output areas

Objectives

1. Explain how overlap increases the productivity of a computer system.

2. Explain why two I/O areas are required for each input and output device if overlap is to take place.

TOPIC 3 Repetitive Processing

In some programs, several fields of a record must be processed in the same way. Rather than repeat similar code for each field, most programmers use looping techniques for repetitive processing.

To illustrate the use of repetitive processing, consider this problem. A payroll program reads an input card that has the format given in figure 5-21. To calculate the number of hours an employee worked during the week, one of the procedures of the program must add the seven daily-hours-worked fields. Although this could be done using the subset presented thus far, figure 5-22 shows how to do it more efficiently using the OCCURS clause, subscripts, and the PERFORM VARYING statement.

The OCCURS clause

The basic format of the OCCURS clause is this:

```
OCCURS integer TIMES
```

This clause may be used to describe any data name that is not on an 01 level. The integer in the clause refers to the number of times a field or group of fields is repeated. In figure 5-22, the OCCURS clause indicates that the WPR-HOURS-WORKED field is repeated seven times in the WEEKLY-PAY-RECORD area.

Subscripts

To process the fields defined with an OCCURS clause, *subscripts* are used. For example, the first daily-hours-worked field in the employee card may be referred to as WPR-HOURS-WORKED (1), the second field as WPR-HOURS-WORKED (2), and so on. In each case, the number in parentheses is called the subscript.

A data name can be used as a subscript in the same way that an integer is. Then, the field that is referred to depends on the value of

Field Name	Employee Data	Daily Hours Worked							Unused
		1	2	3	4	5	6	7	
Characteristics	X(38)	99V9	99V9	99V9	99V9	99V9	99V9	99V9	X(21)
Usage									
Position	1-38	39-41	42-44	45-47	48-50	51-53	54-56	57-59	60-80

Figure 5-21 Employee payroll card format

```
 DATA DIVISION.
x
     .
     .
x
 WORKING-STORAGE SECTION.
x
     .
     .
x
 01   WORK-FIELDS          COMP-3.
x
     05   WEEKLY-HOURS      PIC S99V9.
     .
     .
x
 01   SUBSCRIPTS           COMP          SYNC.
x
     05   WPR-SUB           PIC S9.
     .
     .
x
 01   WEEKLY-PAY-RECORD.
x
     05   WPR-EMP-DATA      PIC X(38).
     05   WPR-HOURS-WORKED PIC 99V9 OCCURS 7 TIMES.
     05   FILLER            PIC X(21).
     .
     .
x
 PROCEDURE DIVISION.
x
     .
     .
     PERFORM 230-TOTAL-WEEKLY-HOURS
         VARYING WPR-SUB FROM 1 BY 1
         UNTIL WPR-SUB GREATER THAN 7.
     .
     .
x
 230-TOTAL-WEEKLY-HOURS.
x
     ADD WPR-HOURS-WORKED (WPR-SUB) TO WEEKLY-HOURS.
     .
     .
```

Figure 5-22   Repetitive processing using subscripts and the PERFORM VARYING statement

the subscript field at the time an instruction is executed. For example, WPR-SUB is a subscript in the following statement taken from the program in figure 5-22:

```
ADD WPR-HOURS-WORKED (WPR-SUB) TO WEEKLY-HOURS.
```

If WPR-SUB contains a 1 at the time of execution, the first daily-hours-worked field is referred to; if it contains a 2, the second daily-hours-worked field is referred to; and so on. Although a data name used as a subscript can be any USAGE, COMP usage (not COMP-3) coupled with the SYNC clause leads to the most efficient object program on the System/360-370.

The PERFORM VARYING statement

To control the repeated processing when subscripts are used, this more advanced form of the PERFORM statement can be used:

```
PERFORM procedure-name-1
    VARYING data-name-1 FROM {integer-1    } BY {integer-2   }
    UNTIL condition.            {data-name-2}    {data-name-3}
```

Data-name-1 is the subscript field, and its initial value is given after the word FROM. Then, each time the procedure named is performed, the value of the subscript field is increased by the amount specified after BY.

When the PERFORM statement in figure 5-22 is executed, it causes the procedure named 230-TOTAL-WEEKLY-HOURS to be executed seven times—once for each of the values of the subscript named WPR-SUB. In other words, by varying the subscript value from 1 to 7 and branching to the procedure named 230-TOTAL-WEEKLY-HOURS, the PERFORM statement causes the seven daily-hours-worked fields to be added together. After the seven WPR-HOURS-WORKED values are added to WEEKLY-HOURS, the processing continues with the statement following the PERFORM.

It is important to note that the condition in the PERFORM is stated as UNTIL WPR-SUB GREATER THAN 7, not UNTIL WPR-SUB EQUAL TO 7, as you might think. This is necessary because the test to see whether the condition has been met is made *before* the procedure named 230-TOTAL-WEEKLY-HOURS is executed. If the condition were stated UNTIL WPR-SUB EQUAL TO 7, 230-TOTAL-WEEKLY-HOURS would only be executed six times, and the seventh daily-hours-worked field wouldn't be added to WEEKLY-HOURS.

Using literals as subscripts

In figure 5-22, you see how the PERFORM VARYING statement can be used in repetitive processing. However, if you have a fixed number of repetitions, it is often just as quick and easy to repeat certain segments of code using literals as subscripts. For example, the PERFORM statement in figure 5-22 could be a simple PERFORM that would execute module 230. Then, module 230 could consist of the following code:

```
ADD WPR-HOURS-WORKED (1)
    WPR-HOURS-WORKED (2)
    WPR-HOURS-WORKED (3)
    WPR-HOURS-WORKED (4)
    WPR-HOURS-WORKED (5)
    WPR-HOURS-WORKED (6)
    WPR-HOURS-WORKED (7)
        GIVING WEEKLY-HOURS.
```

The point is, when you have a small, fixed number of repetitions, it's up to you to decide how to control processing—either by using the PERFORM VARYING statement or by coding the repetitive code using literals as subscripts.

Varied number of repetitions

Sometimes, the number of fields to be operated upon in a repetitive processing loop may vary. For instance, the sixth and seventh daily-hours-worked fields in figure 5-21 may be blank if an employee works only five days. Then, if the coding shown in figure 5-22 is used, program cancellation will occur due to data exception (invalid numeric field).

As an alternative, suppose card column 38 is used to indicate the number of days an employee has worked. Then, the coding in figure 5-23 will perform the repetitive processing only as many times as column 38 indicates is necessary. The key change here is that the condition in the PERFORM statement is UNTIL WPR-SUB GREATER THAN WPR-DAYS-WORKED. In a case like this, the PERFORM VARYING statement must be used to control processing. You can't use literals as subscripts because the number of required subscripts varies with each input record.

Terminology

subscript

```
    DATA DIVISION.
 ::
          .
          .
 ::
    WORKING-STORAGE SECTION.
 ::
          .
          .
 ::
    01  WORK-FIELDS           COMP-3.
 ::
        05  WEEKLY-HOURS      PIC S99V9.
          .
          .
 ::
    01  SUBSCRIPTS            COMP         SYNC.
 ::
        05  WPR-SUB           PIC S9.
          .
          .
 ::
    01  WEEKLY-PAY-RECORD.
 ::
        05  WPR-EMP-DATA      PIC X(37).
        05  WPR-DAYS-WORKED   PIC 9.
        05  WPR-HOURS-WORKED  PIC 99V9 OCCURS 7 TIMES.
        05  FILLER            PIC X(21).
          .
          .
 ::
    PROCEDURE DIVISION.
 ::
          .
          .
        PERFORM 230-TOTAL-WEEKLY-HOURS
            VARYING WPR-SUB FROM 1 BY 1
            UNTIL WPR-SUB GREATER THAN WPR-DAYS-WORKED.
          .
          .
 ::
    230-TOTAL-WEEKLY-HOURS.
 ::
        ADD WPR-HOURS-WORKED (WPR-SUB) TO WEEKLY-HOURS.
          .
          .
```

Figure 5-23 Repetitive processing with a varied number of repetitions

Objectives

1. Given a problem involving repetitive operations, solve it using the elements or techniques presented in this topic.

Problems

1. A deck of cards contains dates and temperatures. Each card can have a maximum of thirteen pairs of four-column dates and two-column temperatures. However, if a four-column date is blank, the rest of the card will be blank also.

   The input area for the card is described as follows:

```
01   TEMPERATURE-RECORD.
     05   TC-TEMP-DATA            OCCURS 13 TIMES.
          10   TC-TEMP-DATE       PIC X(4).
          10   TC-TEMPERATURE     PIC 99.
     05   FILLER                  PIC XX.
```

   Write a routine that adds the temperatures in each card to a field named TEMPERATURE-TOTAL. Use subscripts and the PERFORM statement to control the repetitive processing.

Solutions

1. Figure 5-24 illustrates an acceptable solution.

```
     DATA DIVISION.
x
          .
          .
x
     WORKING-STORAGE SECTION.
x
          .
          .
x
     01   WORK-FIELDS              COMP-3.
x
          05   TEMPERATURE-TOTAL   PIC S9(4).
               .
               .
x
     01   SUBSCRIPTS              COMP        SYNC.
x
          05   TEMP-SUB           PIC S99.
               .
               .
x
     01   TEMPERATURE-RECORD.
x
          05   TC-TEMP-DATA       OCCURS 13 TIMES.
               10   TC-TEMP-DATE  PIC X(4).
               10   TC-TEMPERATURE PIC 99.
          05   FILLER            PIC XX.
               .
               .
x
     PROCEDURE DIVISION.
x
          .
          .
          .
          PERFORM 120-ADD-RECORD-TEMPS
              VARYING TEMP-SUB FROM 1 BY 1
              UNTIL TEMP-SUB GREATER THAN 13.
               .
               .
x
     120-ADD-RECORD-TEMPS.
x
          IF TC-TEMP-DATE (TEMP-SUB) EQUAL TO SPACE
              MOVE 99 TO TEMP-SUB
          ELSE
              ADD TC-TEMPERATURE (TEMP-SUB) TO TEMPERATURE-TOTAL.
               .
               .
```

Figure 5-24 Routine for adding temperatures

PART THREE

Sequential File Handling

This part begins in chapter 6 by presenting the tape and direct-access concepts that are related to sequential files. If you have written programs with tape and direct-access input and output in another language or if you have taken a course that emphasized tape and direct-access concepts, this chapter may be largely review for you. In chapter 7, you will learn how to use COBOL for handling sequential files with fixed or variable-length records.

6

Tape and Direct-Access Concepts
for Sequential Files

If you have had an introductory data-processing course or have
coded tape and disk operations in another language, you may
already be familiar with most of the material in this chapter. Thus,
you may want to check the terminology and objective lists at the
end of each topic to help you decide whether the material is new to
you. Topic 1 describes the characteristics of magnetic tape and tape
equipment, while topic 2 does the same for direct-access devices.
Then, topic 3 describes some programming considerations related to
tape and disk operations.

TOPIC 1   Tape Concepts

Figure 6-1 illustrates a reel of the *magnetic tape* used in computer
operations. Similar to the tape used for tape recorders, it is a continuous strip of plastic coated on one side with a metal oxide. In
general, it is half an inch wide and comes in lengths of 250, 600,
1200, and 2400 feet, wound on plastic reels of varying sizes.
   Data is recorded on the coated surface of the tape in patterns of
magnetized spots called *bits*. A succession of these patterns strung
together forms a *record*—that is, a collection of related data fields.
For example, the data from a file of punched cards can be recorded

319

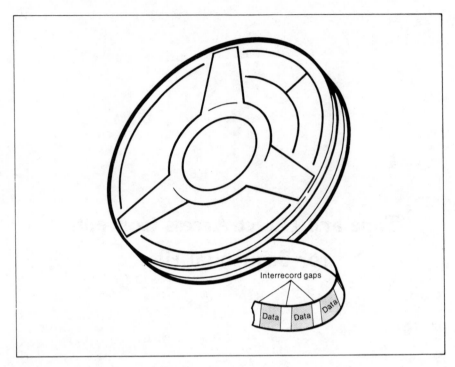

Interrecord gaps

Data Data Data

Figure 6-1   A magnetic tape

on tape so that each tape record corresponds to an individual card. Between individual data records on the tape are spaces where no data is recorded. These spaces, shown in figure 6-1, are called *inter-record gaps*, or *IRGs*. For most uses, a data record can be as short or as long as necessary. An IRG is only .6 of an inch long on most IBM tapes, and this gap is down to .3 of an inch on tapes for the latest tape equipment.

To get a clearer idea of how bits are used to record data on tape, look at figure 6-2. For each letter, number, and special character, there are nine vertical positions on the tape in which a bit may or may not be recorded. In other words, each character is represented by its own code made up of a unique combination of "on" and "off" bits. (In figure 6-2, the on-bits are indicated by a line in a bit position, the off-bits by a space.) The nine vertical bit positions in each code correspond to a byte of System/360-370 storage.

Actually, though, the code for each character uses only eight of the nine bit positions. The ninth bit, called a *check bit* or *parity bit*, is used as a check on the accuracy of tape operations. This bit is set either off or on to make the number of on-bits in the individual codes either all odd or all even, depending on the computer. If a System/360-370 tape character is read that consists of an even

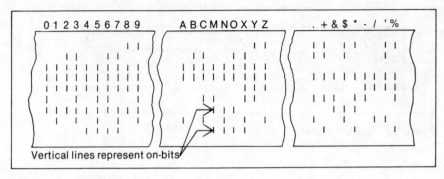

Figure 6-2   Coding on tape

number of on-bits, the computer system has detected an input error. This type of checking is called *vertical parity checking.*

A second type of check is performed in the horizontal direction. At the end of each tape record—the last byte before the interrecord gap—is a *horizontal,* or *longitudinal, check character.* The bits of this byte are set on or off to form a parity check for each of the horizontal tracks. For the System/360-370, for example, the bits of the check character are set so the number of on-bits in each track is odd. Then, if a tape record is read that contains an even number of on-bits in one or more of the tracks, an input error has been detected. With the combination of vertical and *horizontal parity checking,* most tape input errors can be caught. While it isn't necessary for you as a programmer to completely understand parity checking, you should realize that all input and output operations on tape are checked.

The tape in figure 6-2 is called a *nine-track tape* because each vertical position consists of nine bit positions. Most System/360-370s use nine-track tapes, but some also have *seven-track tape* capabilities. This means they can process tapes from older computer systems. Seven-track tapes are recorded in a code called *Binary Coded Decimal,* or *BCD.* In this code, seven bits are used to represent one character of data—six data bits plus one parity bit. Parity checking takes place on seven-track tapes just as it does on nine-track tapes.

Often in tape operations, more than one tape record is recorded between IRGs. This is called *blocking* records. Figure 6-3, for instance, shows how a *block* of five records would look on tape. Here, the *blocking factor* of the file is 5, since five records (often called *logical records*) are stored in each tape block (often called a *physical record*). Because blocking is such a common practice, the IRG is often referred to as an *interblock gap,* or *IBG.* Blocking is commonly used because it increases the storage capacity of a reel of

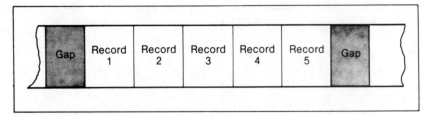

Figure 6-3 Blocked records

tape as well as the speed at which the records on the tape can be read or written.

The tape drive

The *tape drive*, which is shown in figure 6-4, is the hardware unit that reads and writes the data on tape. To mount a tape on one of the older tape drives, the computer operator threads the tape through a read/write mechanism in the center of the unit and then onto an empty takeup reel, as shown in figure 6-5. This process is similar to mounting a tape on a tape recorder. On the newer tape drives, threading of the tape is done by the drive itself so the operator can change tapes more rapidly.

Once the tape is mounted, the operator pushes the start button, and the tape drive locates the first record on the file by searching for a *load-point marker*, which is a reflective spot on the surface of the tape. Tape records can then be read or written under control of a stored program. When data is read from a tape, the data on the tape remains unaltered, so it can be read many times. When data is written on a tape, it replaces (and thus destroys) the data that was on the tape. Before a tape is removed from the tape drive, it is rewound onto the original reel, ready to be read or written again.

During reading operations, input records are checked for vertical and horizontal parity as discussed earlier. In writing operations, output records can be checked for vertical and horizontal parity as soon as a character, record, or block of records is written, because the reading mechanism is located just after the writing mechanism.

Although the basic programmable functions of a tape drive are reading and writing records, there are a number of others. For example, tape drives can be programmed to rewind a tape, to backspace a tape one block of records, and to skip over faulty sections of tape. In addition, some tape drives can be programmed to read tapes backwards, which can increase the speed of tape operations in some applications.

Figure 6-4 The tape drive

Many computer systems use tape drives extensively, even
though their primary I/O form is the disk. For instance, a medium-
sized system frequently includes from two to six tape drives, while
larger systems may have several dozen or more.

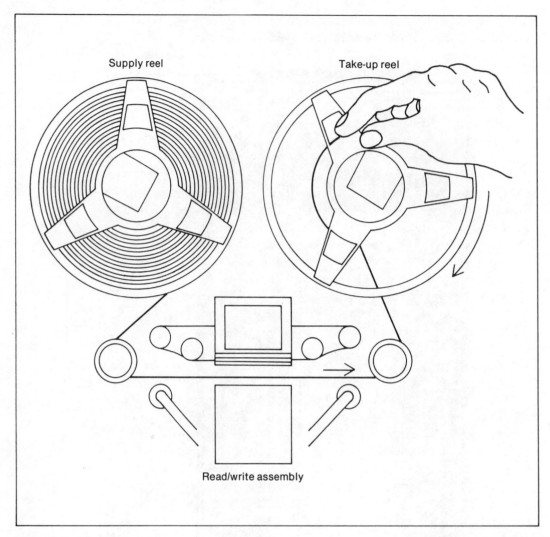

Supply reel

Take-up reel

Read/write assembly

Figure 6-5   Mounting a tape

Tape speed and capacity

One measure of the speed of tape operations is the *transfer rate*, or *transfer speed*, of a tape drive. It measures how long it takes in bytes per second to transfer data from the tape drive to storage, or vice versa. For example, one common model of the IBM 2400/3400 series tape drive has a transfer rate of 60,000 bytes per second. (This speed is often referred to as 60 *KB*, where KB means thousands of bytes per second.) Other tape drives that are used on the System/360-370 have speeds that range from 15 KB all the way up to 1250 KB for the 3420 Model 8 tape drive. To appreciate tape speeds, consider that a transfer rate of 80,000 bytes per second (80

KB) is the equivalent of reading 1000 eighty-column cards per second, or 60,000 cards—a stack 35 feet high—in one minute.

Transfer rate is somewhat misleading, however, because a tape drive actually stops and starts every time that it comes to an IBG. Yet transfer rate does not reflect this *start/stop time.* For several models of tape drives used on the System/360-370, this start/stop time is 8/1000 of a second, or 8 milliseconds. To appreciate the effect of this starting and stopping between each physical record, suppose that a file of 6000 records, each 100 bytes long, is stored on a tape with a blocking factor of 1. At 60 KB, it takes 10 seconds to read the data in the file (600,000 bytes at 60,000 bytes per second). However, the tape also has to stop and start 6000 times. At 8/1000 of a second for each start/stop, this takes an additional 48 seconds. In other words, the tape drive spends 10 seconds reading data and 48 seconds starting and stopping. The effective processing rate is therefore much less than 60 KB.

Now suppose the records are blocked with a blocking factor of 10. Ten seconds are still required for reading the 600,000 bytes of data, but only 4.8 seconds are required for starting and stopping. Since the total time for reading the file is reduced from 58 seconds to 14.8 seconds, you can see the effect of blocking on the speed of tape operations.

The capacity of a reel of tape depends on the length of the tape and the *density* of the tape. Density is a measure of the number of bytes of data that can be recorded on one inch of tape. One model of the IBM 2400 series of tape drives has a density of 800 *bpi* (bytes per inch). At this density, an 80-byte record requires 1/10 inch of tape. One of the IBM 3400 models is a 1600-bpi tape drive. On this drive, an 80-byte record requires only 1/20 inch of tape. And the 3420 Model 8 tape drive has a density of 6250 bpi, which means an 80-byte record requires just a little more than 1/80 inch of tape.

Blocking also affects the capacity of a tape. To illustrate, suppose there is a sample file of 8000 records, 100 bytes each. At 800 bpi, the 800,000 bytes require 1000 inches of tape. With a blocking factor of 1, the 8000 IBGs (at 6/10 inch) use 4800 inches of tape. The total file then requires 5800 inches of tape. If the blocking factor is increased to 10, however, only 800 IBGs are required. Then, only 480 inches of tape is used for IBGs, and the file is reduced from 5800 inches to 1480 inches.

How large can a blocking factor be? On smaller systems, it depends to some extent on the computer's available CPU storage. If, for example, a program is to be run in 16K of storage and the instructions by themselves take 14K, the blocking factors must be kept relatively small. Assuming four files were processed by a program, each requiring two I/O areas, the average block size would have to be 250 bytes (2K divided by eight I/O areas).

On most System/360-370s, however, storage restrictions are not a factor in determining the block size. This is particularly true on the larger systems running under one of the versions of OS or VS. In this case, you choose a blocking factor that will make optimum use of the resources of the computer system. Based on our experience, this means that you should try to use a block size of around 4000 bytes. Thus, to write card records on a tape, 50 would be the best blocking factor (80 bytes per record times 50 records per block equals 4000 bytes).

Terminology

magnetic tape

bit

record

interrecord gap

IRG

check bit

parity bit

vertical parity checking

horizontal check character

longitudinal check character

horizontal parity checking

nine-track tape

seven-track tape

Binary Coded Decimal

BCD

blocking

block

blocking factor

logical record

physical record

interblock gap

IBG

tape drive

load-point marker

transfer rate

transfer speed

KB

start/stop time

density

bpi

Objectives

1. Explain how vertical and horizontal parity checking assure the accuracy of tape I/O operations.

2. Name two benefits derived from blocking records on tape.

3. Describe how the blocking factor for a tape file is determined; specifically, name the factors that must be considered.

TOPIC 2   Direct-Access Concepts

A substantial majority of today's data-processing systems are direct-access systems. Direct-access storage devices *(DASD)* provide large amounts of storage with fast access to any of the stored records. Unlike sequential devices such as a card reader or tape drive, a record on a direct-access file can be read or written without reading or writing the records that precede it. To process the 500th record in a direct-access file, only the 500th record has to be read.

Direct-access devices also differ from tape devices in that they vary considerably in physical characteristics. For example, *disks* record data on platters that are somewhat analogous to phonograph records in a stack, and *drums* record data on the outside of cylindrical (drumlike) surfaces. For each type of device, there are further variations depending on manufacturer and model.

The two primary direct-access devices used on the System/360-370 are the 2314 and the 3330 Direct-Access Storage Facilities. The 2314 is used mainly on the System/360, though it can be used on the System/370 as well. In contrast, the 3330 was designed for the 370 and cannot be used on the 360. Although the two devices are somewhat similar, the 3330 offers greater storage capacity and faster access than the 2314. Both devices are described in greater detail below.

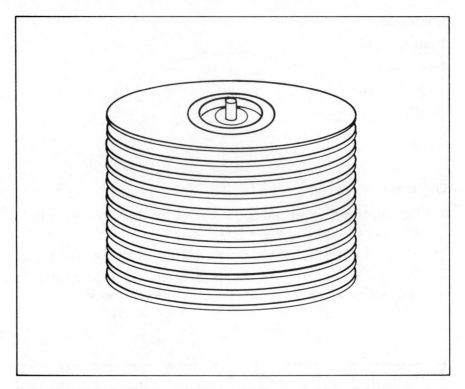

Figure 6-6 The disk pack

The 2314 Direct-Access Storage Facility

The disk pack

The *disk pack* is the device on which data is recorded; the *disk drive* is the I/O unit that writes data on and reads data from a disk pack. The disk pack used with the 2314 disk facility, called the 2316 pack, is schematically illustrated in figure 6-6. It consists of 11 metal disks, each 14 inches in diameter, permanently stacked on a central spindle. When the disk pack is mounted on a 2314, it rotates at a constant speed of 40 revolutions per second while data is read from or written on it. When the disk pack is removed from the disk drive, a protective plastic cover is placed over it for storage.

Except for the top surface of the top disk and the bottom surface of the bottom disk, data can be recorded on both sides of the 11 disks that make up the 2316 pack; this is similar to sound being recorded on both sides of a phonograph record. As a result, this disk pack has a total of 20 recording surfaces, each of which has a magnetic surface coating on which data can be recorded.

On each of the 20 recording surfaces are 200 concentric circles called *tracks*, as illustrated in figure 6-7. These tracks are numbered

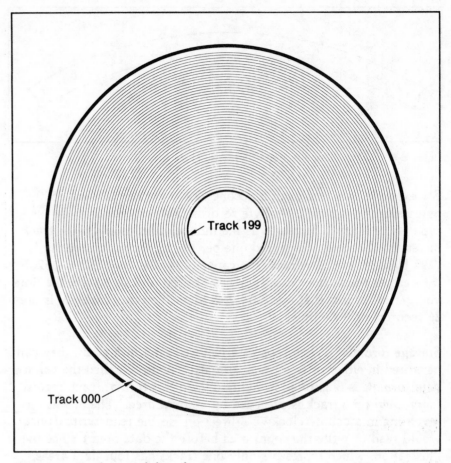

Figure 6-7   Tracks on a disk surface

from 000 through 199. Since there are 20 surfaces and 200 tracks per surface, the 2316 pack has a total of 4000 tracks on which data can be recorded. Although these tracks get smaller toward the center of the disk, each of the tracks can hold the same amount of data, a maximum of 7294 bytes.

Bits are used to record data on a track of a disk pack, just as they are on tape. On disk, the bits are strung together so that eight bits make up one byte of data. To illustrate, suppose that figure 6-8 represents a portion of one track on one recording surface. If 0 represents an off-bit and 1 represents an on-bit, this portion of track contains three bytes of data. In EBCDIC code, which corresponds to DISPLAY usage, the first byte, 11000001, represents the letter A; the second byte, 11110010, represents the digit 2; and the third byte, 01011011, represents the special character $.

The actual number of records on any track of a disk pack for the 2314 varies depending on the size of the records being stored.

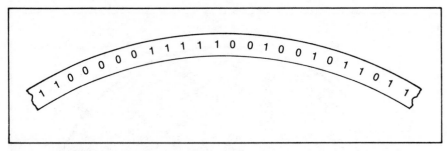

Figure 6-8   Coding on one section of a track

For example, one track can hold one 7294-byte record, two 3520-byte records, or three 2298-byte records. You can see that the capacity of a track decreases as the number of records on the track increases. If records are stored one per track, the track capacity is 7294 bytes; if two per track, the capacity is 7040 bytes (2 × 3520); if three per track, the capacity is 6894 bytes; and so on. By the time you get to records that are 100 bytes long, the track capacity is only 36 records, or 3600 bytes.

Storage formats   When records are stored on a disk pack, they can be stored in either of two track formats. The first, called the *count-data format*, is illustrated in figure 6-9. In this format, each record *(data area)* on a track is preceded by a *count area*. (The disk is revolving in a counterclockwise direction, so the read/write device would read or write the count area before the data area.) Since the illustration, which represents only one track, has four data areas, there are four count areas on the track. These count areas contain the *disk addresses* and lengths of the records following them. Just as a storage address identifies one and only one storage position, a disk address identifies one and only one data area on a disk pack. By using the count area, each of the records on a disk pack can be directly accessed and read or written.

In addition to count areas and data areas, each track in the count-data format has a *home address*. The home address, which comes immediately before the first count area on a track, uniquely identifies each of the tracks on a disk pack. On the 2316 disk pack, there are 4000 different home addresses, one for each of the 4000 tracks.

The second track format that can be used is called the *count-key-data format*. Like the count-data format, there is a home address at the start of each track. However, unlike the count-data format, there is a *key area* between each count and data area as shown in figure 6-10. This key area, which may be from 1 through 256 bytes in length, contains the control data that uniquely identifies a record

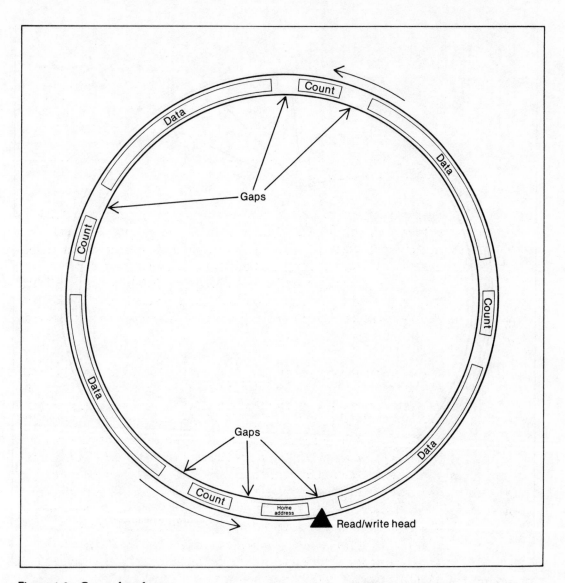

Figure 6-9   Count-data format

in a file. For example, in a file of inventory master records, the part number would logically be recorded in the key area. In a file of master payroll records, the employee number would be recorded in the key area. The difference, then, between count and key areas is that the count area contains a disk address that uniquely identifies a record location on the disk pack, and the key area contains a control field that uniquely identifies a record in a file. As you will see later, both count and key areas can be used to locate records when directly accessing them.

Because the count-key-data format has gaps separating the key from the count and data areas, the track capacity of this format is

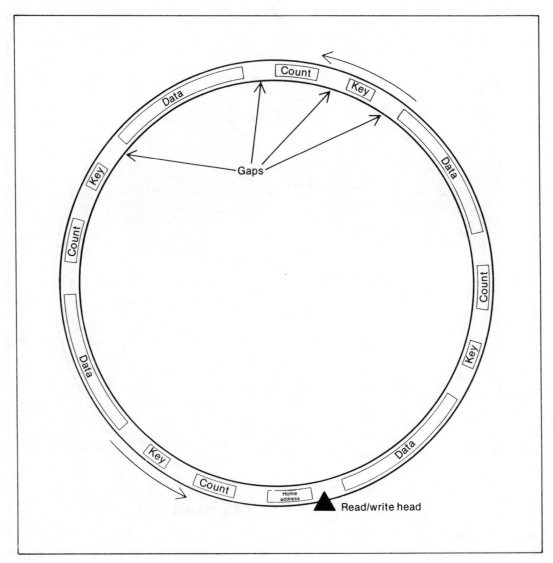

Figure 6-10   Count-key-data format

less than that of the count-data format. For example, with one
record per track (one home address, one count, one key, and one
data area), the track capacity is 7249 bytes. This includes both key
and data areas—say a 10-byte key and a 7239-byte data area. In
contrast, the capacity of a track in count-data format is 7294 bytes.
Similarly, with a 5-byte key and a 95-byte data area (a total of 100
bytes), only 29 records can be recorded per track in contrast to the
36 records possible in the count-data format.

Figure 6-11   The 2314 direct-access storage facility

The disk drive

The 2314 disk facility contains from three to nine independent disk drives, called *modules*. In figure 6-11, for example, a facility with five disk drives, or modules, is shown. For all models of the 2314, at least one module is reserved for backup in case any of the others fail. Thus, a nine-module 2314 can only use eight modules at any one time.

To mount a disk pack on one of the five drives in figure 6-11, the operator pulls out the selected disk drive, places the disk pack on the drive's spindle, and pushes the module back into the facility. In a multidrive device like this, a drive is often referred to as a *spindle*. Thus, the device in figure 6-11 can be called a 2314 with five spindles.

When the operator pushes the start button of the unit, the disk pack begins rotating until it reaches a speed of 40 revolutions per second. At this speed, the drive can read data from or write data on the recording surfaces. When it reads data, the data on the disk pack remains unchanged; when it writes data, the data that is written replaces the data previously stored there.

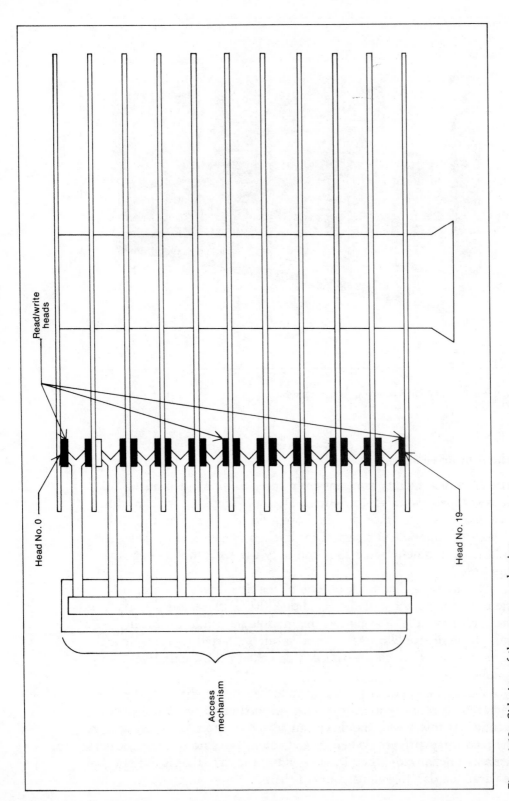

Figure 6-12   Sideview of the access mechanism

The access mechanism   The mechanism used to read and write data on the 2314 is called the *access mechanism* and is illustrated in side view in figure 6-12. It consists of 20 read/write heads, one for each of the 20 recording surfaces. These heads are numbered from 0 through 19. Only one of the 20 heads can be turned on at any one time; thus, only one track can be operated upon at one time. Each of the heads can both read and write data but can do only one operation at a time.

In order to operate on a recording surface, the access mechanism moves to the track that is to be operated upon. When the access mechanism moves, all 20 heads move in unison so that they are positioned at the same track on each of the 20 recording surfaces. Then, these 20 tracks, which are said to make up one *cylinder* of data, can be operated upon, one right after another, without the access mechanism having to move to another setting. In other words, if the access mechanism is positioned at the 75th cylinder, the 75th track on each recording surface can be read or written, one track right after another. Since there are 200 tracks on each surface of the 2316 pack, there are 200 different settings of the access mechanism—and 200 cylinders. In figure 6-12, the access mechanism is positioned at approximately the 65th cylinder.

Accessing a disk record   Any programming references to data records on disk are eventually reduced to cylinder number, head (track) number, and either record number or key. The cylinders are numbered 0 through 199, the heads 0 through 19, and the record number starts at 0 and continues through the maximum number of records that can be stored on the track. Because record number 0 is used by the operating system, data records always begin with record number 1.

When directly accessing and reading a record on a disk, there are four phases that the disk drive goes through. During the first phase, called *access-mechanism movement*, the access mechanism moves to the cylinder that is going to be operated upon. The time required for this movement depends on the number of cylinders moved. If it is just one cylinder—for instance, a move from the 25th to the 26th cylinder—it takes 25 milliseconds (25/1000 second). On the other hand, if the movement is 180 cylinders—say from the 10th to the 190th cylinder—the time required is from 115 to 120 milliseconds, depending on the model used. In any event, the more cylinders moved, the more time required for access-mechanism movement. The average access-mechanism movement when processing a file that uses all 200 cylinders of the disk pack is 75 milliseconds on one model of the 2314, 60 milliseconds on another.

Once the heads are moved to the correct cylinder, the appropriate read/write head must be turned on. This is called *head switching*. If a track on the third recording surface is supposed to be read, head number 2 is turned on. In figure 6-12, head number 2, which is on, is white while the others are black. Since head switching takes place at electronic speeds, it has a negligible effect on the total amount of time required to read or write a record.

After the head is turned on, there is a delay while the appropriate record rotates around to the head. This phase is called *rotational delay* (or *latency*). Since one complete rotation on the 2314 takes 25 milliseconds, the maximum time that rotational delay could be is 25 milliseconds. On the other hand, the appropriate record might just be reaching the head when the head is switched on. In this case, rotational delay would be 0 milliseconds. Since rotational delay will vary between 0 and 25 milliseconds, the average delay is about 12.5 milliseconds.

The last phase in the process of accessing and reading a record is called *data transfer*. Here, data is transferred from the disk to storage in the CPU. On the 2314, data transfer takes place at 312,000 bytes per second, or 312 KB. At this speed, a 312-byte record requires 1 millisecond for data transfer.

When accessing and writing a record, the same four phases are completed. First, the access mechanism is moved; second, the appropriate head is turned on; third, rotational delay takes place; and fourth, the data is transferred from storage to disk. In either a reading or writing operation, access-mechanism movement and rotational delay are by far the most time-consuming phases.

Verifying I/O operations   Like other I/O devices on a computer system, the disk drive checks to make sure that reading and writing take place without error. Although I haven't mentioned it before, there are actually two *cyclic check characters* at the end of each count, key, and data area that are used as a check on accuracy. During a writing operation, these characters are calculated based on the combinations of bits used in the count, key, or data area. Then, when a record is read, the cyclic check characters are recalculated and compared with those that are read. If they don't agree, an input error is indicated.

A writing operation may be checked by using the write-verify instruction. When it is executed following a write instruction, the data that has just been written is read and the cyclic check characters are checked as in a read operation. If there is a discrepancy, it indicates that the writing operation did not take place correctly. Unfortunately, the write-verify is time consuming since the disk must make one complete rotation before the record that has been written can be read. Nevertheless, write-verification is often used when recording permanent files.

I/O commands

The actual *I/O commands* that a 2314 disk can be programmed to execute are many. (I/O instructions on the System/360-370 are called commands.) These commands can be broken down into five types: seek, search, read, write, and write-verify.

The *seek* command causes the access mechanism to be moved to the specified cylinder and the specified head to be turned on. A typical *search* command tries to locate a record by searching a track until it finds a count or key equal to the one specified in the command. If the specified key or count isn't found, the search may be continued on successive tracks in the cylinder.

Once the seek and search have been executed, a *read* or *write* may take place. This is the data-transfer phase of the operation. In a typical business program, data alone or data plus key is transferred during a read or write command. Following the write command, a *write-verify* may be executed as described above.

To illustrate the use of the commands, suppose the 5th record on the 7th track of the 120th cylinder must be accessed and read. The seek command would specify that the access mechanism be moved to the 120th cylinder and the 7th head (head number 6) be turned on. Next, a search command would compare the counts on the track with the count specified in the command. Since the count for a record indicates the cylinder number, head number, and record number on the track, the count for this record would indicate that it is the 5th record on the track. When the count in the command and the count on the track are equal, the read command would be issued, thus causing the data area following the count to be read.

When using the count-key-data format, a slightly different set of instructions may be used instead. First, the seek finds the selected cylinder and turns on the selected head. Second, the search looks for a key on the track that is equal to the one specified in the command. When they match, a read command is issued, thus transferring the data area following the selected key into storage.

The 3330 Direct-Access Storage Facility

The physical characteristics of the 3330 Direct-Access Storage Facility are similar to those of the 2314. Like the 2316 pack, the 3336 disk pack has 11 disks with 20 recording surfaces. The 3330, which consists of up to 9 modules, also rotates this removable pack at a constant speed and reads or writes data through an access mechanism that carries the 20 read/write heads to the same position (cylinder) on each recording surface.

In contrast to the 2314, however, the 3330 offers significantly faster access-mechanism movement, faster data-transfer rate, and from four to eight times the storage capacity, depending on the 3330 model used. For the Model 1 3330, each recording surface is divided into 400 tracks instead of 200 as on the 2314. This accounts in part for the increased storage capacity. In addition, the 3330 track has nearly double the capacity of the 2314 track—13,030 bytes on a fully used 3330 track as compared to 7294 bytes on a 2314 track. However, only 19 of the 20 tracks in each cylinder of the 3330 can be used for storing data. The 20th track is a synchronizing track that helps guide the 20 read/write heads.

Because the pack on the 3330 spins at 60 revolutions per second instead of 40 as on the 2314, its rotational delay averages only 8.4 milliseconds as compared to 12.5 milliseconds on the 2314. Since the 3330 access mechanism also moves faster, the average time for access-mechanism movement is only 30 milliseconds versus 60 or 75 milliseconds on the 2314. Finally, since more data is passing under the heads at a faster rotational speed, the data transfer rate is increased to 806,000 bytes per second, or 806 KB.

The second model of the 3330, the model 11, has twice as many cylinders as the basic model. This, of course, means the storage capacity of each pack is doubled. Otherwise, the operational features are the same as on the Model 1 3330.

Other DASD Devices

Although the 2314 and 3330 are currently the most widely used direct-access devices on the System/360-370, there are others. For instance, the 3350 is sometimes found on large virtual storage systems. Part of this device resembles the 3330, while the other part differs in that there is one read/write head for each track. This means there is no access-mechanism movement on this portion of the device, so the average time to access a record is one-half the time for one revolution of the disk, or about 8.4 milliseconds. Because portions of a program running on a virtual storage system are read from and written on disk, this faster access can mean faster program execution. The applications programmer can use either part of the 3350 for his files, depending on the requirements of his program.

Another device that you may come in contact with on a large system is the 3850 Mass Storage Device. The storage unit on the 3850 is a data cartridge approximately four inches long and two inches in diameter, which contains a 770-inch long spool of tape.

Two of these cartridges can hold as much data as a 3336 Model 1 disk pack. And the 3850 can store up to 4720 of these cartridges in a single unit.

When the System/370 requests the data on a cartridge, the selected cartridge is mechanically moved to a read/write mechanism. Then, the 3850 transfers the data on the cartridge to a 3330 disk drive. This process is called *staging*. Thereafter, the data is treated just as though it were stored on and accessed by a 3330 disk device. Once the data is no longer required, it is *destaged* back onto the data cartridge and the cartridge is returned to its original location.

The 3850, then, is a cross between a tape and a disk device, offering the advantages of direct-access storage at the low cost of tape storage. An additional advantage is that the staging and destaging processes are done automatically, so no operator intervention is required to mount and remove the cartridges. And because of the size and capacity of the cartridges, the 3850 offers an appreciable savings in the amount of space needed to house a conventional tape or disk library.

In addition to these devices, other direct-access devices are available on the System/360-370. Rather than give the characteristics of all the DASDs that you may encounter, however, I just want you to remember one thing. Regardless of the device used, the concept of cylinder, track, and record is followed when addressing a record. So the programming requirements are much the same no matter what devices are used. This is particularly true when you are using sequential file organization.

Sequential File Organization

Although direct-access devices were designed for directly accessing records, they may also store and process records sequentially. In fact, *sequential organization* is the most efficient method for many types of files. As a result, sequential file organization is probably more common than any other method of file organization used on direct-access devices.

Conceptually, a sequential file on a direct-access device is like a sequential tape file. When writing records sequentially on disk, for example, the first record of the file is stored in the first record position on the first track of the first cylinder of the file, the second record is stored in the second record position on the first track of the first cylinder of the file, and so on. Likewise, the records in a sequential disk file are read beginning with the first physical location of the file and continuing consecutively until an *end-of-file record* is read. Because the records in a sequential disk file are almost always processed sequentially, keys aren't needed, and the count-data format is used.

For processing efficiency, the records in a sequentially organized file on disk are usually blocked just as they are on tape. Because more than one record is read or written by a single read or write command when the records are blocked, blocking reduces the time required for these I/O operations. Specifically, only one rotational delay is required for each block of records in contrast to one rotational delay for each record when unblocked records are processed. Thus, by reducing rotational delay, blocking can significantly reduce the time required to read the records in a sequential file.

Blocking also affects the storage capacity of a direct-access device. On the 2314, for example, 7200 100-byte records will take 200 tracks, or 10 cylinders, if the records are unblocked. If they are blocked 9 to a block, however, 7 such blocks may be recorded on each track—a total of 63 records per track. Then, the entire file requires only 115 tracks, or less than 6 cylinders.

In summary, a large percent of all applications programs involve sequential files on direct-access devices. And because of its effect on processing speed and storage capacity, blocking is commonly used on these sequential files. On the 2314 you should choose a blocking factor that leads to blocks of approximately 7294 bytes (a full track) or 3520 bytes (half a track). On the 3330, you should try to create blocks of approximately 3156 bytes (a quarter of a track), 4253 bytes (a third of a track), or 6447 bytes (half a track). You will have to make certain, of course, that your system has adequate main storage for blocks of these sizes.

Terminology

DASD

disk

drum

disk pack

disk drive

track

count-data format

data area

count area

disk address

home address

count-key-data format

key area

module

spindle

access mechanism

cylinder

access-mechanism movement

head switching

rotational delay

latency

data transfer

cyclic check character

I/O commands:

   seek

   search

   read

   write

   write-verify

staging

destaging

sequential organization

end-of-file record

Objectives

1. List and describe the physical operations required by the 2314 or 3330 in order to access and read or write a record from a file (1) in count-data format and (2) in count-key-data format.

2. List the I/O commands that must be executed in order to access and read or write a record on the 2314 or 3330.

3. Explain how blocking can (1) increase the number of records that can be stored on a disk and (2) decrease the time required to read or write a sequential file on disk.

TOPIC 3   Programming Considerations

From a conceptual point of view, sequential files on tape or direct-access devices are much like card and printer files. When reading a sequential file, one record is read after another in the physical sequence of the records on the device just as cards are read one after another in their physical sequence. When writing a sequential file, one record is written after another and it is placed in the next available physical location on the device just as one line follows another line on a printer.

On the other hand, there are some complications with tape and direct-access files that must be handled by programming. Some of the most important of these are error recovery, record blocking and deblocking, and label checking. For the most part, these complications are handled by routines that are part of the operating system, so no special coding is required of the applications programmer. Nevertheless, the programmer should be familiar with what these routines do.

Error-recovery routines

When an error is detected during a reading operation, the error may often be recovered by an *error-recovery routine*. If, for example, a piece of dust or dirt on the surface of the tape or disk causes an error, it may be brushed off as the reading mechanism passes over that part of the recording surface. Then if that area is reread, the data can be transferred to storage without error. (A tape must be backspaced to be reread; a disk record is reread by waiting one complete revolution until the record rotates under the read/write head again.) In a typical error-recovery routine, the record is reread a number of times. If the error persists, an error message is printed so the operator can decide what action to take.

The same type of routine is used in a writing operation. For example, if a writing error is detected on tape, the tape is backspaced and the write instruction is tried again. After a number of attempts, the program may skip a certain amount of tape—the equivalent of a long IRG—and try again. On disk, the error-recovery routine may try to write the record on an *alternate track*. Both the 2314 and 3330 have several cylinders that can be used for alternate tracks. The 2314, for instance, actually has 203 cylinders, with tracks 0-199 used for normal processing and 200-202 for alternate track assignment. In either case, if the attempt to write the record takes place without error, the program continues. Otherwise, an error message is printed for operator action.

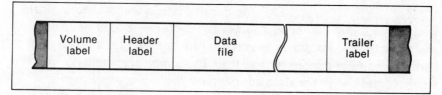

Figure 6-13   Labels for a tape file

Blocking and deblocking routines

When a tape or disk drive executes a read command, it reads an entire block of records into storage. The program, however, is usually written to process only one record at a time. *Deblocking routines* are used to keep track of which record in a block is being processed and to issue read commands to the drive only when a new block of records is required.

A similar situation exists when creating blocked output files. Each time the processing portion of the main program writes an individual record, a *blocking routine* moves the record to the output area. Only when the entire block is filled does the blocking routine actually issue a write command to the tape or disk drive.

Label-checking routines

Tape files   The instructions given to a computer operator for running a job tell him which reel of tape to mount on which tape drive. The reels of tape are identified by external labels on the outside of the reels. Suppose, however, that the operator makes a mistake. He mounts a tape containing current accounts receivable records on a tape drive that is going to write a file of updated inventory records. If this mistake isn't caught, the accounts receivable records will be destroyed.

To prevent this type of error, *internal labels*—labels that are actually records on the tape itself—are used. For example, System/360-370 tape files with *standard labels* contain the three label records shown in figure 6-13. (IBGs aren't shown in this illustration.) The *volume label*, which comes immediately after the load-point marker, identifies the reel of tape. The *header label*, which contains information such as the file name, the date the file was created, and the date after which it can be destroyed, identifies the file. The *trailer label*, found after the data records of the file, contains the same data as the header label plus a block count indicating the number of blocks of data that the file contains.

On the System/360-370, job-control cards are used to indicate what the volume and header labels for each file should be. Then when the OPEN statement is executed for a tape file, a *label-checking routine* processes the labels by comparing the data that the labels contain with the data supplied by the job-control cards. Examples of System/360-370 header labels and related job-control cards are given in chapters 8 and 9.

To appreciate the value of label checking, consider the label processing that is done on the System/360-370 before writing a tape output file. First, the volume and header labels are read and analyzed. If the volume number agrees with the volume number given in the job-control cards and the expiration date has passed, the routine backspaces the tape, writes a new header label for the output file, and begins processing. Otherwise, a message is printed to the operator indicating that he has mounted the wrong file, and thus, what might have been a costly error is avoided.

For input files, the header label is checked to make sure that the identifying information agrees with the information given in the job-control cards. At the end of the file, the block count in the trailer label is compared with a block count accumulated during processing. If the counts are the same, all the input blocks have been processed. If they are different, the routine prints a message to the operator telling him that an error has occurred.

In some cases, a file of records will require more than one reel (volume) of tape. This is referred to as a *multivolume file* and requires additional label-checking routines. When writing a multivolume file, the tape drive must check for a reflective spot near the end of each tape—this is the *end-of-reel marker*. When it is encountered, the label-checking routines write a trailer label, called an *end-of-volume label*, that includes the block count for that reel of tape. The routines then check the labels on the next reel of tape. If the next reel is accepted for processing, a header label is written that contains a volume sequence number indicating the order in which the reels of tape should be read. This switching from one reel of tape to another is called *tape switching*. On the last reel of the multivolume file, the program writes a file trailer label, called an *end-of-file label*, containing the block count for the reel. A four-volume multivolume file and its associated labels are illustrated in figure 6-14.

For multivolume input files, the label-checking routines check the header label of each reel to be sure that the correct file is being processed and that the reels are being processed in sequence. Thus, the first reel in the file must have a volume sequence number 1, the second must have sequence number 2, and so on. If the wrong file has been mounted, a message is printed and the program is halted.

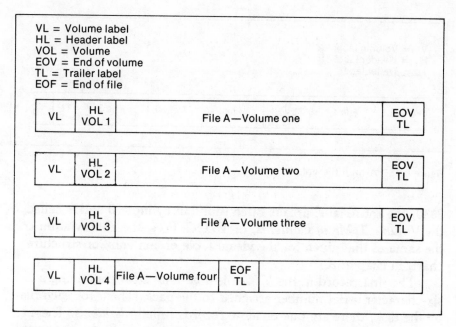

VL = Volume label
HL = Header label
VOL = Volume
EOV = End of volume
TL = Trailer label
EOF = End of file

| VL | HL VOL 1 | File A—Volume one | EOV TL |

| VL | HL VOL 2 | File A—Volume two | EOV TL |

| VL | HL VOL 3 | File A—Volume three | EOV TL |

| VL | HL VOL 4 | File A—Volume four | EOF TL | |

Figure 6-14 A multivolume file

At the end of each reel, prior to tape switching, the program checks the block count in the trailer label against a block count accumulated by the program to determine if all blocks have been read.

One final aspect of tape label-checking routines concerns *multifile volumes (or multifile reels)*. These are reels that have more than one file stored on them—for example, an inventory file, a billing file, and a sales-reporting file. In this case, each file is preceded by a header label and followed by a trailer label, as illustrated in figure 6-15. When reading a file from a multifile volume, the label-checking routines must scan the tape until the correct label is located. When writing a file in any but the first position of a multifile volume, the label-checking routines must locate the correct position for the output file.

Disk Files   A single disk pack normally contains many files, with each file assigned to a particular area on the pack. For example, a pack might have an accounts receivable file in cylinders 1-30, a payroll master file in cylinders 36-55, and other files on the rest of the pack. A second pack could have cylinders 1-10 allocated as a temporary work area for record sorting and cylinders 11-20 assigned to a customer master file. These file allocations are illustrated in figure 6-16.

Again, as on tape, internal labels are used for each file on the disk to protect it from being destroyed by mistake. On the 2314 or

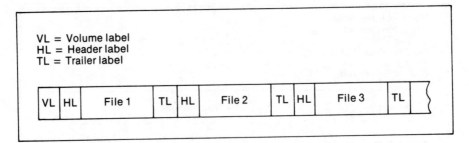

Figure 6-15 A multifile volume

3330, the entire label area is often found in cylinder 0 and is called
the *Volume Table of Contents,* or *VTOC.* (Yes, the abbreviation is
the same as that given for the visual table of contents, or structure
chart, in chapter 3.)

The first record in the VTOC is a *volume label* containing a
six-character serial number assigned to the pack. Then, for each file
on the disk, there are one or more records called *file labels.* These
labels give the name of the file, its organization, its location on the
disk, and its expiration date. The expiration date indicates when a
file is no longer needed so that its area can be assigned to another
file. If a file is to be found in more than one area of the disk—
cylinders 11-20 and 41-49, for example— this information is also
given in the file label. Each area of a file is referred to as an *extent*
of the file; it is expressed as lower and upper limits of the area in
terms of cylinder and head numbers.

Label-checking routines similar to those for tape records compare the data in the labels with data supplied in job-control cards at
the time the program is executed. These job-control cards indicate
which program should be run, as well as which pack should be
mounted on which disk drive and what information the volume and
file labels should contain. They also indicate the extents of each file
that is going to be processed. Chapters 8 and 9 explain in detail the
contents and formats of these cards.

When a disk file is opened for processing, the volume label is
compared to the one supplied in the job-control cards. This is called
volume-label checking. If the six-character volume codes don't
match, the operator is notified by a message and he is thus given the
opportunity to mount the proper pack.

Once the volume label is checked, *file-label checking* takes
place. This level of label processing actually performs two types of
checking. First, the file name is checked. For an input file, the name
of the file as supplied in the job-control cards is compared to the list
of file names on the pack. If an equal name is found, the file is
opened for processing. Otherwise, a message is issued to the

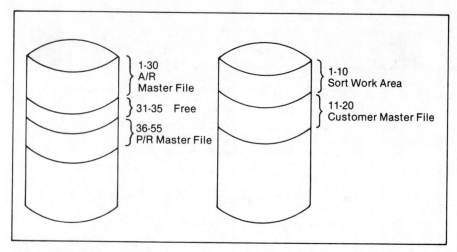

Figure 6-16   Disk pack allocation

operator for appropriate action. For output files, the list of file
names is checked to see if a file with the same name already exists
on the pack. If a duplicate is found, a message is printed on the console typewriter.

If a duplicate name for an output file does not exist, the second
type of file-label checking is performed. The disk extents in the job-
control cards are compared with the extents given in the file labels
of all the other files on the disk pack. As long as the new file does
not overlap any active file, the program continues. If, however, the
new file will overlap an area already assigned to some other file,
processing stops and a message is issued to the operator.

Referring to figure 6-16, suppose that a programmer wanted to
use the free area in cylinders 31-35 on disk 1. By mistake, however,
he assigns cylinders 30-35 for his new file. Extent checking will prevent the last cylinder of the accounts receivable file from being
destroyed. When this new program tries to open the output file, the
overlap with cylinder 30 will be found and the operator will be
alerted to the problem.

When a direct-access file is stored on more than one disk pack,
the labels for all the packs are checked and processed. For a sequentially organized file, this processing takes place when the end of the
first disk pack is reached. Thus, the label-checking routines provide
for switching from one disk pack to the next.

What the programmer must know

As you can see, tape and disk programs can be considerably more
complicated than card and printer programs. Fortunately for the

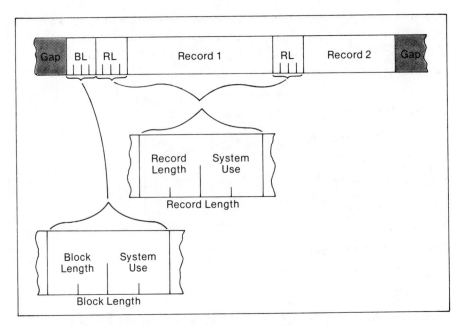

Figure 6-17   Variable-length format on the System/360-370

COBOL programmer, various modules of the operating system contain the code to perform all these tape and disk functions. The programmer need only know how to specify the characteristics of the files to be processed. In general, this means you need only know the blocking characteristics of the file and whether the records of the file are fixed or variable in length.

If all the records in a file have the same number of bytes, the record has a *fixed-length* format. These records can be either blocked or unblocked. In some cases, however, the records in a tape or disk file will be variable in length. *Variable-length records* can also be blocked, resulting in variable-length blocks.

Figure 6-17 shows the System/360-370 format of a variable-length tape file. (A variable-length disk file would be much the same.) As you can see, each of the variable-length records is preceded by a four-byte record-length field. The number of bytes contained in the record, including the four-byte length field, is recorded as a binary (COMP) value in the first two bytes. The second two bytes are reserved for use by the operating system and usually contain blanks. Another four-byte field at the start of the block specifies the total number of bytes in the entire block. It has the same format as the record-length field: bytes 1 and 2 carry the total block length, including the four-byte block-length field, as a binary value, and bytes 3 and 4 are reserved for system use. As a COBOL programmer, you should be familiar with this format so you can properly allocate space to a file of variable-length records.

Terminology

error-recovery routine

alternate track

deblocking routine

blocking routine

internal label

tape label-checking routine

   standard labels

   volume label

   header label

   trailer label

   multivolume file

   end-of-reel marker

   end-of-volume label

   tape switching

   end-of-file label

   multifile volume

   multifile reel

disk label-checking routine

   Volume Table of Contents

   VTOC

   volume label

   file label

   extent

   volume-label checking

   file-label checking

fixed-length record

variable-length record

Objectives

1. Describe the purpose of error-recovery, blocking, deblocking, and label-checking routines.

2. Distinguish between the terms in each of the following pairs:
    fixed-length vs. variable-length records
    multifile volume vs. multivolume file

7

COBOL for Sequential Files

This chapter is divided into two topics. Topic 1 shows you how to process sequentially organized, fixed-length records on tape or direct-access devices. Topic 2 shows how to process variable-length records on tape or direct-access devices. Before beginning this chapter, you should be familiar with the concepts and terminology related to sequential tape and disk files as presented in chapter 6.

TOPIC 1   Fixed-Length Records

Most sequential files consist of blocks of fixed-length records—for example, ten records to a block, each record 120 bytes long. When coding COBOL programs, these files are handled much like card or printer files. Only minor adjustments are required in the Environment, Data, and Procedure Divisions.

From a conceptual point of view, a tape file and a sequentially organized file on a direct-access device are the same. When you read a tape file, you start with the first record and continue sequentially until you reach the end of the file. When you read a sequential file on disk, you read the record in the first physical record location assigned to the file and continue in sequence with the records in the next physical record locations until you reach the end of the file.

The idea is the same when writing a sequential file on tape or disk; you move in sequence from the first physical record to the last.

In terms of COBOL, however, there are some minor variations depending on whether you are coding for a tape file or a direct-access file. This is particularly true of DOS COBOL, which requires that the I/O device number be coded in the system name for a file. In contrast, it is possible to write file-handling programs in OS COBOL so the files can be converted from tape to direct-access devices simply by changing the job-control statements for the run; that is, the program doesn't have to be changed in any way. Since this device independence is a worthwhile goal, the OS program in this topic is coded so it can be run using any available devices.

Figure 7-1 summarizes the COBOL elements that are used for processing sequential files. Because the WRITE statement for sequential files on direct-access devices varies as you move from DOS to OS 68 to OS 74 compilers, these variations are summarized in figure 7-2.

To show you how the COBOL elements for sequential files are actually used, a simple file-to-printer program is illustrated in figures 7-3 and 7-4. Figure 7-3 is a VTOC for this program and, as you can see, the printed output requires no headings, page overflow, or final totals. This will let you concentrate on the coding for the input file. The complete program listing in DOS COBOL is given in figure 7-4.

The Environment Division

DOS system names   The DOS SELECT statement for the item file in figure 7-4 is this:

```
SELECT ITEMIN ASSIGN TO SYS010-UT-2400-S-ITEMIN
```

The only difference between this and a DOS SELECT statement for a card or printer file is the system name. Here, UT stands for utility device and 2400 refers to the IBM 2400 tape drive. The SYS number is SYS010, but any number can be used as long as it is assigned to a tape drive.

A name appears after the S (for Sequential) in the DOS system name. This name, sometimes called an *external name* because it is used in job-control statements, is made up of a maximum of seven letters or numbers and must start with a letter. When the program is run, this name will be used in the job-control card that specifies the data that must be contained in the volume and header labels for the file. As you can see from this example, the external name and the file name may be identical. In fact, this is a good programming practice.

```
    IDENTIFICATION DIVISION.
        .
        .
    ENVIRONMENT DIVISION.
        .
        .
    INPUT-OUTPUT SECTION.
    FILE-CONTROL.
        SELECT file-name ASSIGN TO system-name.
        .
        .
    DATA DIVISION.
    FILE SECTION.
    FD  file-name
        LABEL RECORDS ARE STANDARD
        RECORDING MODE IS F
        RECORD CONTAINS integer CHARACTERS
        BLOCK CONTAINS integer RECORDS.

    PROCEDURE DIVISION.

        OPEN { INPUT file-name  }  ...
             { OUTPUT file-name }

        READ file-name RECORD
            [INTO data-name]
            AT END imperative-statement ...

        WRITE record-name
            [FROM data-name]
            INVALID KEY imperative-statement ...

        CLOSE file-name ...


    NOTE: INVALID KEY is only used when creating files on direct-access devices. It is not
          used when creating tape files. For compiler variations in the WRITE statement,
          please refer to the summary in figure 7-2.
```

Figure 7-1 Syntax summary for sequential file handling

Figure 7-5 gives the format for a DOS system name for a sequential file. To find out which device numbers are acceptable for your compiler, you should refer to the compiler's reference manual. At present, 2400, 3410, and 3420 are typical device numbers for tape drives; 2314, 2319, and 3330 are typical numbers for disk drives.

You might note in figure 7-5 that the external name is optional in a DOS system name, although it is a common practice to use it. When it isn't used, the SYS number must be used in the job-control card for the file. Since a name like ITEMIN is easier to use than a code like SYS010, you should always use external names for tape and direct-access files.

```
DOS Compilers:
WRITE record-name
     [FROM data-name]
     INVALID KEY imperative-statement ...

OS Compilers (1968):
WRITE record-name
     [FROM data-name]
     [INVALID KEY imperative-statement ...].

OS Compilers (1974):
WRITE record-name
     [FROM data-name].
```

Figure 7-2 Summary of WRITE statement variations when creating
sequential files on direct-access devices

OS system names   If the program in figure 7-4 were written for an
OS compiler, the system name might be this:

```
UT-S-ITEMIN
```

This follows the same format recommended in chapter 2 for card
and printer files. Here again, UT means utility device, S stands for
sequential, and ddname (ITEMIN) is the external name that is also
given in the job-control cards used to run the program.

If you look at the OS system name format in figure 7-5, you'll
see that the device may be specified for a sequential file just as it is
under DOS. However, device is optional and should be omitted
from OS system names so the programs are device independent.
Then, a job-control card specifies the device to be used at the time
the program is run. This gives an operator the opportunity to use an
alternate device if the intended device is unavailable. For instance,
an operator can cause a file intended for a 3410 tape device to be
written on a 3330 disk device if the tape device isn't available.

Incidentally, the most recent OS compilers maintain device
independence even if you specify the device in the system name. For
example, the version 4 COBOL compiler treats any device specification as a comment. In other words, the compiler doesn't generate
code for any specific device.

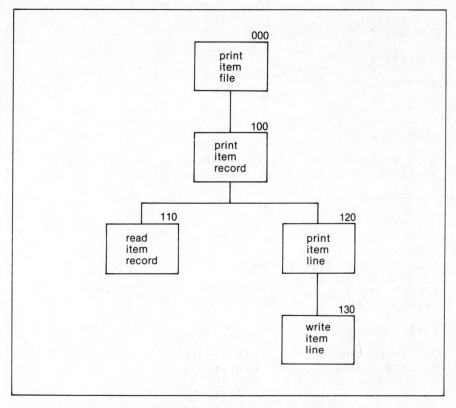

Figure 7-3   VTOC for the sequential file-to-printer program

The Data Division

In the FD statement in the Data Division, the programmer gives the characteristics of the sequential file. In figure 7-4, these characteristics are given:

```
FD   ITEMIN
     LABEL RECORDS ARE STANDARD
     RECORDING MODE IS F
     RECORD CONTAINS 100 CHARACTERS
     BLOCK CONTAINS 40 RECORDS.
```

This code is similar to what you've seen for card and printer files. For a tape or direct-access file, the LABEL RECORDS clause indicates that the labels used are in the manufacturer's standard format. Although the labels can be omitted or can conform to a user's format, they are standard in almost all cases. The RECORDING

```
      IDENTIFICATION DIVISION.
*
  PROGRAM-ID. ITEMLIST.
*
  ENVIRONMENT DIVISION.
*
  INPUT-OUTPUT SECTION.
*
  FILE-CONTROL.
*
      SELECT ITEMIN   ASSIGN TO SYS010-UT-2400-S-ITEMIN.
      SELECT PRINTOUT ASSIGN TO SYS006-UR-1403-S.
*
  DATA DIVISION.
*
  FILE SECTION.
*
  FD  ITEMIN
      LABEL RECORDS ARE STANDARD
      RECORDING MODE IS F
      RECORD CONTAINS 100 CHARACTERS
      BLOCK CONTAINS 40 RECORDS.
*
  01  IT-RECORD.
*
      05  IT-ITEM-NUMBER     PIC X(5).
      05  IT-ITEM-DESC       PIC X(20).
      05  IT-ON-HAND         PIC S9(5)    COMP-3.
      05  FILLER             PIC X(72).
*
  FD  PRINTOUT
      LABEL RECORDS ARE STANDARD
      RECORDING MODE IS F
      RECORD CONTAINS 133 CHARACTERS.
*
  01  PR-RECORD.
*
      05  PR-CC              PIC X.
      05  PR-ITEM-NUMBER     PIC X(5).
      05  FILLER             PIC X(3).
      05  PR-ITEM-DESC       PIC X(20).
      05  FILLER             PIC X(3).
      05  PR-ON-HAND         PIC Z(5).
      05  FILLER             PIC X(96).
*
  WORKING-STORAGE SECTION.
*
  01  SWITCHES.
*
      05  ITEM-EOF-SW        PIC X    VALUE 'N'.
          88  ITEM-EOF                VALUE 'Y'.
*
```

Figure 7-4   A sequential file-to-printer program in DOS COBOL (part 1 of 2)

```
      PROCEDURE DIVISION.
 *
      000-PRINT-ITEM-FILE.
 *
          OPEN INPUT  ITEMIN
               OUTPUT PRINTOUT.
          PERFORM 100-PRINT-ITEM-RECORD
              UNTIL ITEM-EOF.
          CLOSE ITEMIN
                PRINTOUT.
          DISPLAY 'ITEMLIST I  1  NORMAL EOJ'.
          STOP RUN.
 *
      100-PRINT-ITEM-RECORD.
 *
          PERFORM 110-READ-ITEM-RECORD.
          IF NOT ITEM-EOF
              PERFORM 120-PRINT-ITEM-LINE.
 *
      110-READ-ITEM-RECORD.
 *
          READ ITEMIN
              AT END
                  MOVE 'Y' TO ITEM-EOF-SW.
 *
      120-PRINT-ITEM-LINE.
 *
          MOVE SPACE           TO PR-RECORD.
          MOVE IT-ITEM-NUMBER TO PR-ITEM-NUMBER.
          MOVE IT-ITEM-DESC   TO PR-ITEM-DESC.
          MOVE IT-ON-HAND      TO PR-ON-HAND.
          PERFORM 130-WRITE-ITEM-LINE.
 *
      130-WRITE-ITEM-LINE.
 *
          WRITE PR-RECORD
              AFTER ADVANCING 1 LINES.
```

Figure 7-4 A sequential file-to-printer program in DOS COBOL (part 2 of 2)

MODE clause says that the individual records are all the same length (F for fixed-length), and the RECORD CONTAINS clause tells how many characters there are in each record.

BLOCK CONTAINS   The only new code in the FD statement is the BLOCK CONTAINS clause. As you might guess, it gives the blocking factor for the file; that is, the number of records in each block.

If the input file in figure 7-4 were to be processed under OS, the FD statement would look something like this:

DOS:

    `SYSnnn-UT-device-S-[external-name]`

where external-name is made up of seven or fewer letters or numbers, starting with a letter

---

OS:

    `UT-[device-]S-ddname`

where ddname is made up of eight or fewer letters or numbers, starting with a letter

Figure 7-5 System name format for sequential files under DOS or OS COBOL

```
FD   ITEMIN
     LABEL RECORDS ARE STANDARD
     RECORDING MODE IS F
     RECORD CONTAINS 100 CHARACTERS
     BLOCK CONTAINS 0 RECORDS.
```

This is the same as the DOS code except the BLOCK CONTAINS clause specifies zero records. This means that the blocking factor will be set by the job-control statements at the time the program is executed. Once again, the goal is device independence, and this coding allows an efficient blocking factor to be used no matter what device is eventually assigned to the file.

When using an OS system, you should realize that omitting the BLOCK CONTAINS clause implies a blocking factor of one record per block. It doesn't mean that the job-control language will set the blocking factor at the time of program execution. So watch out for this common error.

Because all card and printer files are spooled to direct-access devices on an OS system, you should use the BLOCK CONTAINS clause for all sequential files, including card and printer files. Furthermore, zero records should be specified in this clause. This allows the blocking factor for the spooled files to be set at the time of program execution. Without the BLOCK CONTAINS clause, a factor of one is assumed and spooling takes place less efficiently than it should. This use of BLOCK CONTAINS for card and printer files is illustrated in the next program in this topic, figure 7-8.

Record description After the FD statement for the sequential file in figure 7-4, the record and its fields are described just as is done for a card or printer file:

```
01   IT-RECORD.
     05   IT-ITEM-NUMBER        PIC X(5).
     05   IT-ITEM-DESC          PIC X(20).
     05   IT-ON-HAND            PIC S9(5)        COMP-3.
     05   FILLER                PIC X(72).
```

Regardless of the blocking factor, only one record is described, because all of the records in the file are the same.

Field usages Unlike the fields in card and printer files, the fields in tape and direct-access files can have COMP-3 or COMP usage. In figure 7-4, for example, IT-ON-HAND has COMP-3 usage. The advantage of using computational fields is found in (1) reducing the size of tape or direct-access records (a five-digit COMP-3 field will require only three bytes of tape or disk storage), and (2) reducing the amount of data conversion required during the execution of the COBOL program (IT-ON-HAND can be operated upon arithmetically without first being converted to COMP-3). As a result, you will often use COMP-3 fields within tape and direct-access records.

When COMP fields are used in tape or direct-access records, you must have some concern for boundary alignment. In particular, if an input or output field is specified as COMP SYNC, the compiler will assign this field to a proper boundary in storage. If the field has a picture of from one to four digits, the field will be assigned to a halfword boundary (a storage address that is a multiple of two); if the field has a picture with more than four digits, the field will be assigned to a fullword boundary (a storage address that is a multiple of four). This in turn means that the COMP SYNC input or output field must be located on a proper boundary within the input or output record; otherwise, the data in the input or output record and the storage assignments in the input or output area for the record will *not* correspond, and errors will result when the data is processed.

To illustrate, suppose an input record in a tape file has this format:

Field name	Location	Usage
Customer number	1-5	Display
Customer name	6-25	Display
Amount owed	26-29	COMP
Unused	30-32	Display

However, this record is described like this:

```
01   CUSTOMER-RECORD.
     05   CR-CUST-NUMBER        PIC  X(5).
     05   CR-CUST-NAME          PIC  X(20).
     05   CR-AMOUNT-OWED        PIC  S9(5)V99    COMP    SYNC.
     05   FILLER                PIC  X(3).
```

Since an 01 description always starts on a fullword boundary, CR-AMOUNT-OWED doesn't fall on a proper fullword boundary. As a result, it will be assigned to the next fullword boundary, thus leaving three unused bytes between CR-CUST-NAME and CR-AMOUNT-OWED. Then, when the record is read, the actual amount-owed data will be stored in this undefined area, and CR-AMOUNT-OWED will be filled by the unused area read from the actual tape record. Do you see the problem? The data and the data descriptions don't correspond.

In general, you won't use COMP fields in tape or direct-access records very often for the same reasons that you won't use them in working-storage: COMP-3 is usually more efficient. When COMP is the best usage for a field in a tape or direct-access record, we recommend these coding standards:

1. Make sure that the record length is a multiple of four like 20, 24, 28, or 32. Since an 01 description always starts on a fullword boundary, this means that all of the records within a block will start on a fullword boundary.

2. Whenever possible, assign a COMP field to a proper boundary within the input or output record. If the field is going to be a halfword (four or fewer digits), start it at a location within the record that is a multiple of two (the first byte in the record is counted as byte zero); if it is going to be a fullword (more than four digits), start it at a location that is a multiple of four. Then, use SYNC when you describe the field, provided the entire record has a length that is a multiple of four.

3. Don't use SYNC with a COMP field unless the record length is a multiple of four and the field has a proper boundary location within the record.

You will see a COMP field used properly in the first program in the next topic, figure 7-12.

The Procedure Divison

As you can see from the summary in figure 7-1, OPEN, CLOSE, READ, and WRITE statements are used in the Procedure Division in much the same way that they are used for card and printer files.

There is one exception, the use of the INVALID KEY clause with the WRITE statement, and that will be covered in detail in a few moments. In the program in figure 7-4, the OPEN, READ, and CLOSE statements for the item file are exactly the same as they would be for a card file.

I/O routines What about blocking and deblocking, error-recovery, and label-checking routines? These are all taken care of by the OPEN, CLOSE, READ, and WRITE statements. For example, when an OPEN statement is executed for a tape input file, the volume and header labels are checked to make sure that the correct tape has been mounted. Similarly, the CLOSE statement takes care of checking and creating trailer labels and rewinding files, while the READ and WRITE statements handle error-recovery, blocking, and deblocking routines. If an input or output file requires more than one volume, the READ and WRITE statements also process the trailer labels at the end of one tape and the volume and header labels at the start of the next. In short, though many more machine-language instructions are executed for a tape I/O routine than for a card or printer routine, the COBOL programmer codes them both in approximately the same way.

The idea is the same for sequential files on direct-access devices. For an input file, for example, the appropriate label routines are executed when the OPEN statement is executed: the volume and file labels are checked to make sure that the right pack containing the right file is mounted on the right disk drive. Similarly, the READ and WRITE statements handle error-recovery, blocking, and deblocking routines. If an input or output file requires more than one disk pack, the READ and WRITE statements also process the labels for additional packs. And, if an input or output file is stored on more than one area of the disk, say cylinders 31-50, 81-100, and 121-140, the READ and WRITE statements handle the switching from one area to the next.

INVALID KEY The only variation in the language for sequential files involves the WRITE statement when using direct-access devices. In particular, the INVALID KEY clause is required by some compilers, is optional on others, and is illegal (deleted) in the 1974 compilers. Figure 7-2 summarizes these variations for DOS and OS compilers. In all cases, this clause is illegal for tape files.

When the INVALID KEY clause is used, it is executed when the WRITE statement tries to write a record beyond the extents given for the file. If, for example, cylinders 10-19 are allocated to a sequential disk output file under DOS, the INVALID KEY clause is executed when the program tries to write a record in the first record location in cylinder 20. In a case like this, the statements in the INVALID KEY clause usually display an error message and set a switch so the program can return to module 000 and come to a normal program termination. This is illustrated in the problems for this topic.

Under OS, however, remember that a major goal is to write programs so a sequential file can be stored on any I/O device. As a result, you shouldn't use the INVALID KEY clause because it says that the device that is used must be a direct-access device.

Furthermore, an attempt to write beyond the extents of a file is handled in two other ways by the OS operating systems. First, as you will see in the chapter on OS job-control language (chapter 9), you normally specify a secondary disk-space allocation for a sequential output file. Then, if a file uses all the space in the primary allocation, the operating system will find additional space for the file as specified in the secondary allocation so the INVALID KEY clause isn't executed. In fact, the INVALID KEY clause is only executed after a file uses the space given in the primary allocation plus the space given in 15 secondary allocations.

Second, if INVALID KEY isn't used and the program tries to write a record beyond all of the secondary space allocations, the operating system will print an error message so the job can end. The only difference, then, is that the INVALID KEY clause allows the program to print a more precise error message and to determine exactly how the program should end thereafter. Since you will normally rerun the job from the start when too little space is allocated for a file, it doesn't much matter how the program ends. As a result, we recommend that you keep your OS programs device-independent by not using INVALID KEY, thus letting the operating system handle the error of trying to write beyond the extents for a file.

If you refer once more to figure 7-2, you can see that INVALID KEY for sequential files is dropped entirely from the 1974 standards. As a result, it isn't allowable in the OS 1974 COBOL compiler. And we wouldn't expect it to be allowed on any future DOS or OS compilers that implement the 1974 standards. This is no problem, however, since the DOS or OS operating systems, not the INVALID KEY clause, will handle the beyond-extents error condition.

In summary, you must use INVALID KEY for sequential, direct-access, output files under DOS. You can use it under OS 68 COBOL, but we recommend that you omit it. This will keep your programs device-independent and make it easier for you to convert to a 1974 compiler later on. Finally, you can't use it for sequential output files under OS 1974 compilers (at this writing, that's the OS/VS compiler with the status set to language level 2).

An update program

At this point, you should realize that tape or direct-access input and output presents few coding problems. However, the logic of a tape or direct-access program can become complex because several files can be processed by a single program.

To illustrate, consider a sequential *update program* such as the one described in figure 7-6. As you can see by the system flowchart, there are two input files—a transaction file and an inventory master file—and two output files—an updated, or new, master file and an error file of unmatched transactions. (An *unmatched transaction* is one that doesn't have a master record with the same *control-field* number—in this case, item number.) The program will also produce a printed summary of the update run. In the system flowchart, the tape symbol is used for sequential files, but these files could be stored on tape or a direct-access device.

Figure 7-7 shows a VTOC for this update program. The main control module, 100-UPDATE-INVENTORY-MASTER, causes one transaction and one master record to be read. It then compares the control fields of the two records and performs one or more of four modules depending on the result of this comparison. To control processing in this way, the module relies on the fact that the records in both the transaction and master files are sorted in ascending sequence by item number.

Figure 7-8 is the COBOL listing for this program when run under OS. Perhaps the key here is the action that results when the control field of the transaction record is compared with the control field of the master record in module 100. If the control fields are equal and the transaction item number is not HIGH-VALUE, the transaction is used to update the old master (module 130) and a report line is printed (module 160). In addition, Y is moved to NEED-TRANSACTION-SW to show that another transaction should be read. If the transaction is greater than the master, module 140 is performed. This module uses a WRITE FROM statement to write the master record, which may have been updated if it matched a previous transaction, on the new master file. Then Y is moved to NEED-MASTER-SW so another master will be read. Finally, if the transaction is less than the master, an unmatched transaction is indicated, and the record is written on the error file (module 150). Again, Y is moved to NEED-TRANSACTION-SW so another transaction will be read.

When a program needs two input files, as this one does, eventually all the records in one file will have been read while the other still contains some records to be processed. Note how the update program handles this problem. The AT END clauses in both the

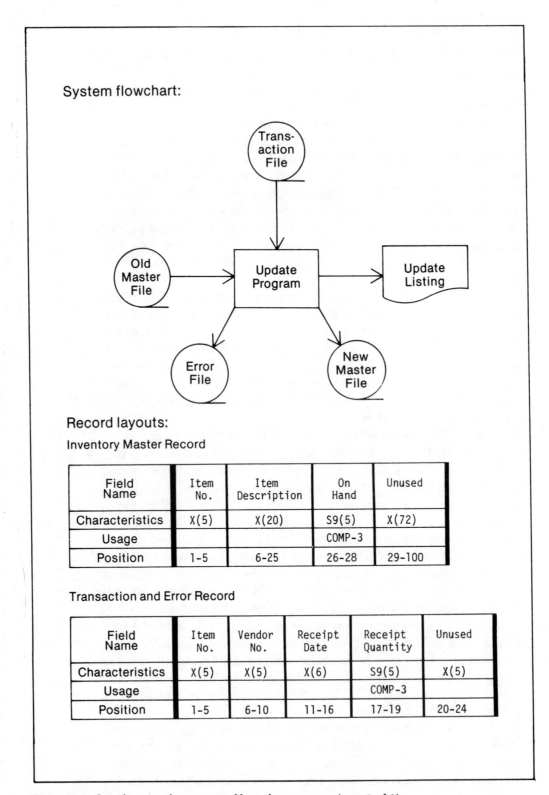

System flowchart:

Record layouts:

Inventory Master Record

Field Name	Item No.	Item Description	On Hand	Unused
Characteristics	X(5)	X(20)	S9(5)	X(72)
Usage			COMP-3	
Position	1-5	6-25	26-28	29-100

Transaction and Error Record

Field Name	Item No.	Vendor No.	Receipt Date	Receipt Quantity	Unused
Characteristics	X(5)	X(5)	X(6)	S9(5)	X(5)
Usage				COMP-3	
Position	1-5	6-10	11-16	17-19	20-24

Figure 7-6 Specifications for a master-file update program (part 1 of 2)

Print chart:

Record Name	1-6	7-10	11-16	17-22	23-28
1					
2 HDG-LINE-1	ITEM	VENDOR	RECEIPT	RECEIPT	
3 HDG-LINE-2	NO.	NO.	DATE	AMOUNT	
4 NEXT-REPORT-LINE	XXXXX	XXXXX	XX XX XX	99999	
5	XXXXX	XXXXX	XX XX XX	99999	
6					
7					
8 TOTAL-LINE-1	99,999 TRANSACTIONS PROCESSED				
9 TOTAL-LINE-2	999,999 UNMATCHED TRANSACTIONS WRITTEN ON ERROR TAPE				
10					
11					
12 ITEMUPDT	ITEMUPDT I I NORMAL EOJ				
13					
14					
15					
16					
17					
18					

Narrative:

1. Use transaction records to update master records by adding the receipt amount in the transaction record to the on-hand amount in the master record. There may be none, one, or several transactions for each master, and both files are in item-number sequence.

2. Print an update report with one line for each valid transaction record showing item number, vendor number, receipt date, and receipt quantity.

3. Write a record on the error file if an unmatched transaction is detected.

4. At the end of the report, print total lines showing the number of transactions processed and the number of unmatched transactions.

Figure 7-6 Specifications for a master-file update program (part 2 of 2)

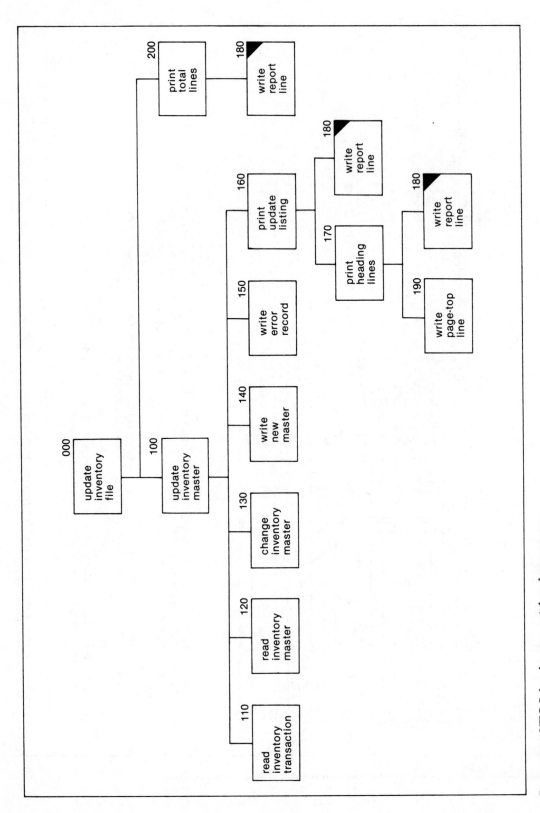

Figure 7-7 VTOC for the sequential-update program

```
    IDENTIFICATION DIVISION.
*
    PROGRAM-ID. ITEMUPDT.
*
    ENVIRONMENT DIVISION.
*
    CONFIGURATION SECTION.
*
    SPECIAL-NAMES.
        C01 IS PAGE-TOP.
*
    INPUT-OUTPUT SECTION.
*
    FILE-CONTROL.
        SELECT TRANFILE ASSIGN TO UT-S-TRANFILE.
        SELECT OLDMAST  ASSIGN TO UT-S-OLDMAST.
        SELECT NEWMAST  ASSIGN TO UT-S-NEWMAST.
        SELECT ERRFILE  ASSIGN TO UT-S-ERRFILE.
        SELECT UPDLIST  ASSIGN TO UT-S-UPDLIST.
*
    DATA DIVISION.
*
    FILE SECTION.
*
    FD  TRANFILE
        LABEL RECORDS ARE STANDARD
        RECORDING MODE IS F
        RECORD CONTAINS 24 CHARACTERS
        BLOCK CONTAINS 0 RECORDS.
*
    01  TR-AREA              PIC  X(24).
*
    FD  OLDMAST
        LABEL RECORDS ARE STANDARD.
        RECORDING MODE IS F
        RECORD CONTAINS 100 CHARACTERS
        BLOCK CONTAINS 0 RECORDS.
*
    01  OM-AREA              PIC  X(100).
*
    FD  NEWMAST
        LABEL RECORDS ARE STANDARD
        RECORDING MODE IS F
        RECORD CONTAINS 100 CHARACTERS
        BLOCK CONTAINS 0 RECORDS.
*
    01  NM-AREA              PIC  X(100).
*
    FD  ERRFILE
        LABEL RECORDS ARE STANDARD
        RECORDING MODE IS F
        RECORD CONTAINS 24 CHARACTERS
        BLOCK CONTAINS 0 RECORDS.
```

Figure 7-8   The sequential-update program in OS COBOL (part 1 of 6)

```
*
 01   ER-RECORD              PIC X(24).
*
 FD  UPDLIST
     LABEL RECORDS ARE STANDARD
     RECORDING MODE IS F
     RECORD CONTAINS 133 CHARACTERS
     BLOCK CONTAINS 0 RECORDS.
*
 01   PRINT-AREA             PIC X(133).
*
 WORKING-STORAGE SECTION.
*
 01   SWITCHES.
*
      05   ALL-RECORDS-PROCESSED-SW    PIC X     VALUE 'N'.
           88  ALL-RECORDS-PROCESSED             VALUE 'Y'.
      05   NEED-TRANSACTION-SW         PIC X     VALUE 'Y'.
           88  NEED-TRANSACTION                  VALUE 'Y'.
      05   NEED-MASTER-SW              PIC X     VALUE 'Y'.
           88  NEED-MASTER                       VALUE 'Y'.
*
 01   COUNT-FIELDS              COMP-3.
*
      05   TRANS-PROCESSED-COUNT   PIC S9(5)    VALUE ZERO.
      05   UNMATCHED-TRANS-COUNT   PIC S9(5)    VALUE ZERO.
*
 01   PRINT-FIELDS          COMP        SYNC.
*
      05   LINE-COUNT        PIC S99       VALUE +99.
      05   LINES-ON-PAGE     PIC S99       VALUE +57.
      05   SPACE-CONTROL     PIC S9.
*
 01   TR-RECORD.
*
      05   TR-ITEM-NUMBER      PIC X(5).
      05   TR-VENDOR-NUMBER    PIC X(5).
      05   TR-RECEIPT-DATE     PIC X(6).
      05   TR-RECEIPT-QUANTITY PIC S9(5)    COMP-3.
      05   FILLER              PIC X(5).
*
 01   MA-RECORD.
*
      05   MA-ITEM-NUMBER    PIC X(5).
      05   MA-ITEM-DESCR     PIC X(20).
      05   MA-ON-HAND        PIC S9(5)    COMP-3.
      05   MA-FILLER         PIC X(72).
*
 01   HDG-LINE-1.
*
      05   HDG1-CC       PIC X.
      05   FILLER        PIC X(1)     VALUE SPACE.
      05   FILLER        PIC X(4)     VALUE 'ITEM'.
```

Figure 7-8 The sequential-update program in OS COBOL (part 2 of 6)

```
            05   FILLER              PIC X(2)      VALUE SPACE.
            05   FILLER              PIC X(6)      VALUE 'VENDOR'.
            05   FILLER              PIC X(4)      VALUE SPACE.
            05   FILLER              PIC X(7)      VALUE 'RECEIPT'.
            05   FILLER              PIC X(2)      VALUE SPACE.
            05   FILLER              PIC X(7)      VALUE 'RECEIPT'.
            05   FILLER              PIC X(99)     VALUE SPACE.
       *
       01   HDG-LINE-2.
       *
            05   HDG2-CC             PIC X.
            05   FILLER              PIC X(2)      VALUE SPACE.
            05   FILLER              PIC X(3)      VALUE 'NO.'.
            05   FILLER              PIC X(4)      VALUE SPACE.
            05   FILLER              PIC X(3)      VALUE 'NO.'.
            05   FILLER              PIC X(6)      VALUE SPACE.
            05   FILLER              PIC X(4)      VALUE 'DATE'.
            05   FILLER              PIC X(4)      VALUE SPACE.
            05   FILLER              PIC X(6)      VALUE 'AMOUNT'.
            05   FILLER              PIC X(100)    VALUE SPACE.
       *
       01   NEXT-REPORT-LINE.
       *
            05   NRL-CC              PIC X.
            05   NRL-ITEM-NUMBER     PIC X(5).
            05   FILLER              PIC X(3)      VALUE SPACE.
            05   NRL-VENDOR-NUMBER   PIC Z(5).
            05   FILLER              PIC X(3)      VALUE SPACE.
            05   NRL-RECEIPT-DATE    PIC 99B99B99.
            05   FILLER              PIC X(3)      VALUE SPACE.
            05   NRL-RECEIPT-AMOUNT  PIC ZZZZ9.
            05   FILLER              PIC X(100)    VALUE SPACE.
       *
       01   TOTAL-LINE-1.
       *
            05   TL1-CC              PIC X.
            05   TL1-TRANS-PROCESSED PIC ZZ,ZZ9.
            05   FILLER              PIC X(23)
                                     VALUE ' TRANSACTIONS PROCESSED'.
            05   FILLER              PIC X(103)    VALUE SPACE.
       *
       01   TOTAL-LINE-2.
       *
            05   TL2-CC              PIC X.
            05   TL2-UNMATCHED-TRANS PIC ZZ,ZZ9.
            05   FILLER              PIC X(23)
                                     VALUE ' UNMATCHED TRANSACTIONS'.
            05   FILLER              PIC X(22)
                                     VALUE ' WRITTEN ON ERROR TAPE'.
            05   FILLER              PIC X(81)     VALUE SPACE.
       *
```

Figure 7-8   The sequential-update program in OS COBOL (part 3 of 6)

```
   PROCEDURE DIVISION.
*
 000-UPDATE-INVENTORY-FILE.
*
     OPEN INPUT  OLDMAST
                 TRANFILE
          OUTPUT NEWMAST
                 ERRFILE
                 UPDLIST.
     PERFORM 100-UPDATE-INVENTORY-MASTER
         UNTIL ALL-RECORDS-PROCESSED.
     PERFORM 200-PRINT-TOTAL-LINES.
     CLOSE OLDMAST
           TRANFILE
           NEWMAST
           ERRFILE
           UPDLIST.
     DISPLAY 'ITEMUPDT   I  1  NORMAL EOJ'
     STOP RUN.
*
 100-UPDATE-INVENTORY-MASTER.
*
     IF NEED-TRANSACTION
         PERFORM 110-READ-INVENTORY-TRANSACTION
         MOVE 'N' TO NEED-TRANSACTION-SW.
     IF NEED-MASTER
         PERFORM 120-READ-INVENTORY-MASTER
         MOVE 'N' TO NEED-MASTER-SW.
     IF TR-ITEM-NUMBER EQUAL TO MA-ITEM-NUMBER
         IF TR-ITEM-NUMBER EQUAL TO HIGH-VALUE
             MOVE 'Y' TO ALL-RECORDS-PROCESSED-SW
         ELSE
             PERFORM 130-CHANGE-INVENTORY-MASTER
             PERFORM 160-PRINT-UPDATE-LISTING
             MOVE 'Y' TO NEED-TRANSACTION-SW
     ELSE
         IF TR-ITEM-NUMBER GREATER THAN MA-ITEM-NUMBER
             PERFORM 140-WRITE-NEW-MASTER
             MOVE 'Y' TO NEED-MASTER-SW
         ELSE
             PERFORM 150-WRITE-ERROR-RECORD
             MOVE 'Y' TO NEED-TRANSACTION-SW.
*
```

Figure 7-8   The sequential-update program in OS COBOL (part 4 of 6)

READ statements move HIGH-VALUE to the item-number fields. If
the transaction file ends first, the rest of the master records will all
have control fields lower than HIGH-VALUE since HIGH-VALUE is
the highest value possible in the computer's collating sequence. So
when the control fields are compared in module 100, the program
will perform the code for a greater-than comparison and write the

```
    110-READ-INVENTORY-TRANSACTION.
*
        READ TRANFILE INTO TR-RECORD
            AT END
                MOVE HIGH-VALUE TO TR-ITEM-NUMBER.
        IF TR-ITEM-NUMBER NOT EQUAL TO HIGH-VALUE
            ADD 1 TO TRANS-PROCESSED-COUNT.
*
    120-READ-INVENTORY-MASTER.
*
        READ OLDMAST INTO MA-RECORD
            AT END
                MOVE HIGH-VALUE TO MA-ITEM-NUMBER.
*
    130-CHANGE-INVENTORY-MASTER.
*
        ADD TR-RECEIPT-QUANTITY TO MA-ON-HAND.
*
    140-WRITE-NEW-MASTER.
*
        WRITE NM-AREA FROM MA-RECORD.
*
    150-WRITE-ERROR-RECORD.
*
        WRITE ER-RECORD FROM TR-RECORD.
        ADD +1 TO UNMATCHED-TRANS-COUNT.
*
    160-PRINT-UPDATE-LISTING.
*
        IF LINE-COUNT GREATER THAN LINES-ON-PAGE
            PERFORM 170-PRINT-HEADING-LINES.
        MOVE TR-ITEM-NUMBER       TO NRL-ITEM-NUMBER.
        MOVE TR-VENDOR-NUMBER     TO NRL-VENDOR-NUMBER.
        MOVE TR-RECEIPT-DATE      TO NRL-RECEIPT-DATE.
        MOVE TR-RECEIPT-QUANTITY  TO NRL-RECEIPT-AMOUNT.
        MOVE NEXT-REPORT-LINE     TO PRINT-AREA.
        PERFORM 180-WRITE-REPORT-LINE.
        MOVE 1 TO SPACE-CONTROL.
*
    170-PRINT-HEADING-LINES.
*
        MOVE HDG-LINE-1 TO PRINT-AREA.
        PERFORM 190-WRITE-PAGE-TOP-LINE.
        MOVE HDG-LINE-2 TO PRINT-AREA.
        MOVE 1 TO SPACE-CONTROL.
        PERFORM 180-WRITE-REPORT-LINE.
        MOVE 2 TO SPACE-CONTROL.
*
```

Figure 7-8   The sequential-update program in OS COBOL (part 5 of 6)

remaining master records on the new master file. If the master file
ends first, the comparison will indicate that the transaction is less
than the master for the rest of the records in the transaction file. So

```
  180-WRITE-REPORT-LINE.
*
     WRITE PRINT-AREA
         AFTER ADVANCING SPACE-CONTROL LINES.
     ADD SPACE-CONTROL TO LINE-COUNT.
*
  190-WRITE-PAGE-TOP-LINE.
*
     WRITE PRINT-AREA
         AFTER ADVANCING PAGE-TOP.
     MOVE ZERO TO LINE-COUNT.
*
  200-PRINT-TOTAL-LINES.
*
     MOVE TRANS-PROCESSED-COUNT TO TL1-TRANS-PROCESSED.
     MOVE TOTAL-LINE-1 TO PRINT-AREA.
     MOVE 3 TO SPACE-CONTROL.
     PERFORM 180-WRITE-REPORT-LINE.
     MOVE UNMATCHED-TRANS-COUNT TO TL2-UNMATCHED-TRANS.
     MOVE TOTAL-LINE-2 TO PRINT-AREA.
     MOVE 1 TO SPACE-CONTROL.
     PERFORM 180-WRITE-REPORT-LINE.
```

Figure 7-8   The sequential-update program in OS COBOL (part 6 of 6)

these unmatched transactions will be written on the error file. After all the records in both files have been read, the comparison will show that the item-number fields are equal. So when the program checks and finds TR-ITEM-NUMBER equal to HIGH-VALUE, Y will be moved to the ALL-RECORDS-PROCESSED switch, and the program will continue with the statements after the PERFORM UNTIL in 000-UPDATE-INVENTORY-FILE.

In order to control processing in this way, you must use the INTO option of the READ statement. Without it, it would be impossible to move HIGH-VALUE into the item-number fields, since fields in an input area aren't available to a program after the AT END clause has been executed. And be sure to move HIGH-VALUE, not all 9s into the control fields when the ends of the files are reached. If you move all 9s to a field in a situation like this, there's always the chance of running into a valid control field of all 9s. Then the comparison would be equal, and the program logic wouldn't work properly.

Because the system names for this OS program don't specify device, because zero records are specified in the BLOCK CONTAINS clauses for the sequential files, and because INVALID KEY isn't used in the WRITE statements for the output files, any devices can be used for the sequential files processed by this program. Note that zero records are specified in the BLOCK CONTAINS clause for the print file so the blocking factor for the spooled print records can be specified at execution time. If this clause were omitted, the print records would be spooled to disk in blocks of one record, thus decreasing output efficiency.

To convert this program to DOS, you would have to make three changes. First, you would have to recode the system names. Second, you would have to code the proper blocking factors in the BLOCK CONTAINS clauses for the files. Third, you would have to code the INVALID KEY clause for any sequential output files that are to be stored on direct-access devices. In short, you would have to find out what type of device would be used for each file before you started coding.

File maintenance

File maintenance refers to the process of changing the fields within the records in a file, adding records to a file, and deleting records from a file. To perform any of these jobs on a sequential file, the file should be rewritten with necessary changes being made as it is written. You have already seen how changes are made to fields in the update program in figure 7-8. To add records, the additional records are inserted in sequence as the file is rewritten. To delete records, all the records in a file except those that must be deleted are rewritten on the new file.

In actual practice, it is seldom efficient to perform only one maintenance operation at a time. If, for example, you had only 10 records to add to a 1000-record file, you'd be wasting computer time to rewrite the entire file. So a single file-maintenance program usually provides for adding, deleting, and changing records in a file.

Although a program like this might appear to be rather complex, the coding involves nothing more than has been illustrated in this topic. Even the design of the program is no more than a variation of the VTOC in figure 7-7. For example, figure 7-9 is a structure chart for a program that does all the file-maintenance chores. Here, module 130 has become the control module that determines which of four modules should be performed based on the control-field comparison. Three of these modules—160, 170, and 180—actually do the work of maintaining the file. The fourth, module 190, controls the creation of the error file. Thus, even the most complicated file-maintenance program will follow the basic pattern of the update program in figures 7-7 and 7-8. (Incidentally, the verb "put" for a tape or disk file is equivalent to the verb "print" for a printer file.)

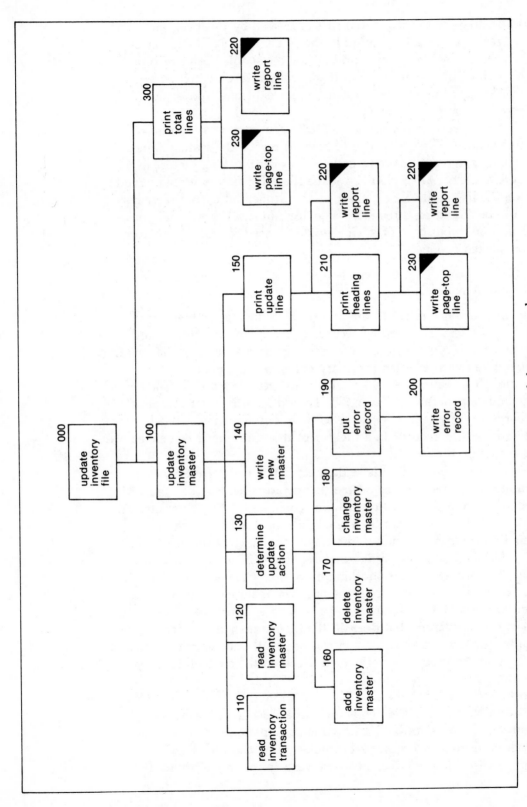

Figure 7-9 A VTOC for a file-maintenance program that adds, deletes, and changes records

Discussion

In keeping with the philosophy of this book, the material presented in this topic is a subset of the COBOL language for sequential file handling. This subset will allow you to code file-handling routines for sequential files using DOS, OS, 1968, or 1974 ANS COBOL compilers. In general, we feel that the language we have omitted isn't something that you should want to use.

For instance, it is possible to update a sequential file on disk by writing the updated records back in their original disk locations. In this case, OPEN I-O is used to open the file, meaning the file is both input and output. Then the READ statement reads the record into storage and the WRITE statement writes the record back into the location it was just read from. We haven't covered this, however, because there are two reasons why it shouldn't be used. First, the logic required to do this ties the update file to a direct-access device and the program is no longer device-independent. Second, since you're going to need a backup file in case the update program fails, you're going to have to copy the master file after each update run. So why not copy the file while creating the new master file and thus keep the update logic similar for all sequential-update programs.

In any event, by using the sequential file-handling subset presented here, you give your programs maximum flexibility. By coding the OS programs as shown, you make them completely device independent. And by coding DOS programs as recommended, you can convert to OS someday simply by changing the system names.

Terminology

external name
update program
unmatched transaction
control field
file maintenance

Objectives

1. Given a problem involving sequential files with fixed-length records, code the COBOL solution. The problem may require more than one input or output file, such as an update program with an output error file.

Problems

1. Code the changes that would have to be made to the DOS program in figure 7-4 in order for it to read the same file stored on a 3330 disk instead of a 2400 tape.

2. Code the changes that would have to be made to the OS program in figure 7-8 in order for it to read the transaction file from a 2400 tape instead of a 3330 disk.

3. Code the changes that would have to be made to the OS program in figure 7-8 in order for it to run under DOS. Assume the blocking factor for the old and new master file is 42, and the blocking factor for the transaction and error file is 131; the I/O device for all four of these files is the 3330. Don't forget that INVALID KEY is required for sequential output files on disk devices under DOS.

Solutions

1. The first SELECT statement would have to be changed as follows:

```
SELECT ITEMIN ASSIGN TO SYS010-UT-3330-S-ITEMIN
```

In addition, you would probably want to increase the blocking factor to 42 in order to make better use of the disk storage space. (Three blocks on a 3330 track have a maximum size of 4253 bytes each.)

2. No changes are necessary. You would simply change the job-control statement for the transaction file, not the program.

3. (1) The SELECT statements must be changed to something like this:

```
SELECT TRNFILE ASSIGN TO SYS010-UT-3330-S-TRNFILE.
SELECT OLDMAST ASSIGN TO SYS011-UT-3330-S-OLDMAST.
SELECT NEWMAST ASSIGN TO SYS012-UT-3330-S-NEWMAST.
SELECT ERRFILE ASSIGN TO SYS013-UT-3330-S-ERRFILE.
SELECT UPDLIST ASSIGN TO SYS006-UT-1403-S.
```

(2) The BLOCK CONTAINS clause in the FD statements for the 3330 files must indicate the proper blocking factors, not zero records. And the BLOCK CONTAINS clause in the FD statement for the printer file must indicate one record or be dropped from the program.

(3) Modules 140 and 150 must use the INVALID KEY clause, perhaps something like this:

```
::
 140-WRITE-NEW-MASTER.
::

    WRITE NM-AREA FROM MA-RECORD
        INVALID KEY
            DISPLAY 'ITEMUPDT A 2 INVALID KEY ON NEWMAST--'
                'ITEM NUMBER = ' MA-ITEM-NUMBER
            MOVE 'Y' TO ALL-RECORDS-PROCESSED-SW.
::
 150-WRITE-ERROR-RECORD.
::

    WRITE ER-RECORD FROM TR-RECORD
        INVALID KEY
            DISPLAY 'ITEMUPDT A 3 INVALID KEY ON ERRFILE--'
                'ITEM NUMBER = ' TR-ITEM-NUMBER
            MOVE 'Y' TO ALL-RECORDS-PROCESSED-SW.
    ADD 1 TO UNMATCHED-TRANS-COUNT.
::
```

Here, the INVALID KEY clauses each print an error message
that indicates which file went beyond its extents and what record was being processed at the time. Then, the ALL-
RECORDS-PROCESSED-SW is turned on so the program will
end when it returns to module 000.

TOPIC 2 Variable-Length Records

Variable-length records provide an important degree of flexibility in
storing data. For example, inventory records that give warehouse
locations are often in variable-length format. A *root segment* of each
record contains the basic item data: item number, description, total
quantity, on hand, and so forth. Then, a variable number of additional segments follow the root. These segments, one for each
warehouse location in which a quantity of the item is stored, specify
the warehouse location (typically, warehouse number and bin
number), the quantity stored there, and maybe even the date it was
stored. An item stored in only one location would have only one of
these location segments attached to the root segment; an item stored
in twenty locations would have twenty location segments. Since a
fixed-length format would have to provide for the maximum number
of warehouse locations possible for an item, a great deal of tape or
disk space could be saved by using the variable-length format.

This type of record design, root segment plus a variable number
of fixed-length segments, is also found in files that store a variable

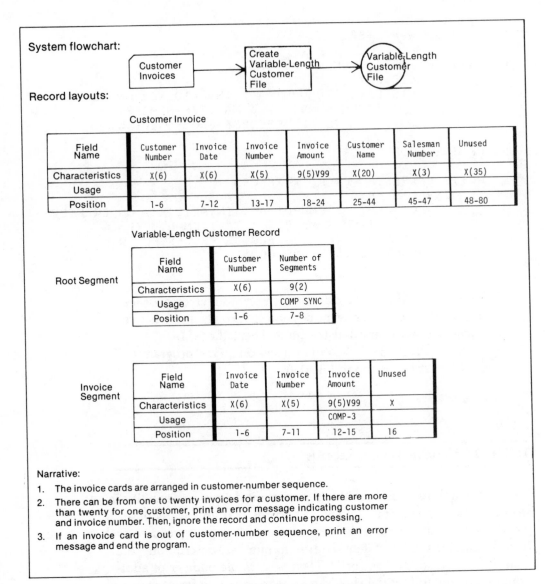

System flowchart:

Customer Invoices → Create Variable-Length Customer File → Variable-Length Customer File

Record layouts:

Customer Invoice

Field Name	Customer Number	Invoice Date	Invoice Number	Invoice Amount	Customer Name	Salesman Number	Unused
Characteristics	X(6)	X(6)	X(5)	9(5)V99	X(20)	X(3)	X(35)
Usage							
Position	1-6	7-12	13-17	18-24	25-44	45-47	48-80

Variable-Length Customer Record

Root Segment

Field Name	Customer Number	Number of Segments
Characteristics	X(6)	9(2)
Usage		COMP SYNC
Position	1-6	7-8

Invoice Segment

Field Name	Invoice Date	Invoice Number	Invoice Amount	Unused
Characteristics	X(6)	X(5)	9(5)V99	X
Usage			COMP-3	
Position	1-6	7-11	12-15	16

Narrative:

1. The invoice cards are arranged in customer-number sequence.
2. There can be from one to twenty invoices for a customer. If there are more than twenty for one customer, print an error message indicating customer and invoice number. Then, ignore the record and continue processing.
3. If an invoice card is out of customer-number sequence, print an error message and end the program.

Figure 7-10   Specifications for a variable-length file-creation program

number of transactions along with some master data. A checking account record, for instance, might contain account number, name, and other master data in the root, followed by one segment for each check written during the month. Each segment might contain check number, amount, and transaction date.

A variable-length file-creation program

To illustrate variable-length processing, figure 7-10 presents a typical file-creation problem. Here, a variable-length file is to be created

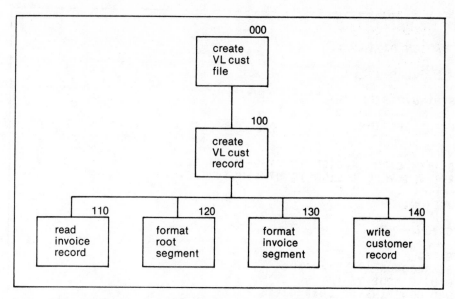

Figure 7-11   VTOC for a variable-length file-creation program

from a deck of invoice cards representing unpaid customer invoices. Although the tape symbol is used in the system flowchart, the file could be stored on tape or a direct-access device. In general, however, variable-length records are more common on tape than on direct-access devices.

The root segment in the master record contains the customer number and a field indicating the number of invoice segments in the record. If, for example, bytes 7 and 8 in the root segment contain a value of 11, the customer has eleven unpaid invoice segments within the record. Because the segment-count field will be used as a subscript in programs that process this file, it has COMP usage. Because the lengths of the root and invoice segments are both multiples of four and because the two-byte segment-count field starts on a halfword boundary within the root segment, SYNC can be used with this COMP field.

Figure 7-11 gives a VTOC for this program, and the COBOL coding is given in figure 7-12. Although a program that operates upon card data should always edit the data before processing it, the edit routines are omitted in this program since its purpose is to show the coding used for variable-length records.

File description   The main element new to you in this program is the coding in the FD statement for the output file:

```
      IDENTIFICATION DIVISION.
    *
      PROGRAM-ID. VLCREATE.
    *
      ENVIRONMENT DIVISION.
    *
      INPUT-OUTPUT SECTION.
    *
      FILE-CONTROL.
          SELECT INVCARDS ASSIGN TO UT-S-INVCARDS.
          SELECT VLINVFLE ASSIGN TO UT-S-VLINVFLE.
    *
      DATA DIVISION.
    *
      FILE SECTION.
    *
      FD  INVCARDS
          LABEL RECORDS ARE STANDARD
          RECORDING MODE IS F
          RECORD CONTAINS 80 CHARACTERS
          BLOCK CONTAINS 0 RECORDS.
    *
      01  CARD-AREA            PIC X(80).
    *
      FD  VLINVFLE
          LABEL RECORDS ARE STANDARD
          RECORDING MODE IS V
          RECORD CONTAINS 24 TO 328 CHARACTERS
          BLOCK CONTAINS 4000 CHARACTERS.
    *
```

Figure 7-12   The variable-length file-creation program in OS COBOL (part 1 of 4)

```
      FD  VLINVFLE
          LABEL RECORDS ARE STANDARD
          RECORDING MODE IS V
          RECORD CONTAINS 24 TO 328 CHARACTERS
          BLOCK CONTAINS 4000 CHARACTERS.
```

Here, the RECORDING MODE clause states that the records are variable (V), not fixed, in length. Then, the RECORD CONTAINS clause gives the minimum and maximum number of characters (bytes) per record (24 characters represents a record with one invoice segment; 328 characters represents a record with 20 invoice segments). Finally, the BLOCK CONTAINS clause gives the maximum number of bytes, including all control bytes for record and block length, that the block may contain. Remember that DOS and OS require four control bytes for each variable-length record and four for each variable-length block. Although this program specifies

```
   01   VL-RECORD.
   *
        05   VL-CUSTOMER-NO        PIC X(6).
        05   VL-INVOICE-COUNT      PIC S99          COMP     SYNC.
        05   VL-INVOICE-DATA       OCCURS 1 TO 20 TIMES
                                   DEPENDING ON VL-INVOICE-COUNT.
             10   VL-INVOICE-DATE  PIC X(6).
             10   VL-INVOICE-NO    PIC X(5).
             10   VL-INVOICE-AMT   PIC S9(5)V99     COMP-3.
             10   FILLER           PIC X.
   *
   WORKING-STORAGE SECTION.
   *
   01   SWITCHES.
   *
        05   CARD-EOF-SW      PIC X          VALUE 'N'.
             88   CARD-EOF                   VALUE 'Y'.
        05   FIRST-RECORD-SW PIC X           VALUE 'Y'.
             88   FIRST-RECORD               VALUE 'Y'.
   *
   01   CONTROL-FIELDS.
   *
        05   OLD-CUSTOMER-NO      PIC X(6).
   *
   01   COUNT-FIELDS.
   *
        05   INVOICE-COUNT       PIC S99      VALUE ZERO COMP SYNC.
   *
   01   CARD-RECORD.
   *
        05   CR-CUSTOMER-NO       PIC X(6).
        05   CR-INVOICE-DATE      PIC X(6).
        05   CR-INVOICE-NO        PIC X(5).
        05   CR-INVOICE-AMT       PIC 9(5)V99.
        05   FILLER               PIC X(56).
   *
```

Figure 7-12   The variable-length file-creation program in OS COBOL (part 2 of 4)

4000 bytes, you should code it as zero if you want to keep your OS program device-independent. Then, you can adjust the block size at execution time by using a JCL statement.

As you have seen in the previous programs in this chapter, the BLOCK CONTAINS clause can specify RECORDS rather than CHARACTERS. If, for example, it is coded as

```
BLOCK CONTAINS 12 RECORDS
```

the compiler will create an I/O area of 3988 bytes. This size is 12 maximum record lengths (12 × 328) plus 12 times the control bytes for record length (12 × 4) plus four bytes for block-length indica-

```
    PROCEDURE DIVISION.
*
  000-CREATE-VL-CUST-FILE.
*
      OPEN INPUT  INVCARDS
            OUTPUT VLINVFLE.
      PERFORM 100-CREATE-VL-CUST-RECORD
            UNTIL CARD-EOF.
      CLOSE INVCARDS
            VLINVFLE.
      DISPLAY 'VLCREATE  I  1  NORMAL EOJ'.
      STOP RUN.
*
  100-CREATE-VL-CUST-RECORD.
*
      PERFORM 110-READ-INVOICE-RECORD.
      IF FIRST-RECORD
          MOVE CR-CUSTOMER-NO TO OLD-CUSTOMER-NO
          MOVE 'N' TO FIRST-RECORD-SW
      ELSE
          IF CR-CUSTOMER-NO GREATER THAN OLD-CUSTOMER-NO
              PERFORM 120-FORMAT-ROOT-SEGMENT
              PERFORM 140-WRITE-CUSTOMER-RECORD
              MOVE CR-CUSTOMER-NO TO OLD-CUSTOMER-NO
          ELSE
              IF CR-CUSTOMER-NO LESS THAN OLD-CUSTOMER-NO
                  DISPLAY 'VLCREATE  A  2  CUSTOMER NO. '
                      CR-CUSTOMER-NO ' HAS OUT OF SEQUENCE CARD.'
                      ' JOB STOPPED.'
                  MOVE 'Y' TO CARD-EOF-SW.
```

Figure 7-12   The variable-length file-creation program in OS COBOL (part 3 of 4)

tion. In this case, each block will receive 12 records regardless of the actual size of the records. Because this option leads to smaller actual blocks than the CHARACTERS option when the I/O areas are comparable in size, CHARACTERS is recommended for variable-length files.

OCCURS DEPENDING ON   The other code that is new to you is the OCCURS DEPENDING ON clause in the record description:

```
05  VL-INVOICE-DATA       OCCURS 1 TO 20 TIMES
                          DEPENDING ON VL-INVOICE-COUNT.
```

Here, the minimum and maximum number of times a group or elementary item should appear is given in the clause. Then, the DEPENDING ON option refers to a field that tells the actual number of times the variable field or fields will occur. Quite logically, the

```
        IF NOT CARD-EOF
            IF INVOICE-COUNT LESS THAN 20
                PERFORM 130-FORMAT-INVOICE-SEGMENT
            ELSE
                DISPLAY 'VLCREATE  A  3  OVER 20 '
                    'OPEN ITEMS--INVOICE NO. '
                    CR-INVOICE-NO ' FOR CUSTOMER NO. '
                    CR-CUSTOMER-NO ' IS IGNORED.'.
*
   110-READ-INVOICE-RECORD.
*
        READ INVCARDS INTO CARD-RECORD
            AT END
                MOVE 99999 TO CR-CUSTOMER-NO
                MOVE 'Y' TO CARD-EOF-SW.
*
   120-FORMAT-ROOT-SEGMENT.
*
        MOVE OLD-CUSTOMER-NO TO VL-CUSTOMER-NO.
        MOVE INVOICE-COUNT   TO VL-INVOICE-COUNT.
        MOVE ZERO TO INVOICE-COUNT.
*
   130-FORMAT-INVOICE-SEGMENT.
*
        ADD 1 TO INVOICE-COUNT.
        MOVE CR-INVOICE-DATE TO VL-INVOICE-DATE (INVOICE-COUNT).
        MOVE CR-INVOICE-NO   TO VL-INVOICE-NO (INVOICE-COUNT).
        MOVE CR-INVOICE-AMT  TO VL-INVOICE-AMT (INVOICE-COUNT).
*
   140-WRITE-CUSTOMER-RECORD.
*
        WRITE VL-RECORD.
```

Figure 7-12   The variable-length file-creation program in OS COBOL (part 4 of 4)

DEPENDING ON field must always originate in the root segment of a record, and the root segment must precede the variable segments.

As you might guess, the DEPENDING ON clause is required for a variable-length output file like this since it gives information that lets the I/O routine figure out how long each record is. On the other hand, it isn't required for variable-length input files with the root-plus-fixed-segments format. And since OCCURS DEPENDING ON leads to extremely inefficient object code, we recommend that you avoid it for input files.

To read a file like the invoice file, then, the input area should describe the maximum record length. If you use a READ INTO statement, the record area in working-storage should also describe the maximum-sized record. To process the varying number of segments in each record, you write your own control routine. You'll see this type of routine in the problem for this topic.

The Procedure Division The rest of the program in figure 7-12 should be fairly easy to follow. After the program reads the first invoice record and sets up the control field, OLD-CUSTOMER-NUMBER, it constructs the first variable segment (module 130) for the first customer in the file. Then, as long as the following card records are for the same customer number, additional invoice segments are added to the record.

INVOICE-COUNT is the field used to keep track of the number of invoice segments per record. It is set to zero (in module 120) before the processing for each master record begins and is increased by one (in module 130) before the construction of each variable segment. Thus, it can be used as a subscript to refer to the fields within the variable segments. For instance,

```
MOVE CR-INVOICE-NO TO VL-INVOICE-NO (INVOICE-COUNT)
```

moves an invoice number to the fifth variable segment when INVOICE-COUNT contains a value of five. If INVOICE-COUNT ever reaches 20, any additional invoices for a customer are skipped since this represents an error condition. Note that INVOICE-COUNT has COMP usage since this is the most efficient usage for a subscript.

When the first card record for a new customer number is read (CR-CUSTOMER-NO GREATER THAN OLD-CUSTOMER-NO), module 120 is performed. This module formats the root segment of the output record and resets INVOICE-COUNT to zero in preparation for the next set of customer invoices. Then, the master record is written out (module 140), the value of OLD-CUSTOMER-NUMBER is changed, and the variable-segment construction process repeats for the next customer record. If an out-of-sequence card is ever read, module 100 prints an error message and moves Y to CARD-EOF-SW so the program will end.

Block sizes One thing you should realize when coding variable-length file programs is that the number of characters given in the BLOCK CONTAINS clause of the FD statement represents only the maximum block size. The actual block size will vary. As the master records are written by the WRITE statement, the associated blocking routine checks the space remaining in the block it is currently building. In the program in figure 7-12, if a maximum size record doesn't fit in the remaining block space without exceeding the 4000-byte maximum given in the BLOCK CONTAINS clause, the current block is written and another block is started.

Suppose, for example, that the first 20 customers have 11 invoices each. Since these records are each 188 bytes long (184 bytes for the record itself plus 4 bytes for record length), the block is 3764 bytes long at this point:

    4 bytes—block length
 3760 bytes—20 master records
 3764 bytes

If the next record is the maximum length allowed (328 bytes plus 4 control bytes), it will cause the block to exceed 4000 bytes. So this 3764-byte block is written out, and the next block is started.

APPLY WRITE-ONLY To increase the actual block sizes on the System/360-370, an extension to the ANS standards—the APPLY WRITE-ONLY statement—can be used. For the program in figure 7-12, it would be coded as follows:

```
I-O-CONTROL.
    APPLY WRITE-ONLY ON VLINVFLE.
```

This paragraph is placed in the Environment Division after the FILE-CONTROL paragraph. Then, a variable-length block is written out only if the next record to be added to the block doesn't fit in the space remaining. As you can imagine, this can significantly increase the average actual block size for a variable-length file. When using this APPLY statement, the FROM option must be used with the WRITE statement; then, the output area following the FD statement for the file describes the maximum record length only.

Another type of sequential file with variable-length records

Although the root-plus-fixed-segments record is the most common type of variable-length record, there is another type that you may occasionally encounter. In this case, the file consists of more than one type of record, and each type has a different record length. For instance, the file may consist of records with lengths of 50, 100, and 500 bytes.

To create this type of file, you can describe each record type after the FD statement as shown in figure 7-13. The effect of describing multiple record types in this way is similar to that of the REDEFINES clause. Here, only one input area is used for all three record types, but different data names are used to refer to various storage positions within that area. In other words, the input area is redefined by each set of record descriptions. As a result, you must make sure that the longest record is described first.

To write the records in a file like this, you must use a different WRITE statement for each record type. This is one of the cases in which you must use more than one WRITE statement for a single output file.

```
        ENVIRONMENT DIVISION.
            .
            .
        FILE-CONTROL.
            SELECT TRANRECS ASSIGN TO UT-S-TRANRECS.
            .
            .
        DATA DIVISION.
            .
            .
        FD  TRANRECS
            LABEL RECORDS ARE STANDARD
            RECORDING MODE IS V
            RECORD CONTAINS 18 TO 128 CHARACTERS
            BLOCK CONTAINS 4000 CHARACTERS.
        *
        01  HEADER-RECORD.
        *
            05  HDR-RECORD-CODE      PIC X.
            05  HDR-FIELD-1          PIC X(30).
            05  HDR-FIELD-2          PIC X(30).
            05  HDR-FIELD-3          PIC X(30).
            05  HDR-FIELD-4          PIC X(30).
            05  HDR-FIELD-5          PIC S9(7).
        *
        01  DETAIL-RECORD.
        *
            05  DET-RECORD-CODE      PIC X.
            05  DET-FIELD-1          PIC X(6).
            05  DET-FIELD-2          PIC X(6).
            05  DET-FIELD-3          PIC S9(5).
        *
        01  TRAILER-RECORD.
        *
            05  TLR-RECORD-CODE      PIC X.
            05  TLR-FIELD-1          PIC X(50).
            05  TLR-FIELD-2          PIC S9(6).
            05  TLR-FIELD-3          PIC S9(7).
        *
            .
            .
            .
        PROCEDURE DIVISION.
            .
        WRITE HEADER-RECORD.
            .
        WRITE DETAIL-RECORD.
            .
        WRITE TRAILER-RECORD.
            .
            .
```

Figure 7-13 Generalized code for creating a file that contains several different
lengths of records (version 1)

If you want to use APPLY WRITE-ONLY in the I-O-CONTROL paragraph, you must use the FROM option of the WRITE statement. Then, the input area describes the maximum-sized record. This is illustrated by the code in figure 7-14. As you can see, you still have to use one WRITE statement for each type of record in the file. Notice that the RECORD CONTAINS phrase isn't used in the FD statement for a variable-length file that is written with the FROM option.

To read this type of file, you can use one of two basic techniques. One way is suggested by the code in figure 7-15. Here, a maximum-sized record is described in the input area following the FD statement and the records are moved into working-storage before processing. Another way to read a file like this is to describe the different records immediately following the FD statement as in figure 7-13; the program then operates on the data in the input area itself.

Discussion

When using variable-length records, the use of INVALID KEY follows the same rules as for fixed-length records. For output files on direct-access devices under DOS, INVALID KEY is required and it is executed when the program attempts to write beyond the extents of the file. Under 1968 OS, it is optional and should not be used if you want the program to be device-independent. Under 1974 OS, it is illegal.

In actual practice, variable-length records aren't used much. One reason for this is that variable-length sorts are much slower than fixed-length sorts. So if a file is going to need sorting, a systems designer must question whether the file wouldn't be more efficient with fixed-length records than with variable-length records.

For instance, the records in the invoice file described in this topic could be treated as fixed-length records of 328 bytes each. Then, if a record contained the data for only one invoice, the last 19 invoice segments would contain blanks or zeros. Although this means wasted storage space on tape or direct-access devices, it also means you don't need OCCURS DEPENDING ON to create the file and the file can be sorted more efficiently.

Which approach is better? It depends, of course, on other considerations. How much do the records vary in length . . . if most of the records are near the maximum length, why not treat them as fixed-length records? How limited is storage space . . . is it a small system with limited disk space available to it? And how much sorting does the file require? While these considerations may rule out variable-length records in a large shop, they may reveal the need for variable-length records in a small shop.

```
     ENVIRONMENT DIVISION.
         .
         .
     FILE-CONTROL.
         SELECT TRANRECS ASSIGN TO UT-S-TRANRECS.
         .
     I-O-CONTROL.
         APPLY WRITE-ONLY ON TRANRECS.
         .
         .
     DATA DIVISION.
         .
         .
     FD  TRANRECS
         LABEL RECORDS ARE STANDARD
         RECORDING MODE IS V
         BLOCK CONTAINS 4000 CHARACTERS.
  ::
     01  OUTPUT-AREA                 PIC X(128).
  ::

         .
         .
     WORKING-STORAGE SECTION.
         .
         .
     01  HEADER-RECORD.
         .
     01  DETAIL-RECORD.
         .
     01  TRAILER-RECORD.
         .
     PROCEDURE DIVISION.
         .
         WRITE OUTPUT-AREA FROM HEADER-RECORD.
         .
         WRITE OUTPUT-AREA FROM DETAIL-RECORD.
         .
         WRITE OUTPUT-AREA FROM TRAILER-RECORD.
         .
         .
```

Figure 7-14 Generalized code for creating a file that contains several different lengths of records (version 2)

```
      ENVIRONMENT DIVISION.
            .
            .
      FILE-CONTROL.
          SELECT TRANRECS ASSIGN TO UT-S-TRANRECS.
            .
            .
      DATA DIVISION.
            .
            .
      FD  TRANRECS
          LABEL RECORDS ARE STANDARD
          RECORDING MODE IS V
          BLOCK CONTAINS 4000 CHARACTERS.
 ::
      01  TRANSACTION-RECORD.
 ::
          05  TR-RECORD-CODE      PIC X.
              88  HEADER                        VALUE 'H'.
              88  DETAIL                        VALUE 'D'.
              88  TRAILER                       VALUE 'T'.
          05  FILLER             PIC X(127).
 ::
            .
            .
      WORKING-STORAGE SECTION.
            .
            .
      01  HEADER-RECORD.
            .
            .
      01  DETAIL-RECORD.
            .
            .
      01  TRAILER-RECORD.
            .
            .
      PROCEDURE DIVISION.
            .
            .
          READ TRANRECS
              AT END
                  MOVE 'Y' TO TRAN-EOF-SW.
          IF NOT TRAN-EOF
              IF HEADER
                  MOVE TRANSACTION-RECORD TO HEADER-RECORD
              ELSE IF DETAIL
                  MOVE TRANSACTION-RECORD TO DETAIL-RECORD
              ELSE IF TRAILER
                  MOVE TRANSACTION-RECORD TO TRAILER-RECORD
              ELSE
                  MOVE 'Y' TO INVALID-TRAN-SW.
            .
            .
```

Figure 7-15 Generalized code for reading several different types of records from a
single file

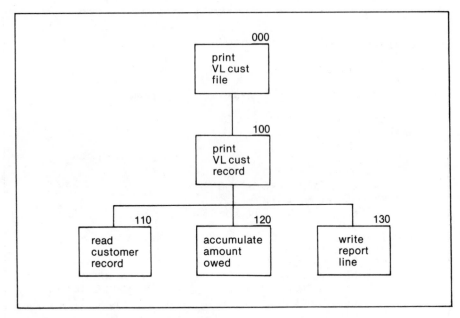

Figure 7-16 VTOC for the variable-length file-to-printer program

Terminology

root segment

Objectives

1. Given a problem involving variable-length records, code a
    COBOL solution. The problem may involve one or more input
    or output files as in an update program with an output error
    file.

Problems

1. a. Design a VTOC for a file-to-printer program for the
        variable-length file created by the program in figure 7-12.
        Quite simply, the program should print one line for each
        customer record in this format:

Field	Print Positions	Picture
Customer number	1-6	X(6)
Total amount owed	12-20	ZZ,ZZZ.99

Because the purpose of this program is to familiarize you
with variable-length coding techniques, you can omit
headings and forms overflow for the listing.

```
        IDENTIFICATION DIVISION.
   *
        PROGRAM-ID. VLPRINT.
   *
        ENVIRONMENT DIVISION.
   *
        INPUT-OUTPUT SECTION.
   *
        FILE-CONTROL.
            SELECT VLINVFLE ASSIGN TO UT-S-VLINVFLE.
            SELECT VLINVLST ASSIGN TO UT-S-VLINVLST.
   *
        DATA DIVISION.
   *
        FILE SECTION.
   *
        FD  VLINVFLE
            LABEL RECORDS ARE STANDARD
            RECORDING MODE IS V
            RECORD CONTAINS 328 CHARACTERS
            BLOCK CONTAINS 4000 CHARACTERS.
   *
        01  VL-AREA                 PIC X(328).
   *
        FD  VLINVLST
            LABEL RECORDS ARE STANDARD
            RECORDING MODE IS F
            RECORD CONTAINS 133 CHARACTERS
            BLOCK CONTAINS 0 RECORDS.
   *
        01  PRINT-AREA              PIC X(133).
   *
```

Figure 7-17   The variable-length file-to-printer program (part 1 of 3)

   b.   Code the program using the VTOC in figure 7-16. Do *not*
         use OCCURS DEPENDING ON.

2.   Code the changes that would have to be made to the program in
      figure 7-12 in order for APPLY WRITE-ONLY to be used on the
      variable-length output file.

Solutions

1.   a.   Figure 7-16 is an acceptable solution.

      b.   Figure 7-17 is an acceptable solution.

2.   Four changes would have to be made: (1) the I-O-CONTROL
      paragraph with the APPLY WRITE-ONLY statement must be
      added to the Environment Division; (2) the description for VL-

```
      WORKING-STORAGE SECTION.
      *
      01  SWITCHES.
      *
          05   CUSTOMER-EOF-SW      PIC X     VALUE 'N'.
               88  CUSTOMER-EOF               VALUE 'Y'.
      *
      01  TOTAL-FIELDS              COMP-3.
      *
          05   AMOUNT-OWED          PIC S9(5)V99.
      *
      01  SUBSCRIPTS               COMP      SYNC.
      *
          05   INVOICE-SUB          PIC S99.
      *
      01  VL-RECORD.
      *
          05   VL-CUSTOMER-NO       PIC X(6).
          05   VL-INVOICE-COUNT     PIC S99           COMP      SYNC.
          05   VL-INVOICE-DATA      OCCURS 20 TIMES.
               10   VL-INVOICE-DATE PIC X(6).
               10   VL-INVOICE-NO   PIC X(5).
               10   VL-INVOICE-AMT  PIC S9(5)V99      COMP-3.
               10   FILLER          PIC X.
      *
      01  NEXT-REPORT-LINE.
      *
          05   NRL-CC               PIC X.
          05   FILLER               PIC X(10)         VALUE SPACE.
          05   NRL-CUSTOMER-NO      PIC X(6).
          05   FILLER               PIC X(10)         VALUE SPACE.
          05   NRL-AMOUNT-OWED      PIC ZZ,ZZ9.99.
          05   FILLER               PIC X(97)         VALUE SPACE.
      *
```

Figure 7-17   The variable-length file-to-printer program (part 2 of 3)

RECORD must be moved to working-storage; (3) the output area description that follows the FD statement for VLINVFLE must describe a maximum-sized record, something like this:

```
      01  OUTPUT-AREA            PIC X(328).
```

and (4) the WRITE statement in module 140 must be something like this:

```
      WRITE OUTPUT-AREA FROM VL-RECORD.
```

```
     PROCEDURE DIVISION.
*
 000-PRINT-VL-CUST-FILE.
*
     OPEN INPUT  VLINVFLE
          OUTPUT VLINVLST.
     PERFORM 100-PRINT-VL-CUST-RECORD
         UNTIL CUSTOMER-EOF,
     CLOSE VLINVFLE
           VLINVLST.
     STOP RUN.
*
 100-PRINT-VL-CUST-RECORD.
*
     PERFORM 110-READ-CUSTOMER-RECORD.
     IF NOT CUSTOMER-EOF
         MOVE ZERO TO AMOUNT-OWED
         PERFORM 120-ACCUMULATE-AMOUNT-OWED
             VARYING INVOICE-SUB FROM 1 BY 1
             UNTIL INVOICE-SUB GREATER VL-INVOICE-COUNT
         MOVE VL-CUSTOMER-NO TO NRL-CUSTOMER-NO
         MOVE AMOUNT-OWED     TO NRL-AMOUNT-OWED
         MOVE NEXT-REPORT-LINE TO PRINT-AREA
         PERFORM 130-WRITE-REPORT-LINE.
*
 110-READ-CUSTOMER-RECORD.
*
     READ VLINVFLE INTO VL-RECORD
         AT END
             MOVE 'Y' TO CUSTOMER-EOF-SW.
*
 120-ACCUMULATE-AMOUNT-OWED.
*
     ADD VL-INVOICE-AMT (INVOICE-SUB) TO AMOUNT-OWED.
*
 130-WRITE-REPORT-LINE.
*
     WRITE PRINT-AREA
         AFTER ADVANCING 1 LINES.
*
```

Figure 7-17   The variable-length file-to-printer program (part 3 of 3)

PART FOUR

DOS and OS
Job-Control Language

This part shows you how to use DOS or OS job-control language for compiling and testing COBOL programs. It can be studied any time after you complete part 1, but you probably won't want to cover it until you complete part 2. Chapter 8 is for DOS and DOS/VS systems. Chapter 9 is for all types of OS systems (MFT, MVT, VS1, and VS2).

8

DOS Job-Control Language

In order to run a program on a System/360-370 operating under DOS, you have to code the proper job-control statements. This chapter is designed to teach you DOS *job-control language (JCL)* for compiling and testing programs involving sequential files. Topic 1 covers very basic JCL setups for compiling and executing card-to-printer programs. Topic 2 covers DOS JCL in more detail, enlarging on some of the job-control statements introduced in topic 1. Topic 3 then shows how to code the JCL to run sequential tape and disk programs.

TOPIC 1 Basic DOS Job Decks for Compiling and Testing

This topic gives you simple JCL setups that will allow you to compile and run your first programs. If you are already familiar with job-control language, you should be able to use the job decks in figures 8-1 and 8-2 without any explanation. Then, you can go on to topic 2 for additional information on DOS job-control language as it applies to COBOL programs.

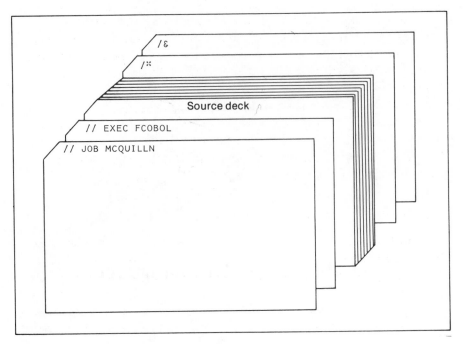

Figure 8-1   DOS job-control cards for COBOL compilation

Compiling a program

Figure 8-1 illustrates the DOS job-control cards needed to compile a
COBOL source deck. It begins with a JOB card, which gives a *jobname* to the *job* that is to be performed. Its format, which is typical
of many DOS job-control cards, begins with two slashes (columns 1
and 2) followed by one or more blanks and the *operation*—in this
case, JOB. This is followed by one or more blanks and the *operand*
or operands—in this case, the jobname MCQUILLN, which is a
shortening of the programmer's name, MCQUILLEN. After one or
more blanks, the operands of a job-control card can be followed by
comments (any data), which are ignored by the operating system.

The jobname can be up to eight alphabetic or numeric characters long but must start with a letter. Usually, each installation has
its own standards for creating acceptable jobnames. Beyond this, an
installation may require that additional information be given in the
JOB card. So find out what the standards are in your shop for
coding a JOB card and follow them.

The second card, // EXEC FCOBOL, causes the COBOL compiler to be loaded into storage and executed. FCOBOL is the name
given to the compiler stored in a library of the system-residence
device. When the compiler is executed, the source deck, which
follows the EXEC FCOBOL card, is read and the source listing along
with diagnostics is printed.

As you saw in chapter 2, the /* card (slash in column 1, asterisk in column 2) indicates the end of the input data. In figure 8-1, then, it tells the compiler that there are no more source cards. The /& card (slash in column 1, ampersand in column 2) indicates that the job is completed.

In DOS, a job may consist of one or more *job steps*. For each job step, there is one EXEC card between the JOB card, which is always the first card for a job, and the /& card, which is always the last card for a job. The job in this example consists of one job step since there is only one EXEC card.

Compiling and testing a program

As you learned in topic 4 of chapter 1, an object program must be processed by the linkage-editor program before it can be executed. The linkage editor stores the object program in one of the libraries of the system-residence device in a form that can be loaded by the supervisor. Compiling and testing a DOS COBOL program, then, is actually done in three steps: first, the source deck is compiled into an object program that is stored on disk; second, the linkage-editor program converts the object program into a form ready for execution and stores it in one of the DOS libraries; third, the object program is loaded and executed.

Figure 8-2 shows the DOS job-control cards required for compiling and executing a COBOL program that involves card input and printer output. The cards for the first job step are as follows:

```
// JOB MCQUILLN
// OPTION LINK
// EXEC FCOBOL
   (Source deck)
/*
```

The OPTION card will be explained in more detail in topic 2. Here, it simply says that the object program resulting from the compilation is to be stored on disk so that it can be link-edited. Outside of the OPTION card, the job-control statements are the same as they were in figure 8-1. So this JCL causes the compilation to take place with the resulting object program stored on disk.

The second job step is executing the linkage-editor program. The following is the job-control card for this step:

```
// EXEC LNKEDT
```

In other words, LNKEDT is the name for the linkage-editor program. It is loaded from the system-residence device and executed. When this job step is finished, the object program to be tested is

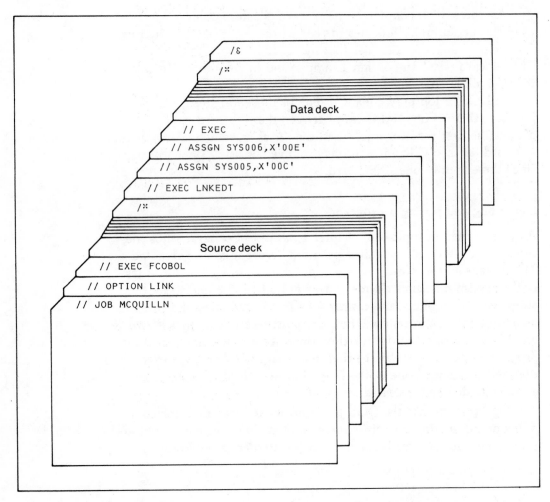

Figure 8-2 DOS job-control cards for compiling and testing a card-to-printer program

stored in one of the libraries of the system-residence device, ready
for execution.

The third job step is testing the program. The job-control cards
for this step are these:

```
// ASSGN SYS005,X'00C'
// ASSGN SYS006,X'00E'
// EXEC
   (Data deck)
/*
```

Here, the ASSGN cards assign specific I/O devices to the SYS
numbers used in the system names in the COBOL program. For
the System/360-370, X'00C' is always the card reader and X'00E' is
always the printer. As you have already seen, the COBOL programs

illustrated in this book use SYS005 for the reader and SYS006 for
the printer, so the ASSGN cards shown will work for any of the
programs in this book that have card input and printer output.
You will learn more about how and when to use ASSGN cards in
topic 2.

After the ASSGN cards, the EXEC card indicates that the program should be loaded and executed. Because the EXEC card doesn't
specify a program name (as in // EXEC FCOBOL or // EXEC
LNKEDT), it indicates that the program can be found in a temporary library area on the system-residence device. When the next
program to be tested is link-edited, it will replace this first program
in the temporary library area.

Summary

Although this has been a brief introduction to DOS job-control
language, the job setups shown in figures 8-1 and 8-2 should allow
you to compile and test your first programs on a System/360-370. In
general, a compilation setup alone (figure 8-1) is used until all
diagnostics have been corrected. Then, a compile and test setup
(figure 8-2) is used for a series of test runs. Each time an error is
debugged, the source deck is changed, and the program is recompiled and tested again.

Terminology

job-control language
JCL
jobname
job
operation
operand
job step

Objectives

1. Make up job decks for compiling or compiling and testing a
    COBOL program with card input and printer output. Follow
    your shop's standards when coding the JOB cards.

TOPIC 2 The EXEC, OPTION, CBL, and ASSGN Statements

You have already seen the formats for the JOB, EXEC, end-of-file (/*), and end-of-job (/&) cards and have been briefly introduced to the OPTION and ASSGN cards for running COBOL programs under DOS. This topic will explain the EXEC, OPTION, and ASSGN statements in more detail. It will also present the CBL statement, which is similar to the OPTION statement; it sets options for the COBOL compiler.

Executing a program from the core-image library

In topic 1, I mentioned that the EXEC card causes a program to be executed from a library of the system-residence device. To be more specific, object code must be stored in the *core-image library* before it can be executed on a DOS system. This library has two sections: a temporary one in which programs are stored for one-time use and a permanent one in which commonly used programs are kept.

When a program is compiled and tested using a job deck like the one in figure 8-2, it is stored in the temporary section of the core-image library after the link-edit step. It is then executed immediately by use of the single statement, EXEC. However, if a program is to be used over and over again, it is stored in the permanent section of the library under a *phase name* that uniquely identifies it. (Each program in the permanent part of the library is called a *phase.*) For example, the phase name for the COBOL compiler is FCOBOL; the phase name for the linkage-editor program is LNKEDT. To execute a program from the permanent section of the library, you must use an EXEC card that specifies the phase name. Thus, as we have already seen in figures 8-1 and 8-2,

```
// EXEC FCOBOL
```

executes the COBOL compiler. Likewise,

```
// EXEC LNKEDT
```

executes the linkage editor.

Suppose now that you want to run the card-to-printer program in figure 8-2. This time, though, the program is stored in the core-image library under the phase name PRTCARD. Since it has already been compiled and link-edited, you no longer need the compile and link-edit steps in your job deck. This, in turn, eliminates the need for the OPTION card and the source deck in figure 8-2. However, you do have to specify the phase name in an EXEC card so the

```
// JOB ADDNGTON
// ASSGN SYS005,X'00C'
// ASSGN SYS006,X'00E'
// EXEC PRTCARD
   (Data deck)
/*
/&
```

Figure 8-3 Executing a program from the core-image library

operating system will know which program in the library to execute. As a result, the job setup in figure 8-3 will cause the card-to-printer program to be executed from the library.

There are other internal libraries besides the core-image library. Book two in this series describes them in detail and shows how to store library entries. For this course, though, all you need to know is how to use the EXEC statement to execute programs from the core-image library.

The OPTION statement

When a DOS system is generated, certain system parameters are set, which provide for *standard options* to be automatically performed by the system. These options determine what optional compiler output—for example, an object deck—will be produced when a program is run. They also determine whether or not a storage dump is to be printed when a program check occurs.

The standard options are in effect for all jobs unless overridden by an OPTION statement. Thus, the purpose of the OPTION statement is to reset system parameters, thereby affecting compilations, link-edit runs, and test runs. When an OPTION statement is used, the options it specifies are in effect until the end of the job or until reset by another OPTION statement. At the end of the job, all options revert to their standard settings.

A partial list of the valid OPTION operands is given in figure 8-4. A typical DOS system might have the following standard options set up at the time of system generation:

```
NOLOG,DUMP,NOLINK,NODECK,LIST,NOLISTX,NOSYM,XREF,ERRS
```

If you wanted to test a program on this system, then, you would have to use an OPTION card like the one in figure 8-2

```
// OPTION LINK
```

Operand	Meaning
LOG NOLOG	Print (log) all job-control statements on the system printer.
DUMP NODUMP	Print a storage dump if an abnormal program end occurs.
LINK NOLINK	Save the object program for immediate input to linkage-editor program. Used whenever the programmer is ready to test a program.
DECK NODECK	Punch the object program in cards.
LIST NOLIST	Print a source program listing.
LISTX NOLISTX	Print a Procedure Division map during a COBOL compilation, including global tables, literal pool, and register assignments.
SYM NOSYM	Print a Data Division map for COBOL compilations.
XREF NOXREF	Print a cross-reference listing.
ERRS NOERRS	Print a diagnostic listing.

Figure 8-4 DOS OPTION statement operands

to override the NOLINK standard option. This would cause the object program created during the compilation to be stored on disk so it could be link-edited. Likewise, if you wanted the JCL statements to print on the printer (they always print on the console typewriter), you wanted to link-edit the resulting object program, and you didn't want a storage dump to print, you would need an OPTION card like this:

```
// OPTION LOG,LINK,NODUMP
```

The operands can be given in any sequence, but they must be separated by commas with no intervening blanks.

Since an OPTION card is required only when you want to change a standard option, you need to know the standard options on your own system to decide when to use an OPTION statement. Once you find out what the standard options are, you can use the OPTION statement to adjust the options as desired.

In general, when you are compiling a program for the first time, it will be in a compile-only job. Then, you will normally want the options set this way:

```
NOLINK,NODECK,LIST,NOLISTX,NOSYM,XREF,ERRS
```

In other words, you don't want the object program to be saved for the linkage editor and you don't want an object deck punched. Similarly, because the Procedure Division map and Data Division map are used for debugging, you don't want them to print (NOLISTX,NOSYM). On the other hand, you do want the source listing, the cross-reference listing, and the diagnostic listing to print. So if these options aren't your system's standard options, you should use an OPTION statement to change them whenever you run compile-only jobs.

When you run compile-and-test jobs, the LINK option must be on. Otherwise, for the purposes of this book, the options would remain as they are for compile-only jobs. Later on, when you learn more about debugging, you may want to turn the LISTX and SYM options on for your compile-and-test jobs. You will also want to make sure that the DUMP option is on for your test runs.

The CBL statement

Besides the options in the OPTION statement, there are a number of other options that relate to the COBOL compiler. A programmer can control these options by using the CBL statement.

Unlike the DOS job-control statements we've seen so far, the CBL statement does not begin with two slashes. Instead, CBL is coded starting in column 2. After at least one blank, the statement operands are coded, separated by commas just as in the OPTION statement. The CBL statement isn't really a job-control statement; it is processed by the COBOL compiler. As a result, the CBL card must come directly after the // EXEC FCOBOL card in the job deck and before the first card of the source deck.

A partial list of valid CBL operands along with recommendations for their use is given in figure 8-5. The underlined values are the ones IBM recommends as standard, or default, options. However, a system's default options are set according to the installation's needs at the time the system is generated, so you will have to find out what the default values are on your system.

Two of the CBL options can cause particular problems when you run COBOL programs. One is the ZWB option. If it is on, the compiler will remove the sign from a numeric field with DISPLAY usage before comparing it with an alphanumeric field. Thus, a -5 could be found to be equal to a $+5$. Rather than code NOZWB, however, you should always leave this option at its default value on your system. If you start switching it around, you may run into problems as you work with programs that have already been tested and put into production in accordance with the default value. In other words, ZWB is one option that should be set the same for

Operand	Meaning	Recommendation
SEQ NOSEQ	Check the sequence of the source statements. If an out-of-sequence statement is detected, print a diagnostic message.	Use SEQ.
FLAGW FLAGE	FLAGW means that all diagnostic messages are to be printed on the diagnostic listing. FLAGE means warning messages are not to be listed.	Use FLAGW.
SUPMAP	If an E-level diagnostic occurs, do **not** (1) print a Procedure Division map or a condensed Procedure Division map (suppress it), (2) punch an object deck, or (3) produce an object program.	Use SUPMAP whenever you use LISTX or CLIST.
SPACEn	Tells how the output listing should be spaced. You can specify n as 1 (single spacing), 2 (double spacing), or 3 (triple spacing). The default value is 1.	Use SPACE1.
CLIST	Print a condensed Procedure Division map. This option overrides the LISTX or NOLISTX option in the OPTION statement.	CLIST can be used in test runs to produce debugging output; it's not necessary in compile-only runs.
QUOTE APOST	Indicates whether quotation marks (") or the apostrophe (') are to be used in setting off non-numeric literals.	APOST is used on most IBM systems.
NOTRUNC TRUNC	Only has meaning in a MOVE or arithmetic statement in which the receiving field has COMP usage. TRUNC means the compiler will generate code to cut off digits in the sending or intermediate result field (or truncate the field) to make it conform to the PICTURE of the COMP receiving field.	**Always** use NOTRUNC.
ZWB NOZWB	Remove the sign from a numeric field with DISPLAY usage if it's compared to an alphanumeric field.	Use the default value on your system.

Figure 8-5 DOS CBL statement operands

every program in an installation, and the easiest way to do this is to leave the option at its default value.

The other troublesome option is TRUNC, which applies only when the receiving field of a MOVE or arithmetic statement is a COMP field. In a MOVE statement, the compiler will cut off digits in the sending field (or *truncate* the field) to make it conform to the

PICTURE of the receiving field. In an arithmetic statement, the final intermediate result field will be truncated before its value is placed in a COMP receiving field. At first glance, this might seem like a fairly useful function. However, because of the way COMP fields are stored internally, a COMP field can have a value containing more digits than are given in its PICTURE. For example, a COMP field with a PICTURE of 9(2) can have a value of up to 32,767. In practice, then, TRUNC is confusing and inefficient, and it can result in pages of diagnostics. So although TRUNC is the recommended value under the ANSI standards, you should always make sure this option is set to NOTRUNC.

To illustrate the use of the CBL statement, suppose that you are to run a compile-only job on a system with these default values:

```
SEQ,FLAGW,SUPMAP,SPACE1,APOST,TRUNC,NOZWB
```

You will want to code this CBL statement before running the program:

```
CBL NOTRUNC
```

As you already know, this will prevent the compiler from truncating any field that is to be moved into a COMP field by a MOVE or arithmetic statement.

The ASSGN statement

The ASSGN statement is used to assign the files defined in your program to physical I/O devices. To help you understand how I/O device assignments work, consider the typical system shown in figure 8-6. This schematic represents a System/360 Model 40 with 128K storage, a 2540 reader/punch, a 1403 printer, a 1052 typewriter, four 2401 tape drives, and a five-spindle 2314 disk facility.

Each of the physical I/O units on a System/360-370 is assigned a *device address* expressed in three digits in hexadecimal notation. (Hexadecimal, or hex, notation is commonly used to represent the contents of System/360-370 storage.) In figure 8-6, for example, the 2540 is assigned device addresses hex 00C for the reader and hex 00D for the punch. (The 2540 is considered to be two devices, even though both are housed in one physical unit.) Each tape drive is assigned an individual address (hex 180 to 183), as is each disk spindle on the 2314 (hex 130 to 134).

The programmer, however, doesn't refer to I/O units by their physical addresses. Instead, he refers to *logical units* (also called *symbolic units*). In the SELECT statements, for example, the system name starts with a logical unit such as SYS005.

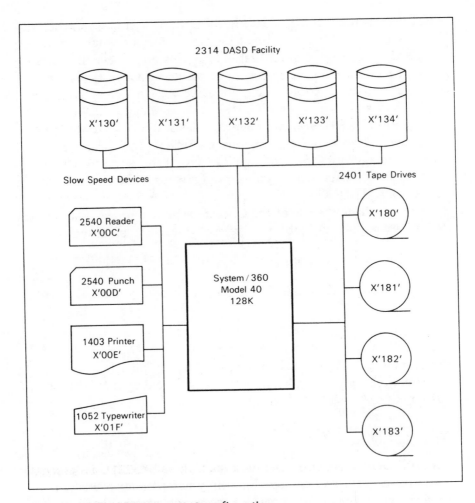

Figure 8-6 A typical System/360 configuration

When a system is generated, the physical addresses of the I/O units are assigned to various logical units. These are referred to as *standard assignments.* Figure 8-7, for example, shows the standard assignments that might be generated for the System/360 configuration in figure 8-6. The *system logical units* are referred to by the DOS control programs (like the linkage editor), but they can also be referred to by user programs. The *programmer logical units* are to be used by user programs.

Since the system-residence device is usually the disk spindle with the lowest hex address (hex 130 in figure 8-6), figure 8-7 indicates that SYSLNK and SYSRES are assigned to the system-residence device. Furthermore, SYS001 through SYS004 are also assigned to the system-residence device. These logical units represent work areas used by the language translators. Although they could be on another disk spindle, they are usually on the system-residence device.

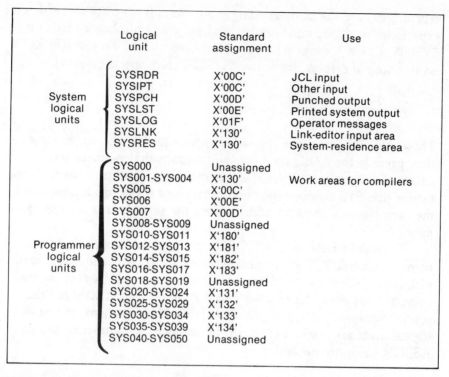

	Logical unit	Standard assignment	Use
System logical units	SYSRDR	X'00C'	JCL input
	SYSIPT	X'00C'	Other input
	SYSPCH	X'00D'	Punched output
	SYSLST	X'00E'	Printed system output
	SYSLOG	X'01F'	Operator messages
	SYSLNK	X'130'	Link-editor input area
	SYSRES	X'130'	System-residence area
Programmer logical units	SYS000	Unassigned	
	SYS001-SYS004	X'130'	Work areas for compilers
	SYS005	X'00C'	
	SYS006	X'00E'	
	SYS007	X'00D'	
	SYS008-SYS009	Unassigned	
	SYS010-SYS011	X'180'	
	SYS012-SYS013	X'181'	
	SYS014-SYS015	X'182'	
	SYS016-SYS017	X'183'	
	SYS018-SYS019	Unassigned	
	SYS020-SYS024	X'131'	
	SYS025-SYS029	X'132'	
	SYS030-SYS034	X'133'	
	SYS035-SYS039	X'134'	
	SYS040-SYS050	Unassigned	

Figure 8-7   Typical standard assignments

From SYS005 on up to the highest numbered logical unit specified in the supervisor (it can go as high as SYS221), assignments are made to best serve the programming requirements of the particular installation. A set of assignments similar to that in figure 8-7 is common. Notice that some of the logical units are unassigned; these are used to accommodate special situations or to provide for later addition of more I/O units.

As shown in the following example, the ASSGN card is used to temporarily override the standard assignments:

```
// ASSGN SYS005,X'182'
```

The first operand names the logical unit and the second specifies the physical address of the device to which the logical unit is to be assigned. This assignment is in effect from the time the ASSGN card is read until the end of the job or until another ASSGN card changes the assignment of the logical unit. When the job ends, the logical unit reverts to its standard assignment.

Suppose the sample configuration of figure 8-6 running under the standard assignments of figure 8-7 is used for a program named REPRO that was originally written for another system. REPRO

reproduces card decks by reading input cards from SYS006, which it
expects to be a 2540 card reader, and punching duplicate cards on
SYS008, which it expects to be a 2540 card punch. To run REPRO
on the sample system, these two ASSGN cards are necessary:

```
// ASSGN SYS006,X'00C'
// ASSGN SYS008,X'00D'
```

These ASSGN cards can appear anywhere in the job step as long as
they precede the EXEC card for the program that requires the
changed assignments. Thus the programmer logical unit for the card
reader (the SYS number specified in the user program) is assigned to
the card reader's physical address, and the same is true for the card
punch.

In most installations, a COBOL programmer codes the system
name of his SELECT statements with a logical unit whose standard
assignment refers to the proper device. For example, a programmer
using the system in figures 8-6 and 8-7 would use SYS006 for the
printer because that is the printer's standard assignment. When the
logical units are used as given in the standard assignments, no
ASSGN cards are needed.

Terminology

core-image library

phase name

phase

standard option

device address

logical unit

symbolic unit

standard assignment

system logical unit

programmer logical unit

Objectives

1. List the standard options for your installation.

2. List the standard assignments for the logical units on your
   system.

3. Given a job that requires a program be executed from the core-
   image library, write a proper EXEC statement.

4. Given a job that requires changes in options or assignments, create job-control decks that use OPTION, CBL, or ASSGN statements to make the changes.

Problems

1. (Objective 4) Suppose a system has these standard options:

```
DUMP,LINK,NODECK,LIST,LISTX,SYM,XREF,ERRS
```

and the COBOL compiler has these standard options:

```
SEQ,FLAGW,SUPMAP,SPACE1,APOST,TRUNC,ZWB.
```

Suppose too that you are running your first compile of a program and want only the source listing, cross-reference listing, and diagnostic listing as output from the compile-only job. Create an efficient job deck for this job.

Solutions

1. Your JOB statement should, of course, conform to your installation standards. Otherwise, the following JCL will work:

```
//   JOB MURACH
//   OPTION NOLINK,NOLISTX,NOSYM
//   EXEC FCOBOL
  CBL NOTRUNC
     (Source deck)
/*
/&
```

Note that there's no point in turning off the DUMP option since the operations department would want a dump if the compiler abnormally terminated.

TOPIC 3   DOS JCL for Sequential Files

In topic 1, you saw the basic DOS JCL needed to run a simple card-to-printer program. This topic introduces the JCL statements you will need to run other types of sequential programs. The topic is divided into two parts: the first part covers DOS JCL for tape files, and the second part deals with DOS JCL for disk files.

JCL for Tape Files

To prevent accidental destruction of tape files, most DOS installations use the standard tape label facility (LABEL RECORDS ARE STANDARD in a COBOL program). As a result, label information must be supplied to the operating system at the time a program involving tape files is executed. This requires the use of the LBLTYP and TLBL statements.

The LBLTYP statement

The LBLTYP statement for a tape file is coded like this:

```
// LBLTYP TAPE
```

It says that the linkage editor must provide an 80-byte tape label area at the start of the user's program. This area is then used in conjunction with the label information given in the TLBL card. The LBLTYP card must come before the EXEC LNKEDT card.

The TLBL statement

Figure 8-8 shows the format of the tape label record, the format of the TLBL card, and an explanation of each of the TLBL operands. Notice the relationships between the TLBL operands and the fields of the tape label. As you will see later, the first operand (file name) refers to the external name given in the system name of the SELECT statement in the COBOL program. Thus, the TLBL statement is matched with a specific file in the COBOL program.

For input files, the operands in the TLBL statement are compared to the corresponding fields of the tape label. If they are equal, the file is opened and processing can begin. If they aren't equal, a message is printed or displayed to tell the operator that the wrong tape is mounted. Since you can selectively code the optional operands of the TLBL card for an input file, only certain fields need be checked. In the example in figure 8-8, only the file identifier, the date, and the serial number are checked.

For output files, the label processing is different. First, the volume serial number, if coded in the TLBL statement, is compared to the tape volume label. Often, this TLBL operand is omitted for output files to allow any available tape to be used. Then, if the tape already holds a file, the *expiration date* in its label is compared to

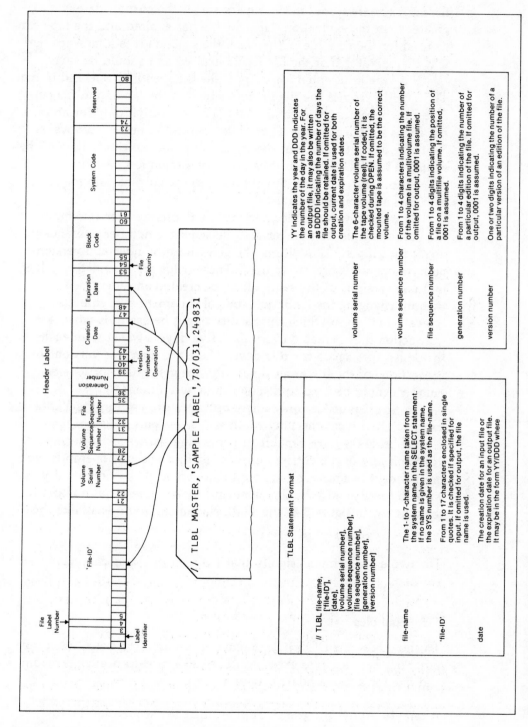

Figure 8-8   Standard tape label and TLBL statement format

the current date stored in the supervisor. If the current date is greater than the expiration date, the file has expired and the tape can be used for the new file. Otherwise, the system gives a message that tells the operator that the file hasn't expired and should be saved.

If a tape is accepted for output, the file identifier operand in the TLBL card becomes the file identifier field in the label, and the current date becomes the creation date. The expiration date for an output file is supplied by the TLBL date operand in one of two ways. First, the date operand can specify an absolute expiration date in the format YY/DDD. Second, it can specify a retention period as a number of days, DDDD; this is added to the current date to calculate an expiration date.

Since multivolume files and multifile volumes aren't common, the volume-sequence number and file-sequence number operands aren't used much. In addition, the generation-number and version-number operands are rarely used. These fields are intended to allow multiple versions of the same file to be created and identified without changing the TLBL job-control statement everytime. A typical situation in which this facility might be useful is when a transaction file is created every day, five days a week, with each of the daily tapes saved for five days. There are then five versions or generations of the file at all times, and the generation or version numbers could be used to distinguish between them.

In actual practice, only a few operands are used in the TLBL card, so DOS label-checking routines process only a few of the several fields they are capable of processing. However, whenever you omit any of the entries between the first and last operands, you must code a comma for each omitted operand. For example, if you were to specify only the file name and the volume serial number for the tape file in figure 8-8, the TLBL statement would look like this:

```
// TLBL MASTER,,,249831
```

The two extra commas signify that the identifier and date have been omitted.

Two examples

To show how the DOS JCL statements are used for executing a tape program, here are two examples: one for a tape-to-printer program and one for a tape-update program.

A tape-to-printer program   Suppose that the sequential file-to-printer program in figure 7-4 were to be used to print the contents of a tape file. Then, the JCL cards in figure 8-9 could be used to compile, link, and execute the program. The OPTION card says that the

```
// JOB TAPEPRT
// OPTION LINK
// EXEC FCOBOL
   (Source deck)
/*
// LBLTYP TAPE
// EXEC LNKEDT
// TLBL ITEMIN,'INVENTORY MASTER',78/079,507196
// EXEC
/&
```

Figure 8-9   DOS JCL for a tape-to-printer program

object program is to be link-edited. The LBLTYP card specifies that extra storage is needed for label information. And the TLBL card supplies the label information that will be checked against the tape label to make sure that the proper tape is mounted. Assuming the standard assignments in figure 8-7, no ASSGN cards are needed. And since no input cards are to be processed, there is no data deck after the last EXEC card.

If you look at the external name for the tape file in the SELECT statement in figure 7-4, you'll see that the file name in the TLBL statement is exactly the same. (If no external name has been coded in the SELECT statement, the SYS number would have been used as the file name in the TLBL statement.) After the file name, the programmer specified only three of the optional operands in the TLBL statement: the file identifier ('INVENTORY MASTER'), the date the file was created (78/079, that is, March 20, 1978), and the volume serial number (507196). If these operands match those in the tape label field, the file will be opened for processing. If not, a message will be given to indicate that the wrong tape is mounted.

A tape-update program   Figure 8-10 illustrates the JCL to compile, link, and test the update program in figure 7-8, assuming the program is used to update a tape file. Since figure 7-8 is for an OS system, assume the program has the following SELECT statements under DOS:

```
SELECT TRNFILE ASSIGN TO SYS010-UT-2400-S-TRNFILE.
SELECT OLDMAST ASSIGN TO SYS011-UT-2400-S-OLDMAST.
SELECT NEWMAST ASSIGN TO SYS012-UT-2400-S-NEWMAST.
SELECT ERRFILE ASSIGN TO SYS013-UT-2400-S-ERRFILE.
SELECT UPDLIST ASSIGN TO SYS006-UR-1403-S.
```

```
// JOB TPUPDTE
// OPTION LINK
// EXEC FCOBOL
   (Source deck)
/*
// LBLTYP TAPE
// EXEC LNKEDT
// ASSGN SYS011,X'181'
// ASSGN SYS012,X'182'
// ASSGN SYS013,X'183'
// TLBL TRNFILE,'TRANSACTIONS',78/102,003414
// TLBL OLDMAST,'INVENTORY ITEMS',,008432
// TLBL NEWMAST,'INVENTORY ITEMS',30
// TLBL ERRFILE,'ERROR TAPE',10
// EXEC
/&
```

Figure 8-10   DOS JCL for a tape-update program

Also assume that blocks in the master files contain 40 records, and blocks in the transaction and error files contain 165 records. The printer records are unblocked.

Before the EXEC LNKEDT card in figure 8-10, the LBLTYP card indicates that the 80-byte label area must be reserved at the start of the user's program. Assuming the standard device assignments given in figure 8-7, three ASSGN cards are needed to assign logical units SYS011, SYS012, and SYS013 to drives X'181', X'182', and X'183'. Since logical unit SYS010 has a standard assignment of X'180', it doesn't require an ASSGN card.

In the TLBL card for the transaction file, the file-ID, the date, and the volume serial number are specified, so these fields will be checked; for the input master file, only file ID and serial number will be checked. In the TLBL cards for the output files, the volume serial numbers are omitted, so any available tapes can be used. The expiration date for the new master file will be thirty days from the current date; for the error tape, it will be ten days from the current date.

JCL For Sequential Disk Files

The DLBL and EXTENT statements

Sequential disk files, like tape files, generally have standard file labels. So these labels can be checked, DLBL and EXTENT job-control statements must be included in the JCL for programs that use disk files. Figure 8-11 shows the format of the file label stored on a disk and the format of the DLBL and EXTENT statements. It also shows the correspondence between the statement operands and the label fields.

The file name in the DLBL card corresponds to the external name in the system name of the SELECT statement for the file in the COBOL program. The file-ID and date operands are similar to those of the TLBL card; the exception is that the file-ID operand must always be present for disk input files so the proper disk label for the file can be found in the Volume Table of Contents. If a file has sequential organization, the code operand in the DLBL card can be omitted; otherwise, it must indicate the file organization. Since the only file organization you'll work with in this course is sequential, you don't have to worry about this operand.

While some of the operands in the DLBL statement are optional, internal commas are required to indicate omitted operands, just as they are in the TLBL statement. For example, in the sample DLBL statement in figure 8-11, you can see that two commas follow the file identifier. The second comma signifies that the date operand has been omitted and that the next operand will be the file organization code. If the programmer had omitted the code, too, no commas would have been required after the identifier.

The EXTENT statement (or multiple EXTENT statements) can be considered an extension of the DLBL information and must always be placed directly after the DLBL statement. The first EXTENT operand names the logical unit on which the file is to be found. The next operand, the volume serial number, is optional, but it is almost always coded so the OPEN routine can check to see that the proper pack has been mounted. The type operand is coded 1 (or omitted) for all *extents* (disk areas) of sequential files. If the type operand is omitted, it is called a default and a value of 1 is assumed. The extent-sequence-number operand is also frequently omitted, in which case the default value of 0 is used. The relative-track operand identifies the starting track of the file as a track number relative to the first track of the disk pack, track 0 of cylinder 0. On a 2314, for example, a file starting in the thirtieth cylinder would have a relative track value of 600 (30th cylinder $\times$ 20 tracks per cylinder = 600th track). The last operand of the EXTENT statement specifies the number of tracks allocated to this particular extent. For most sequential files, only one EXTENT statement is used, so the number of tracks specified represents the entire file. The number of tracks is usually given in even cylinder multiples (for example, in multiples of 20 on the 2314). As in the DLBL statement, a comma must replace

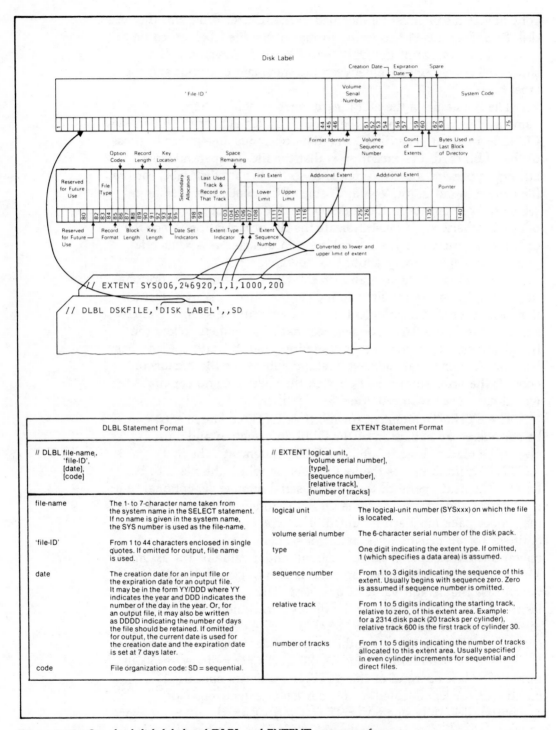

Figure 8-11   Standard disk label and DLBL and EXTENT statement formats

```
// JOB DSKCREAT
// OPTION LINK
// EXEC FCOBOL
   (Source deck)
/*
// EXEC LNKEDT
// DLBL ARTRANS,'ACCTS RCV TRANS'
// EXTENT SYS023,CMP060,,0,1200,100
// EXEC
   (Data deck)
/*
/&
```

Figure 8-12 DOS JCL for a card-to-disk program

any EXTENT operand that is omitted between the first and last
operands specified.

Two examples

To illustrate how the DLBL and EXTENT statements are used,
suppose a program is to create a sequential disk file from a deck
of accounts-receivable transaction cards. The programmer has
decided to put the file on disk volume CMP060 and has found
cylinders 60 through 64 free to hold it. The JCL for this program is
given in figure 8-12. Here, the DLBL statement gives the file name,
ARTRANS, and the file identifier that is to become the label of the
file. Since the date operand is omitted, the file will be assigned a
retention period of seven days. Since the code operand is also
omitted, SD is assumed.

The EXTENT statement indicates that the file is to be found on
logical unit SYS023, which you would expect to be assigned to a
disk device, and the volume serial number of the disk to be used is
CMP060. When the type operand is omitted as in this example, the
value for a sequential file (1) is assumed; thus, it is correct for this
file. The sequence number is 0, which is usual for a sequential file.
Since the extents of the file are given as relative track 1200 and 100
tracks in length, the five cylinders from 60 through 64 are used.

Now suppose a different program reads this same sequential

file. Because the file label is stored on the disk this time, some of the entries in the JCL cards can be omitted as follows:

```
// DLBL ARTRANS,'ACCTS RCV TRANS'
// EXTENT SYS023,CMP060
```

The file-name and file-ID operands must both be present in the DLBL cards so that the file label can be found in the Volume Table of Contents. On the EXTENT statement, however, only the logical unit is actually required, but the volume serial number has also been coded so that it will be checked. When the file is opened, the volume serial number of the disk found on SYS023 will be compared to CMP060. If they are the same, processing continues. If different, a message is issued to tell the operator that the wrong pack is mounted. If the serial number is omitted, this check isn't performed. If the type, sequence-number, relative-track, and number-of-track operands are omitted for an input file, these values are retrieved by the OPEN routine from the file label on the disk and are used without being checked.

Incidentally, the EXTENT operands can be omitted for an input file only when using the more recent versions of DOS—specifically, those versions starting with release 27. If an installation has not yet switched to this release or a later one, all EXTENT information may be required. In such a case, the job-control program will print a message indicating an invalid EXTENT statement if you omit any of the operands. You can correct this by duplicating the extent information used by the file-creation job in any job that requires the file as input.

Terminology

expiration date

extent

Objectives

1. Given the description of a job that fits one of the patterns of job-control cards described in this chapter, make up job-control cards that will cause the intended sequence of programs to be executed.

Problems

1. Suppose a sequential disk master file is to be created from a file of tape records. The creation program must be compiled and link-edited before it is executed. The tape file has the file name ITMTRAN, the file identifier ITEM TRANSACTIONS, volume serial number 459031, and a creation date of 78/059. It will be mounted on 2400 tape drive X'180'. The disk file, which is to be mounted on 2314 spindle X'131', has the file name ITMMSTR, the file identifier ITEM MASTER FILE, and should be stored in cylinders 10-55 on the pack with the volume serial number 103111. The new disk file is to be kept 30 days.

    To make sure the file is created properly, the programmer will run a disk-to-printer program to print the contents of the file immediately after the creation program. This program is stored in the core-image library under the name DSKPRT. Assuming the standard assignments in figure 8-7, write the JCL statements for running these two programs in a single job.

2. Suppose the file created in problem 1 is used as the old master file for testing the sequential update program in figure 7-8. Assume the SELECT statements on a DOS system are as follows:

```
SELECT TRNFILE ASSIGN TO SYS020-UT-2314-S-TRNFILE.
SELECT OLDMAST ASSIGN TO SYS021-UT-2314-S-OLDMAST.
SELECT NEWMAST ASSIGN TO SYS022-UT-2314-S-NEWMAST.
SELECT ERRFILE ASSIGN TO SYS023-UT-2314-S-ERRFILE.
SELECT UPDLIST ASSIGN TO SYS006-UR-1403-S.
```

    The transaction file, which is to be mounted on 2314 spindle X'132', has the file identifier ITEM TRANSACTIONS and can be found in cylinders 11-20 of the pack with volume serial number 219109. It was created on January 12, 1979. The error file, which is to be written on a pack mounted on spindle X'134', has cylinders 151-152 as its extents and will be saved five days. The old master file will be mounted on spindle X'131', as in problem 1. The new master file will be written in cylinders 1-46 on pack 237562, which will be mounted on spindle X'133'. It will be saved 30 days. Assuming the standard assignments given in figure 8-7, write the JCL statements for compiling and testing the update program.

```
// JOB DSKTEST
// OPTION LINK
// EXEC FCOBOL
   (Source deck)
/*
// LBLTYP TAPE
// EXEC LNKEDT
// TLBL ITMTRAN,'ITEM TRANSACTIONS',78/059,459031
// DLBL ITMMSTR,'ITEM MASTER FILE',30
// EXTENT SYS020,103111,,,200,920
// EXEC
// DLBL ITMMSTR,'ITEM MASTER FILE'
// EXTENT SYS020,103111
// EXEC DSKPRT
/&
```

Figure 8-13 A job deck for running a tape-to-disk program and a disk-to-printer program

Solutions

1. Figure 8-13 is an acceptable solution. Since each EXEC statement indicates one job step, this job consists of four job steps. In the first step, the tape-to-disk program is compiled and the object program is saved on disk. In the second step, the program is link-edited and the 80-byte label area is provided. The third EXEC statement causes the program to be run using the tape and disk label information given in the three preceding job cards. And the fourth job step executes the disk-to-printer program that is stored in the core-image library, using the disk label information in the two preceding job cards. Note that you must give some disk label information in each job step in which a file is used, although you don't have to include all the same operands each time.

```
// JOB DKUPDAT
// OPTION LINK
// EXEC FCOBOL
   (Source deck)
/*
// EXEC LNKEDT
// ASSGN SYS020,X'132'
// ASSGN SYS022,X'133'
// ASSGN SYS023,X'134'
// DLBL TRNFILE,'ITEM TRANSACTIONS',79/012
// EXTENT SYS020,219109
// DLBL OLDMAST,'ITEM MASTER FILE'
// EXTENT SYS021,103111
// DLBL NEWMAST,'UPDATED ITEM MASTER FILE',30
// EXTENT SYS022,237562,,,20,920
// DLBL ERRFILE,'ERROR FILE',5
// EXTENT SYS023,,,,3020,40
// EXEC
/&
```

Figure 8-14   A job deck for running a disk-update program

2.   Figure 8-14 is an acceptable solution. Note that only three
     ASSGN statements are needed because the old master file and
     the update listing are already assigned to the correct I/O
     devices. Also note that I omitted the track operands for the
     transaction and old master files. Since they are input files in this
     program, you don't have to specify their extents.

9

OS Job-Control Language

In order to compile and test a program under OS, you must be able
to create the required job-control cards. Because job-control cards
require specifications that are in a sense a language of their own, the
code used in job-control cards is often referred to as *job-control
language,* or *JCL.* This chapter, then, is designed to teach you OS
JCL. Each topic covers JCL at a greater level of difficulty, and can
be read at any time throughout the course.

Topic 1 covers the elementary JCL required to compile and
test programs using only card and printer files. Thus, it is just
enough to get you going with your first programs. Then, topic 2
goes over most of the OS JCL statements in greater detail. Finally,
topic 3 covers the JCL requirements needed to use sequential files on
tape or disk; it should be read before testing the programs you write
in part 3.

TOPIC 1   Basic OS Job Decks for Compiling and Testing

In order to compile and test a COBOL program, you must know
how to create the necessary job-control cards. So, this topic is
designed to give you the bare minimum you need to compile or test
a program involving card input and printer output under OS. Additional specifications for OS job-control language are given in the rest
of this chapter.

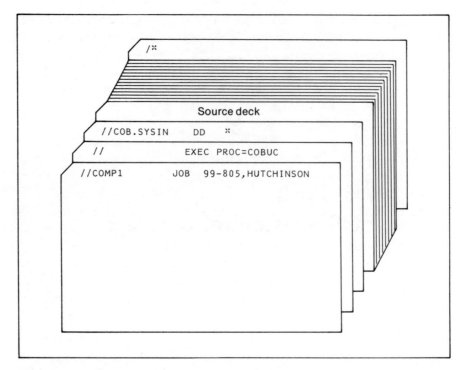

Figure 9-1 A job deck for a COBOL compilation

Compiling a Program

Figure 9-1 illustrates the job-control cards needed to compile a COBOL program. This job deck consists of four types of JCL cards: the JOB card, the EXEC card, the DD card, and the /* card.

The JOB card   The first card in the job deck is a *JOB card* which gives a *jobname* to the *job* that is to be performed. The format of the JOB card is typical of nearly all OS job-control cards. Slashes in columns 1 and 2 are followed by a one- to eight-character name field—in this case, the jobname COMP1. One or more blanks then separate the name field from the *operation code,* JOB. Then, again after one or more blanks, come the *operands* of the control card, separated from each other by commas if there are more than one. The operation code must start in or before column 16, and nothing can be coded beyond column 71.

    The characters of the jobname can be letters, numbers, or certain special characters (@, $, or #), but the first one must be a letter. The jobname is printed in large letters on the first and last pages of the job output, so it is often used by operating personnel. Thus, your installation is likely to have standards for forming jobnames.

For example, our installation uses the first three characters to identify the programmer, while the last five characters are used by the
programmer to identify the program. The listings are filed according
to the first three characters. Then, when the programmers pick up
their listings, they can identify a program by the last five characters.
Thus, a jobname like DALUPDAT belongs to Douglas A. Lowe
(DAL), and the program is UPDAT.

There are ten possible operands for the JOB card, but only two
are coded in most OS installations. (Topic 2 explains some of the
others, and you can refer to the IBM manuals on OS and OS/VS
job-control language for the complete list.) The first operand,
accounting information, is used as an identification code so that the
OS system can keep a record of who uses the system and for how
long. It's usually just an account number as shown in figure 9-1
(99-805), but it may also include other information. For example, the
following JOB card has an account number (2009) and a maximum
time limit (2 minutes) coded in the accounting information operand:

```
//SAMPLE  JOB  (2009,2),MEADOWS
```

In this case, the accounting information is enclosed in parentheses and its parts are separated by commas with no intervening
blanks. Since the format of the accounting information operand is
unique to each installation, you'll have to find out what's correct for
your system.

The second standard JOB card operand is the programmer name
field, which can be up to 20 characters long. If it contains any
characters other than letters, numbers, or periods, it must be
enclosed in apostrophes, as in this example:

```
//CM047  JOB  0932,'CLARK & MURPHY'
```

The EXEC card   The second control card in figure 9-1, the *EXEC
card* (execute card), follows the same basic format given for the JOB
card. If a name is coded in the name field, it has the same character
limitations as a jobname. Then, the name becomes the name of the
job step; that is, the *stepname*. Again, one or more blanks must
precede and follow the operation code.

The operand of the EXEC card in figure 9-1 names a *cataloged
procedure* (PROC=COBUC). A catalogued procedure is a list of frequently used job-control cards that is stored in a library on disk so
that instead of recoding, repunching, and rereading these cards every
time they are required, they are retrieved from the disk library when
referred to by an EXEC card. Some procedures cause only one program to be executed, but others cause several programs to be executed in sequence. In figure 9-1, the procedure is named COBUC

and it causes just the COBOL compiler to be executed. With few exceptions, the COBUC procedure is standard for all OS systems. Within the catalogued job-control statements for COBUC is an EXEC card that assigns the name COB to the compile step.

The DD card   The third card in the job-control deck in figure 9-1 is a *DD card*, which stands for Data Definition. Each DD card gives information about one input or output file. Because the compiler is able to read data from any input device, a DD card must be used in every compile step to indicate the location of the COBOL source program.

The characters in the name field of the card form the *ddname* (pronounced dee-dee-name). In this case, the name is COB.SYSIN, which is made up of the stepname of the compile step (COB) and the file identification name required by the compiler (SYSIN). When two names are combined like this, it's called a *concatenation* and the names are separated by a period. Later in this chapter, you'll see concatenations used to specify other parts of job-control statements.

In any event, the ddname COB.SYSIN refers to the input file that contains the source program. Then, the operand is the asterisk (*). This operand indicates that the input file is a card deck that immediately follows the DD card.

The /* card   The last card of the compile job is the standard OS *end-of-data card*. It has a slash in column 1 and an asterisk in column 2. In conversation, it is usually called the *slash-asterisk card*, and it's used to indicate the end of all types of card input files.

Compiling and Testing a Program Using OS

Figure 9-2 shows typical OS job-control cards for compiling and testing a COBOL program. Here, the procedure name is COBUCG, which refers to a procedure that compiles an object program, loads it, and executes it (sometimes called a compile, load, and go, or just compile and go). The procedure consists of two steps: one named COB (for compiling) and the other named GO (for executing).

The first step of the procedure compiles the object program and stores it on disk. Like the compile-only procedure, a DD card is required to identify the input file that contains the source program. Once again, the ddname is COB.SYSIN and the asterisk operand indicates that the source deck immediately follows the DD card.

The second step of the COBUCG procedure, which is assigned the stepname GO by the control statements for the procedure, combines the loading of the object program into storage and the actual test execution of the COBOL program. In this step, the *loader pro-*

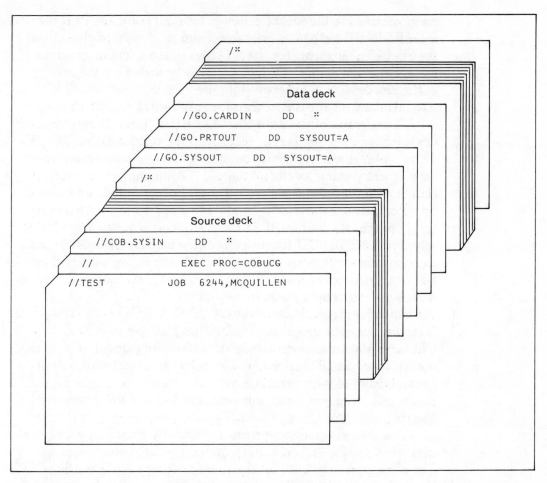

Figure 9-2   A job deck for a COBOL compilation and test run

gram, an OS system program, reads the object program from the
disk area where it was stored by the compiler, places it in storage,
and then branches directly to its first instruction. Once this branch is
made, the COBOL program is in execution.

After the end-of-data card for the source program, these DD
cards describe the output files for the load-and-execute (go) step:

```
//GO.SYSOUT     DD    SYSOUT=A
//GO.PRTOUT     DD    SYSOUT=A
//GO.CARDIN     DD    ::
```

Because the first card in this group, the GO.SYSOUT card, has a
special purpose, I'll come back to it. The other two cards define the
printer output file and the card input file used in the COBOL program. Here again, the ddnames are a concatenation of the stepname
(GO) and the file identification used in the COBOL program. For

the print file, the file identification is PRTOUT; for the card file, it is CARDIN. These names are taken from the system names coded in the SELECT statements for the I/O files in the COBOL program itself. For example, GO.ORDLST would be coded for the printer file in the reorder-listing program in figure 2-24 because the SELECT statement assigns the file to the system name UT-S-ORDLST.

The operand of the print-file DD card is coded in the standard OS form for directing output records to the printer: SYSOUT=A. This means "direct the output records to the system output device (usually the printer) as class A output." Although other output classes exist, you can use class A for all printer output unless told to do otherwise.

Like the DD card for the source program input in the compile step, the CARDIN DD statement uses the asterisk operand to indicate that the input cards for the CARDIN file immediately follow the DD card. Also according to standard practice, the end of the input deck is indicated by a slash-asterisk card.

Now, let me get back to the GO.SYSOUT DD card. This card is required if your program uses DISPLAY statements. Since DISPLAY statement output should be standard printed output, the operand for this DD statement is SYSOUT=A (standard output). Because most of your programs will use one or more DISPLAY statements, your job decks will normally include a DD statement like this.

You should realize that there are actually two printer output files when DISPLAY and WRITE statements are used in a program. The ddname for the DISPLAY statement output is always SYSOUT; the ddname for the WRITE statement output is taken from the system name in the SELECT statement for the file. As your program is executed, the separate print files are spooled to disk before printing. Later on, the files are printed independently. You should now have a better understanding of how DISPLAY and WRITE output are separated by the OS operating system.

One final point to note in figure 9-2 is the sequence of the job-control cards. Within each job step, the card-file DD statement and the data cards are usually last. The order of the other DD statements isn't important, but they usually come before the card file.

Summary

Although this has been a brief introduction to OS job-control language, the job setups shown in figures 9-1 and 9-2 should help you to compile and test your first programs on a System/360-370. In general, a compile-only setup (figure 9-1) is used until all diagnostics have been corrected. Then, a compile-and-go setup (figure 9-2) is used for a series of test runs. Each time an error is debugged, the source deck is changed, and the program is recompiled and tested again.

Terminology

job-control language

JCL

JOB card

jobname

job

operation code

operand

EXEC card

job step

stepname

cataloged procedure

DD card

ddname

concatenation

end-of-data card

slash-asterisk card

loader program

Objectives

1. Make up OS job decks for compiling or compiling and testing a COBOL program requiring card input and printer output.

Problems

1. Code the JCL required to compile and test the investment-listing program in figure 2-27.

Solutions

1. Acceptable code follows:

```
//SREINV     JOB  99-805,EHLERS
//           EXEC PROC=COBUCG
//COB.SYSIN  DD   *
       (Source deck)
//GO.SYSOUT  DD   SYSOUT=A
//GO.INVLST  DD   SYSOUT=A
//GO.BFCRDS  DD   *
       (Data deck)
/*
```

Did you use the correct ddnames in your DD cards for the GO step? Is your accounting information operand in the JOB card coded to meet the specifications of your system?

TOPIC 2   OS Job-Control Statements

Topic 1 presented some basic forms of OS JCL statements so you could compile and test card and printer programs. Specifically, you were introduced to the JOB statement, the EXEC statement, the DD statement, and the end-of-data (/*) statement. Also, you were introduced to two of the basic COBOL procedures, COBUC and COBUCG.

This topic builds on that base of knowledge by giving expanded explanations of the JOB, EXEC, and DD statements. In addition, the COBOL procedures COBUC and COBUCG will be discussed in detail. From this information, you should be able to better understand the JCL used in topic 1.

The JOB statement

Figure 9-3 illustrates the format of the JOB statement and presents the valid formats for its operands. In addition to the accounting information and programmer name operands that were presented in topic 1, the JOB statement has four optional operands. Each of these optional operands is normally assigned a default value when the OS system is generated. As a result, they should be coded only when you want to specify some value other than the default value.

Before getting into the optional operands, consider the first operand in figure 9-3—accounting information. As explained in topic 1, it can consist of more than one item of information separated by commas and enclosed in parentheses. If only account number is

```
Statement format:

//jobname        JOB   (account-number,additional-accounting-information),
                       programmer-name,
                       MSGLEVEL=(x,y),
                       CLASS=job-class,
                       PRTY=nn,
                       REGION=nnnK

Examples:

//SABINVST       JOB   (1766,2),BATES,MSGLEVEL=(1,0)

//TOHPAY         JOB   (1812,2),SYSPROG,CLASS=X,PRTY=10

//MMAMULTI       JOB   (56,8),'MM&A'

//JSEJOB         JOB   048-9038,J.S.ENGLEBERG,CLASS=E,REGION=200K
```

Figure 9-3   The JOB statement

used, however, the parentheses are omitted and the account number
is followed by one comma and the next operand.

Remember also from topic 1 that the programmer name, the
second required operand, can be up to 20 characters. If it contains
any characters other than letters, numbers, or periods, it must be
enclosed in apostrophes as in example 3 of figure 9-3.

MSGLEVEL   The first of the optional operands is the MSGLEVEL
operand. It controls the appearance of the JCL statements and
system allocation messages in the printed output of the system. If the
first entry in parentheses is coded as 1, all the job control-statements
used by the job will appear in the output; if the first entry is coded
as 0, only the JOB statement will appear. Likewise, if the second
entry is 1, the system allocation messages will appear, while if it's 0,
they won't be printed. (In figure 4-6, the allocation messages begin
with IEF236I and IEF237I.) If MSGLEVEL=(1,1), both the job-
control and allocation messages will be printed.

You can determine the default setting for MSGLEVEL on your
system by running a job without this operand and examining the
first page of output from your test runs. If the system allocation
messages aren't printed there, you don't have to worry about them
since they won't mean anything to you at this point. In contrast, a

listing of all the JCL statements for a job is useful for two reasons. First, it provides printed documentation of each of your test runs. And second, it can be valuable when debugging JCL and program errors. So if printing the JCL statements isn't the default value on your system, I recommend you add MSGLEVEL=(1,0) to all your JOB statements.

CLASS The CLASS operand specifies the job class that determines which partition (OS/MFT and OS/VS1) or region (OS/MVT and OS/VS2) the job runs in. This in turn determines a job's priority relative to other jobs waiting to be executed. The valid codes for job class include the letters A to Z and digits 0 to 9, but most OS installations use only a small subset, typically letters A to E or F.

If the CLASS operand is omitted from the JOB card, the job class is set to the default value, A. Job class A is normally used for the most common type of job run in an installation. If, in your installation, your test jobs can run as class A, you can omit this operand from your JOB statement. Otherwise, you must find out the proper class and code the CLASS operand accordingly.

PRTY The PRTY operand is used to specify a job priority within job class. The valid codes are decimal digits 0-13. While the PRTY operand can be used to cause a job to be executed before others of equal class, it is usually omitted so that all the jobs of a given class execute in the sequence in which they were submitted to the system. If you should ever want to code PRTY, check your installation's standards first. In many cases, this operand has been disabled; that is, it's not available for a programmer to use.

REGION In MVT and VS2 systems, the JOB statement may also request a region size. Normally the REGION operand is coded only for programs that require a region larger than the default value that was specified for each job class when the system was generated. If it is required, it is coded as a multiple of 2K bytes (1024 times 2). A typical example is REGION=256K.

The EXEC statement

The format of the EXEC statement and its six possible operands are illustrated in figure 9-4. Here, the first operand is required, but the others are optional.

The first operand specifies either a procedure name or a program name. In the examples in topic 1, procedure names are used, which means that a series of job-control statements representing that procedure are *invoked* from a library of procedures. (The term

```
Statement format:


//stepname    EXEC ⎧ PROC=procedure-name, ⎫
                   ⎨ procedure-name,       ⎬
                   ⎩ PGM=program-name,     ⎭

              PARM='values',

              COND=((code,operator,stepname),...),

              ACCT=(accounting-information),

              TIME=(minutes,seconds),

              REGION=nnnK
```

```
Examples:


//            EXEC PROC=COBUC,PARM.COB='XREF,NOSTATE,NOFLOW'

//MMAREORD    EXEC COBUCG

//STEP2       EXEC PGM=TAPPRT,COND=(4,LT,STEPA)
```

Figure 9-4 The EXEC statement

invoke means to call upon or summon. It is used here so you will be familiar with it when you see it in IBM manuals.)

If you check the format in figure 9-4, you'll see that a procedure can be specified in one of two ways: either by PROC= followed by the procedure name or by the procedure name without any code preceding it. These methods are illustrated in the first two examples of figure 9-4. In this book, you will always see procedure names preceded by PROC= in the EXEC statement, but you should remember that either form invokes a procedure. Thus,

```
//        EXEC PROC=COBUC
```

and

```
//        EXEC COBUC
```

are equivalent.

The other option in the first EXEC operand is to use PGM= followed by the name of the program to be executed. For instance, the COBUC procedure includes an EXEC statement with this operand:

```
PGM=IKFCBL00
```

Parameter	Meaning
SOURCE NOSOURCE	Print the source listing.
CLIST NOCLIST	Print a condensed Procedure Division map. This option can't be used when PMAP is used.
DMAP NODMAP	Print a Data Division map.
PMAP NOPMAP	Print a complete Procedure Division map. This option can't be used when CLIST is used.
VERB NOVERB	Print procedure names and verb names on the Procedure Division map. This has meaning when CLIST or PMAP is in effect.
LOAD NOLOAD	Store the object program on a direct-access device or tape so it can be used as input to the loader or linkage-editor program.
DECK NODECK	Punch an object deck.
SEQ NOSEQ	Check the sequence of the source statements. If an out-of-sequence statement is detected, print a diagnostic message.
LINECNT = nn	Specifies the number of lines to be printed on each source listing page (from 01 to 99). If omitted, 60 is assumed.
FLAGW FLAGE	FLAGW means that all diagnostic messages are to be printed on the diagnostic listing. FLAGE means warning diagnostics are not to be listed.
SUPMAP NOSUPMAP	Do not print the Procedure Division map or condensed Procedure Division map (suppress it) if an E-level error is detected during compilation.
QUOTE APOST	Indicates that quotation marks ('') or the apostrophe (') are to be used in setting off non-numeric literals.
XREF NOXREF	Print a cross-reference listing. Arrange the items in order of their occurrence in the program.
SXREF NOSXREF	Print a sorted cross-reference listing; that is, arrange the items in the listing in alphabetical order.

Figure 9-5   OS COBOL compilation parameters (part 1 of 2)

This indicates that the program named IKFCBL00 (a COBOL compiler) is to be executed. Within each procedure, there must be at least one EXEC card that specifies a program name.

Although most of the jobs you run for this course will require EXEC statements that name one of the COBOL procedures, there

Parameter	Meaning
STATE NOSTATE	Save the statement number of the last statement executed. Used with the debug feature (not covered in this text).
FLOW NOFLOW	Save the last 50 paragraph names entered in the COBOL program. Used with the debug feature (not covered in this text).
TRUNC NOTRUNC	Only has meaning in a MOVE or arithmetic statement in which the receiving field has COMP usage. TRUNC means the compiler will generate code to cut off digits in the sending or intermediate result field (or truncate the field) to make it conform to the PICTURE of the COMP receiving field.
ZWB NOZWB	Remove the sign from a numeric field with DISPLAY usage if it's compared to an alphanumeric field.

Figure 9-5 OS COBOL compilation parameters (part 2 of 2)

will be cases in which you will use the PGM= form. Most likely, the program named will be one of the OS utility programs, although it could be a program written by you or another programmer. In either case, the program must have been stored in some type of program library on disk.

PARM   There are many options associated with an OS COBOL compiler. For instance, much of the compiler output, such as object decks and cross-reference listings, is optional. In addition, some of the features of the compiler, such as the debug features, are optional.

Figure 9-5 is a partial list of the OS options related to COBOL compilations. These options can be controlled by using the PARM (parameter) operand in an EXEC statement. For example, the statement

```
//      EXEC PROC=COBUCG,PARM.COB='XREF,LINECNT=60'
```

will cause a cross-reference listing to be printed by the compiler, and it will cause a maximum of 60 lines to be printed on each page of the compiler output. Because the COBUCG procedure consists of two job steps, COB (the stepname of the first job step) follows PARM and one period to indicate that the options apply only to the compilation step.

Before a programmer can start using the PARM operand to control options, however, he must be aware that there are two previous

```
*STATISTICS*    SOURCE RECORDS =   202      DATA DIVISION STATEMENTS =    67      PROCEDURE DIVISION STATEMENTS =    45
*OPTIONS IN EFFECT*        SIZE =  116000  BUF =   18000  LINECNT = 54  SPACE1, FLAGW,    SEQ,    SOURCE
*OPTIONS IN EFFECT*        DMAP, NOPMAP,    CLIST,   SUPMAP, NOXREF,   SXREF,   LOAD, NODECK, APOST, NOTRUNC, NOFLOW
*OPTIONS IN EFFECT*        NOTERM, NONUM,    BATCH, NONAME, COMPILE=01, NOSTATE, NOLIB,    VERB,    ZWB, SYST
```

Figure 9-6   OS option listing (compiler output)

levels at which options can be set. First, when a system is generated, the options of a system are given default values. In figure 9-5, the underlined options are the default values that are recommended by IBM. In actual practice, however, the default values will be adjusted to meet the requirements of a given installation. If none of the options are changed by the PARM operand for a program, the default values will be in effect during the execution of the program.

The second level at which options can be set is within a procedure. In other words, when a procedure is invoked, the EXEC card within the procedure may have its own PARM operand to modify some of the default parameters. The options set by this PARM card are called *procedure options.*

Now back to you, the programmer. Whenever you code the PARM operand in an EXEC statement, your PARMs replace the ones in the procedure you invoke. So if you want one or more of the procedure options to remain in effect, you must code them in your PARMs; otherwise, they will revert to their default values. For example, suppose that you want to use the PARM operand to set certain options when you invoke the COBUCG procedure. Suppose, too, that one of the COBUCG procedure options is LOAD but the default value of your system is NOLOAD. You must then code LOAD along with your other PARMs or else your object program won't be saved for loading in the GO step. You will see this in more detail later on.

To find out what the default values of your system are, you can run a program with this EXEC card:

```
//  EXEC  PROC=COBUCG,PARM.COB=' '
```

Because the PARM operand is given, the procedure options will be overridden. But since there aren't any PARMs listed between the two quotation marks, the default values will be the only ones printed on the listing of output options that you get with your compiler output. An example of the option listing is given in figure 9-6. By studying this listing, you will know for sure what the default values are on your system. Notice that there are many more options than are given in figure 9-5.

To find out what the procedure options are for one of the procedures you are using, you can study the procedure JCL given on the

JCL and message listing that is always the first page of your OS output. In figure 4-6, for example, the lines beginning with XX are JCL statements taken from the procedure. Thus, the PARM card for the COB step (the seventh line of figure 4-6) specifies only the LOAD option:

```
XXCOB    EXEC   PGM=IKFCBL00,PARM='LOAD'
```

By combining your knowledge of the procedure options with your knowledge of the default values, you will be able to figure out when you need to use PARMs.

In a later book in this series, you will learn how to use some of the compiler output that is helpful in debugging, such as the condensed Procedure Division map and the Data Division map. For now, however, you should only require the source listing, a cross-reference or sorted cross-reference listing, and the diagnostic listing with all warning messages printed. As a result, you can use PARMs to turn off any of the other options if you are getting them either by default or by procedure options. Remember, however, that the LOAD option must be on in a compile-and-go procedure. And be aware that the SUPMAP option has no meaning unless the CLIST or PMAP option is on. So oftentimes there is no reason to turn SUPMAP on.

Three options that you should definitely turn off if they happen to be default values on your system are the STATE, FLOW, and TRUNC options. The STATE and FLOW options are designed to aid the programmer when debugging, but you won't learn how to use them in this book. If these options are on, they will seriously impair the efficiency of your object program.

TRUNC applies only when the receiving field of a MOVE or arithmetic statement is a COMP field. In a MOVE statement, the compiler will cut off digits in the sending field (or *truncate* the field) to make it conform to the PICTURE of the receiving field. In an arithmetic statement, the final intermediate result field will be truncated before its value is placed in a COMP receiving field. At first glance, this might seem like a fairly useful function. However, because of the way COMP fields are stored internally, a COMP field can have a value containing more digits than are given in its PICTURE. For example, a COMP field with a PICTURE of 9(2) can have a value of up to 32,767. In practice, then, TRUNC is confusing and inefficient, and it can result in pages of diagnostics. So although TRUNC is the recommended value under the ANSI standards, you should always make sure this option is set to NOTRUNC.

One other option that can cause problems is the ZWB option. If it is on, the compiler will remove the sign from a numeric field with DISPLAY usage before comparing it with an alphanumeric field.

Thus, a −5 could be found to be equal to a +5. Rather than code NOZWB, however, you should always leave this option at its default value on your system. If you start switching it around, you may run into problems as you work with programs that have already been tested and put into production in accordance with the default value. In other words, ZWB is one option that should be set the same for every program in an installation, and the easiest way to do this is to leave the option at the installation's default value.

COND   To avoid unnecessary use of computing time, the COND (condition) operand can be coded in an EXEC statement to cause the operating system to determine whether a job step should be executed. At the normal completion of a job step (if a step terminates abnormally, the succeeding steps are usually bypassed anyway), a processing program can pass a *return code* to the operating system. It is always a numeric value in the range 0 to 4095. This return code plus the return codes of other job steps can then be tested by the operating system to determine if any of the conditions specified in the COND operand are met. If so, the job step is bypassed.

The format of the COND operand is this:

```
COND=((code,operator,stepname),(code,operator,stepname),...)
```

Each of the (code,operator,stepname) groups refers to one previous step whose return code is to be tested. The stepname suboperand identifies the step to be tested, the operator specifies one of the six logical relationships given below, and the code specifies a value from 0 to 4095 against which the return code set by the earlier step is to be tested. If any of the conditions coded in this way are met (from one to eight tests can be specified), the step is bypassed.

The allowable operators for the COND operand are as follows:

Operator	Meaning
GT	Greater than
GE	Greater than or equal to
EQ	Equal
NE	Not equal
LE	Less than or equal to
LT	Less than

As a result,

```
COND=(12,LT,STEP1)
```

is interpreted like this: "If 12 is less than the completion code returned by STEP1, bypass this step." Similarly, the statement

```
//STEP4 EXEC PGM=PROG4,COND=((12,GT,STEP1),(8,LE,STEP2))
```

is interpreted like this: "If 12 is greater than the return code of
STEP1, or 8 is less than or equal to the return code of STEP2,
bypass STEP4."

While the COND operand is not widely used by programmers,
you will see it in many of the cataloged procedures. For instance, the
COBUCG procedure conditions the execution of the load-and-
execute step based on the return code set by the compilation step.
The value of the return code is determined by the seriousness of the
errors in the source program that is compiled. The EXEC statement
for the load-and-execute step then tests this return code. If it's
greater than a specific value, such as 4, the load-and-execute step
is bypassed.

Although you probably won't often need to pass completion
codes from one program to another, you may be interested to know
how it's done. In the COBOL program, the programmer gives the
completion code in the MOVE statement using the reserved word
RETURN-CODE. Thus, the statement

```
MOVE 16 TO RETURN-CODE
```

will pass a completion code of 16 back to the operating system. In
conventional usage, a code of zero indicates normal termination of a
program, and other codes are generally specified in multiples of four
to a maximum value of 4095.

ACCT, TIME, and REGION   Three more optional operands for the
EXEC statement are shown in figure 9-4: ACCT, additional accounting information; TIME, a specific CPU time limit for the job step;
and REGION, a request for a special REGION size for the step
(OS/MVT and OS/VS2 only). These operands are included in the
illustration so you will know what they are if you see them.
However, they are seldom used and, for most programs, they can be
ignored.

The DD statement

Every time a program is executed, the JCL must include a DD statement for each of the files used by the program. In topic 1, you were
introduced to the formats of the DD statement for card and printer
files. The following are typical examples:

```
//GO.CARDFLE   DD *

//GO.PRINTFLE DD SYSOUT=A
```

```
Statement format:

//ddname        DD    DSNAME=data-set-name,

                      UNIT=address or type or group,

                      VOLUME=SER=serial-number,

                      LABEL=(sequence-number,code),

                      DISP=(status,normal-action,abnormal-action),

                      DCB=(...),

                      SPACE=(units,(quantity,increment),RLSE,CONTIG)

Examples:

//GO.SYSIN      DD    *

//GO.SYSPRINT   DD    SYSOUT=A

//TAPEOUT       DD    DSNAME=ACCTFILE,UNIT=TAPE,DISP=(NEW,CATLG),
//                    DCB=BLKSIZE=1600

//TAPEIN        DD    DSNAME=TABLE,UNIT=TAPE,VOLUME=SER=004921,DISP=(OLD,KEEP)

//DSKOUT        DD    DSNAME=ACCTTAB,UNIT=2314,VOLUME=SER=114560,
//                    DISP=(NEW,CATLG,DELETE),SPACE=(CYL,(5,1)),
//                    DCB=BLKSIZE=1780
```

Figure 9-7   The DD statement

For tape and disk files, you must code more elaborate DD statements using the format and operands illustrated in figure 9-7. As you will see, all of the operands shown are optional under one condition or another.

Before explaining the DD operands, though, let me define some terms that must be used in any discussion of OS disk and tape files. First, in OS terminology, files are called *data sets*. Thus, the terms file and data set are used interchangeably in the remainder of this topic.

Second, data sets can be either permanent or temporary. A *permanent data set* is usually a special system file, a program library, a master data file, in short, any file that is used by multiple jobs in the course of a day, week, or some other period. The qualifying point is that the file continues to exist from one job to another.

In contrast, a *temporary data set* exists only within the boundaries of a single job. It is usually created by one job step, then used in one or more following steps, and finally deleted at the end of the job. A typical example of a temporary data set is the object module created by the COBOL compiler when the COBUCG procedure is used. This data set is created in the compilation step and is then passed to the load-and-execute step. After the test step is executed, this temporary data set is deleted.

The third concept I want to introduce is the OS *data set catalog facility*. Information concerning the status and location of permanent data sets within the system can be stored in a special system file called the *data set catalog*. The basic purpose of this facility is to make it as easy as possible to refer to permanent sets and to avoid possible JCL errors. When information about a data set is stored in the data set catalog, the data set is said to be *cataloged*. Data sets are cataloged or uncataloged (that is, the entry for the data set is added to or deleted from the catalog file) by one of the DD statement operands, the disposition (DISP) operand.

DSNAME   The DSNAME operand (often abbreviated DSN) specifies the *data set name* or *label* of an existing data set or the label to be assigned to a data set that is being created. It can be coded in any of three forms: (1) as a permanent name, (2) as a temporary name, or (3) as a backward reference. It can also be omitted, thus causing the OS supervisor to create and assign a temporary name.

The permanent name form is used for permanent files. It can be from one through eight alphabetic or numeric characters but must start with a letter. A typical example is DSNAME=INVMSTR, which might represent an inventory master file. If a data set is to be cataloged, it must be assigned a permanent name.

A temporary data set is indicated by using the temporary name form. It follows the same name formation rule as the permanent name, with the exception that it must be preceded by two ampersands (&) as follows:

```
DSNAME=&&TEMPFILE
```

Whenever a data set is assigned a temporary name, it is deleted at the end of the job.

The backward reference form is used to refer to a data set that was first defined in a previous job step. It has this form:

```
DSNAME=*.stepname.ddname
```

Here, stepname must be coded with the name of the job step in which the data set was first defined, and ddname must be coded with the ddname used for the first definition. The main feature of this form is that you don't have to know the actual data set name of the file.

To illustrate, suppose that you wanted to test a disk-to-printer program but first needed to create a test file. You could make the test run a two-step job in which the first step executes a card-to-disk program to create the test file and the second step tests the disk-to-printer program. If the stepname in the EXEC card for the card-to-disk step was CRDDISK and the ddname of the disk file it created was DSKOUT, you could use this backward reference in the DD statement for the disk file in the disk-to-printer step:

```
DSNAME=*.CRDDISK.DSKOUT
```

Thus, the appropriate temporary file is referred to even though you don't know its name.

When the backward reference form is used to refer to a data set that was first defined by part of a cataloged procedure, it must be in a slightly expanded form:

```
DSNAME=*.stepname.procstepname.ddname
```

In this form, stepname refers to the stepname coded on the EXEC card that invokes the procedure, and procstepname refers to the name of the step within the procedure. You'll see backward references used in the JCL examples in topic 3.

UNIT   The UNIT operand specifies the type of I/O device that is used for the file. It can have one of three forms: (1) a physical address, (2) a device-type code, or (3) a group specification.

The physical address form is always a three-digit number in hexadecimal notation. (Hexadecimal, or hex, notation is commonly used to represent the contents of System/360-370 storage.) If a physical address is used, it must be a valid device address for one of the I/O devices attached to the system. A typical example would be 282, which is a common address for a tape drive. This type of unit specification means that the file is to be found on that specific device.

The physical address form of unit specification is almost never used, however. A device-type code specification is much more common because OS provides automatic assignment of I/O devices. If, for example, the UNIT operand were coded with a device code of 2400, OS could select any available 2400 tape drive for mounting the tape rather than wait for drive 282 to be available. Since you will use this operand mostly for tape or disk files, you need to know the tape or disk device codes for your system in order to code the operand properly. If you're using a System/360, the tape drive code will probably be 2400, 2400-3, or 2400-4, and the disk drive code will be 2314. For System/370, it will probably be 3400 for tapes and 3330 for disk.

A group specification, such as UNIT=TAPE or UNIT=SYSDA, is an even more general form of the unit operand and is valid on most systems. It is usually defined during system generation. Then, you don't have to specify an individual device code. When this type of UNIT operand is coded, a data set can be assigned to any of the tape or disk devices on a system. On many System/370s, for example, both 3330 and 2314 disk devices are present. If you requested space for a temporary file with UNIT=3330 but no space was available, the program would have to wait. If you coded UNIT=SYSDA, however, the program would be run if space were available on either a 2314 or a 3330 disk. Because of this flexibility, you should find out the valid group specifications for your own system and use them as the normal UNIT code.

VOLUME   The VOLUME operand (usually abbreviated VOL) should be coded whenever you want to refer to a specific tape reel or disk pack. This is most commonly required when you are retrieving a permanent data set. (If the data set has been cataloged, it's not necessary to specify the volume operand because this information has already been recorded in the catalog file.) Although there are several forms of this operand, you will probably always use this one:

```
VOLUME=SER=XXXXXX
```

The entry *xxxxxx* must be coded with the six-character volume serial number of the disk pack or tape reel. For instance,

```
UNIT=3330,VOL=SER=TSTPAK
```

indicates that the file being described is to be found or stored in a 3330 disk pack with a serial number of TSTPAK.

LABEL   The LABEL operand is used to tell the OS system which type of label processing is to be performed for the file defined by the DD statement. You will rarely see it coded on a DD statement, however, because standard labels are used for most tape and disk files in OS installations, and standard label processing is the default value for this operand.

In testing tape programs, though, it is sometimes useful to have multiple files on one reel of tape. To refer to the second, third, fourth, or some other file on a tape volume, you must use the sequence number parameter of the label operand. As you can see in figure 9-7, the label operand has this format:

```
LABEL=(sequence-number,code)
```

Here, the sequence-number entry specifies the position of the file on the tape reel, and the code indicates the type of label processing to be performed. Since SL, for Standard Labels, is the default option for the label-processing code, the code entry is normally omitted. To refer to the third file on a standard label tape, then, you would code

```
LABEL=3
```

Notice that the parentheses can be omitted since only the sequence number is required. Otherwise,

```
LABEL=(3,SL)
```

accomplishes the same thing.

DISP   The disposition operand, DISP, tells OS what the current status of the file is, what to do with the file upon successful completion of the job step, and what action to take if the job step terminates abnormally. The DISP operand is coded like this:

```
DISP=(status,normal-action,abnormal-action)
```

If an action entry is omitted, the data set will remain in the status it had before the job was executed. Figure 9-8 summarizes the valid parameters for the DISP operand.

   The DISP operand is usually coded in regular combinations. For instance, to retrieve an existing data set and maintain its previous cataloged or uncataloged status, you would code

```
DISP=(OLD,KEEP)
```

When creating a new permanent data set, you might want to catalog it if the step proceeds normally but delete it if the step fails:

```
DISP=(NEW,CATLG,DELETE)
```

In a program test, you might create a temporary data set in one step and pass it to a later step. The DISP operand in the first step would be

```
DISP=(NEW,PASS,DELETE)
```

and in the later step, it would be

```
DISP=(OLD,DELETE)
```

You'll see the DISP operand illustrated in these and other patterns in the JCL examples in this chapter.

   In general, you won't be using the CATLG parameter when testing your programs. This parameter causes the name of the file just

```
                          Status Parameter

  Code      Meaning
  OLD       The data set exists and may or may not be cataloged.
  NEW       The data set is to be created.
  SHR       The data set exists and can be shared with other programs during
            processing.
  MOD       The data set exists and records are going to be added on to the end of
            the data set.

                     Termination-Action Parameter

  Code      Meaning
  KEEP      The data set is saved, and if already cataloged, it remains so.
  DELETE    The data set is not saved, and if cataloged, it is deleted from the
            catalog.
  CATLG     The data set is saved and cataloged (if not already cataloged).
  UNCATLG   The data set is saved, but it is deleted from the catalog.
  PASS      The data set is passed to succeeding job steps and retains its previous
            status. This is valid only for normal termination action.
```

Figure 9-8   Summary of valid parameters for the DISP operand of the DD statement

created to be stored in the systems catalog with other information about the file such as the UNIT and VOLUME information. Thereafter, the file can be found by giving the data set name only in the DD statement. Because most of the files you use in testing will be stored for only a short time, you shouldn't clutter the systems catalog with information about these test files. As a result, the CATLG parameter is used primarily by the operations department in conjunction with production (tested) programs.

When a file isn't cataloged, you must code the UNIT and VOLUME parameters in the DD statement for the file. And this is the way you will normally access files when testing your programs. If, for example, a file is created with these parameters:

```
DSNAME=TESTMST,UNIT=SYSDA,VOL=SER=TESTPK,DISP=(NEW,KEEP,DELETE)
```

you can access it later with these parameters:

```
DSNAME=TESTMST,UNIT=SYSDA,VOL=SER=TESTPK,DISP=(OLD,KEEP)
```

Here, the system first finds the right disk volume; then, it finds the file's location by searching the disk labels in the disk's VTOC. Note that you won't be able to create two files with the same name on the same volume, so you must be careful to delete a file before trying to recreate it with the same name.

DCB   When a COBOL program is compiled under OS, a *data control block* (DCB) is created for each file processed based on information taken from the SELECT and FD statements for the file. Each DCB is a table in storage that is used by various routines for controlling I/O operations. To increase its flexibility, OS allows certain data set information to be supplied at execution time by the DCB operand in the DD statement rather than by the COBOL program itself. This makes it possible for a file to exist in various forms and still be processed by the same programs.

One parameter often supplied by the DCB operand is block size. This can be done if the FD statement for a file states

```
BLOCK CONTAINS 0 RECORDS
```

Then, the block size to be used is specified in the DD statement as follows:

```
DCB=BLKSIZE=800
```

Here, the block contains 800 bytes. Thus, if the record size is 80 bytes, the block contains 10 records. This allows the block size of a file to be changed without recompiling all the programs that process this file. And it also allows you to write a sequential program without knowing what I/O device will be used to run it (you code BLOCK CONTAINS 0 RECORDS for all the files). Then, at execution time, you can use whatever device is available and code the BLKSIZE parameter to make the best use of the space on that device.

While BLKSIZE is the most common DCB parameter to be used in the DD statement, it isn't the only one. For instance, when using utility programs (programs supplied with an operating system to perform certain tasks, such as printing a disk file), you are often required to supply the Record Form (RECFM) and the Logical Record Length (LRECL), as well as the block size in the DCB parameter for a file. Thus, one utility program can be used for many different types of files. For example, this DCB parameter specifies a sequential file with Fixed-length Blocks of records (FB), a record length of 80 bytes, and a block size of 400 bytes:

```
DCB=(RECFM=FB,LRECL=80,BLKSIZE=400)
```

Note that when multiple entries are used in the DCB operand, they are separated by commas and the entire list is enclosed in parentheses.

SPACE   The SPACE operand is used to request direct-access space for a new file:

```
SPACE=(units,(quantity,increment))
```

The units entry can specify cylinders (CYL), tracks (TRK), or blocks specified as a decimal number of bytes. (If the block-size form is used, OS will calculate the disk space required to hold the blocks.) The quantity entry then specifies how many of these units are to be reserved as the initial disk space area, or *primary allocation*, for the file. If you're not sure that the primary allocation will be enough to hold all the records or if you want to allow more space for file increases at some later time, you can code the increment entry. It indicates the number of units of disk space that OS will add to the file as a *secondary allocation* each time the file area is filled up. Up to 15 secondary allocations can be added. The size of the increment quantity is usually something like 5 to 20 percent of the primary allocation.

Suppose, for example, you wanted to create a sequential file on a 3330 and expected about 500 4250-byte blocks. The SPACE operand of the DD statement for the file could be coded in several ways:

```
SPACE=(CYL,13)
SPACE=(TRK,260)
SPACE=(4250,500)
```

Each of these SPACE operands reserves about the same amount of space for the file. If you wanted to include the increment entry for secondary allocations, these same SPACE operands would be coded like this:

```
SPACE=(CYL,(13,1))
SPACE=(TRK,(260,20))
SPACE=(4250,(500,38))
```

Each of these increment entries specifies a secondary allocation of about one cylinder.

Following the quantity and increment entries, the SPACE operand can include either or both of two positional entries:

```
SPACE=(units,(quantity,increment),RLSE,CONTIG)
```

The first one, RLSE, causes any unused portion of the initial allocation for a new file to be released. This means, for example, that if
the initial allocation for a file was ten cylinders but the loaded
records filled only eight cylinders, the remaining two cylinders
would be released so that they would be available for some
other file.

The CONTIG entry requests that the space allocated for a new
file be a continuous disk area. For a three-cylinder file, for instance,
this means that instead of assigning one available cylinder in one
area of the disk, another cylinder in some other area, and the third
in still another area, an area of three adjacent cylinders is assigned.

Continuation cards

If you look at the examples of DD statements in figure 9-7, you will
see that some of the statements are too long for a single JCL card. In
this case, continuation cards can be used. Because the use of continuation cards is one of the major sources of errors when coding
JCL, you should give extra attention to this explanation.

To use a continuation card, you interrupt the statement at the
end of a complete operand or parameter, including the comma that
follows it. The continuation card must then have slashes in columns
1 and 2, and the statement must continue starting anywhere between
column 4 and column 16. In no case can a job-control statement go
beyond column 71 of a JCL card.

If you omit the comma at the end of a line of a statement that is
going to be continued, the operating system will assume that the
statement is completed and an error will result. Similarly, if you
accidentally put a space between two operands in a line of a statement that is to be continued, the operating system will assume that
the statement ends as soon as it encounters the space unless the last
character before the space is a comma. As a result, the statement

```
//TAPEOUT    DD    DSNAME=ACCTFILE,  UNIT=TAPE,DISP=(NEW,CATLG),
//                  DCB=BLKSIZE=1600
```

will be treated as a continuation, but the UNIT and DISP operands
will be treated as comments rather than as part of the statement (the
first space in the operand portion of the line ends the line with any
additional coding being treated as comments). On the other hand,
the statement

```
//TAPEOUT    DD    DSNAME=ACCTFILE ,UNIT=TAPE,DISP=(NEW,CATLG),
//                  DCB=BLKSIZE=1600
```

```
Programmer job-control language:

//SALCOMP        JOB   048-9038,LOWE,MSGLEVEL=(1,0)
//               EXEC  PROC=COBUC,PARM.COB='NOLOAD,XREF'
//COB.SYSIN      DD    ::
                 (Source deck)
/::


Cataloged COBUC procedure:

//COB            EXEC  PGM=IKFCBL00,PARM='NOLOAD'
//SYSPRINT       DD    SYSOUT=A
//SYSUT1         DD    DSNAME=&&SYSUT1,UNIT=SYSDA,SPACE=(460,(700,100))
//SYSUT2         DD    DSNAME=&&SYSUT2,UNIT=SYSDA,SPACE=(460,(700,100))
//SYSUT3         DD    DSNAME=&&SYSUT3,UNIT=SYSDA,SPACE=(460,(700,100))
//SYSUT4         DD    DSNAME=&&SYSUT4,UNIT=SYSDA,SPACE=(460,(700,100))


Effective job-control language:

//SALCOMP        JOB   048-9038,LOWE,MSGLEVEL=(1,0)
//COB            EXEC  PGM=IKFCBL00,PARM='NOLOAD,XREF'
//SYSPRINT       DD    SYSOUT=A
//SYSUT1         DD    DSNAME=&&SYSUT1,UNIT=SYSDA,SPACE=(460,(700,100))
//SYSUT2         DD    DSNAME=&&SYSUT2,UNIT=SYSDA,SPACE=(460,(700,100))
//SYSUT3         DD    DSNAME=&&SYSUT3,UNIT=SYSDA,SPACE=(460,(700,100))
//SYSUT4         DD    DSNAME=&&SYSUT4,UNIT=SYSDA,SPACE=(460,(700,100))
//SYSIN          DD    ::
                 (Source deck)
/::
```

Figure 9-9 A typical COBUC (compile only) procedure

will be treated as though it ended after the DSNAME operand. So watch out for inadvertent spaces in your coding. And make sure a comma follows the last operand in a line that is to be continued. These guidelines apply to JOB and EXEC statements as well.

COBOL Procedures

With the background you now have for the JOB, EXEC, and DD statements, you should be able to better understand the two basic procedures presented in topic 1: COBUC and COBUCG.

The COBUC procedure

Figure 9-9 illustrates the COBUC procedure and its use. Here, the procedure name, COBUC, is used in the programmer's EXEC card, so the cataloged procedure is invoked from the procedure library. In this procedure, which is made up of one job step, there is an EXEC card for the COBOL compiler, a DD card for the printed compiler output file, and four DD cards for work files used by the compiler (SYSUT1, SYSUT2, SYSUT3, and SYSUT4). All four work files have temporary names (beginning with two ampersands). They can be assigned to any direct-access device (SYSDA), and they consist of 700 460-byte blocks of storage with 100 block increments if needed.

Because the compiler also requires an input file, referred to as SYSIN, that contains the COBOL source statements, the programmer has supplied a DD statement with the ddname SYSIN. The operand is an asterisk, indicating the file is in deck form immediately following the DD card. Notice that the stepname COB followed by a period is used to indicate that this data set is used in the step named COB. (COB is the stepname given in the EXEC statement in the COBUC procedure.) Since there is only one job step, it isn't really necessary to indicate the stepname on the DD statement, but in procedures with multiple steps, it is.

The bottom portion of figure 9-9 shows the effect of the programmer's JCL on the invoked procedure. Because the programmer's EXEC card has specified the NOLOAD and XREF parameters, these are the parameters for the execution of the COBOL compiler. In other words, the procedure options are replaced by the programmer's parameters. So if the programmer didn't duplicate the NOLOAD parameter of the procedure, the LOAD/NOLOAD option would revert to its default value, probably LOAD. The SYSIN DD card supplied by the programmer has the effect of following the DD statements of the invoked procedure.

The COBUCG procedure

Figure 9-10 illustrates the use of the COBUCG procedure. This two-step procedure consists of a COBOL compilation followed by the execution of the loader program. This loader program combines the COBOL program with required object modules from the OS systems library. The loader program then transfers control to the complete COBOL program so it can be executed.

Because the COBOL object program must be input to the loader program, the compilation requires a data set with the ddname SYSLIN. This data set is given the temporary name LOADSET in the procedure and is passed to the next job step since the DISP operand specifies PASS. Because the COBOL compiler also requires

Programmer job-control language:

```
//MRMTEST      JOB  048-9038,MURACH,MSGLEVEL=(1,0)
//             EXEC COBUCG,PARM.COB='SXREF'
//COB.SYSIN    DD   *
               (Source deck)
/*
//GO.SYSOUT    DD   SYSOUT=A
//GO.PRINTFLE  DD   SYSOUT=A
//GO.CARDFLE   DD   *
               (Data deck)
/*
```

Cataloged COBUCG procedure:

```
//COB          EXEC PGM=IKFCBLOO,REGION=120K
//SYSPRINT     DD   SYSOUT=A
//SYSUT1       DD   DSNAME=&&SYSUT1,UNIT=SYSDA,SPACE=(460,(700,100))
//SYSUT2       DD   DSNAME=&&SYSUT2,UNIT=SYSDA,SPACE=(460,(700,100))
//SYSUT3       DD   DSNAME=&&SYSUT3,UNIT=SYSDA,SPACE=(460,(700,100))
//SYSUT4       DD   DSNAME=&&SYSUT4,UNIT=SYSDA,SPACE=(460,(700,100))
//SYSLIN       DD   DSNAME=&&LOADSET,DISP=(MOD,PASS),UNIT=SYSDA,
//             SPACE=80,(500,100)
//GO           EXEC PGM=LOADER,PARM='MAP,LET',COND=(5,LT,COB),REGION=120K
//SYSLIN       DD   DSNAME=*.COB.SYSLIN,DISP=(OLD,DELETE)
//SYSLOUT      DD   SYSOUT=A
//SYSLIB       DD   DSNAME=SYS1.COBLIB,DISP=SHR
```

Effective job-control language:

```
//MRMTEST      JOB  048-9038,MURACH,MSGLEVEL=(1,0)
//COB          EXEC PGM=IKFCBLOO,PARM='SXREF',REGION=120K
//SYSPRINT     DD   SYSOUT=A
//SYSUT1       DD   DSNAME=&&SYSUT1,UNIT=SYSDA,SPACE=(460,(700,100))
//SYSUT2       DD   DSNAME=&&SYSUT2,UNIT=SYSDA,SPACE=(460,(700,100))
//SYSUT3       DD   DSNAME=&&SYSUT3,UNIT=SYSDA,SPACE=(460,(700,100))
//SYSUT4       DD   DSNAME=&&SYSUT4,UNIT=SYSDA,SPACE=(460,(700,100))
//SYSLIN       DD   DSNAME=&&LOADSET,DISP=(MOD,PASS),UNIT=SYSDA,
//             SPACE=(80,(500,100))
//SYSIN        DD   *
               (Source deck)
/*
//GO           EXEC PGM=LOADER,PARM='MAP,LET',COND=(5,LT,COB),REGION=120K
//SYSLIN       DD   DSNAME=*.COB.SYSLIN,DISP=(OLD,DELETE)
//SYSLOUT      DD   SYSOUT=A
//SYSLIB       DD   DSNAME=SYS1.COBLIB,DISP=SHR
//SYSOUT       DD   SYSOUT=A
//PRINTFLE     DD   SYSOUT=A
//CARDFLE      DD   *
               (Data deck)
/*
```

Figure 9-10 A typical COBUCG (compile and go) procedure

an input data set named SYSIN, the programmer again indicates that it is in deck form following its DD statement. Here, the stepname must precede SYSIN, as in

```
COB.SYSIN
```

because two job steps are involved.

The second EXEC card in the COBUCG procedure causes the loader program to be executed and gives the name GO to this procedure. It also gives two parameters that apply to the loader program. (The parameters aren't covered in this text.) Because the loader program should be executed only if E-level errors aren't detected during compilation, the condition parameter specifies no execution if 5 is less than the return code in the compile step. In addition to the data sets required by the COBOL program, the loader step requires data sets named SYSLIN (for the COBOL object module), SYSLOUT (for the printed output of the loader program), and SYSLIB (for various system object modules that are to be linked to the COBOL program). The SYSLIN DD card uses a backward reference to SYSLIN in the COB procedure. The DD statement for SYSLOUT simply specifies standard printer output. And the DD statement for SYSLIB refers to an object library named SYS1.COBLIB.

For the data sets required by the COBOL program, the programmer has specified stepname followed by a period followed by ddname. As a result, the programmer's DD statements have the effect of being inserted in the job-control statements for the GO step. Again, the appropriate stepname can be taken from the EXEC card in the cataloged procedure.

Other data sets used by COBUC and COBUCG

Although figures 9-9 and 9-10 illustrate the data sets normally required by the COBOL compiler and loader program in the COBUC and COBUCG procedures, others are sometimes required. For example, if the compilation is supposed to punch an object deck (PARM='DECK'), a data set named SYSPUNCH is required. This would normally be coded as follows:

```
//COB.SYSPUNCH  DD   SYSOUT=B
```

You will rarely want to punch an object deck, however.

If you want a storage dump to be printed in case of abnormal program termination, a data set named SYSUDUMP is required. Although a storage dump can be helpful when debugging, you won't learn how to use one until a later book in this series. As a result, you shouldn't want to use this data set right now either.

The only extra set that you will use now, then, is the SYSOUT data set for DISPLAY statement output. This data set is included in figure 9-2. And it is included in the programmer JCL in figure 9-10. Whenever you use DISPLAY statements in one of your programs, be sure to include this data set in your JCL. Otherwise, your program will terminate the first time it tries to execute a DISPLAY statement.

Discussion

This has been only an introduction to the job-control language of OS. Quite frankly, there are many more parameters that can be used on the JOB, EXEC, and DD statements, and there are many complex ways in which the job-control statements can be combined. This beginning, however, should help you in doing the basic tasks of compiling, linking, and executing. Then, if you are interested in more advanced uses of OS JCL, you can study the appropriate manuals as well as the procedure listings used on your system. These listings can give you much greater insight into the details of OS JCL.

Because this topic has been concerned with the practical application of OS JCL, it is easy to overlook the complexity of the OS operating system itself. Take a minute, then, and consider everything that OS is doing as you run programs. As you create and delete data sets, OS keeps track of data set locations, file label information, expiration dates, available disk areas, and so on. If necessary, OS will split a data set over several areas of a disk, but the user doesn't know this is happening. (Remember the CONTIG entry in the SPACE operand of the DD statement?) Furthermore, spooling, multiprogramming, and virtual storage take place even though the user treats the system as if his program were the only one running. The JCL specifications presented in this topic, then, in no way completely indicate the facilities and features of the operating system.

Terminology

invoking a procedure

procedure option

return code

data set

permanent data set

temporary data set

data set catalog facility

data set catalog

cataloged data set

data set name

data set label

data control block

primary allocation

secondary allocation

Objectives

1. Given the description of a compile-only or a compile-and-go job, create JCL for it. The COBOL program will require card input and printer output, and may also require DISPLAY statement output.

Problems

1. Figure 2-27 is the COBOL listing for a program that prints an investment report. (The specifications for the program are given in figure 2-25.) Suppose that you are going to compile this program for the first time on a system that has these default values:

```
SOURCE,NOCLIST,NODMAP,NOPMAP,NOVERB,LOAD,NODECK,
SEQ,FLAGW,NOSUPMAP,APOST,NOXREF,NOSTATE,NOFLOW,
NOTRUNC,NOZWB
```

The procedure options in the COBUC procedure are as follows:

```
DECK,NOLOAD,SUPMAP
```

Write the JCL needed to compile this program.

2. From the information given below, write the *effective* job-control language (as in figures 9-9 and 9-10):

Programmer JCL:

```
//MMAPROC      JOB  048-9038,'MMA-LOWE',MSGLEVEL=(1,0)
//           EXEC PROC1
//S1.CARDIN  DD
             (Data deck)
/*
```

Cataloged Procedure (PROC1):

```
//S1        EXEC PGM=UPD0998,REGION=128K
//WORK1     DD   UNIT=SYSDA,SPACE=(100,(100,10)),DISP=NEW
//PRINTOUT  DD   SYSOUT=A
```

Solutions

1. Your JOB statement should, of course, conform to your installation standards. Otherwise, the following JCL will work:

```
//JATINVST   JOB  (048-9038,COBOL),TAYLOR,MSGLEVEL=(1,0)
//           EXEC PROC=COBUC,PARM.COB='XREF,NOLOAD'
//COB.SYSIN  DD   *
             (Source deck)
/*
```

Do you understand why the PARMs are coded this way? First, you need a PARM card in order to get a cross-reference listing. However, using a PARM card overrides the procedure options and causes the system to revert to its default values for those options. Since you want to retain the procedure option NOLOAD (you don't want to save the object program because you're not testing it in this job), you have to recode it in your PARM statement. The DECK option, on the other hand, has reverted to its default value, NODECK. Since you don't want an object deck punched, you don't want to reset this option. As for SUPMAP, it too has reverted to its default value, NOSUPMAP. You could reset it in your PARM card, but it wouldn't affect your compilation because neither the CLIST or PMAP option is on.

2. Here is the effective job-control language:

```
//MMAPROC    JOB  048-9038,'MMA-LOWE',MSGLEVEL=(1,0)
//S1         EXEC PGM=UPD0998,REGION=128K
//WORK1      DD   UNIT=SYSDA,SPACE=(100,(100,10)),DISP=NEW
//PRINTOUT   DD   SYSOUT=A
//CARDIN     DD   *
             (Data deck)
/*
```

TOPIC 3   OS JCL for Sequential Files

Once you are familiar with the operands of the DD statement, JCL for sequential tape and disk files should present no particular problems. However, depending on the characteristics of a file, there are many different ways in which the operands can be used, so a number of examples follow.

```
//RKATPPRT     JOB  (048-9038,COBOL),'MMA-ADDINGTON',MSGLEVEL=(1,0)
//             EXEC PROC=COBUCG,PARM.COB='SXREF,NODECK,NOTRUNC'
//COB.SYSIN    DD   *
               (Source deck)
/*
//GO.SYSOUT    DD   SYSOUT=A
//GO.ITEMIN    DD   DSNAME=INVFILE,UNIT=TAPE,VOL=SER=004905,
//             DISP=(OLD,KEEP)
//GO.PRINTOUT  DD   SYSOUT=A,DCB=BLKSIZE=133
```

Figure 9-11   OS JCL to test a tape-to-printer program

Permanent Files

Testing a tape-to-printer program

Figure 9-11 illustrates the OS JCL for compiling and testing a
sequential file-to-printer program like the one in figure 7-4, assuming
the program were used to print the contents of a tape master file.
We'll also have to assume that the program was written for an OS
system, in which case the SELECT statements would be something
like this:

```
SELECT ITEMIN   ASSIGN TO UT-S-ITEMIN.
SELECT PRINTOUT ASSIGN TO UT-S-PRINTOUT.
```

And the BLOCK CONTAINS clause for both files would be this:

```
BLOCK CONTAINS 0 RECORDS
```

With the exception of the DD statements, the JCL in figure 9-11
should be easy to follow. For the tape DD statement, there are four
points to note.

First, the DSNAME operand has a permanent name entry
because this file was created by an earlier program and saved as a
permanent file. Naturally, the name used (INVFILE) must be exactly
the same as the DSNAME used when the file was created.

Second, the UNIT operand is coded with a group specification—
TAPE. As mentioned earlier in the description of this operand, this
allows the OS I/O device assignment routine to select whatever tape
drive is available and then instruct the operator to mount the tape
on it.

Third, the volume serial number of the tape is coded in the
VOLUME operand so that the operating system can tell the operator
which tape is to be mounted on the selected tape drive. If this permanent file had been cataloged at the time it was created, the infor-

```
//GMBDKCRT    JOB   (048-9038,COBOL),'MMA-BARTLETT',MSGLEVEL=(1,0)
//            EXEC  PROC=COBUCG,PARM.COB='SXREF,NODECK,NOTRUNC'
//COB.SYSIN   DD    *
              (Source deck)
/*
//GO.SYSOUT   DD    SYSOUT=A
//GO.MASTER   DD    DSNAME=MASTER,UNIT=3330,VOL=SER=TESTPK,
//                  DISP=(NEW,KEEP,DELETE),DCB=BLKSIZE=3156,SPACE=(TRK,5)
//GO.CARDIN   DD    *,DCB=BLKSIZE=800
              (Data deck)
/*
```

Figure 9-12 OS JCL to test a card-to-disk program

mation would have been stored in the catalog file and thus would
not have to be coded in the DD statement.

Finally, the first entry of the DISP operand specifies that the file
already exists. This means that the operating system must first check
the labels on the tape to make sure that it contains the file requested.
The second DISP entry specifies that the file is again to be saved
when the job is completed.

The only complication in the DD statement for the printer file is
the use of the DCB operand. It should be coded to give the block
size of the printer file, since the COBOL program has the BLOCK
CONTAINS 0 RECORDS clause. In this case, the programmer has
assigned the file a block size of 133 bytes. Since each record is 133
bytes long, there will be one record to a block. Although this is fine
for testing, you should select a more efficient block size for the file
once the program is put into production.

The DCB operand could have been coded for the tape file, too.
However, since the file is old and the DCB operand is omitted, the
operating system will look up the block size on its own. Actually,
it's a good practice to omit this operand when coding the DD statement for a file that already exists. Then you don't have to worry
about making a coding error that will lead to an abnormal termination of your program.

Testing a card-to-disk program

Figure 9-12 illustrates the JCL necessary to compile and test a typical
card-to-disk program. Here again, the main points of interest are the
DD statements. The DSNAME operand for the disk file is coded in
permanent form because the file is to be used later in a disk update
program. The UNIT operand is coded 3330 because the pack to be

used is a 3330 device, and the VOLUME operand specifies the volume serial number of this special pack for testing—TESTPK.

Since the disk file is being created in this program, the first entry in the DISP operand is coded NEW. OS then knows that it should expect a SPACE operand and must find space on the TESTPK disk for the file. It will also check to see that no other file with the same data set name already exists on this disk pack. The second and third entries of the DISP operand specify that the file is to be saved if the job step completes successfully (indicating that the file was probably created as intended), but that in the event of abnormal termination, the data set is to be deleted. By coding these DISP entries, the bad file is automatically scratched (deleted), so when the program is corrected and tried again, there will not be the problem of attempting to create a new data set with the same name as one already on the disk.

After the DISP operand, the DCB operand says each block will contain 3156 bytes. This is only a quarter of a track; however, in your test runs, you may want to create even smaller blocks, depending on the amount of space your test data requires. Because this file will be a small set of test data, the SPACE operand requests only five tracks and no secondary allocation entry is needed. It's a good idea to avoid tying up disk space unnecessarily during test runs. So keep your disk allocations small in size.

The DD statement for the card file includes a DCB operand to give the file a block size of 800 bytes. Since a card record contains 80 characters, each block will consist of 10 records. Though the blocking factor you choose for an input card file doesn't matter too much during testing, you should choose an efficient block size once the program is put into production.

Temporary Files

Sometimes, a file is only needed for one job. In this case, it is usually best to create a temporary file. In topic 2, you saw that a temporary file can be created by coding the DSNAME with two ampersands. Thus, DSNAME=&&TEMP defines a temporary data set.

When a DD statement for a temporary file is processed, the operating system creates a complicated DSNAME consisting of the date, the time, the jobname, some other system information such as the system configuration, and the DSNAME supplied by the DD statement. However, if the DSNAME is not specified in the DD statement, the system will generate a number to make the name unique. Thus, for temporary data sets, it is common to leave out the DSNAME and to use backward references to refer to the file. When creating a temporary data set, then, all you need to code on the DD

```
//DALUPDT        JOB  048-9038,'MMA-LOWE',MSGLEVEL=(1,0)
//UPDAT          EXEC COBUCG,PARM.COB='SXREF,NODECK,NOTRUNC'
//COB.SYSIN      DD   *
                 (Source deck)
/*
//GO.SYSOUT      DD   SYSOUT=A
//GO.TRANFILE    DD   DSNAME=TRANFILE,UNIT=TAPE,VOL=SER=TESTTP1,
//                    DISP=(OLD,KEEP)
//GO.OLDMAST     DD   DSNAME=ITEMMSTR,UNIT=TAPE,VOL=SER=TESTTP2,
//                    DISP=(OLD,KEEP)
//GO.NEWMAST     DD   DSNAME=&&NEWMAST,UNIT=TAPE,VOL=SER=TESTTP3,
//                    DISP=(NEW,PASS,DELETE),DCB=BLKSIZE=4000
//GO.ERRFILE     DD   UNIT=TAPE,VOL=SER=TESTTP4,
//                    DISP=(NEW,PASS,DELETE),DCB=BLKSIZE=3960
//GO.UPDLIST     DD   SYSOUT=A,DCB=BLKSIZE=133
//               EXEC PGM=MSTRPRNT
//TAPEIN         DD   DSNAME=&&NEWMAST,DISP=(OLD,DELETE)
//LIST           DD   SYSOUT=A
//               EXEC PGM=ERRPRNT
//TAPEIN         DD   DSNAME=*.UPDAT.GO.ERRFILE,DISP=(OLD,DELETE)
//LIST           DD   SYSOUT=A
```

Figure 9-13 OS JCL to test a tape-update program

statement are the UNIT operand, the DCB operand for the block size, and, if the file's on disk, the SPACE operand.

Testing a tape-update program

To illustrate the use of temporary data sets, consider the JCL in figure 9-13. It could be used to test the sequential update program in figure 7-8 if a tape file were to be updated. After the inventory file (ITEMMSTR) is updated in the first job step, the new master file is printed by a special program called MSTRPRNT. Then, the error file that is created by the update program is printed in the third job step by a special program named ERRPRNT.

Notice how the new master and the error files are defined in the first job step. Because this is only a test run, the new master file (NEWMAST) is created as a temporary data set. Here, the DSNAME is coded as $$NEWMAST. The error tape is also a temporary file, but it is not given a DSNAME. Because each of the error records is 24 bytes long, a block of 3960 bytes will contain 165 records.

In the second job step, the MSTRPRNT program is executed to print the new master file. The input to this program is a file called TAPEIN, and the DD statement for TAPEIN specifies DSNAME= &&NEWMAST. Since the DISP operand specifies OLD and

```
//DALUPDT       JOB   048-9038,'MMA=LOWE',MSGLEVEL=(1,0)
//UPDAT        EXEC  COBUCG,PARM.COB='SXREF,NODECK,NOTRUNC'
//COB.SYSIN    DD    *
               (Source deck)
/*
//GO.SYSOUT    DD    SYSOUT=A
//GO.TRANFILE  DD    DSNAME=TRANFILE,UNIT=TAPE,VOL=SER=TESTTP1,
//                   DISP=(OLD,KEEP)
//GO.OLDMAST   DD    DSNAME=ITEMMSTR,UNIT=TAPE,VOL=SER=TESTTP2,
//                   DISP=(OLD,KEEP)
//GO.NEWMAST   DD    SYSOUT=A,DCB=BLKSIZE=100
//GO.ERRFILE   DD    SYSOUT=A,DCB=BLKSIZE=24
//GO.UPDLIST   DD    SYSOUT=A,DCB=BLKSIZE=133
```

Figure 9-14   OS JCL to test the tape-update program using SYSOUT=A

DELETE, the file will be deleted at the end of the job step.

For the third job step, a backward reference is used to print the error tape. Here, the DSNAME is coded like this:

```
DSNAME=*.UPDAT.GO.ERRFILE
```

As a result, this program processes the file that had the ddname ERRFILE in the procedure step GO in the job step UPDAT.

Testing a tape-update program using SYSOUT=A

If you have special programs like MSTRPRNT and ERRPRNT, a job like the one in figure 9-13 is fine. But sometimes special programs aren't available, and you won't want to take the time to write your own. In this case, you may want to take advantage of the fact that OS allows you to treat any sequential file as standard printer output (SYSOUT=A). In other words, you can print the newly created files directly, rather than write them on tape or disk and then print them.

Figure 9-14 illustrates the use of SYSOUT=A for testing the same sequential update program that is tested by the JCL in figure 9-13. Here, the input files—the old master file and the transaction file—are treated just as they are in figure 9-13. However, the operand in the DD statement for the new master file and the error file is SYSOUT=A. This means these temporary files are spooled out to tape or disk areas, after which they are printed.

When using this technique, the printed output is a straight listing of the contents of the file, one line of print for each record in the file. For instance, the 100-byte records in the NEWMAST file will be printed in the first 100 print positions in each output line. This means this technique is limited. In fact, if your records are over 132 bytes long, if your records contain COMP or COMP-3 fields, or if you want to space the output fields, this technique shouldn't be used at all.

Objectives

1. Given a description of a job that fits one of the patterns described in this chapter, make up job-control cards that will cause the intended sequence of programs to be executed.

Problems

1. Suppose a sequential disk master file is to be created from a file of tape records. The tape file is a permanent file on tape 437046 with the ddname ITEMTRAN. The disk file consists of 100-byte records. It has the ddname ITEMMSTR and should be stored in six cylinders on a disk pack called TESTPK, which will be used on a 3330 device. It should be saved, but not cataloged, if it's created properly.

    To check the contents of the disk file after the creation program is run, the programmer will run a disk-to-printer program called DSKPRT. This program expects an input file named DISKIN and an output file called PRTOUT. Write the JCL statements for running these two programs in a single job.

2. Suppose the file created in problem 1 is used as the master file for testing the sequential update program in figure 7-8. The transaction master, new master, and error files will all be on 3330 devices and should be saved for further processing. The transaction file can be found in three cylinders on disk pack 219109. The error file is to be written on pack 555033 and will require one cylinder. The new master file will be written on TESTPK. Write the JCL statements for compiling and testing the update program.

Solutions

1. Figure 9-15 is an acceptable solution Your JOB card should conform to your own installation's standards. And you should code the PARMs you would use on your own system. To retrieve the disk file for printing in the second job step, you must code the DSNAME (it must be the same as the name used when the file was created), UNIT, VOL, and DISP operands.

```
//DALTPDK        JOB  049-9038,'MMA-LOWE',MSGLEVEL=(1,0)
//               EXEC PROC=COBUCG,PARM.COB='SXREF,NODECK,NOTRUNC'
//COB.SYSIN      DD   *
                 (Source deck)
/*
//GO.SYSOUT      DD   SYSOUT=A
//GO.ITEMTRAN    DD   DSNAME=ITEMTRAN,UNIT=TAPE,VOL=SER=437046,
//               DISP=(OLD,KEEP)
//GO.ITEMMSTR    DD   DSNAME=ITEMMSTR,UNIT=3330,VOL=SER=TESTPK,
//               DISP=(NEW,KEEP,DELETE),DCB=BLKSIZE=6400,SPACE=(CYL,6)
//               EXEC PGM=DSKPRT
//DISKIN         DD   DSNAME=ITEMMSTR,UNIT=3330,VOL=SER=TESTPK,
//               DISP=(OLD,KEEP)
//PRTOUT         DD   SYSOUT=A,DCB=BLKSIZE=133
```

Figure 9-15   OS JCL to run a tape-to-disk program and a disk-to-printer program

2. Figure 9-16 is an acceptable solution. Again, your JOB card and PARMs should conform to your installation's standards. Since the transaction and old master files are already stored on disk, the first DISP parameter is OLD, and no DCB is required. The operating system will look up the block sizes for these files. The error and new master files, however, require DCB operands to

```
//DJZUPDT        JOB  049-9038,'MMA-ZOLDOSKE',MSGLEVEL=(1,0)
//               EXEC PROC=COBUCG,PARM.COB='SXREF,NODECK,NOTRUNC'
//COB.SYSIN      DD   *
                 (Source deck)
/*
//GO.SYSOUT      DD   SYSOUT=A
//GO.TRANFILE    DD   DSNAME=TRANFILE,UNIT=3330,VOL=SER=219109,
//               DISP=(OLD,KEEP)
//GO.OLDMAST     DD   DSNAME=ITEMMSTR,UNIT=3330,VOL=SER=TESTPK,
//               DISP=(OLD,KEEP)
//GO.NEWMAST     DD   DSNAME=ITEMMST2,UNIT=3330,VOL=SER=TESTPK,
//               DISP=(NEW,KEEP,DELETE),DCB=BLKSIZE=6400,SPACE=(CYL,6)
//GO.ERRFILE     DD   DSNAME=ERRFILE,UNIT=3330,VOL=SER=555033,
//               DISP=(NEW,KEEP,DELETE),DCB=BLKSIZE=3144,SPACE=(CYL,1)
//GO.UPDLIST     DD   SYSOUT=A,DCB=BLKSIZE=133
```

Figure 9-16   OS JCL to run a disk-update program

give the block sizes because they're new files with BLOCK
CONTAINS 0 RECORDS in the COBOL program. Note that
the DSNAME for the new master file must be different from the
DSNAME for the old master file, in spite of the fact that the
new master is just an updated version of the old master.

PART FIVE

Programming Techniques

This part presents the proper sequence of program development in a COBOL shop in industry. It also presents techniques for coding and testing programs on a top-down basis. You can study this part any time after you complete part 2, but you will probably get more from it if you wait until you have completed all of the other parts in this book.

10

Structured Program Development

As you have already seen, structured programming is a general term that includes techniques for design, documentation, and coding. And yet structured programming doesn't stop there. In topic 1 of this chapter, I'm going to show you how structured programming should infiltrate all phases of program development. In topic 2, I'm going to show you how you can use top-down coding and testing to improve your efficiency and morale during the coding and testing phases of program development.

TOPIC 1 Structured Development for Small, One-Programmer Projects

In many cases, a programmer will use structured design, documentation, and coding, but he won't use top-down coding and testing as described in topic 2. This is particularly true on small, one-programmer projects. For my purposes here, you can think of a small project as consisting of 1500 lines of COBOL code or less and taking three months or less from the start of the project to the finish.

Figure 10-1 lists the preferred sequence of development for small, one-programmer projects. In this topic, I'm going to discuss each of these phases in the context of structured programming.

1. Get complete specifications
2. Get related source books and subprograms
3. Design the program
4. Code the JCL
5. Create the test plan
6. Create the test data
7. Code the program
8. Test the program

Figure 10-1   The eight phases of structured program development

Because structured programming puts the emphasis on planning, a structured programmer should do each of these phases in a more orderly manner than they have been done in the past.

Get complete specifications

Today, as in the past, the specifications that come down to a programmer are likely to be heavy with detail, even though they omit one or more important aspects of the problem. As a structured programmer, your first job should be to make sure that you have complete specifications. To do this, you must wade through the pages of detail and summarize. Create record layouts and print charts for all input and output files. List all of the major functions that appear to be required by the specifications.

As part of this summary, you may want to use the IPO form. For instance, figure 10-2 gives an overview of what the edit program that was discussed in chapter 3 requires. Although it is similar to the IPO for module 000 of this program, the process box doesn't in any way imply procedural steps. Instead, the programmer has simply listed what he thinks the major functions of the program are. Later on, this list can aid in the development of the VTOC for the program.

After you have summarized all of the specifications that you have been given, look for omissions. Do you have all the information you need to decide when a line should be printed on the output listing? Do you know how the part-number table should be arranged so it can be used most efficiently? The point here is, look beyond the obvious. If you don't get specifications that give you a clear idea of what the problem is, even structured programming can't save you. In fact, you will usually find that you can't create an adequate VTOC if the major functions aren't clearly specified.

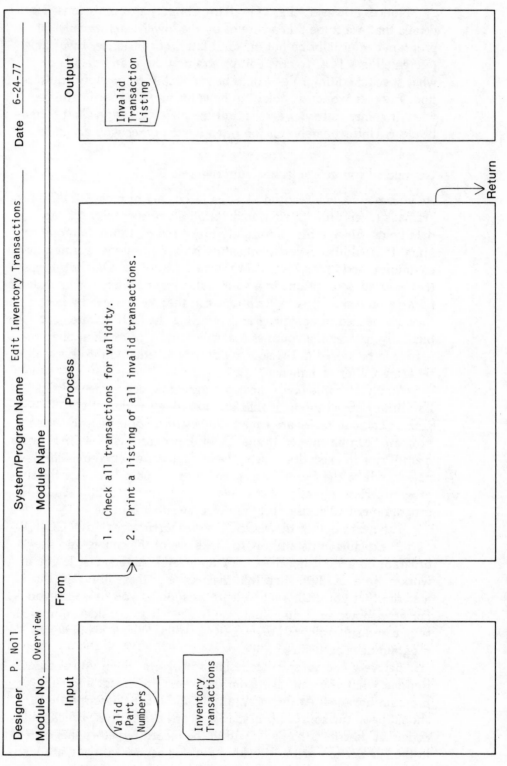

Figure 10-2 Use of HIPO form for summarizing program requirements

Notice, however, that I'm talking about major omissions. The details that are to be taken care of by the lower-level modules of a program can usually be put off until later. For instance, I was able to create the VTOC for the edit program without any details on what specific editing rules would be for each type of input transaction. In other words, it's okay to have incomplete specifications when it comes to trivial details, but the major functions had better be clear. Unfortunately, all too often it's the other way around.

Get related source books and subprograms

As you may have already noticed, a large part of most COBOL programs is taken up with routine descriptions of files, records, and data fields. Since a file is normally processed by more than one program, it would be useless duplication if each program repeated the common descriptions. To avoid this, a typical COBOL shop keeps the repeated descriptions in a *source-statement library* (or just *source library*) on disk. These descriptions can then be retrieved whenever they are needed in new programs by using the COPY statement. Similarly, processing routines that are used by more than one program can be stored in the source library and entered into programs by using COPY statements.

Along the same lines, most programming departments keep libraries of object modules that are useful in a wide variety of programs. These libraries are called *subprogram libraries*, and the subprograms can be entered into a COBOL program with a CALL statement. Prior to execution, then, the linkage editor combines the object code of the COBOL program with the object code of the subprogram. Here again, programmer productivity goes up because the programmer makes use of a previously written routine.

The next book in this COBOL series *(Structured ANS COBOL, Part 2)* explains in detail how to make use of the source and subprogram libraries using the COPY and CALL statements. If you are working in a COBOL shop that makes use of these libraries, this is material that you will want to learn as soon as you finish this book. For now, however, I just want you to see where consideration of the source and subprogram libraries fits into the normal sequence of program development.

Before you even start to design a program, then, you should find out what you can take from the source-statement and subprogram libraries. At the least, all file and record descriptions should be in the source library. (By record description, I mean all code that describes the fields within the record, whether this code is in the File Section or the Working-Storage Section of the Data Division.) So if you're writing the first program that processes a certain file, see to it that the file and record descriptions are entered into the source library. On the other hand, if your program is going to use files that have already been placed in the source library, get listings of the code so you can use the proper names when you create HIPO diagrams.

Beyond file and record descriptions, you may find processing modules that apply to your program. For instance, we have a date-conversion module in our installation that is in both the source and subprogram libraries. This module converts a date in the form month/day/year to the form day/year; thus, 02/15/78 would be converted to 046/78. A module like this could be used in the produce-ATB-report program described in figure 3-41.

In any event, find out what might be applicable to your program and get listings of these source books or subprograms. Then, after you design the VTOC for the program, you can decide whether or not you will use any of these modules. It's important to get copies of these modules before you start to design the program, however, because in some cases they will affect your design.

Design the program

This step, of course, is what topics 2 and 3 of chapter 3 have covered in detail: developing the VTOC and making HIPO diagrams for each module in the VTOC. The only point I want to make here is to be aware of available source books or subprograms and use them if they apply to your problem. If, for example, your program requires a date-conversion routine and it is available in the source library, use it. On your VTOC, you should make a note indicating the name of the existing module. This name can then be transferred to the related IPO diagram.

Code the JCL

Now that your program is designed, you should code the job-control language that will be used to run it. This establishes the interface between your program and the operating system. Figure 10-3, for example, shows the OS JCL that I used for compiling and testing the reorder-listing program in figure 2-24. It also shows the JCL that will be used to run the program when it is put into production.

In order to cut down the amount of JCL that must be submitted each time a production program is run, most of the JCL is stored as a production procedure in a procedure library on an OS system. For example, the production procedure in figure 10-3 is the JCL that would be stored to run the reorder-listing program. The production JCL can then be kept at a minimum because it simply calls for the

```
Test JCL:

//MMAORD        JOB  048-9038,'MMA-NOLL',MSGLEVEL=(1,1),CLASS=N
//              EXEC PROC=COBUCG
//COB.SYSIN     DD   *
                (Source deck)
/*
//GO.SYSOUT     DD   SYSOUT=A
//GO.ORDLST     DD   SYSOUT=A
//GO.BALCDS     DD   *
                (Data deck)
/*



Production procedure:

//F55           EXEC PGM=F55
//STEPLIB       DD   DSN=SYS1.PGMLIB,DISP=SHR
//SYSOUT        DD   SYSOUT=A
//ORDLST        DD   SYSOUT=A
//SYSUDUMP      DD   SYSOUT=N



Production JCL:

//MMAF55        JOB  048-9038,'MMA-NOLL',MSGLEVEL=(1,1),CLASS=A
//              EXEC PROC=F55
//BALCDS        DD   *
                (Data deck)
/*
```

Figure 10-3   The JCL interface between the reorder-listing program and IBM's OS/VS

production procedure and provides the input data. In figure 10-3, for instance, the production JCL consists of only four cards plus the data deck. Coding the test and production JCL like this will help prevent any misunderstanding about what the interfaces are between your program and your operating system.

Create the test plan

The next step in developing a program is to develop a *test plan* for it. As in all phases of structured programming, the idea behind the test plan is to put the emphasis on planning.

But let's back up a minute. In general, most programs are tested in three phases: unit test, systems test, and acceptance test. The *unit test* is the programmer test in which the programmer should make sure that all modules in his program are tested. Since he knows his program better than anyone else, he is best qualified to create the test plan for the unit test.

The *systems test* is designed to test the interfaces between the programs within a system. For instance, if I'm writing an update program, the systems test will determine whether or not the edit programs create transaction files that are acceptable to my program. But if the test data used for the edit programs is incomplete, the output from the edit programs will be an inadequate test of my program. So I can't rely on the systems test to test all aspects of my program.

The *acceptance test* is designed to determine whether the instructions to operations are clear so the programs that are tested can be run without any help from the developers. Although the data for the acceptance test should be developed by a creative person with plenty of testing experience, this isn't always the case. So you can't count on this phase of testing to test all aspects of your program either.

To a large extent, then, the burden of proof is on the programmer in the unit test. As a result, the test plan should be made with a maximum of planning. To begin with, the programmer should go through each of the HIPO diagrams for the program. For each module that he reviews, he should list all of the conditions that must be tested. When he's finished, he will have a list of all of the conditions for all of the modules. As a result, if data is created that tests for all of these conditions, the programmer can be sure that every line of code in the program is tested.

Figure 10-4 is a list of conditions that I developed for the edit program that was described in chapter 3. It gives all of the conditions that should be tested for each module in module-number sequence. Although making a list like this can be a laborious job if the program is large and the modules are many, what choice do you have? Your job as programmer is to prove that your program works for all possible conditions. How can you do this without knowing what they are? As you will see, however, your test data usually won't have to be extensive just because your list of conditions is long.

One of the fringe benefits of making a list like this is discovering conditions that your program didn't provide for. For instance, look at the condition for module 110 in figure 10-4: What happens if the table file is empty? Granted the possibility is obscure, but all transactions will be invalid if this does happen. Depending on the

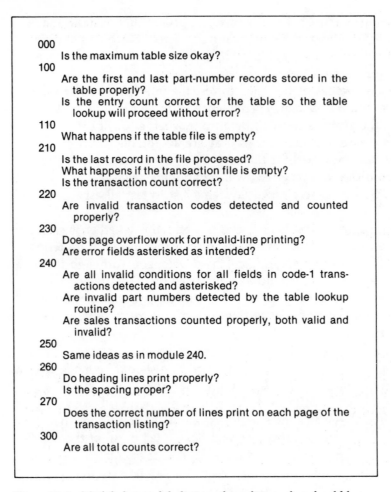

Figure 10-4 Module-by-module listing of conditions that should be covered by the edit program

way the part-number file is created, then, you may want to change module 000 so the program ends if the part-number count is zero after module 100 is executed. Since the cost of correcting an error increases the farther you progress in the program-development sequence, finding one condition that hasn't been provided for can more than pay for the time you spend listing the conditions.

After you have made your list of conditions, you are ready to create the test plan. Specifically, you want to decide in what sequence the conditions should be tested. The intent here is to discover the major problems first. So you don't want to start by testing to see whether the branch-number field is edited properly. You want to start by testing to see whether the major modules are entered properly and whether control passes from one major module to another as intended.

Test phase	Data	Data source
1. Valid transactions	Three valid part-number records; two valid transactions, one for each transaction code, and one with the first part number in the table, one with the last part number	Self
2. Single errors	Invalid transactions that will test all possible causes of invalid fields	Self
3. Contingencies	Mixed data from test runs 1, 2, and 3; any new records that might cause a contingent error	Self
4. Page overflow and maximum table size	As many part-number records as the program is supposed to provide for; 150 transactions, with enough invalid transactions to cause page overflow	Test data generator

Figure 10-5   A test plan for the edit program

In general, your test plan should have four main parts to it. First, the major modules of the program should be tested using only valid data; that is, no error conditions will be tested. Second, independent error conditions should be tested, one at a time (I call these *single errors*). Third, error conditions should be tested together to see whether one error condition has an effect upon another (I call these *contingencies*). In general, these three types of tests can be made with a low volume of input data. Then, in the fourth phase of testing, conditions that depend upon volume can be tested. I'm thinking now of things like page overflow and maximum table size. If testing a volume condition like maximum table size is impractical in the unit test and you know it will be tested in the systems or acceptance test, you may simply want to review your code for these conditions, perhaps with an associate, and then make sure the condition actually is tested later on.

As you create your test plan, you should also decide where the test data will come from. Will you code the data yourself and create the proper input files using utilities? Will you use a test data generator (a utility that is available in many COBOL shops)? Can you copy some "live" data for your volume test? Has another program that is in development created test data that you can use? Here again, make these decisions in a thoughtful, controlled manner since they can have a significant effect on the efficiency and effectiveness of your unit test.

Figure 10-5 gives a test plan for the edit program in this book.

Although the program is limited, I think it will give you the idea of what a test plan should look like. As I've just described, this plan starts by testing with only good data, then adds single errors, then adds contingencies, and ends up by testing the volume conditions of page overflow and maximum table size. Notice that I haven't covered every condition that is listed in figure 10-4, but I considered them all.

Create the test data

Too often in the past, test data was created without any test plan. Is it any wonder, then, that programs were put into production with dozens and even hundreds of bugs? Is it any wonder that bugs have been found years after a program was put into production? In contrast, it is a relatively easy task to create test data with the test plan as a guide. Furthermore, your planning will give you a solid basis for believing that your program is bug-free after it proves itself on the data you have created. At the least, you will know that every line of code has been executed during the test runs.

As you create the test data, you should also determine what output to expect. It still amazes me that programmers don't always know what output they are looking for as they test a program. But not long ago a programmer asked me to help him with a debugging problem. When I asked him what output he expected, he gave an embarrassed shrug and said he wanted the output to look like a report . . . no particular values in the report, just a report. So this is the time to determine what the output should be; in some cases, doing this will help you uncover problems in your specifications, design, or documentation.

I also want to point out that the test data used in the early test runs should be low in volume, often just a couple of records for each input file. That way, determining the expected output won't be a laborious task. For instance, in the test plan for the edit program in figure 10-5, two valid transactions are enough for the first testing step. Then, for step 2, a dozen or so transactions should be enough to test all of the invalid conditions that are possible in both transaction types. By using low-volume test files, you will keep your early test runs manageable and help to simplify the debugging process. Larger test files should only be introduced after all of the major bugs have been corrected.

Code the program

As shown throughout this book, the paragraphs in your COBOL program will be in sequence by module number. That doesn't mean,

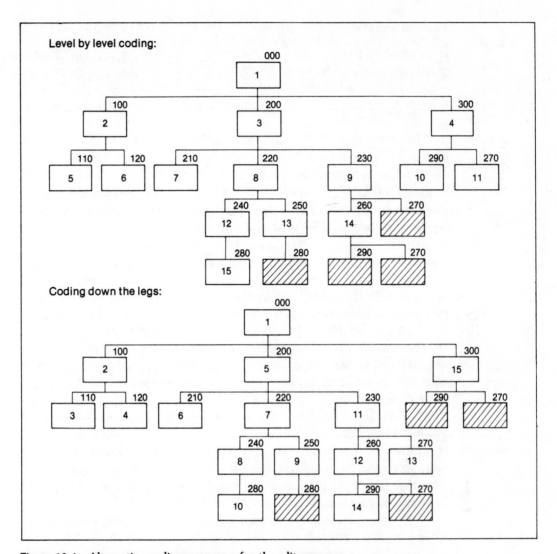

Figure 10-6   Alternative coding sequences for the edit program

however, that you should code them in module-number sequence. Although a structured program is always coded from the top down, the programmer has considerable leeway as to the actual module sequence he will use.

The basic rule for coding sequence is this: never code a module before you code its calling module. As a result, one of the most common coding sequences is level-by-level from the top down. On the other hand, you may prefer to code down one of the branches or legs of the program. That is all right too. Figure 10-6 illustrates two different sequences in which the edit program could be coded: the first is level-by-level, the second is leg-by-leg. And, of course, the legs could be coded in other sequences as well.

Test the program

In most cases today, all of the modules in a small, one-programmer program are tested at once. In the next topic, I'm going to show you what I think is a better way of coding and testing programs. Nevertheless, testing all modules at once is acceptable, particularly on programs of 500 lines or less.

In preparation for testing, you will usually want to place debugging statements in your program. At the least, you will want to know when each module has been called. To do this, you can simply place a DISPLAY statement at the start of each module using a literal to give the module name. For example, this statement could be used for module 100 of the edit program:

```
DISPLAY '100-LOAD-PART-NUMBER-TABLE'.
```

When you've completed this preparation, you're ready for the first test run indicated by your test plan.

Some of the major benefits of structured programming come to the fore during the testing phase of program development. First, because you've taken the time to design and document your program correctly, your program just won't have as many bugs as it would have otherwise. Second, because you are using structured (GOTO-less) COBOL, all modules will have only one entry and one exit point, so your program will be executed in a controlled manner from the top down. As a result, if there is a bug, it should be relatively easy to isolate the module in which it can be found. (Compare this with unstructured code that branches from page 7 of your listing to page 31, back to page 15, and so on.) Third, because you have created a test plan based on conditions developed from the IPOs for your program modules, all of the modules in the program will be adequately tested. This will contribute to the reliability of the program after it goes into production. And finally, since your test plan has arranged the conditions in a sequence that is designed to uncover the major errors first, you won't necessarily be testing all of the modules of your program at once. Because your program is structured, your test data itself can determine which of the modules are actually entered. In the edit program, for example, my first test run will use only valid test data, so the print-invalid-line leg of the program will never be executed. And this too will make it easier to find the cause of any bug.

Discussion

In actual practice, you usually won't find the phases of programming done in the sequence shown in figure 10-1, even in shops that use structured programming. In many cases, programmers code the

JCL and create their test data as the last step before testing. And they check the source and subprogram libraries just before coding.

Regardless of these variations, I believe that the sequence given in figure 10-1 is the most efficient one. Why check source and subprogram libraries before designing? Because available modules may have an effect on design. And names taken from source books should be used when the modules are documented. Why code JCL and create a test plan and test data before coding? Because these activities may point up problems that will affect your coding. So try this sequence on the next program you develop and see if it isn't both logical and professional.

Terminology

source-statement library

source library

subprogram library

test plan

unit test

systems test

acceptance test

single errors

contingencies

Objectives

1. List the eight phases of structured program development in the sequence that I have recommended. (And develop your next programs in this sequence.)
2. Explain how to create a test plan for a structured program.
3. Given the specifications, VTOC, and module documentation for a program, create an efficient test plan for it. Then, create test data that corresponds to the test plan.

Problems

1. (Objective 3) The VTOC for the reorder-listing program is given in figure 2-23 and the program listing is given in figure 2-24. Using the code itself, do the following:

   a. List the conditions that must be tested in each module.

   b. Create an efficient test plan for this program. Because this program is short and simple, you may want to combine two or more of the four parts you would normally have in your test plan.

c.   Create test data that corresponds to your test plan.

Solutions

1. a.   An acceptable list of conditions is given in figure 10-7.

    b.   An acceptable test plan is given in figure 10-8. Because the program is so simple, I have listed only two steps. First, the normal functions of the program are tested. Second, single errors, contingencies, and volume conditions are tested.

    c.   Figure 10-9 gives the test data for each step in the test plan. For step 1, I have coded only 3 cards to cover these major processing conditions:

Condition	Comment
1. On order + on hand < reorder point	Printed output
2. On order + on hand = reorder point	No printed output
3. On order + on hand > reorder point	No printed output

Notice that in the item-description field of each record, the code tells what condition is being tested.

For step 2, I have coded only 5 additional records; they cover these conditions:

Condition	Comment
1. Size error and maximum values in numeric fields	Display message
2. Maximum values in all fields; on order + on hand < reorder point	Printed output
3. Maximum values in all fields; on order + on hand = reorder point	No printed output
4. Minimum values in all fields; on order = 0, on hand < reorder point	Printed output
5. Minimum values in all fields; on hand = 0, on order > reorder point	No printed output

To provide a test for page overflow, I will duplicate the 3 cards that produce printed output 20 times and then combine the two decks for a total of 65 input cards. This combined deck will be used for step 2 of the test plan.

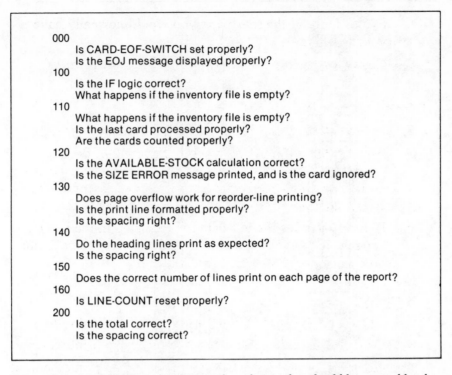

```
000
     Is CARD-EOF-SWITCH set properly?
     Is the EOJ message displayed properly?
100
     Is the IF logic correct?
     What happens if the inventory file is empty?
110
     What happens if the inventory file is empty?
     Is the last card processed properly?
     Are the cards counted properly?
120
     Is the AVAILABLE-STOCK calculation correct?
     Is the SIZE ERROR message printed, and is the card ignored?
130
     Does page overflow work for reorder-line printing?
     Is the print line formatted properly?
     Is the spacing right?
140
     Do the heading lines print as expected?
     Is the spacing right?
150
     Does the correct number of lines print on each page of the report?
160
     Is LINE-COUNT reset properly?
200
     Is the total correct?
     Is the spacing correct?
```

Figure 10-7   Module-by-module listing of conditions that should be covered by the reorder-listing program

Test phase	Data	Data source
1. Normal functions	3 inventory records in which AVAILABLE-STOCK is less than reorder point, equal to reorder point, and greater than reorder point	Self
2. ON SIZE error, contingencies, and page overflow	All records from phase 1; one inventory record that will cause a size error; records with minimum and maximum values in all fields; enough records with items that have to be reordered to cause page overflow	Self

Figure 10-8   A test plan for the reorder-listing program

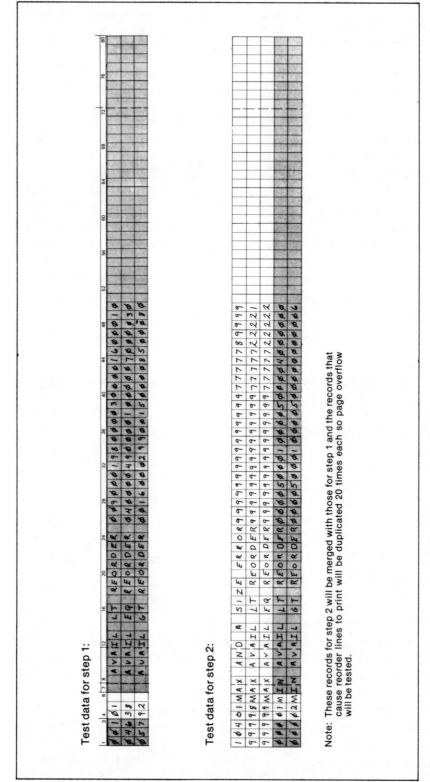

Figure 10-9   Test data that corresponds to the test plan in figure 10-8

TOPIC 2   Top-Down Coding and Testing

Although you will sometimes code and test all of the modules of the structured program at once, as described in topic 1, I think there's a better way to do it. This better way is called *top-down coding and testing*. In fact, I recommend that top-down coding and testing be used on all COBOL programs of 1000 lines or more. After you see its advantages, you may even want to use this technique on programs of less than 1000 lines.

When you use top-down coding and testing, you don't code the entire program and then test it. Instead, you code and test in phases. You normally start by coding and testing the top-level module and one or more of the level-1 modules. Then, after correcting any bugs, you add one or more modules to this coding and test again. When this much of the program runs without bugs, you code a few more modules, add them to what you have, and test again. You continue in this way until all of the modules have been coded and you are testing the entire program. Because top-down coding and testing always go together, the phrase *top-down testing* implies top-down coding as well.

To illustrate top-down testing, figure 10-10 gives the complete VTOC for the edit-inventory-transactions program presented in chapter 3. Rather than test all 15 modules at once, however, the programmer has decided to code and test only modules 000, 100, and 200 in the first phase of testing as shown in figure 10-11. After they run without error, the programmer will continue with subsequent modules. As you will see later, the programmer has considerable choice as to the modules that he codes and tests next. For instance, he could code modules 110 and 120 next, or modules 210 and 220, or modules 230, 260, 270, and 290. And whether he adds one, two, or more modules at a time will depend on the length and complexity of the modules and program.

In order to use top-down coding and testing, the programmer must code *program stubs*, or *dummy modules*, for all modules called by the modules that are being tested. In figure 10-11, for example, modules 110, 120, 210, 220, 230, and 300 are program stubs in the first phase of testing. The coding for program stubs, as you will see, varies depending on whether the modules supply input, process data, or give output.

When you use top-down coding and testing, the sequence of program development will be much the same as that listed in figure 10-1. The primary difference is that the coding phase and the testing phase will be overlapped. In addition, when you create your test plan, you will have to decide not only what conditions are to be

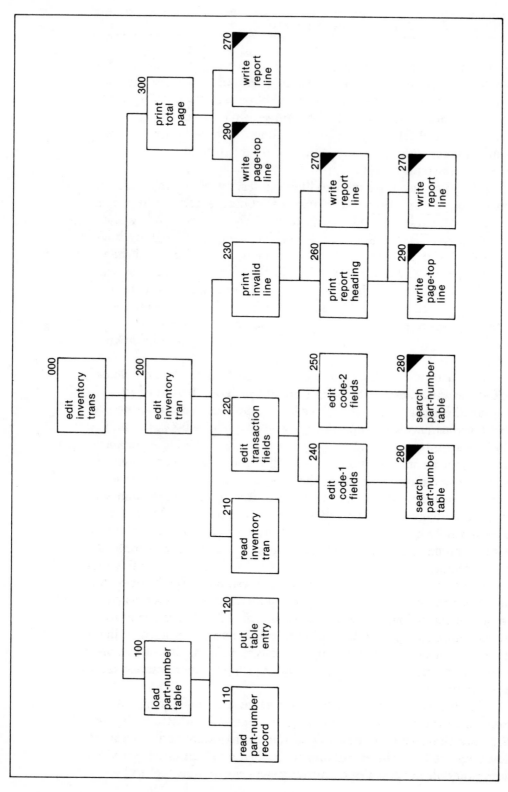

Figure 10-10 Complete VTOC for the edit-inventory-transactions program

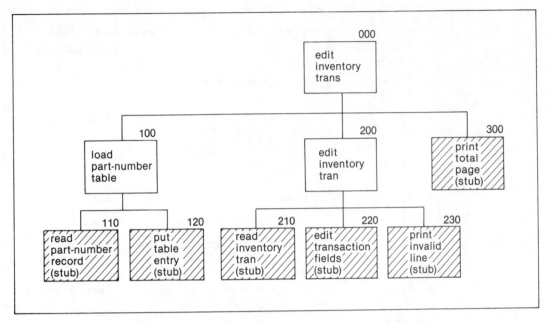

Figure 10-11   First phase of coding and testing for the edit program (modules 000, 100, and 200)

tested, but also what modules are to be tested.

To illustrate, figure 10-12 gives a possible top-down test plan for the edit-inventory-transactions program. In each of the first four test phases, new modules are being tested. Then, the entire program is tested in the last two phases. Note that the first test run doesn't require any data at all because both input modules are stubs.

The primary advantage of top-down testing is that testing proceeds in manageable steps. Although the edit-inventory-transactions program is so short that top-down testing won't contribute much to its development, imagine a program of 2000 cards or more with 1000 statements in the Procedure Division. If you test the entire program at once with all of its bugs, there is a good possibility that the first few days of testing will be very inefficient. If, for example, a couple of minor clerical errors cause some part of the program to execute improperly, it may be difficult to determine just where in the program the bug originates. And this in turn can lead to backtracking: the addition of extra debugging statements, an unnecessary test run or two, etc.

But if this program is tested from the top down, testing will proceed in increments of a few modules, perhaps 150 statements or less, at a time. As a result, it should be easy to locate the source of any bugs that are discovered during testing. They almost have to be in the modules just added or in the interfaces between the old

Test phase	Data	Data source
1. Modules 000, 100 and 200	None	Not applicable
2. Add modules 110 and 120	Three part-number records	Self
3. Add modules 210, 220, 240, 250 and 280	Two valid transactions, one for each transaction code, and one with the first part number in the table, one with the last part number	Self
4. Add modules 230, 260, 270, 290, and 300	Invalid transactions that will test all possible causes of invalid fields	Self
5. Contingencies	Mixed data from steps 3 and 4; any new records that might cause contingent errors	Self
6. Page overflow and maximum table size	As many part-number records as the program is supposed to provide for; 150 transactions, with enough invalid transactions to cause page overflow	Test data generator

Figure 10-12 A test plan for the edit program using top-down coding and testing

modules and the new. By the time all 1000 statements are tested together, all of the major control modules should be error free, so any additional errors will be relatively trivial. In short, an unwieldy test run is turned into a series of easily-managed steps.

To use top-down testing, you need to know (1) how to code program stubs, (2) under what conditions to use top-down testing, and (3) in what sequence to code and test the modules of a program. After I give you some ideas in these areas, I will describe instances in which you may want to overlap coding and testing with design and documentation.

How to code program stubs

In general, there are three types of program stubs: input stubs, processing stubs, and output stubs. An *input stub* replaces a module that is supposed to supply data to a program. For instance, modules 110 and 210 in figure 10-10 are input modules, so their replacements are input stubs. A *processing stub* replaces a module that operates upon the data within a program such as module 120, 220, 240, 250, or 280 of figure 10-10. And an *output stub* replaces a module that produces output in a program such as module 230, 260, 270, 290, or

```
Input stubs:

110-READ-PART-NUMBER-RECORD.
    DISPLAY '110-READ-PART-NUMBER-RECORD'.
    MOVE 'Y' TO PART-NUMBER-EOF-SW.

210-READ-INVENTORY-TRAN.
    DISPLAY '210-READ-INVENTORY-TRAN'.
    IF FIRST-RECORD
        MOVE 'C1AAAAAAAAAA05247811222333334444455555' TO TR-RECORD
        MOVE 'N' TO FIRST-RECORD-SW
    ELSE
        MOVE 'Y' TO TRAN-EOF-SW.


Processing stubs:

120-PUT-TABLE-ENTRY.
    DISPLAY '120-PUT-TABLE-ENTRY'.

220-EDIT-TRANSACTION-FIELDS.
    DISPLAY '220-EDIT-TRANSACTION-FIELDS'.
    MOVE 'N' TO VALID-TRAN-SW.


Output stubs:

230-PRINT-INVALID-LINE.
    DISPLAY '230-PRINT-INVALID-LINE'.
    DISPLAY TR-RECORD.

300-PRINT-TOTAL-PAGE.
    DISPLAY '300-PRINT-TOTAL-PAGE'.
    EXHIBIT NAMED VALID-SALES-COUNT.
    EXHIBIT NAMED VALID-RETURN-COUNT.
    EXHIBIT NAMED INVALID-SALES-COUNT.
    EXHIBIT NAMED INVALID-RETURN-COUNT.
    EXHIBIT NAMED INVALID-TRAN-CODE-COUNT.
    EXHIBIT NAMED TRANS-PROCESSED-COUNT.
```

Figure 10-13   Examples of program stubs for the first test phase of the edit program

300 in figure 10-10. How you code any of these three types of stubs will depend upon the requirements of the program and upon your test plan.

To illustrate some typical program stubs, I have coded the stubs that I would use for the first test phase of the edit program as shown in figure 10-11. These stubs are shown in figure 10-13. In columns 73 through 76 of these cards I would code STUB so the cards can easily be removed from the deck when the stubs are replaced by the actual modules.

The minimum amount of code that an input stub should contain is shown in figure 10-13 for module 110. This stub simply displays the module number and indicates that the last record in the file has been read. A step up from this is the code shown for module 210.

This simulates the reading of one input record the first time the module is executed and sets the end-of-file switch the second time the module is executed. Beyond this level, you may want to use a counter to simulate the reading of several records before setting the end-of-file switch. Or you may want to take records one at a time from a table that you created for the stub and pass them back to the calling module. At some point, of course, it becomes more practical to code the actual module and use actual input data than to code an extensive stub that will be thrown away later. So you must have solid reasons for going beyond the levels of detail shown in figure 10-13.

A processing stub should supply the codes or answers that the calling modules look for, but they don't have to be the right codes or answers. For instance, the code for module 220, the edit module, in figure 10-13 moves an N into the valid-transaction switch. It will do this whether the transaction is valid or invalid. Nevertheless, this is all that module 200 needs in order to continue processing. Similarly, a calculate module may pass a constant value back to the program each time it is executed. For instance, a stub for a gross-pay calculation may return a constant value of $100.00 each time it is entered. Since this will allow the calling module to continue, it is acceptable. In those cases where a calling module doesn't require any processing at all from a processing stub, it is enough to indicate that the stub was entered and that's all. This is illustrated by the coding for module 120 in figure 10-13.

For an output stub, you will generally use a DISPLAY or EXHIBIT statement. These are illustrated in the code for modules 230 and 300 in figure 10-13. For module 230, the DISPLAY statement is used to print the contents of the entire transaction record. For module 300, the EXHIBIT statement is used to give the values of the fields named. (The EXHIBIT statement is covered in detail in the next book in this COBOL series, *Structured ANS COBOL, Part 2.*)

Notice that each program stub will display the paragraph name before doing any dummy processing. This will help the programmer determine whether all modules were called as intended.

In some cases, due to the test data used, a program stub should never be reached at all. If, for example, only good transaction data is used to test the edit program, as it would be in phase 3 of the test plan in figure 10-12, module 230 should never be executed. In such a case, the stub should consist of a single statement that displays the module number so the error will be obvious if the module is called.

When to use top-down testing

As I mentioned earlier, the primary reason for using top-down testing is to simplify debugging. In addition to simplified debugging, however, there are several other reasons for considering top-down testing.

I think the second biggest reason for using top-down testing is programmer morale. To me, variety is the spice of life, so it gets depressing to be involved in a large project in which the coding phase alone will take a couple of months or more. While you are coding, you have to wonder whether you have any major omissions or logical deficiencies. And because you're not getting any feedback, your mind tends to get jumbled up as thoughts about one module interfere with thoughts about another. Because this is still the normal way of developing programs, it's no wonder to me that studies of programmer morale indicate widespread dissatisfaction.

How much better it is to code a couple hundred lines of code and test them before going any further. Besides giving a little variety to the project, it clears the mind. Once you know the top levels of the program are okay, you have more confidence that you're on the right track and you can code the next modules with honest enthusiasm. Furthermore, by proceeding in this way, you know that you won't be facing the awesome task of debugging the entire program when you complete the coding. Instead, you will only have to debug the last modules that you added, which will probably be a less difficult task than testing some of the higher-level modules was.

Another reason for using top-down testing is to get around incomplete specifications. For instance, when I presented the original specifications for the edit program in figure 3-6, I said the edit rules for each field would be presented later. And this isn't unrealistic at all. Nevertheless, this omission in specifications shouldn't stop you from designing the program and documenting all of the modules except the ones with incomplete specifications. Furthermore, by using program stubs, you can code everything but these modules. In this case, you can code and test all of the modules except modules 240 and 250 even though the specifications are incomplete. So your productivity shouldn't be affected at all.

You may also choose to use top-down testing to get around a module or a group of modules that seem overwhelming to you. For example, you haven't yet learned about the table-handling feature of COBOL. As a result, modules 100, 110, and 120 in the edit program probably bother you. To clear the air, then, you can code a stub for module 100 using code with subscripts (presented in chapter 5) as shown in figure 10-14. This allows you to forget about these modules until you have time to research the table-handling feature and code them properly. Meanwhile, your coding and testing can continue without interruption.

When a program is getting more attention than it deserves

```
100-LOAD-PART-NUMBER-TABLE.
    DISPLAY '100-LOAD-PART-NUMBER-TABLE'.
    MOVE 00001 TO PN-TABLE-ENTRY (1).
    MOVE 55555 TO PN-TABLE-ENTRY (2).
    MOVE 99999 TO PN-TABLE-ENTRY (3).
    MOVE 3 TO PN-ENTRY-COUNT.
    MOVE 'Y' TO PART-NUMBER-EOF-SW.
```

Figure 10-14   Program stub that simulates the functions of modules 100, 110, and 120 in the edit program

because the user is concerned about it, you have another good reason for using top-down testing. In this case, you can stub off all of the modules that the user isn't worried about, and test the ones he is worried about. If he's worried about the output format, code these modules early in your development sequence. Then, you can show the user a sample of the output he will be getting and get reactions to it early in the game. If problems are discovered, you have saved yourself some headaches later on. As in all cases, the earlier you discover problems in specification or design, the better off you are.

How to decide on the coding sequence

As you may have realized by now, you can develop the modules in a program in many different sequences when you use top-down coding and testing. If there are no outside influences, your goal should be to use the sequence that will be most efficient in terms of coding and testing. When you develop your test plan, then, you should ask questions like: Where are the major module interfaces in the program? Where, if anywhere, in the VTOC do I have doubts about the design? In what modules do I have doubts about how the coding relates to the HIPO diagram (whether it can be done as planned)? Once again, you should attempt to detect the major errors first.

   If you have no particular concerns about your program or module designs, you have great flexibility as to your development sequence. After you test the first two or three levels, it becomes a case of mop up. Eventually, you have to code and test all of the modules, so you may as well take them one leg at a time, introducing data that applies to each leg as you go along.

   In some cases, however, you will have to plan your module-development sequence based on outside influences. For instance, a user may want to see output early to make sure it will be usable, so you will develop the output leg early in the sequence of development. The operations department may doubt that a certain phase of the program can be done efficiently, so you will develop this leg sooner in the sequence of development. Or management may insist that you put a trainee to work on your project. So you will move a relatively easy leg up in the sequence of development and let the trainee work on it while you code a more difficult leg of the program.

The point, of course, is flexibility. Unlike the traditional program, you can adjust the development of a structured program to the demands made by a wide range of influences. Another advantage of structured programming? You bet.

Discussion

In one form or another, I have already given most of the advantages of top-down coding and testing: simplified debugging, improved programmer morale, high programmer productivity in spite of difficult modules or incomplete specifications, and early visibility of the program for user reaction. One other advantage is that test time on the computer is more evenly distributed from the start of the project to the finish. Rather than following up three months of coding with two months of intensive testing, for example, your test runs will be spread over the entire five months. When a package of several programs is developed over the same time period, this can be a significant advantage from the point of view of operations.

By far, however, the primary advantages of top-down testing are simplified debugging and improved programmer morale. And these advantages take on more and more significance as the size of a project increases. As a programmer, then, I would make top-down testing a way of life. It is simply a more enjoyable way of developing programs.

Terminology

top-down coding and testing

top-down testing

dummy module

program stub

input stub

processing stub

output stub

Objectives

1. Given the specifications, VTOC, and module documentation for a program, create an efficient top-down test plan for it.

Problems

1. (This problem assumes that you have completed chapter 7. If you haven't, return to this problem later.)

    Figure 7-6 gives the specifications for a sequential update program. The VTOC and the coding for this program are given in figures 7-7 and 7-8. Based on this documentation, create an efficient top-down test plan for this program.

Solutions

1. Figure 10-15 is an acceptable test plan for the sequential update program. In phase 1, I plan to test the six modules that perform the basic update function. After I know that the master file is being updated properly, I can test the legs that (1) write the error file, (2) print the update listing, and (3) print the totals. Finally, I can test the entire program for contingencies and page overflow.

Test phase	Data	Data source
1. Modules 000, 100, 110, 120, 130, and 140.	A master file consisting of 10 records; 15 valid transactions including one for the first master and one for the last master (there will be more than one transaction for some masters, none at all for others)	Self
2. Modules 150, 160, 170, 180, 190, 200 (mop up)	Two valid transactions taken from phase 1; two unmatched transactions	Self
3. Contingencies	Combinations of transactions, like a valid transaction for the last master record followed by two invalid transactions	Self
4. Page overflow	Enough valid transactions to cause page overflow	Test data generator

Figure 10-15   A test plan for the sequential-update program using top-down testing

Index

Comment Form

Your opinions count

If you have comments, criticisms, or suggestions, I'm eager to get them. Your opinions today will affect our products of tomorrow. If you have questions, you can expect an answer within one week from the time we receive them. And if you discover any errors in this book, typographical or otherwise, please point them out so we can make corrections when the book is reprinted.

Thanks for your help.

Mike Murach
Fresno, California

fold

fold

Book Title: Structured ANS COBOL (part 1)

Dear Mike: _____

_____

_____

_____

_____

_____

_____

_____

fold

fold

_____

_____

_____

_____

_____

Name and Title _____

Company (if any) _____

Address _____

City, State, & Zip _____

Fold where indicated and staple.
No postage necessary if mailed in the United States.

NO POSTAGE
NECESSARY
IF MAILED
IN THE
UNITED STATES

fold   fold

fold   fold

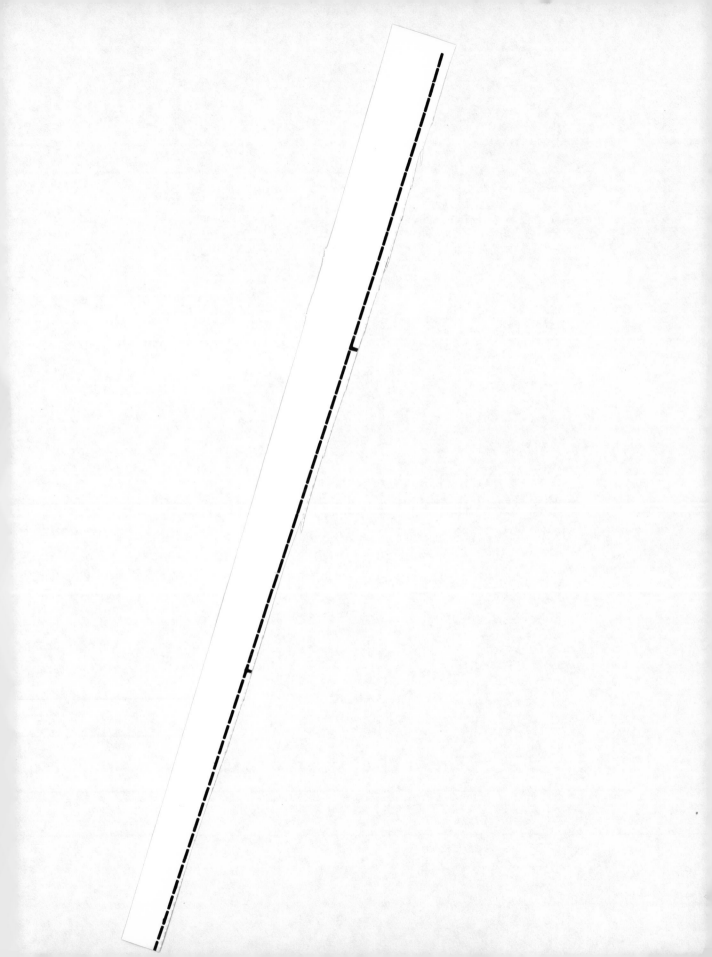